Practice Basics

CORPORATE COUNSEL GUIDES

CORPORATE COUNSEL GUIDES

Practice Basics

STEVEN L. LOVETT

AMERICAN BAR ASSOCIATION
Solo, Small Firm and
General Practice Division

Cover by Jill Tedhams/ABA Publishing.

The materials contained herein represent the opinions of the authors and editors, and should not be construed to be the views or opinions of the law firms or companies with whom such persons are in partnership with, associated with, or employed by, nor of the American Bar Association or the Solo, Small Firm & General Practice Division unless adopted pursuant to the bylaws of the Association.

Nothing contained in this book is to be considered as the rendering of legal advice for specific cases, and readers are responsible for obtaining such advice from their own legal counsel. This book is intended for educational and informational purposes only.

Printed in the United States of America

17 16 15 14 13   5 4 3 2 1

Library of Congress Cataloging-in-Publication Data

Lovett, Steven L.
    Corporate counsel guides : practice basics / By Steven L. Lovett.—First edition.
    pages cm.
Includes bibliographical references and index.
    ISBN 978-1-61438-828-9 (print : alk. paper)
    1. Corporate legal departments—United States. 2. Practice of law—United States. 3. Corporation law—United States. I. Title.
    KF1425.L69 2013
    3446.73'066—dc23

                                                                    2012046544

Discounts are available for books ordered in bulk. Special consideration is given to state bars, CLE programs, and other bar-related organizations. Inquire at Book Publishing, ABA Publishing, American Bar Association, 321 North Clark Street, Chicago, Illinois 60654-7598.

www.ShopABA.org

CONTENTS

ACKNOWLEDGMENTS

As a lawyer, the ability to discuss law while having free rein to use your own voice can be a rare thing, unstilted by the formalities of a brief, the cautiousness of a "corporate statement," or the academic prose of a journal article. There are times, though, when using your own voice is not as successful as you would like it to be. I take full responsibility for whatever portions of this book might lack an effective, engaging voice.

For everything that is well said, well organized, and worthwhile, the credit goes entirely to my editor, Erin Nevius. Her tireless encouragement—even when I was sure I had exhausted her patience—was a constant support to me.

I also want to thank each of my law partners—Raul, Karen, and Daniel—who unknowingly drive me to become just a little bit better every day at what I do as a lawyer and advisor.

Lastly but most warmly, I want to thank my family. They may have no real interest in business law, yet they have every interest in me. That is a humbling, treasured gift.

PREFACE

In 2006 there were approximately 18,000 companies in the United States that employed between 49,000 and 61,000 in-house lawyers.[1] The top 200 domestic companies' corporate law departments employed as many as 27,000 lawyers.[2] Citigroup employed 1,500 lawyers. General Electric employed 1,200 lawyers. Liberty Mutual employed 775 lawyers. State Farm employed 720 lawyers. Allstate employed 700 lawyers. Exxon Mobil employed 600 lawyers.

Those figures are six years old and do not include the hundreds of thousands of lawyers engaged as outside counsel. Today, in 2012, a reasonable estimate is that eight to ten percent of all persons who earn a living practicing law do so as business lawyers: lawyers who are in management and/or who are employed by companies. Perhaps another ten to twenty percent of lawyers have corporate law as an appreciable component of their daily practices.

As a consequence of this massive professional demographic, most state bar associations, as well as the American Bar Association, maintain committees and sections dedicated to the nuances of practicing corporate law, or as it is interchangeably called, *business law*. Independent professional organizations have also sprung up to augment traditional, bar-associated affiliations. The Association of Corporate Counsel, dedicated to "serving the professional and business interests of lawyers who practice in the legal departments of corporations," currently boasts the active membership of "a diverse mix of more than 29,000 in-house lawyers who represent more than 10,000 companies in the United States and 75 countries around the world."[3] Indeed, there is almost an overwhelming multitude of resources available to the practicing corporate lawyer: articles, CLE programs, organizations, newsletters, reports, magazines, Web sites, and books. *Inside Counsel*, a monthly magazine available in print and online, has a circulation of 40,000 consumers, including 22,384 chief legal officers, vice presidents, and general counsel.[4]

The world of business in which corporate lawyers work, both domestic and international, spins ever more quickly on an axis of intrinsic complexity. In an effort to remain competitive and to grow—to simply get a product or a service off of their shelves and into the marketplace—companies face a dizzying array of enigmatic constellations: employment issues, regulatory oversight, litigation, contract creation and enforcement, transactional concerns, multijurisdictional interests, intellectual property rights, media relations, and an ever-evolving, rarely satisfied, demand-side consumer. Reading these stars better than a competitor reads them—all while the world of business spins at light speed—can usually forecast a company's success or its ultimate failure.

The corporate lawyer has become a key participant in this commerce astronomy, and businesses more than ever before recognize the tactical importance of obtaining and retaining competent, effective, and efficient legal counsel. Indeed, many businesses integrate their corporate lawyers into their executive levels, embedding them within the decision-making matrix of their companies. Every day, corporate clients of all sizes and from every industry continue to seek out knowledgeable and dedicated corporate counsel. In 2007, when Steve Jobs, the iconic founder of Apple, was struggling to find someone to build the right kind of legal department within Apple Inc., he found Daniel Cooperman, who was then the General Counsel of Oracle Corporation. Once Mr. Cooperman set up shop at Apple (with the blessing of Larry Ellison, the CEO of Oracle), he led the way to building a legal department that is "integral to the company's $300 billion business—from protecting its signature logo and coordinating worldwide product launches to waging war over smartphones patents. Apple's top lawyers 'are part of the senior management team[.]'"[5]

A rapidly multiplying number of businesses, whether public or private, for profit or nonprofit, ask themselves, "What is the optimal number of lawyers for our company, given our industry, our mission, our strategic plans, and our particular appetites for risk?"[6] This is a question beyond the mere benchmarking practice of stocking legal departments with the right number of lawyers by using a formulaic lawyer-to-revenue ratio.[7] Savvy businesses now evaluate their needs for in-house counsel and outside counsel (as well as the effectiveness of their legal departments) by thinking more in terms of a rate-of-investment (ROI) evaluation.

Does our business investment in a corporate lawyer minimize costs, maximize profits (or output), and avert or better manage risks?

Bottom line? Businesses expect to see a correlation: *good* corporate counsel should universally *improve* the bottom line.

This book was born out of a presumption underpinning that conclusion: to improve a business's bottom line, corporate lawyers need to be good at what they do.

The presumption is simple; the reality can sometimes be far different. On average, lawyers report they practice law for approximately six years before being hired into an in-house counsel position.[8] At that point, they enter a hardscrabble reality of learning their trade on a steep and unforgiving curve, handling and contributing to a single yet multifaceted and expectant client. These corporate lawyers may understand their previous area of practice quite well, but the growing uniqueness of an in-house practice requires a much more robust, general skill set and an uncommon professional perspective.

Instead of running their own practice or associating with a firm where *law* is the business, these corporate lawyers become an operational and managerial resource within a company where *law* is only a supporting (or damning) element of business. Client interaction is not event driven; it is constant, usually diverse, and subservient to a greater goal: the *business* of the business. Thinking about law—about what it means to be a corporate lawyer—undergoes several paradigmatic changes when a lawyer "goes in-house." Neither law school nor traditional law practice offer substantive training grounds for these paradigm shifts, but nearly all of the materials available to corporate lawyers presume that those paradigm shifts have already taken place or are understood. To be good at what you do—to deliver top-flight legal services to your employer-company—you have to understand the practice basics underpinning the role of practicing as a corporate lawyer.

The objective of this book is to help illuminate those underpinnings: to identify, develop, and discuss those paradigmatic changes from a practical and an assimilated point of view. Thankfully, there is a wealth of resources addressing the mechanics of day-to-day practice for a corporate lawyer, but there are far fewer resources focusing on *how* and *why* a corporate lawyer must retrain his or her mind to acclimate to this unique area of law. My intention is to keep that focus as the centerline for this book.

Chapter 1 takes a look at what being a corporate lawyer (whether in house or as outside counsel) functionally means. **Chapter 2** suggests a thoughtful way for you to analyze your relationship with your corporate client and looks at the foundational elements of that relationship. **Chapter 3** explores three basic business environments, and it discusses how those business environments might affect your contributive role as corporate counsel. **Chapter 4** investigates the ins and outs of a typical company's legal department while examining the participatory role a corporate lawyer should strive to fill. **Chapter 5** evaluates topical areas of law in which you are likely to practice, and how those areas of practice influence your company's broader business concerns. **Chapter 6** discusses risk management, preventive measures, and where the landmines of liability may be hidden for your corporate client and yourself. **Chapter 7** provides a helpful starting place for identifying important resources used by corporate lawyers.

Whenever and wherever possible throughout the book, I have attempted to quote and highlight the voices, suggestions, and experiences of those lawyers, executives, consultants, professors, and reporters who are or have been in the trenches. There is nothing more valuable than learning from those who have been there. Additionally, I have mostly sought to assemble these observations from resources that can easily be accessed by anyone at little or no cost and with little or no effort. The idea has been to demonstrate how painless it can be, even on a tight department's budget, to find good advice on almost any issue facing a corporate lawyer.

Though the overall focus of this book leans toward the nuances of practicing as an in-house lawyer, the platitudes for representing a single, corporate client should be equally beneficial to outside counsel. As vital as it is for an in-house lawyer to fully understand his or her role in light of a single, corporate employer, it is similarly important for outside counsel to competently grasp the inner workings, thought processes, tasks, risks, and goals of their brethren who live and work within the walls of the castle. Indeed, the role of outside counsel is to act temporarily, or specifically (with expertise), as a surrogate for a company's in-house lawyer. Strategic partnering between the two camps has never been more crucial to delivering overall value to the company-client. Moreover, much of the power balance has shifted over the past twenty-five years from the hands of outside counsel and into the hands of in-house counsel: "the once almost singular relationship that existed between the primary outside law firm and the corporation is the distinctly minority approach today."[9] As more corporate legal departments develop and maintain a fold of outside counsel, an arena of competition is created wherein outside counsel want to, and need to, demonstrate an extra edge of attractiveness to obtain and repeat business. How better to do that than to understand their client (and their client's employed lawyers) from the inside out?

Brian Burton, General Counsel of Daimler Trucks North America LLC, made the following remarks: "[U]nderstand how a business works. It's not like a law firm. . . . [L]earn about the business so that if you're in-house, you won't have to learn from scratch, you'll be ready to go."[10] Burton's maxim is applicable to both inside and outside counsel.

This book is devised to act as a beginning and a framework for a long-lasting career and client relationship: a loom on which you can pull together all of the wildly disparate issues of corporate law while representing a single business client. From here you can springboard into researching and studying the specific practicalities that plague, or bless, the everyday life of a corporate lawyer.

Whether you have just begun your career, or whether you have a number of years already under your belt and are looking to expand your base of knowledge, this book will serve as a concise and rigorous primer for practicing law as general counsel, in-house counsel, or outside corporate counsel.

I wish you, and your client-company, the very best!

—Steven Lovett, May 2012

Notes

1. Association of Corporate Counsel, *Profile of In-House Counsel*, Dec. 2006, at 4.
2. *See Analysis of the Legal Profession and Law Firms*, Harvard Law School Program on the Legal Profession, http://www.law.harvard.edu/programs /plp/pages/statistics.php (last visited Jan. 21, 2012); U.S. Bureau of Labor Statistics, Occupational Outlook Handbook (2010–11 ed.).
3. Association of Corporate Counsel, Membership, http://www.acc.com /aboutacc/membership/index.cfm (last visited Jan. 17, 2012).
4. InsideCounsel, About Us, http://www.insidecounsel.com/pages/aboutus .php (last visited Jan. 17, 2012).

5. Catherine Dunn, *Working Under an iCon*, CORPORATE COUNSEL, Dec. 2011, at 15.
6. *Reading the Tea Leaves: What's the Current Thinking on How Many Lawyers a Company Should Have?*, Sender Legal Research (January 29, 2010), http://www.senderlegalsearch.com/archives/62.
7. *Id.*
8. *Id.* at 7.
9. Carl D. Liggio, Sr., *A Look at the Role of Corporate Counsel: Back to the Future—or Is It the Past?*, 44 ARIZ. L. REV. 621, Fall/Winter 2002, at 631–32.
10. Shirley Li, *Daimler Trucks GC Discusses His New Role as Head of the Legal Department*, INSIDECOUNSEL, Dec. 2011, *available at* http://www.insidecounsel.com/2011/12/01/daimler-trucks-gc-discusses-his-new-role-as-head-o?t=careers.

CHAPTER 1

AN INTRODUCTION— "SO YOU'RE A WHAT?"

TABLE OF SECTIONS

You made it! The meeting or phone call has taken place, and your mind is racing with the names of people to excitedly tell or round up for a celebratory dinner. A corporation—a *single* client—thinks well enough of your legal abilities to pay you full-time to exclusively capture all your professional expertise, judgment, and intelligence. They might have hired you from within, as is many times the case for a general counsel, or your résumé might have fought its way through stiff competition to get you through the door and securely onto the company's in-house legal team. Or perhaps, if you are working for a private law firm, the white whale has finally been harpooned, and the majority (if not all) of your time will be spent dedicated to the needs of this unwieldy, titanic client (with titanic fees). Regardless, there is a new title on your door, or you have a new door altogether, and it should feel great.

As wine glasses (or whiskey tumblers, if you're of my ilk) are clinked together to applaud your new job, one of your party guests, with an interested look on her face, asks, "So what does this mean for you?" Because you have the linguistic alacrity that can come with a slightly smug feeling of genuine success, you quickly reply, "More money!" Everyone laughs, and the wine (or whiskey) continues to flow.

Interestingly enough, your jest may be right: your new title could come with a financial increase.[1] (Certainly, this is likely if you are billing the white whale as outside counsel or if you've graduated from less-than-lucrative government work.) Gradually but with noticeable traction throughout the late 1980s, 1990s, and early 2000s, the compensation of in-house lawyers began to become much more competitive with the compensation of lawyers employed by private law firms. It is quite possible that your new position might add something to your financial bottom line. Even so, this spry response did not offer a very meaningful answer to the heart of the question being asked by your enthusiastic celebrant. Yet each of us (one can safely assume) would be able to generally discuss what we think being a corporate lawyer means.

So why do we need to define these roles? How do we define these roles?

§ 1.1 Defining Your Role

Although many lawyers have a conversational grasp of what entails serving as a general counsel, an in-house lawyer, or a corporate lawyer, it is probably a safe prediction that most such conversations would become anemic if they started to delve into sometimes-byzantine issues such as privilege, budgets, valuation models, governance, lobbyists, internal investigations, compliance, and one of the most confounding issues of all: exactly *who* the client really *is*. I do not believe this naiveté—or simply the lack of an in-depth grasp of these topics (among so many others)—is a reflection of poor education, laziness, or arrogant obliviousness. The reality is, the role of a corporate lawyer is complex and demanding, involving numerous topics that typically lie well beyond what many well-seasoned lawyers have had to deal with all at once.

The purpose of defining a corporate lawyer's role is to give us working parameters and stable reference points, which we can turn to when we need to bring our focus back to the full spectrum of our responsibilities—a 50,000-foot view far above any specific area of practice. Our definitions enable us to address critical fundamentals, just as our first year of law school gave us the core subjects from which we could build a functional knowledge of the law.

What does your corporate lawyer job mean for you? How has your perspective as a lawyer changed? What new professional challenges are you facing? What are your new goals, if any? What are your goals for your client? What *are* you now? If enough wine or whiskey flowed during your congratulatory dinner, you might have collapsed into your bed much later than usual that night, and before drifting off into an excited but fitful sleep, you might have taken a mindful pause and found yourself asking some of those same self-reflective questions.

Defining and understanding our roles as lawyers is an ongoing part of our professional life. Designating a person as a partner, associate, judge, lead counsel, division chief, co-counsel, client, or clerk comes from an ability and a need (on some level) to define and understand what that person does—what that person's job *means* and what it means to the pursuit of our own jobs. Most of our professional rules discuss some of the definitional differences, and consequences, between acting as a counselor, advocate, or officer of the court. Defining roles—the functional meaning of those roles—gives us our compass points as we navigate through an endless ocean of legal and professional issues. With defined roles, (1) we know what to expect; (2) employees know what to expect; (3) the client knows what to expect; (4) other lawyers know what to expect; and (5) the public, the government, and other parties know what to expect. Our sense of what our role means in any given situation is what acts as a rudder, steering the course of our conduct and our decisions. The more firm and comprehensive our sense of meaning, the more precisely and predictably that critical rudder will pilot us. Your role's underlying purpose will formulate your behavior, your rights, your obligations, your decision matrix, your ethos, and ultimately your principal usefulness to your employer.

Defining roles also establishes the pragmatics of function and procedure, including (1) vertical and horizontal structure, (2) processes for workflow, and (3) efficiency of work management. Your ability to define your role as a general counsel, an in-house lawyer, or a company's corporate lawyer is essential to dictating your level of overall success when working with and for a corporation. Though it is important to have a job description—if, in fact, one is available—it is even more imperative to grasp what that job *means.*

What will act as your personal mission statement as you plunge into this new endeavor? This inquiry need not become too esoteric, but if you are unable to have a 360-degree view of your role, then you are probably unable to be the best business investment for your company-client, and you are likely to find yourself staring into the abyss of some very unfortunate situations.

Obtaining a truly comprehensive view of your role is a challenge—hence this book—and a dynamic, malleable invention. It is also an exciting and engaging way to practice law. Carl Liggio Sr., who is now Of Counsel at McCullogh, Campbell & Lane after twenty-two years as General Counsel to Arthur Young/Ernst & Young, said, "Subject to more demands, the new general counsel will be more consigliore than just lawyer. The new role will call for a broader set of skills that will extend far beyond the law. This truly is the start of the platinum age for the general counsel."[2]

For those readers who might like a shortcut, a quick search of *Black's Law Dictionary* can leave one scratching his or her head if hunting for the terms *general counsel, in-house counsel,* or *corporate counsel.* Interestingly, the editors of this esteemed resource[3] have left these terms undefined, perhaps because these phrases are viewed as being too unspecific in their substantive meaning, or because they are viewed as being too imprecise when used as professional designations. A good argument can be made for either position. Therefore, as a working thesis, let us take the *absence* of traditional definitions as the scaffolding for this book, beginning with this first chapter, and extract practical, visceral substance from the vaporous apparition of what it really means to be a corporate lawyer.

§ *1.1.1 Defining* General Counsel

Succinctly put, "the general counsel is an employee-officer of the corporation charged with overall responsibility for how the corporation's legal matters are handled."[4] More succinctly put, a general counsel is a company's most senior lawyer. As simple as that sounds—and it *is* simple in some respects and *should* be simple in some respects—the role of general counsel (shared to a certain extent by other in-house lawyers) is also one of the most ambiguous and difficult roles one can pursue in the legal profession. Whether you are hoping to fulfill that aspiration someday, or whether you find yourself now holding it and marveling at its weight and breadth, you had better be at the top of your game when you walk onto the field. Although the rewards of your hard work—your integral contribution to the successful progression of a corporate enterprise—can be gratifying, the risks and potential hazards to your career are tenfold.

Keeping in mind the adage warning a person to beware of taking away hope from another human being,[5] I intend to begin gently and first discuss how the role of general counsel is a simple one. This concept, in fact, is the sorcerer's stone to understanding the role of a general counsel (and all in-house lawyers).

Professor Deborah DeMott's article on the roles of a general counsel discusses four likely reasons why a lawyer may seek to hold the position of general counsel.[6] All four of Professor DeMott's ideas are convincing; I would like to deferentially posit a fifth. This fifth reason is a more elemental hypothesis: the *simplicity* hypothesis.

What is readily apparent and so strikingly simple about the role of general counsel is that a general counsel has a *single* client.[7] Though this can often be the very thing that makes a general counsel's role complicated, it should also bring a refreshing straightforwardness to the job. That straightforwardness is in itself an attractive challenge (much like Fermat's Last Theorem: the equation looks invitingly simple, but solving it can sometimes appear impossible[8]).

For many other lawyers, the single-client phenomenon can occur in a modified way in private practice, usually in larger law firms when one is burrowed within a particular practice division and when one is working on a particularly complex, single transaction or piece of litigation. You wake up in the morning and enter your office fully consumed with the needs and wishes of a single client. A general counsel does much the same thing. But when the private practitioner walks into the office in the morning, his or her mental resources are typically bent toward a limited (even if large and multipart) task from a client with a knowable terminus, such as a multimillion-dollar bond issuance, defending a class-action derivative lawsuit, or working on a merger deal between two companies. In contrast, when a general counsel walks into the office, his or her mental resources are charged with addressing and/or being responsible for the full spectrum of his or her employer company's liabilities, business operations, and current projects—past, present, and future. How then does this equal simplicity? Instead of thinking in terms of having a single client, think in terms of how *working* for a single client, as a general counsel does, should affect your professional worldview.

A general counsel can concentrate on one industry,[9] a single group of employees and employment issues (even when the employment pools are large), a single corporate philosophy, a single board of directors, and a single management group. A general counsel can look to a single corporate history (unless dealing with a new venture) and the history of a single industry for guidance and some level of future predictability about the scope of his or her job. A general counsel can look to an identifiable group of regulatory agencies and become a pseudo-expert on a fairly particular body of laws and regulations while still practicing as a generalist. The attractiveness of a general counsel's position is that a lawyer can go into work and face a *known* universe.[10] True, a general counsel may face an immense amount of work, involving a host of difficult and various issues, but he or she can do so while keeping in mind that everything that needs to be done is predicated upon practicing law and working for *one* client within *one* universe.

Why is this important to consider when talking about defining the role of a general counsel? Because the act of defining the role of a general counsel is born out of this one element: *that a general counsel has a single client.* As rudimentary as it sounds, if that one element is forgotten or mislaid, or if it fades too far into the background, then the defined role, and the ultimate success, of a general counsel quickly begins to come unhinged. All else should fall into line behind that one element. If a general counsel, an in-house lawyer, changes or forgets this first element—the *primoris elementum*—then the entire definition of *general counsel* will disintegrate. By way of simple proof, let us revisit Professor DeMott's definition but remove the *corporate* term: "A general counsel is an employee-officer of the _____ charged with overall responsibility for how the _____'s legal matters are handled."[11] Immediately, we can see that the client component of the definition is not an elective. It directly affects *who* and *what* a general counsel is and does. Woe to any general counsel (or in-house counsel) who forgets that he or she works for a *single* client.

This, then, must be the building block on which we frame all of our construction about how a general counsel is defined: *you cannot conceive the many without the one.*[12]

Advisor, Counselor, Pundit

Now that we have identified our arena—the single, corporate employer—we can leap into action and face the first, and biggest, challenge of a general counsel's role: as an advisor, Mr. Liggio's "consigliore." A general counsel is the ultimate *legal advisor* to a corporation, bearing the ultimate responsibility for *all* of a corporation's legal matters.[13] In spite of acts of delegation, or the participation of outside-counsel specialists, a general counsel bears the true onus of insuring that a company is receiving appropriate and quality legal counseling on all necessary issues. In this primary capacity, a general counsel is *the* legal advisor to senior management (or sometimes not-so-senior management), *the* legal advisor to the board of directors and its committees, and *the* legal advisor to the whole of the corporation, staying dutifully abreast of the body of laws—and pieces of litigation—which have an impact on all of a company's business enterprises. Lastly, as the singularly responsible legal advisor to a corporation, a general counsel's role must also be to champion the ethical conscience of the corporation.[14] "In rendering advice, a lawyer may refer not only to law but to other considerations such as moral, economic, social and political factors, which may be relevant to the client's situation."[15]

Corporate Counsel

Unless there is simply a changing of the guard as a general counsel retires or moves on, there are times when a new general counsel is hired because of an immediate issue the corporation believes needs some proven expertise, or a prominent reputation, to successfully handle. A lawyer might be hired as general counsel to help steer a company out of a strategic setback and to position itself to regain its market momentum.[16] A general counsel might be hired to restore market or governmental confidence in a corporation that has struggled with regulatory issues or enforcement actions.[17] A general counsel might be selected to restore public confidence in its brand name or public image.[18] A general counsel might be employed on an interim basis—one that could stretch for many months or longer—as a permanent replacement search is underway.[19] A general counsel might be hired for his or her neutrality and grit as a corporation deals with putting an end to corrupt or harmful internal practices and the painful exodus and replacement of various senior-level and management-level personnel.[20]

I mention these kinds of situations because they can present one of the greatest hurdles to a general counsel's role as a corporation's legal advisor. A real temptation is for a general counsel to have a "pet" area of practice while giving other vital areas of practice negligible attention. When that happens, a corporation has only hired itself another in-house counsel, or another outside, corporate lawyer. What a company truly *needs* from its general counsel is an epicenter, sitting directly above and to the center of all of its legal demands and resources.

Although a corporation may go shopping for a lawyer because it is looking for a particular set of experiences or for a particular reputation, any person who is hired as a general counsel will ultimately be *the* lawyer of the corporation—its *general* lawyer. That lawyer may have been a top-notch litigator, but he or she will now also need to give competent legal advice on compliance issues. The new hire might have been awesome at mergers and acquisitions, but he or she will now also need to give competent legal advice on employment and human-resource issues. The new general counsel, brought on board for his or her regulatory background, will now also need to give competent legal advice on intellectual property issues. The point is not a trivial one. A general counsel is ultimately responsible for *all* of a corporation's legal advice and legal activities. Unfortunately, most lawyers, and most clients, routinely think in terms of being *event*-driven; that is, legal services are provided due to a single event or series of events. Not so with the role of a general counsel. A general counsel needs to be thinking well beyond the scope of whatever particular event(s) ushered him or her into the halls of the company. A general counsel needs to be thinking in terms of 360 degrees and for the long term.

True, many of a general counsel's duties can be, or will be, performed by other persons. Other lawyers within the legal department, outside counsel, special counsel (such as counsel who might be hired by and for a board's audit committee), reporting services (such as compliance review services), and quasi-legal persons (such as consultants or compliance officers) may all be part of the alphabet soup of legal resources who handle many of the practical, day-to-day advisory functions for the corporation, but a general counsel is the proverbial bowl in which the alphabet soup sloshes and splashes. His or her ultimate responsibility as *the* legal counsel for the company is never a charge to be taken lightly, even if reviewing arcane financial statements lies well beyond a lawyer's pre–general counsel litigation background.[21] Relying on others is critical, and it is a healthy function of delegation, but a general counsel must at all times remember that he or she bears the final responsibility for what information, documents, or advice other persons or entities are providing. In the final analysis, a corporation (and other, more menacing entities, such as a court) will look to a general counsel as the source and sieve of all of a company's legal advice and activities.[22] The corporate client depends on that gatekeeping function as an essential part of a general counsel's advisory role.

"O Captain, My Captain!"[23]

A general counsel's managerial and administrative role requires as much of a rodeo roundup as it does square-dance calling. Sometimes you are herding cats and other times you are barking out dance steps. If you are doing neither at some meaningful level, then something is fundamentally wrong.

Most corporate law departments utilize some kind of hierarchical, vertical structure for their organizational purposes. Even when the structure comprises no more than the general counsel, a small staff pool, and one associate or deputy lawyer, part of a general counsel's role is going to be to act as the senior (and only) administrative partner of this unique "law firm." Larger administrative issues—such as hiring and firing, budget requests and projections, and departmental reports— typically fall within the purview of a general counsel's personal attention (or the personal attention of a deputy general counsel, but keep in mind there is still only one "end of the line"—one lawyer of the company). Day-to-day administrative duties are often assigned away from a general counsel's desk, but again, this is an area where a general counsel has final accountability, and he or she should have oversight mechanisms in place to superintend these duties. A well-built, well-thought-out departmental structure is the backbone to effective administration and management. It defines areas of responsibility, both horizontally and vertically, and it provides a quick roadmap for identifying exactly where something is inefficient or missing.

Administrative matters, in fact, can take up a significant amount of a general counsel's time (as we shall see in Chapter 4), but to a certain extent, they should. If you are too far removed from *why* your department uses the amount of paper it does, or *why* a contract review project has not been assigned to anyone yet, or *why* you recently spent $10,000 on an associate's continuing legal education, or *why* you spent $50,000 in litigation-support expenses (*expenses*, mind you, not fees), then your function as an administrator is not where it should be. Any single inefficiency does not usually spell doom, but it can be the canary in the coal mine, signifying that there is a much more systemic problem with the overall supervision and/or delivery of your legal services to your employer. Keep in mind that a general counsel and a company's legal department are a *business investment*. As a general counsel, you should administer your department—both its personnel and resources—in cost-effective and project-effective ways. Delivering effective and positive cost-benefit legal services to your corporate client, your employer, should be the basic objective of a legal department—*your* department.

You cannot expect your department simply to run on its own or to run successfully with too much democracy (at least insist upon a constitutional monarchy!). Input and an appropriate level of self-autonomy from your division leaders, associates, and staff is important and should be encouraged, but each person has to understand his or her chain of command, and all chains of command have to eventually lead to your door. There need to be systems in place (the simpler, the better) that keep track of your resources, your departmental needs (current and projected), your department's actual usages, and the volume/activity of your department's "docket"—that is, the work it performs in a repetitive manner, the special- or event-driven projects it has, and the projects it is supervising in other departments or through outside counsel. Without this kind of data, and without the data being easily producible in a regular and uncomplicated manner, proper administration of a legal department cannot occur. Budgets cannot be written. Expenses cannot be controlled. Productivity cannot be measured. Services cannot be efficiently and effectively provided to other business departments or divisions. Outside counsel cannot be properly monitored. And eventually, when push comes to shove, a general counsel would be unable to make sure there are enough of the right kind of "beans and bullets" to get the job done right. Worst of all, an employer's business investment in you and your staff will have been needlessly squandered.

A corporation depends upon its general counsel—its chief legal officer—to be its chief legal administrator. In the spirit of one of the basic paradigms of the U.S. military, your staff needs to understand, and therefore be capable of supporting and completing, your department's goals. This begins with good administration. You, leading from the front, have to make sure your entire department is being run, and has been organized, in an accountable, productive way. When properly trained and appropriately supervised, your lawyers and staff will be able to execute the kind of mission accomplishment desired by you and needed (required) by your company. The bottom line is a general counsel has to "manage upward, to justify the department's budget to the CEO and CFO."[24]

Administration might seem to be a mundane part of your role, but developing and administrating a successful legal department is a key function of the department's head—the general counsel—a *business* executive.

Executive

Crewmember

Not too many lawyers can boast they have held the title Senior Vice President, Football Operations, but Sashi Brown can. Mr. Brown was promoted to the position within the National Football League's Jacksonville Jaguars from his previous job as the Jaguars' senior vice president, digital media, and assistant general counsel.[25] Though many of us might have the tendency to see a general counsel's *executive* title and station as superfluous—quickly skipping past its import and its rightful obligations—I thought Mr. Brown's uniquely memorable title might help to slow us down for a moment. You, as did I, might have paused to ask yourself: What the heck is a senior vice president of football operations?[26] Whatever this rare job might entail, Mr. Brown is just as much responsible for its successful prosecution as he is for acting as the Jaguars' most senior lawyer. He is one of the Jaguars' executive crewmembers.

Many general counsel have some kind of nonlegal executive title as a companion role (or doppelgänger, depending on who you ask) to their position as their company's senior legal officer. Because these professionals stand at the top of the legal food chain within their corporations, most outsiders—and many lawyers—unthinkingly gloss right over the "executive" part of the title. It can seem gratuitous, intended to act more as a gauge of the management level of a general counsel within a corporation rather than as a true operational title. In one respect, such a presumption might be correct—it does denote a senior-level position—but to see the executive side of a general counsel's job predominantly as mere window dressing is a risky point of view.

Historically, a general counsel also bore the duties of acting as the corporate secretary, and many times, that is still the case today. Because of a corporate secretary's natural responsibility to ensure the corporate records reflect the proper exercise of the board's fiduciary duties, the corporate secretary is also in a position to provide advice and resources to the board's directors for discharging their duties under state and federal law.[27] A corporate secretary is more than "a combination of scrivener and custodian."[28] The need for core competency in governance issues—corporate and securities law—has made this corporate-officer position a cozy fit for a general counsel. But despite the cozy fit, this executive position, as all others, is distinguishable from the duties of acting as general counsel, especially when a corporate secretary is delivering managerial advice, as opposed to legal advice.[29] And like all other executive positions, it deserves and requires studious attention to its own realm of responsibilities.

Most general counsel (and many assistants and deputies) find themselves wearing two different shoes at the same time: one shoe as a lawyer and one shoe as a company executive. One foot might be heeled with a dress shoe and the other with a running shoe, but at no time can a general counsel impetuously hop along on only the legal shoe while ignoring the equal weight and attention the other shoe—the executive shoe—also needs: such is a risky game. Indeed, Texas and Delaware— two states that prolifically deal with the concerns of leadership roles within corporations—have recognized that "a corporate officer owes fiduciary duties of care, good faith and loyalty to the corporation, and may be sued in a corporate derivative action just as a director may be."[30] Even though a general counsel may keep a tidy house within the legal department, he or she can become woefully exposed to nonlawyer liabilities if other executive responsibilities are not competently met.

Paradoxically, a general counsel, who sports a nonlawyer executive shoe, needs to look into his or her own mirror when providing advice to directors and other officers about their actions, duties, and fiduciary obligations. As with other senior-level colleagues, an executive general counsel's own actions may be the focus of particular scrutiny by shareholders, regulators, creditors, or other businesses, especially when he or she is involved in executive compensation, affiliated-party transactions, business-to-business interactions, corporate insolvency, or illegal activities (say it isn't so!).[31] Finding oneself as a potential target for the crosshairs of leadership liability—*aside* from the liability of malpractice—can be an unsettling proposition, but it can also be a useful incentive to make sure your contribution as a nonlawyer executive is meaningful and principled.

A general counsel's role as a company executive should, in fact, be another opportunity in which he or she decides to lead by example, not just by proselytizing to other senior officers about what they should or should not be doing. This is easier said than done, of course, and the duality of the role as a general counsel and an executive can sometimes lead to discordant interests and goals: all the more reason for a general counsel to work with the tenacity to apply ethics to business.[32]

To use a well-worn proverb: the best defense is a good offense. Just as a general counsel must understand his or her functions and duties as the company's lawyer, it is equally necessary to understand the functions and duties of acting as a company executive. Alongside the legal department, there might be an entirely different division or department you are responsible for running. Indeed, it might be these duties, hand in hand with your lawyerly responsibilities, that are grooming you for a full-flight executive post. Harkening back to one of Professor DeMott's reasons by which a lawyer may be attracted to the role of general counsel, the C-suite may be calling your name.[33] In January 2012, Laura Quatela found herself rising from the role of Eastman Kodak Company's general counsel, chief intellectual property officer, and senior vice president to the role of president. As a general counsel, Ms. Quatela created a profit center for Kodak through patent licensing, earning the company hundreds of millions of dollars in licensing income.[34] Ms. Quatela's business acumen, integrated with her responsibilities as general counsel, led her from working as a lawyer/executive to a full-time executive.[35]

Learn to run with both of your shoes in rhythm (or at least in such a manner as to avoid tripping over your laces). Fulfilling the role as an executive of your corporation—whether directly tied to the office of general counsel or as a distinct, stand-alone position—can be an exciting new career, and it warrants your careful and diligent attention.

Emissary, Agent, Proxy

As a lawyer, I am guided by rules of professional conduct that adopt this same principle, cautioning that, at all times, I am an "officer of the court," and as such, a representative of the judicial system at large, above and beyond the way in which I represent any individual client. Like most humans, naturally egocentric in my worldview, I have found it a difficult concept to keep in mind at all times: that I am almost *constantly representing something greater than myself.* As the most senior lawyer of a company—sometimes a multibillion-dollar, very high-profile company—a general counsel would do well to tattoo that concept on the inside of his or her eyelids and to blink often.

Once we become caretakers of any kind of professional identity, we must always be "on," always aware that we are emissaries, speaking and acting for whomever or whatever we represent. A general counsel, as a visible and operative *agent* (in both the legal and public-image sense of the word) of a corporation, possesses the interface role by which many third parties acquire their view of, and information about, a corporation's litigation policy, its regulatory/compliance posture, its employment culture, its bargaining and collaborative prowess, and its public image.

Certainly other employees of the client-company look to a general counsel as an agent of the corporation. These employees include members of the legal department, who literally view a general counsel as their boss, and they include employees from other departments (including management), who work with, or rely on, the legal department to get their own work done. Indeed, when a legal department is fully functional and is truly running as a support system for the rest of the company's departments, there are very few, if any, employees who do not interact with, or who are not familiar with, the legal department and the general counsel.

Unfortunately, all of those same employees can also see a general counsel as part of the machinery for terminating their employment, affecting their rights to benefits, and affecting their promotions, demotions, or transfers into other departments. And they are right: many times a general counsel (or the legal department) *is* included, and *should* be included, in those kinds of activities and decisions, and for many of those kinds of activities and decisions, a general counsel can be seen as (or suspected of being) the company's hatchet man. It is reasonable to presume most people's collective sense of the law is that it is a dispassionate and pitiless endeavor. In a mocking twist of fate, the legal profession is popularly seen as a source of *in*justice, and fairly or not, a general counsel, viewed by other employees of the client-company, can easily be tarred and feathered with the same attitude.

It is a general counsel's responsibility to see the primary audience as being his or her fellow employees. A general counsel who is accessible, solicitous, patient, thorough, and well organized is going to make a substantial impact on how a company's employees view the legal department's usefulness, aptitude, and decisions. There will also be a substantial impact on broader cultural principles. An employee's jaded view of the law, or an employee's otherwise-irritated view of the legal department's interference with his or her area of responsibility, can be significantly and positively changed by a general counsel's attitude, channeled as leader of the legal department at large. Remember too that this does not have to be achieved only through direct contact. Opinions are just as easily formed through anecdotal word of mouth or disinterested observation. If a general counsel is regularly seen stalking through the hallways with only the barest of personable greetings to any "underlings," then even the kindest and gentlest soul will be mistaken for an uptight ogre. The role of a diplomat lies as much in passive perception as it does in active negotiation.

Do not think for a moment this need for your role as an ambassador is limited to your company's larger workforce or to your department's immediate pool of employees. The need to remember your role as a representative of your company extends perhaps most importantly to your fellow executives, those in your command chain, the board, and the owners (or other stakeholders). Regardless of the level of expertise you may bring to any particular issue, your *representative attitude* can still exhaust them, alienate them, or entirely estrange them from you. How is this different from remembering your role as a crewmember? There is a distinction in a general counsel's job between acting as a team member and acting as a representative of the company *to* the company. For instance, this can become terribly apparent if you are involved in, or at the head of, an internal investigation. Though you may typically fill the role of co-executive, you now also, in clear distinction, fill the role of the legal arm of the company, acting as its voice of query, concern, or sanction. At this point, a general counsel's sentences might usually begin with "The company's position on this matter is . . . ," which cements a general counsel's position as the company's spokesperson. Never is the art of diplomacy more critical than when a general counsel is wearing the emissary's hat and speaking to a board member, another executive, or a shareholder. For any employee—and certainly for senior management, a board member, or a significant stakeholder—the cold-water shock of having *your* company speak *to you* through the voice of the *company's lawyer* is an experience that can begin a butterfly effect of emotions and consequences.

A general counsel, just by the nature of the profession, swings a heavy, psychological bat. A misstep of tact with those who are inside the company may inadvertently create the kinds of internal schisms that are the hardest and messiest to heal. "Remember who you are."

A general counsel's secondary audience (but perhaps the first one that leaps to mind) is outside counsel. Over the past thirty years, the meaning of a general counsel's role, as compared to the role of outside counsel, has changed as most general counsel have now become the taskmasters and gatekeepers of outside counsel. Instead of being members of a "second-class citizenship," as they were when outside counsel was viewed as the landed gentry of the corporate, legal world, general counsel are now seen to be at the top of the profession's social order.[36] Nowadays, outside counsel may feel the need to pay a certain amount of homage to a general counsel in order to retain consistent and well-paid work. That shift in power (which is not, of course, always a very clear shift) does not mean a general counsel should act the part of an elitist. On the contrary, it is in this role—as a benevolent sovereign over many outside counsel resources—that a general counsel can deliver one of the greatest assets to his or her employer: access to competent, specialized, and attentive legal representation by selectively pairing specific outside counsel to specific projects or problems.

No one wants to work for a draconian dictator; likewise, few good professionals want to work for a sloppy, weak, and unpredictable manager. A general counsel, as a proxy for the corporation, must be able to set the overall tone for the company's approach to each of its legal issues, competently manage those activities, and knowledgeably evaluate the outcomes and effectiveness of the end results. At each stage, a general counsel must guide outside counsel with a firm hand, but one that does not micromanage. A general counsel must be as attentive to the needs of outside counsel (that is, for discovery, statements, depositions, document retention, and so forth), as a general counsel expects outside counsel to be attentive to the unique needs of the corporation. And like a medical internist, a general counsel needs to successfully orchestrate all outside counsel in concert with each other, especially in those matters that have multiple fronts, such as employment litigation tied to an ongoing internal investigation involving governance issues. Elbert Hubbard, an American editor and writer, once said that wisdom is knowing when to be generous and when to be firm. This is never truer than when selecting and dealing with outside counsel. As you make your decisions and take actions involving outside counsel, you must at all times remember you are speaking and acting for your company at large, and the consequences of what you say and do are much broader than the four corners of your own office.

Your third audience, as the *emissary* of your company, is global. This audience rightfully stands outside of your company's doors and receives information, well groomed or not, without any basic loyalty to your employer. This audience consists of regulators, clients and customers, creditors, policy makers, business partners, business rivals, journalists, pundits, bloggers, tweeters, talking heads, court jesters, and the unpredictable public.

We have all had our moments. Moments that torture us at night as we relive them in painful, vivid detail. Moments when we said something or did something we wish we could take back. Hopefully, most of your own bloopers have occurred in front of a limited audience, a friendly audience, an audience who could laugh with you in a supportive, sympathetic way. But alas, the faux pas that really give each of us the night sweats are probably those that occur in the public arena. These gaffes are irretrievably embarrassing and, worst of all, possibly damaging and destructive. In this sense, in which actions and words are at the mercy of outsiders, strangers, and foes, a general counsel must truly understand his or her role as a representative of the company.

Deals can fall apart, stock prices can dip, investigations can begin, contracts can be breached, lawsuits can be filed, images can be tainted, and congressional subpoenas can be issued when a corporation's senior legal officer says or does the wrong thing. Of course, the opposite can occur, too. A general counsel's words and actions can rally a sinking stock price, save a merger, avoid or quietly settle a lawsuit, improve a corporate image, and bring balance and composure to an otherwise worrisome situation. Your words and actions, whether you like it or not, reflect the legal brain trust of your employer. Indeed, as we noted earlier in this section, the very act of simply hiring a general counsel might be part of a corporation's public effort to handle a sticky situation. The moment a corporation's general counsel speaks, there is meaning, and there is an impact.

Thomas Saenz, the president and general counsel of the Mexican American Legal Defense and Educational Fund (MALDEF), who graduated from Yale University summa cum laude and from Yale Law School, who clerked for a federal district court and the Ninth Circuit Court of Appeals, and who has had a distinguished legal career as a civil rights advocate, reportedly made this comment on Arizona immigration laws: "If every state had its own laws, we wouldn't be one country; we'd be fifty different countries."[37]

Although Mr. Saenz was likely intending to explain the MALDEF's opinion on the importance of a single, federal immigration law over the haphazardness of individual state laws, this sound bite created some choppy water for his employer's political position and public image. In response to this innocent slipup, a politically conservative blog, Moonbattery, made Mr. Saenz's remark its "stupid quote of the day," coupled with an acerbic comment about the MALDEF.[38] A reader of the *Orange County Register* rhetorically opined, "How is it possible for an attorney such as Saenz, born here in Southern California and educated at Yale, to make such an ignorant statement?"[39] Regardless of political affiliations or opinions, any lawyer who reads Mr. Saenz's quote should feel a wince of empathy. We have all been there. No one is exempt from the occasional disconnect between the brain and the tongue.

A company depends on its general counsel to convey the level of its legal intellect, as well as the breadth of its business judgment. When a general counsel's words or actions call those qualities into question, a corporation can suffer. Conversely, when a general counsel's aplomb and diplomatic skill advance the perception of those qualities, a corporation can greatly benefit. By keeping in mind the three spheres of audiences when writing emails, drafting memorandums, providing advice, making decisions, speaking with the press, or simply walking down the hall, a general counsel is capable of delivering another invaluable resource to his or her corporate employer: that of a consummate ambassador.

A general counsel who possesses the deep rudder guidance of the *single*-client phenomenon—and who possesses an effective sense of his or her role as an advisor, administrator, team member, and corporate representative—will have the professional self-perception necessary to be a success and to remain an appreciated business investment of the company.

> *The aspects of things that are most important for us are hidden because of their simplicity and familiarity.*[40]

§ 1.1.2 *Defining* In-House Counsel

A general counsel is (almost always) an apex species of in-house counsel.[41] Every definitional trait of a general counsel carries the same DNA as carried by every in-house lawyer; it is only a matter of degree and application that distinguishes the two. Just as a successful general counsel must understand the four-point compass of his or her role, a successful in-house lawyer must also appreciate his or her role as an advisor, administrator, teammate, and corporate representative (and all points in between). Consequently, the previous section's discussion of those four roles is a must-read for every in-house lawyer, regardless of day-to-day duties or position. Whatever other expectations or responsibilities are involved in a particular area of in-house legal work, an in-house lawyer also shares the same expectations and responsibilities as a corporation's most senior lawyer. A deputy or associate in-house lawyer's success, and a general counsel's success, are entwined and should be mutually supporting. As in private practice, the limelight might follow a senior partner, but his or her glory rests on the shoulders of others: the legal team, standing in the shadow. The relationships and roles are synergetic with each other.

How then does the task of defining an in-house lawyer differ from the task of defining a general counsel?

The task of defining the role of an in-house lawyer must focus on the value and creation of a team concept. If a general counsel sits at the tip of the corporate spear, then an in-house lawyer, regardless of the rung of the ladder on which his or her upward mobility now rests, comprises the body of the spearhead and some of its incisive edges. The role of a successful in-house lawyer—what it *means* to be an in-house lawyer, aside from those basic components discussed in the previous section—is best described by his or her contributions to a corporation's legal team. This outlook is not simply a feel-good, rah-rah refrain of popular team-building endeavors. This outlook actually provides an in-house lawyer with value far beyond the temporary peaks of a successful project or event.

Eric Esperne, counsel for Dell Healthcare & Life Sciences, shared some practical wisdom on working as an in-house lawyer in an article for *InsideCounsel* magazine.[42] One of Mr. Esperne's ten pieces of advice is to "turn hierarchy into collegiality" by looking for opportunities to make "your reporting into the law department as 'flat' as possible."[43] This advice is referring to a type of organizational structure in which middle management (or superfluous hierarchical structure) is replaced with direct reporting to the person(s) who will actually perform the task— "flat reporting" (for example, a staff lawyer reviews a vendor purchasing agreement and submits the reviewed contract directly to the purchasing department, instead of routing it to a senior lawyer for dissemination). The point is that an in-house lawyer should look for ways to work as a team player, instead of merely grinding away as a back-office worker bee. "[O]ffering to help other lawyers in your department," as suggested by Mr. Esperne, is a quintessential hallmark of the role of an in-house lawyer. Your mission—your *role*—is defined by the value you bring to the legal department, and thus to your company as a whole. Even when a general counsel decides to structure his or her legal department along regimented, hierarchical lines, an in-house lawyer's desire and ability to bring initiative and substantive value by looking for opportunities to laterally contribute will always be welcomed.

Preceding his piece of advice to look for direct-effect opportunities, Mr. Esperne also delivers another important morsel of advice: don't worry about specializing.[44] Many in-house lawyers, and many general counsels, have built their reputations by focusing on distinct areas of law.[45] There is nothing inherently wrong with developing a specialization, but as an in-house lawyer, for most companies, specialization can reduce the value of your advice to your company-client. As Mr. Esperne urges, "specialize in knowing your company."[46] An in-house lawyer should be a "Swiss army knife,"[47] possessing enough knowledge to competently contribute, lead, and evaluate as part of a corporation's legal brain trust. "Improvements in [the] reputation and skill of in-house lawyers mark a watershed in legal demographics."[48] This observation is the result of the noticeable legal prowess of many in-house lawyers, but it is also the result of in-house lawyers delivering a better, overall business product to their employers.

What are the practical ways to meet that goal—the role of value contributor? There are a multitude of books on the market that address successful management. I would urge you to find a few (some are highlighted in Chapter 7) for nightstand reading. There are few better ways to understand how to contribute value than to understand what your management team needs from you from *their* perspective. Interestingly though, there are fewer books focused on the subject of being a team player, which should be your immediate concern, almost regardless of how far or how near you might sit under a general counsel.[49] Certainly, it is even more difficult to find a book that specifically centers on the subject of being a team player within a corporate legal department. Instead, you may find Cameron Stracher's nonfiction exposé on the rancorous life of an associate in a high-powered corporate law firm to be the only frank input on the matter, but Mr. Stracher's book would hardly constitute "good" advice (which perversely recommends it as a must-read).[50]

Just as law school may not do much to prepare a lawyer for the day-to-day practice of law or the business of running a law firm, law school also may not do much to formulate what it means to be an in-house lawyer (nor are most law schools designed to do so). After law school, once a lawyer has moved out of private practice and into an in-house setting, there are few who can look back on any kind of substantive training they received on how to bring real value to a large client. They find themselves working in a legal department (a quasi-law firm) for a single client as that client's employee. Most lawyers have not attended seminars or sat through meetings on corporate teamwork. Their minds, understandably, are probably still driven by the equation of task success equaling professional success. Although that equation has an obvious enough place, an in-house lawyer, just as a general counsel, must redefine what it means to practice law as a corporate employee.

Left therefore to our own devices, we need to formulate the value-contributor role of an in-house lawyer by recognizing several key elements of collaboration. These elements, together with a general counsel's four-point compass, will give an in-house lawyer the basis of her or her role.

Adaptability[51]

Harkening back to my days as a U.S. Marine—the archetypal embodiment of team ethos—there is a single trait, above all others, that defines an in-house lawyer's role: to be *adaptable*. We leathernecks used to say: "adapt and overcome." A corporation by its nature is a creature of surprising diversity and complexity. On any given day of the week (including weekends), a corporate lawyer will find him- or herself staring straight into the eyes of a question, an issue, or a bet-the-company lawsuit that had not existed a few moments before. Consequently, it is an in-house lawyer's ability to "adapt and overcome" that delivers the single greatest measure of value to the legal department and to the company. There will come the day when your entire company is looking to its in-house lawyers to hit a high-right, fast curveball out of the ballpark. If an in-house lawyer has a habit of contentedly shuffling papers in his or her own corner without keeping his or her head up and go-to place on the team sharp, then that wicked curveball will likely drill a hole through the legal department and the client-company.

When working as counsel for a regional hospital group, which was literally in the final hours of signing the paperwork for a hard-fought $97 million bond issue, I received an email alerting me to a series of medical malpractice lawsuits that had just been filed against the hospital and a long string of related defendants. Immediately, decisions had to be made about what to do. Of course, the preliminary official statement had already been circulated to institutional bond investors from the underwriter's trading desk, and the entire deal hung in the balance of a single sentence of disclosure, regarding "no pending litigation . . . of . . . any substantial risk of material liability." Within hours, all the energy of the deal went into strategic damage control, even to the point of finding myself on a conference call with institutional traders who were looking for a better sense of what the number of mounting lawsuits meant to the hospital's ability to repay the bonds (no script, notes, or prep time). Handling a variety of concerns and interpositions of the issuer's counsel, underwriter's counsel, bond counsel, and trustee's counsel, among others, kept things at a frenetic pace. Ultimately, the lawsuits rolled up the bond deal, but the adaptability and promptness of our legal team, working together for the client, gave our company valuable time and options.

Make sure you are adaptable. Fight the urge to become too territorial; this only pours concrete around your feet. Look for opportunities to exercise your adaptability on smaller, less consequential events. Wake up in the morning with a to-do list for the day, but on the way out of your front door, remind yourself to "adapt and overcome." An in-house lawyer's ability to calmly and decisively adapt to whatever storm hits the legal department will bring more value—practically and emotionally—to your corporate client than a year's worth of noble paper shuffling (which I am *not* belittling).

Dedication

One of the enticing qualities of working as an in-house lawyer is probably the predictability of being an employee of a company versus a law firm. In-house lawyers are, in my experience, very hardworking, but there is also the temptation to fall into an employment rut. Income is certain, business hours are set, and vacations are foreseeable, all of which are phenomena that can be disturbingly uncertain in private practice. Without the urgency of billing hours and the pressure of rainmaking, an in-house lawyer might unintentionally find him- or herself acting like a bureaucrat, feeling ruffled when asked to go the extra mile. Dedication (slightly different than loyalty) means an in-house lawyer is going to complete the work that is expected but then look around to find what else might need to be done. Your dedication is to the company at large. All events and tasks touched by the legal department are within your responsibility. You, as much as a general counsel, are a lawyer of the company.

Dedication does not always need to come in the form of late nights or painfully early mornings. Dedication also does not mean stretching yourself too thin or thrusting your nose into situations too far above your pay grade or too far beyond your level of competency. However, a genuine question of "How may I help?" always shows you are ready and willing. You are dedicated. An in-house lawyer who is dedicated to the functions and goals of the legal department is an invaluable asset to a general counsel and to a successful company.

Dependability

It would be embarrassing if you asked, "How may I help?" only to have to later explain your unavailability when you were needed because you decided to take an extra-long lunch. Dependability is only earned in one way: *being reliable*. It does no good to have initiative if you cannot be relied upon for follow-through. Unforeseeable things happen to everyone (and everyone likes a long lunch when they can take it), but your dependability means the legal department, the general counsel, and the company can depend on you to be present and accountable. Presumably, your company decided to invest in employing a full-time lawyer when they hired you. That must mean, aside from possible cost savings, they wanted the advantage of having reliable legal counsel 24/7.

Unfortunately, I knew of a general counsel of a fairly large financial institution who would disappear from her office for hours at a time on random days and at random times. The institution (as is sometimes the case) was late to the game when it finally decided to hire its first in-house lawyer, and it made some critical judgment errors when it decided to hire this particular general counsel. This newly installed general counsel seemed incapable of exhibiting one of the most basic traits of employment: dependability. Out of all the complaints her tortured staff eventually disclosed about her, the fact that she was unaccountable, employed in absentia, was one of the most damning. Her lack of dependability had all kinds of ramifications: meetings could not be scheduled, deadlines could not be met (or set), interdepartmental questions were left unanswered, and confidence in the legal department dropped precipitously. For those and other reasons, she was eventually fired. Other employees, to say nothing of in-house lawyers, can and should be shown the door for being undependable. It is impossible to provide competent, timely, and valuable legal services—to be adaptable and dedicated—when you are unable or unwilling to be a dependable member of an in-house legal team.

Stick with routines. Everyone can work with a routine. Share your calendar; let other staff lawyers and staff members know where you are and for how long you plan on being there. Develop consistency with certain activities; predictable turnaround times with commercial contract reviews, for example, would allow a company's commercial lending department to reliably schedule its own tasks and representations to its customers. As much as anyone might like a sense of adventure, dependability—not erraticism—is a valued part of your role as an employee-lawyer.

Mission Orientation

The U.S. Marines impart two primary objectives to leadership, implemented at every level of every unit throughout the Corps: "mission accomplishment and troop welfare." Rarely are civilian situations as dire as those faced by hard-bitten Marines, but the pragmatism of the Corps' first objective has a clear application to the world of an in-house lawyer.[52] To get the job done, the mission has to come first. If there is a clarion call for an in-house lawyer, it is: *support the mission*.

When an in-house lawyer understands and helps to effectuate the overarching goal of a legal department, then value contribution is a natural result. This applies to a legal department as a whole—to deliver necessary, competent, legal counsel to the corporation—just as it applies to internal divisions, projects, or daily tasks. If you do not understand or have not bothered to learn the goal—the mission—then you cannot possibly be acting at 100% capacity as an in-house lawyer, nor can you deliver the return on investment your corporate employer anticipated when it hired you.

Heeding the greater mission will probably require you to think outside the legal box and import an external point of view into your law-based analysis. Take for instance the simple matter of advising your company's IT department on a software provider's service contract's choice-of-law provision. Forgetting for a moment all the myriad other legal issues that might affect your advice on this issue, you should know that any good transactional lawyer, and any good litigation lawyer, will practically demand that the choice-of-law provision name your company's home state, or your company's preferred venue, for purposes of contract interpretation (and litigation, if necessary). There are, admittedly, very good reasons for insisting on a home-court advantage in case your company finds itself in a contract dispute with the software provider. However, an in-house lawyer must also include within his or her analysis the question: What is the big picture? Sometimes the big picture is that your company may need the service contract more than it needs to stubbornly argue over a choice-of-law provision. After all, the overall goal of your company is its business, not a possibly deal-breaking tug-of-war over a single contract. The choice-of-law provision can be important, and it is certainly an item on which to provide thorough and suitable advice, but the point is that an in-house lawyer's role is to weigh his or her legal counsel in balance with the greater mission.

There may be those of you who are kindly (or not so kindly) thinking that it is a lawyer's primary function to provide *objective* advice to a client, and legal advice that pays too much attention to a nonlegal goal strips a lawyer of precious objectivity—the vaunted argument for the independence of outside counsel. A compromise of objectivity can certainly occur if an in-house lawyer fails to deliver advice in a balanced and thorough manner. It can also be true of outside counsel, who may pound his or her fist on the table with righteous conviction over a legal issue while forgetting the corporate client needs advice that assists in promoting, expanding, and strengthening its core business. Risks may have to be taken or endured.

For those in doubt, Willie Miller, deputy general counsel of Kraft Foods, Inc., made this remark about Jeanne Gills, a partner at Foley & Lardner and outside counsel for Kraft: "She listens to the conversations, to the discussions we're having, and then she responds in a manner that helps us to get to where we want to go."[53] All counsel, both in-house and outside, are best fulfilling their roles when they understand and look to help implement the overarching mission of the corporate client.

In-House

Preparedness

The drollness of Benjamin Franklin gives us a pithy grasp of the importance of being prepared: "By failing to prepare, you are preparing to fail." This simple truism, like each of the other elements of an in-house lawyer's role, should come as no surprise. Most lawyers were born with words in their mouths, ready to make an argument or fashion an opinion at the drop of a hat. Most of us are improvisers by nature, a helpful characteristic indispensable to adaptability. But when taken to an extreme, a knack for improvisation can regrettably encourage a lack of preparedness.

When someone pokes his or her head into your office and begins a request with "whenever you get the chance," the offhand invitation to take as long as you want is an illusion. If the request did not matter, the person would not have asked. More likely than not, your phone routinely buzzes with pressing questions or issues needing immediate attention or at least a quick turnaround. By staying as prepared as possible, you are better able to address either scenario promptly and knowledgeably. If you have to say, "I don't know, but I will find out," then be brave enough, and wise enough, to say it. And then find the answer as quickly as you can. Over the long run, your client will respect your honesty and your diligence, and your candor will lend credibility to your work.

There are a few keys to staying as prepared as possible, some of which you might already be doing without knowing it.

1. LISTEN: Many in-house lawyers' intelligence inhibits their ability to listen. They hear only the first half of the question, or they so quickly jump to a stock legal rule, practice, or position that they forget to listen to the entire question, weighing the goal of their client against the backdrop of the law.

2. KNOW THE LAW: Staying current on the laws, regulations, and litigation that affect your company and your company's industry is vital to providing good advice. Set up your electronic devices and information streams so that you are effortlessly fed a steady diet of current and relevant legal information. Daily (or weekly) canvassing of a few key web sites and legal newswires is an excellent technique for keeping up with the curve.

3. KNOW THE INDUSTRY: As important as the law is to your company, how the law fits (usually reactively) with your company's core business activities is the knife edge of where you sit as an in-house lawyer. Most industries have their own trade journals (many times online) and news outlets or resources. If you fail to keep pace with market trends, supply-side issues, delivery systems, demand-side issues, customer demographics and trends, and the myriad of other topics that may affect your corporation's operations, you will fall woefully short of meeting a corporation's needs, as would even the best-prepared legal mind.

4. KNOW THE COMPETITION: As part of staying current on industry matters, your capacity to keep your company's competition

in your sights is essential. Not only will the actions, news releases, employment issues, public-image issues, acquisitions or divestments, success, and failure of the competition give you a wealth of contextual information, it might also prove valuable when you need to attack or join its efforts.

5. KNOW YOUR COMPANY: As an employee-lawyer, this last bit of guidance is really your first step to being prepared for most issues that may walk through your door. You must keep your finger on the pulse of the corporation. As closely as you can, watch what is going on at every level (or on as many as you can manage). Drop by different departments, ask if you may sit in on meetings, attend company functions, participate in committees outside the legal department (if you can), and let everyone you speak with know that you are there to help (*not* interfere) and to support their jobs and operations. Preparedness is in lockstep with prevention. It is also in lockstep with progression. Your corporation will better be able to achieve success, stay competitively nimble, and generate good press when its in-house lawyers know what strategies, procedures, and methods are in place, as well as what the overall goals are.

Being prepared is a long-term project. It involves a healthy desire for self-improvement, coupled with a desire to benefit your company and your department. For most in-house lawyers, being prepared is (and should be) fairly generalized. Remember: you demonstrate your level of dedication by the dependability of your preparedness, and being prepared means you are better equipped to adapt to unexpected situations within critical timeframes. (Did you catch how these characteristics of an in-house lawyer's role just braided themselves together?)

Remedy Orientation
The popular perception, certainly held within the business world for a long time, is that lawyers are doomsayers. We warn of disaster, predict devastation, and use the word "no" far too often. No need to become defensive; the naysayer task is an indispensable part of good lawyering. A mild obsession over possible pitfalls is proactive risk management, and your corporate employer will always need you to shine a light in dark corners and say, "I wouldn't do that if I were you." Of course, our words

of caution need balance. Constant refrains of "no" and "be careful" will eventually erode the perception of your objectivity, and the impact of your advice might be lessened at times when it is needed the most.

To deal with this situation, decide to take an active part in finding a good or positive remedy[54] to whatever might be the problem or issue. Too often, an in-house lawyer's analytically risk- or loss-averse mind rushes only to defend against, or to warn away from, possible hazards. Like an unmoving sentinel, the oft-naysaying in-house lawyer can become so intent on protectionism that he or she forgets to help pursue a remedy. Neither function, though, is mutually exclusive from the other. A supportive in-house lawyer must be able to identify risks, threats, and liabilities, as well as generate or collaborate on curative resolutions. A corporate client needs its hawks to also be its doves (or at least its creative thinkers). An in-house lawyer can bring to bear the invaluable asset of his or her trained and battle-ready mind on a corporation's question of "how do we get this done?" instead of stopping at "don't do it."

The encouraging fact is, a majority of lawyers regularly execute this one-two punch combination on a micro scale. If you care to perform an Internet search with the search term "solution-oriented lawyer," you are very likely to see page after page of law-firm web sites that feature their law shops as solution oriented. Many of their marketing claims may be true. Every day, lawyers encounter drafting problems, regulatory proscriptions, procedural obstacles, or litigation complications, and they deftly find their way around the issue (or through it). Part of an in-house lawyer's role is to take his or her well-worn micro-habit and layer it with a macro-habit. Because an in-house lawyer's relationship with his or her client is not event driven, an in-house lawyer's legal practice is concerned both theoretically and practically with the entire corpus and lifespan of the corporate employer. An in-house lawyer's thinking cap must be large enough to troubleshoot discrete tasks, and it also must be large enough to see those tasks as they exist within the greater universe of the corporation as a whole.

Janice Block, executive vice president, general counsel, and chief compliance officer for Kaplan Higher Education, said "we need to be able to prioritize both the problems and the solutions, and implement action plans for putting those solutions firmly into place."[55] After watching her elementary school daughter take part in a growing international problem-solving program,[56] Ms. Block identified six steps to generate a remedy for any situation. They are to find and develop:

1. all possible problems with any given scenario,
2. the most important underlying problem,
3. remedies to solve the underlying problem,
4. measurements by which to evaluate the remedies,
5. the best remedy, and
6. a plan for implementing the remedy.

Even if an in-house lawyer does nothing more than grab the closest legal pad and take a few minutes to loosely jot down ideas for each of these steps, he or she will not only have identified inherent hazards but also will have unwittingly walked through a process designed to build-in a global point of view. An in-house lawyer's perspective must encompass more than just a panorama of the law; it must lie within a greater landscape of the company's condition and goals. When an in-house lawyer begins to regularly take even a few moments to step back from an issue or problem—or actually create an intradepartmental procedure for problem solving—and to systematically explore possible remedies, then his or her advice to the corporate client is going to have a much more valuable scope.

Instead of adding another disjointed opinion to the mix, when other employees, department heads, executives, or board members are sitting around a table trying to come to grips with a problematic issue—an issue impeding the company's business—an in-house lawyer's role should be to present the legal aspects while collaboratively augmenting efforts to find the best remedy. As Henry Ford said, "Don't find fault. Find a remedy."

What is the role of an in-house lawyer?
Beyond individual job descriptions, your role is to act as an advisor, administrator, colleague, and corporate representative; more essentially, your role is to be an adaptable, dedicated, dependable, mission-oriented, prepared, and remedy-oriented lawyer-employee. Your role is defined by your teamwork, as a lawyer and an employee, and your ability to deliver valued contributions to your company as a whole. An in-house lawyer's professional life is not guided by billable hours, rainmaking, or the next big case. Working inside of a corporation means to practice law

as a tool—a critical tool—for the advancement of a business enterprise. Undergird all of your assignments and responsibilities with the core definitional characteristics we have discussed, and you will consistently deliver value to your client-company.

§ *1.1.3 Defining* Outside Corporate Counsel

There are those lawyers who have picked up this book to take a long, hard look inside the window of an in-house lawyer's world. Or they have picked up this book because they make camp just outside the doors of corporate America. These are the long ranks of blue-suited corporate lawyers, the ubiquitous "outside counsel."

Much has been made of the traditional friction and competition between in-house counsel and outside counsel,[57] but to a large extent, the competitive acrimony has done little to make either group a better value, or a better sell, to corporations. Mudslinging detracts credibility from both factions.[58] Cynicism and negativity do not yield positive opinions, and corporate clients do not favor their outside counsel or their in-house counsel as a result of one slinging enough mud at the other. Putting that checkered history (what *should* be a historical attitude) behind us, an objective observer would acknowledge that outside counsel and in-house counsel now reside in a much more symbiotic, rather than antagonistic, state. They are, and should be, complementary to each other's function and purpose, although there may still be some quibbling over just how to get the job done.

The role of outside corporate counsel is iterative of the roles—the *meaning*—of a general counsel and of an in-house counsel. Most of the characteristics of in-house counsel are equally crucial for outside corporate counsel to digest and live by. Outside corporate counsel, even if in a more limited, unique way, act as advisors and representatives of a company. They need to be mindful of their adaptability, dedication, dependability, preparedness, and remedy orientation. Not only will a corporate client look to its outside counsel for legal advice and representation as defined by these traits, but in-house peers and colleagues will also need to know the outside corporate counsel is just as driven by the goal of value contribution as they are. Mere subject-matter experience, and even a solid understanding of the industry and the individual client's goals, are not enough. Being a successful outside counsel (for the long term) means more than that.

Loyalty

Some time ago, I took a call from one of a client's senior banking executives, who was hoping to develop a creative lending strategy for a large construction-company customer. She wanted the customer's business, but she was rightfully concerned about compliance issues, how certain deal structures might affect the bank's statement of condition (its balance sheet), and what kind of structure would protect the bank in the future. Because of internal lending policies and requirements, and because inventive transactional work can only (legally) cure so many ills, I had to finally tell her the suggested strategies were recipes for eventual failure. I could not take advantage of an opportunity for easy fee generation and claim I was an honest broker when I knew that whatever lending maneuvers could be created would very likely compromise the bank later on. Sounding almost relieved, even though she was going to lose some business at my direction, the banker thanked me and promised to call again soon with more business. And she did.

When asked what makes the partnership between UPS and one of its outside counsel, Alston & Bird, so strong, Richard Rufolo, a UPS vice president and in-house lawyer, said, "trust. . . . It goes beyond just the legal advice," Mr. Rufolo said. "It drives the relationship." [59] For outside counsel, legal advice and the relationship with a corporate client must go beyond subject-matter expertise, and it must go beyond simply identifying with a corporate client's goal. Your attitude, actions, and decisions must tell the client, "you come first, and your ability to rely on our loyalty comes first." If you step back and objectively look at a corporate client's need for loyalty—allegiance to the client first—you will have discovered the key ingredient to creating and maintaining a successful, long-lasting business relationship. For lawyers in private practice, who are more often trained in an event-driven mentality, this sometimes takes a conscious effort.

Sarah Feingold, general counsel of Etsy, an e-commerce company that has grown to eight hundred thousand sellers and twelve million buyer accounts,[60] related an unfortunate experience she had with a hopeful outside counsel.[61] As Ms. Feingold was finishing an introductory call with a very promising outside counsel candidate, the lawyer asked where to send his bill for the telephone call.[62] In less than a minute, he had communicated to Ms. Feingold, the general counsel of a company with which he hoped to do business, that his fees were more important to him than the relationship he was about to build. Ms. Feingold summed up the unhappy result of missing that key ingredient:

> My company and I were excited about the prospect of starting a new long-term relationship with a law firm that comprehended our goal. In one minute, however, all of that was thrown away. The attorney's short-sighted view of legal fees and, in turn, how to generate business, proved to me that I had to continue my legal search.[63]

Loyalty means something more than simply being committed. For outside counsel, loyalty is much more akin to the fiduciary duty of good faith imposed upon corporate directors (and officers): "to not allow . . . personal interest to prevail over that of the corporation."[64] Even more obviously than an in-house lawyer's loyalty, your loyalty to your corporate client, and the client's ability to rely on it, is loyalty to an *ambition*—the ambition of a long-term connection, driven by the success of the company and your desire to remain a part of that success. The fees will roll in, but first and foremost, a corporation has to know you put them first.

Outside Counsel

Independence
An in-house lawyer's likelihood of receiving some kind of equity-based compensation is a growing trend and has been for years.[65] Because of this, and simply because an in-house lawyer is an employee of a corporate client, outside counsel can bring a sense of independence to the legal services being provided to the client. The "not independent

enough" critique is, in fact, one of the globs of mud sometimes thrown at in-house counsel. In truth, the difference in independence between in-house lawyers and outside counsel should be illusory. All lawyers, by virtue of their role as advisors, are compelled to strive to "exercise independent professional judgment and render candid advice."[66] However, outside counsel does not usually have the unique, single-client financial exposure faced by an in-house lawyer, although the detachment of an outside counsel could also be undermined by the potential of large fees.[67]

As attractive as it may be to be ushered through the front doors and whisked upstairs to the executive suites, outside counsel does better to preserve the value of its objectivity by mindfully keeping issues beyond his or her engaged purpose at a good arm's length. When sitting in a meeting or on a conference call that appears to be outside the reasons for which you were engaged, take a quiet moment to ask yourself, "Why am I here?" Any simple answer may be frustratingly difficult to pin down because an outside counsel *should* make sure his or her advice and representation is in concert with broader-reaching goals. In many instances, an outside counsel's purpose of engagement is also generalized, even if it initially springs from a particular event, and you may have a long-term interest in staying in the loop of a company's day-to-day operations. Just be cautious as you tread. It is far too easy to be drafted as a partisan in the internal squabbles precipitated by a certain executive or board member (or other faction). It is far too easy to be viewed as taking someone's side, instead of preserving the above-the-fray significance of a professional point of view. The best insulation is to let your route to the company always go through the door of the general counsel's office or the legal department. There are specific instances when this will not work—such as when you have been hired directly by a board's internal audit committee—but in those instances, it is all the more necessary for outside counsel to be seen as an operating device, not a decision-making authority.

Independence is not synonymous with impassivity. Your client needs your zealous representation and your passion for balanced advice. Abraham Maslow,[68] a professor of psychology at Brandeis University in Brooklyn and Columbia University, said, "Dispassionate objectivity is itself a passion, for the real and for the truth."

Let dispassion be your passion.

Specialization

I use the word *specialization* logically instead of as a designation, realizing that many state bar associations do not allow lawyers to use that descriptor unless board certifications or other accreditations have first been met. Though most in-house lawyers should "specialize" in generalization, an outside counsel should be an area-specific doyen. An outside counsel's ability to devote his or her energy and concentration within a single area of law affords the company-client the shrewdness of a specialist. In several areas of law, such as intellectual property, employment, mergers and acquisitions, bankruptcy, securities, and tax (to name only a few), subject-matter expertise *is* the commodity.

There are certainly law firms large enough, with enough divisions and departments, to act as a one-stop shop for a corporation, but in most circumstances, outside counsel should concentrate the efforts of his or her representation on one, or a limited number, of practice areas and excel in them. Engaging in too many areas for a single corporate client may invite conflict, or the perception of conflict. Imagine a firm's governance division presenting a best-practices policy to a board regarding FASB[69] pronouncements for revenue recognition procedures, while the company's general counsel is, at the same time, using the same law firm's international division to defend a lawsuit based on the company's historical use of the International Accounting Standards involving revenue recognition procedures (which can conflict with domestic standards). Sound complicated? It can be, so beware.

Simply put, part of the role of outside counsel is to provide a corporate client with independent, objective legal representation and guidance. Resist the temptation to compromise that commodity, and wisely take pains to preserve it. Michael Porter, the Bishop William Lawrence University Professor at Harvard Business School, provides a nicely packaged perspective: "A 'strategy' delineates a territory in which a company [such as a law firm] seeks to be unique."[70]

Standard-Bearer

Like a general counsel and other in-house lawyers, outside counsel is a unique, civic agent of a client-company. Zealous representation—even when dispassionately underwritten—is a cornerstone principle of every lawyer's legal practice. This principle extends well past the courtroom, perhaps most importantly *beyond* the courtroom, when outside counsel, many times more vividly than most, has the opportunity to exhibit a true attitude of *esprit de corps*. In-house lawyers by the nature of their direct association with a corporation wear a company's badge openly. However, outside counsel live their lives further afield, routinely attending functions, going to conferences, engaging other clients, and plying their trade in a variety of forums, none of which may have anything to do with a corporate client. But it all *affects* a corporate client.

Judges, other members of the bar, and the public at large may view a corporate client through the lens of an outside counsel's activities. An outside counsel must not think of him- or herself solely within the framework of his or her law firm. An outside counsel must realize reputation, action, success, or failure may impugn a client-company, too. This, of course, can be a wonderful sweetener for a corporation. If, for instance, a chagrined adversary of Facebook, Inc., decided to file suit against the social-networking giant, it might find itself facing Gibson, Dunn & Crutcher—*The American Lawyer*'s choice for Litigation Department of the Year in 2010 and 2011—which Theodore Ullyot, general counsel of Facebook, has described as having "the complete game. They're aggressive and tenacious—they're incredible trial lawyers and superb on appeal. They really dig deep and nail down facts, and then they come up with the best legal and factual arguments."[71]

Reputation: a thousand years of consequence based upon the conduct of a single moment.[72]

Outside corporate counsel is, in a very concrete way, the principal prosthesis of an in-house lawyer. Most in-house legal departments have more work than they can rightfully handle, and they look for a loyal, independent, and specialized "extra set of hands" to deliver the best, most efficient, and talented legal product for their corporate employer. After her employer, MIPS Technologies, Inc., earned $82 million in revenue during the 2010–2011 fiscal year, Gail Schulman, the company's vice president, general counsel, and corporate secretary, recognized the benefit of having top-flight outside corporate counsel at her company's disposal.[73] Ms. Schulman runs an energetic but small (three full-time lawyers) in-house shop that depends on the abilities of its outside counsels' extra sets of hands. Speaking of her outside counsel peers, her comments reveal the appreciation and the underlying core trait a general counsel, and any in-house lawyer, has for exceptional legal support: they "really understand" the needs of her company and her company's industry.[74]

There is a close collaboration between in-house lawyers and their successful outside counsel. The role of outside counsel—their *raison d'être*—is to ensure their part in the collaboration is value contributive and ultimately a trustworthy business investment for the corporate client.

§ *1.1.4 Your Employment Contract*

The first section of Chapter 5 will focus on the area of employment law. A pervasive part of that area of law has always been—especially for corporate lawyers—the notorious or unwieldy employment contract. A corporate lawyer will likely have the opportunity, or burden, to draft various employment contracts, reviewing them and perhaps litigating over them. Employment issues can present many minefields, and employment contracts represent a singular, but not impassable, type of minefield. As is natural with other employment-law issues, employment contracts personally affect in-house lawyers as *employees*, especially a general counsel, who is also an executive and who is likely to be employed under executive contract. Because it should also be one of the first exercises of an in-house lawyer's ability to professionally balance personal interest and opinion with the interests of the corporate employer, it is a good idea to run through some of the idiosyncrasies of *your* particular patch of mines at the outset, especially if employment contracts are something new to you.[75]

This section will not be an effort to map out an exact contract. This is also not intended to be legal advice, nor is it to take the place of good legal advice (or tax advice). Instead, this section is intended to provide some working insights, suggestions, and bits of caution about the uniqueness of employment contracts for in-house lawyers. Though there are numerous good examples of employment contracts readily available, every employment situation is distinct enough that one size does not fit all, especially as an employee-lawyer.

This may be a wise time to seek personal counsel at least to review your contract and to recommend a few salient points of discussion for you to have with your new employer (or current employer if you are renegotiating or newly instituting an employment contract). Lawyers do not always provide themselves with very objective or well-reasoned advice. Many times the executive recruiting and hiring process also encompasses the negotiating process for an in-house lawyer's employment contract. This can be unnerving, and there can be the tendency to be less thorough and thoughtful in the eagerness to seal the deal. Do not give in or give up. It is a friendly negotiation, and there is (and should be) real value on the table for both parties. Work jointly together to draft an employment contract that will protect you both and that will deliver the most value for you both.

You *Need* a Contract

As exciting as a new employment opportunity can be, especially one that has been long awaited and precipitously career enhancing, it is prudent to pause, take a deep breath, and think about your future. Your employer *wants* you to think of your future (even if the employer does not consciously know it). The future is not years away; it consists of every moment after you begin your new job. What are your expectations, and your employer's expectations, while you work for your client-company, and what are your expectations, and their expectations, after you move on? If there is not a four-cornered document addressing all of those expectations, then when the ground shifts—and it *will* shift in some unpredictable way— you might find that you have built this part of your career on sand. Your employer will find it has built its investment in you on sand. Either way, it will not be pretty. This, therefore, should be the most obvious of all of the elements of an employment contract—*it should exist*.

I have personally seen at least one company with a balance sheet of almost $2 billion that had *no* substantive employment contracts in place for its executives (or its general counsel). When various executive employment relationships ultimately came to an end (unfortunately, a contentious end), there were no contractual processes or expectations to light a path forward. The road to a more peaceful, predictable parting of ways was nervously dark.

Your Contract

Most businesses are built and developed on a loom of assorted contracts, yet adequate employment contracts—especially for those persons whose job it is to dominate such a significant part of a business's growth and success—often seem frustratingly ill conceived, clumsy, or entirely nonexistent. Do not set an example of poor legal representation by allowing your own employment to proceed without a contract. As critical as engagement letters (or legal-services contracts) are to outside counsel, an employment contract is equally critical to in-house counsel. If approached with a positive attitude, your corporate employer will appreciate your initiative and/or thoughtful input.

Commencement Dates and Renewal

Seemingly insignificant, and not part of the real meat on the bone, are the terms of your commencement date (when you officially begin your duties) and the options, if any, of renewal. As is the case with all other "routine" parts of a contract, these items can become suddenly relevant and scrutinized under certain circumstances.

Your commencement date is a *contractual* concept; when you physically begin working might be irrelevant if your contractual start date is ever part of any employment question. Your commencement date can passively affect several kinds of activities, such as your eligibility for benefits, the vesting of your retirement plan, and the timing for you to exercise equity-based compensation derivatives or the sale of company stock. Your commencement date might also have an effect on your own tax situation. For your company's part, the commencement date might affect disclosure filings or something as practical as payroll procedures. Pause and think through the "if, then" scenarios of any particular commencement date. It is a small exercise, but your commencement date is *the* starting point for everything else.

The renewal (or not) of your employment contract also begins its clock from your commencement date. The functional design of a renewal provision is to provide an end date, necessary for statutory or common law elements of a contract, but to do so in a way that allows for some kind of perpetuity. Interestingly, it also gives you (and your company) a window in which to evaluate the benefits of your relationship and decide whether it is worth continuing. A renewal provision can also establish a hypothetical term of damages in case of breach (a painful but still obligatory thought). Renewal provisions can contain arrangements for a renewal bonus, or they can contain severance arrangements if your contract is not renewed. It is an interesting question to ask of yourself and of the company: Which arrangement is, or should be, larger? If they are the same, then renewal can be seen (except for future income) as a zero-sum game. If one is larger than the other, then it might create an incentive, or disincentive, to renew.

Titles and Responsibilities

"As to my Title, I know not yet whether it will be honourable or dishonourable, the issue of the War must Settle it." Abraham Clark, a signer of the Declaration of Independence and a member of the Second and Third U.S. Congresses, hit upon the singular truth of all titles: *their meaning can have little to do with their label*. Whatever your title might be, it is *how* you execute your *role* that will have lasting impact on your company, its perception of you, and your career.

Having said that, a title does convey (at least on the surface) certain obligations, responsibilities, involvements, and potential liabilities. Particularly in a corporate context, and much more so in a *public* corporate context, a title that places you in a management or executive tier can be as perilous as it is flattering. Be aware of that effect. As a lawyer, you automatically carry a heightened expectation of professional responsibility; a lofty title and its trappings can add to that. Your title, of course, emanates from the client: who it is and how it is organized.

Interestingly enough, what most contracts are unlikely to contain is a good description of *who* the client is. This may seem a bit redundant; common sense says your employer is your client. But since when are contracts bastions of common sense? Though the contract will certainly identify the name of your employer, it is well worth the extra sentence or two to articulate, in black and white, that you are being engaged by—providing legal counsel to—the corporation as an *entity*. As we will see later in Section 2.1.2, the need for everyone, not just you, to understand whom you will be representing. Whom you will *not* be representing is fundamental and can be confusing. Outside counsel would not dare to enter into a legal-services contract, or to issue an engagement letter, unless the paperwork clearly stated who the client was. Likewise, your engagement letter, your contract, should tack out similar language, perhaps following the description of representation of an entity provided in the rules of professional conduct. This will help to put everyone on notice of what underlying obligation should be driving your decisions and advice, regardless of to whom you report or who has hiring and firing authority over you.

From this, your responsibilities and job description will influence your professional accountability. This is the area of your contract that may prove to be the most interesting yet vague. Ironically, a typical description of responsibilities relies on the abstraction of your title: "As Chief Legal Officer, you shall have the powers and duties commensurate with such position, including but not limited to . . ." A few notable responsibilities or obligations may then be listed, but there is usually a scarcity of substance. Constructively, this scarcity leaves elasticity in a position that probably has too many day-to-day responsibilities to list without the risk of leaving something out. However, you should find out what is commensurate with the position you are taking, specifically as those things relate to the norm in your client-company's industry.

You should also take the time to discuss various tasks and perhaps have them written in. For an in-house lawyer, a company's organizational chart is more fluid under certain circumstances. An in-house lawyer's ultimate duty is to the corporate client, and the execution of his or her responsibilities to that client might step outside the conventional lines of the chain of command. Most other employees would not experience that kind of anomaly except in rare circumstances of reporting fraud or something of that nature, but an in-house lawyer has a consistent, ever-present professional duty to provide competent legal advice to the corporation as a whole. On a daily basis, this function is usually performed through specific conduits, such as a chief executive officer, but frequently, a general counsel (and as necessary, other in-house lawyers) should provide legal advice directly to a client-company's board.[76]

It is imprudent to leave the description of your responsibilities and obligations too vague, too loosely hung upon a common title. Aside from the rules of professional conduct that govern your actions as a lawyer, it is this section of your employment contract that will govern your actions as a lawyer-employee.

Full-Time Attention and Other Activities

Naturally, you should expect your employer will want your full-time attention. Your company-employer will be your sole client, and the business of running a business is understandably a round-the-clock endeavor. This provision of your contract will most likely have some variation of standardized language describing the expectation that you will devote your "best efforts" and "full-time business attention" to your job. This is prefatory to your contract's allowance, or prohibition, of "other activities."

In-house lawyers are, in many cases, uniquely positioned to pursue activities that are commonly part of most lawyers' careers. These activities, such as teaching, writing, professional membership participation, and guest or public speaking, can also benefit a lawyer's corporate employer: a more well-rounded, widely respected in-house counsel is a public-image booster for a company.[77] These other involvements are also likely to improve your professional network and your level of subject-matter proficiency. It is good to talk about these kinds of opportunities, even if they are not part of your present experience or detailed in your contract. At some point, they are likely to divert some of your attention or time, but this could be something that your employer views as an advantage. As an example, your participation in the leadership of the American Bar Association's standing committee on environmental law may add indirect clout to your client-company's position on a business-related issue being considered by the U.S. Senate Committee on Environment and Public Works. Executives routinely are encouraged by their employers to sit on civic committees or on the boards of other companies when invited to do so.

The cautionary aspect of this provision in your employment contract, and specifically for lawyers, is that none of your extracurricular pursuits should conflict, or be perceived to be in conflict, with your legal representation of your client-company. For most other employees, conflicts can be more obvious. They, obviously, should not perform work that is competitive with the company's business. Executives are also usually barred from owning securities of any publicly traded competitor. However, you should exercise even more discretion. If your client-company finds itself in a litigious or potentially litigious situation with its distribution-services vendor—one in which you or your immediate family owns stock—you should disclose your equity position to your employer. You may need to liquidate it, or you may need to obtain a waiver of conflict of interest from your employer if you want to keep your investment.[78]

Lawyers in private practice usually think of conflicts of interest in terms of representation. As an in-house lawyer, you must consciously think more broadly than that. Conflicting representation will rarely be an issue, but acquiring "an ownership, possessory, security, or other pecuniary interest adverse to"[79] your corporate employer might take some thoughtful care.

Compensation

It is rare that the issue of compensation is not a well-tilled part of almost any negotiated employment contract. The hiring process's carousel ride has (almost) come to a close for you, and all that's left is to grab the brass ring. Even if the parleying is not vigorous between a company and a new hire, this provision probably receives the most readership attention, whether the attention comes from the two bargaining parties or from scrutinizing "outsiders"—shareholders, regulators, or (wince) the unsparing public.[80] In a society consumed by wealth and privilege, executive pay, in all its sundry forms, is no longer a private matter for compensation committees and senior management, and especially in publicly traded companies, it never should have been thought of in that way.[81]

Borrowing again from Eric Esperne's practical dollops of in-house counsel wisdom, "Don't chase the money."[82] Approach compensation fairly—for you and your client-company—and more money will almost surely follow you down the road. Your base salary should reflect a normative amount earned by other similarly situated peers in other comparable professional positions. There are good resources, readily available, to help you and your employer find the right set of upper and lower poles between which you can bargain for your salary.[83]

Any kind of achievement or performance bonus should also reflect an industry norm, and, most important, it should be aligned with a determinable metric of the company's (or your department's) performance. In 2011, the "top lawyers did pretty well for themselves," says Shannon Green in her article for *Corporate Counsel*, "as long as their boards and CEOs thought they did right by their companies."[84] The embattled national economy took a lot of pepper out of bonuses and performance compensation, but as recessive numbers are coming back up, cash—a "non-equity incentive"—has largely taken the place of traditional stock options. For integrity's sake (or perception) as previously discussed in Section 1.1.3, *not* having an equity stake in your client-company might actually be preferable for an in-house lawyer. On the other hand, an executive or senior manager who does not have an ownership interest in his or her own company can make investors, and maybe other managers, nervous. Aligning personal interests with corporate interests is not always a bad thing.[85]

Another type of bonus you may find tantalizingly included in your employment contract is a transaction bonus or retention bonus. If so, it is perfectly all right to feel momentarily flattered. These kinds of bonuses are typically used to entice and retain key employees in the event a client-company entertains the desire to merge with, or be acquired by, another company. This type of bonus can also be used as a defensive measure—a "poison pill"—to help a company ward off unsolicited bids for acquisition: ideally, compensation packages become too big for the acquiring company to absorb. A transaction bonus is typically cojoined to other severance protections, and it can come in the form of cash or pre–change-in-control (CIC) stock awards. They are usually awarded as fixed dollar values, percentage-of-equity deal values, or a fixed number of shares. Bonuses arising from CIC transactions can become complex, and in spite of having each provision spelled out in your contract, their future value—and therefore any present incentive to you—may remain vague and unpredictable. Even if you are an old hand at the mergers and acquisitions game, a transactional bonus provision might be a good reason for you to hire a lawyer.[86]

The withholdings portion of your employment contract will most likely be fairly standard, referencing applicable federal, state, and local taxes. If your position will be overseas, and if you remain overseas long enough to qualify for the bona fide residence test or the physical presence test, then you may be able to exclude almost seven figures of your wages from U.S. taxation. An additional exclusion amount may also be for your housing.

Expense Allowances and Fringe Benefits

Raising the issue of vacation time during an interview might kill the deal, but before inking your employment contract, make sure you have covered this base. If the company works you to death, you are going to need some time in the sun.

For this section of your contract, you might ask to speak directly with a client-company's human resources representative or a benefits representative. Make sure you understand all the available programs—health and life insurance and pension and savings plans—and how they affect or do not affect your paycheck, as well as when or how they accrue and vest. (Don't forget tax consequences.)

A more involved employment contract will also discuss company loans and business-expense reimbursements. Depending on the industry, such as banking, you will need to research regulatory limitations and restrictions if you are not already familiar with them. Take a close look at the client-company's policies and guidelines *before* taking advantage of either of these kinds of benefits. Assumptions can be catastrophic. You also need to understand how these benefits will be handled in the event of a change in control at the company or a "significant event," which should be defined.

For lawyers, it is wise to discuss professional-liability insurance as an additional paid or participatory benefit. If you are an officer of the company, your business decisions as an officer should be covered by the client-company's directors' and officers' policy ("D&O," directors and officers, or "E&O," errors and omissions, insurance), but because providing legal advice may distinctly fall outside of covered duties as an officer, and because many in-house lawyers are not company officers, a professional-liability policy may need to be included. If an insurable error is made, your client-company—its officers, directors, and shareholders—would have some financial recourse, and you could rest more easily. Your company is your employer, but your company is also your legal client. Insurance concerns might also be pointedly critical if your position would place you in the crosshairs of the Responsible Corporate Officer Doctrine,[87] which has budded up in certain areas of law, such as the Environmental Protection Act, the Stark Law, the Securities Exchange Act, and the Foreign Corrupt Practices Act. This formidable (and, some would argue, unconstitutional) doctrine imposes *strict criminal liability* (that is, without *mens rea*) on unsuspecting corporate officers, including general counsel.[88]

Likewise, do not forget the expense of bar dues and continuing legal education. Most companies will accommodate professional licensing costs, but be careful to distinguish this benefit from other reimbursable expenses, such as general expense account expenditures, if necessary. (By the way, remember that your perks should come exclusively from your employer. Being handed box-seat tickets by a customer or an associative business might be exciting, but as a lawyer, you must always be thinking beyond company policy and examining everything in light of the professional rules of conduct and other governing regulations. Conflicts of interest or violations of applicable regulatory restrictions can occur unwittingly and within the blink of an eye.)

Confidentiality, Noncompetes, and Nonsolicitations

For lawyers, client confidentiality is second nature, and the insertion or omission of a contractual provision about proprietary information is almost pointless—except that your employer may later have a breach-of-contract claim against you, as well as a professional-liability claim, if your tongue should slip.

Noncompete clauses are also less relevant to most in-house lawyers, although some states have begun to enforce noncompetes against lawyers.[89] These kinds of provisions, or attached agreements, are treated differently depending on your employer's state of residence. Though the primary trend in most states favors nonenforcement of noncompete clauses because they interfere with potential clients' ability to freely choose legal counsel, you need to make sure you are aware of any controlling law or decisions that might indicate otherwise.[90]

Nonsolicitation clauses, or agreements, might prove more applicable than noncompete agreements, even though they also are not universally enforceable. Nonsolicitation provisions are typically more focused, prohibiting solicitation of employees (that is, asking a fellow employee to leave his or her employment and go work for you elsewhere), or prohibiting solicitation of customers, clients, or other companies on whom you have called while employed, or who have had business dealings with your employer.[91] As with noncompete provisions, you need to pay particular attention to scope, duration, and breadth.

Termination and Separation

For better or for worse, at some point, your employment relationship with your client-company will come to an end. If the end arrives on good terms—or at least unpredictable terms, such as death or disability—then you should be looking at measures of goodwill in your termination provision. Accrued salary, earned bonus compensation, vested retirement plans, paid-for benefits (or eligible-for benefits), accrued vacation, and other severance compensation may apply.

If the end arrives on dismal terms—for cause, or when either you or the client-company exercises an at-will right to terminate your employment—then you need to know exactly what will happen and what to expect, because your employment contract, and its enforceability, may be the only parachute you have. Not only will these provisions discuss severance (if any) and other related matters, they may also contain restrictions you will need to follow, such as not engaging in any business activity that is competitive with your former employer while severance benefits are being paid, not exercising certain issues of stock options, or not selling certain amounts of company stock for a certain period of time. The point is: tread carefully.

Many times the end arrives constructively. But you still need to be prepared. A change in control (carefully defined, one hopes) can herald an end to your services. Constructive termination also has its nuances of severance and restrictions.

Your employment contract is your client engagement letter and your job description all rolled into one. You need one, and it needs to be well drafted, thoroughly discussed, reviewed, and carefully followed. Use the previous suggestions and comments to make sure you are on solid, predictable footing with your employer. Consult with your own counsel as you see fit. Your new employment relationship will run more smoothly, and any thoughts about your future should be put more at ease.

§ 1.2 A FEW WORDS BEFORE YOU ROLL UP YOUR SLEEVES

You have a good sense of who you are, and your freshly executed employment contract is tucked under your arm. You are ready to go: sharpen the pencils and roll up the sleeves.

So what are the take-away points before the practical work begins?
I am reminded of a remark made by the Honorable Lewis A. Kaplan, United States District Judge for the Southern District of New York, regarding the fate of the unhappy defense counsel for KPMG's beleaguered former vice chairman of tax. The defense lawyers were no longer being paid their legal fees by their client, and they had sent notice to the court that they were withdrawing as defense counsel. Judge Kaplan had a different opinion. "Having signed on for the voyage, they are on for the voyage unless relieved by the court."[92]

Practicing corporate law can be an exquisitely demanding, and rewarding, career. Both in-house and outside counsel will find themselves in situations where a multitude of jobs are on the line, millions (or billions) of dollars are at stake, the media is less than kind, and regulatory enforcement or criminal prosecution is only one bad decision away; and there are always twenty-five hours of work to accomplish in a twenty-four hour day. Even the most well-prepared, focused corporate lawyer is going to pitch high out of the water from time to time, with his or her rudder fully clear of navigable water, ready to quit and move on. But if you remember who you are—a dedicated and necessary emissary, advisor, crewmember, and advocate for your corporate client—you will remember that you are your *client's* best rudder, and your client-company *needs* you (even if your client doesn't know it) in order to be a success over the long haul.

Reminded of that responsibility and privilege, I encourage you to weather the storm, go back to the basics—*your role for the benefit of the client*—and, unless ethically compelled to do otherwise, remain "on for the voyage unless relieved by the court."

NOTES

1. Association of Corporate Counsel, *Profile of In-House Counsel*, Dec. 2006, at 8. As reported in 2006, the base salary for an average in-house counsel lawyer was $165,000. The recent financial crisis disrupted the upward trend of many in-house salaries, but it appears that any step backward may be reversing its course. Kayleigh Roberts and Ashley Post, *In-House Salary Report*, InsideCounsel, Feb. 2011, *available at* http://www.insidecounsel.com/2011/02/01/building-worth-inhouse-salary-report.

2. *Reading the Tea Leaves: What's the Current Thinking on How Many Lawyers a Company Should Have?*, Sender Legal Research 634–35 (January 29, 2010), http://www.senderlegalsearch.com/archives/62.

3. As simple as it may sound, I highly recommend that you always keep a copy of *Black's Law Dictionary* on your bookshelf. I still have my circa–law school edition and have used it many times throughout the years. Language—the iron ore of wordsmiths—is weak and useless unless you can comprehensibly define the words you are using. This is especially vital in a business setting, where millions or billions of dollars may hinge solely upon the correct choice of words and phrases. The core, and wonderful, purpose of any dictionary, much less one whose focus is law, is to give us exactly the right kind of ore from which to fashion our arguments, ideas, opinions, and documents. *Sine qua non—without which, there is none.*

4. Deborah A. DeMott, *The Discrete Roles of General Counsel*, 74 FORDHAM L. REV. 955, 955 (2005).

5. Oliver Wendell Holmes.

6. DeMott, *supra* note 4, at 961–65. Professor DeMott thoughtfully proposes four hypotheses, namely: "(1) the fit between the general counsel's position and an individual lawyer's talents (the 'fit' hypothesis), (2) the prospect that service as general counsel may furnish a good launching pad into other positions within senior management (the 'launching pad' hypothesis), (3) the position's anticipated economic rewards (the 'economic' hypothesis), and (4) the contrast with partnership in a large law firm (the 'law firm contrast' hypothesis)."

7. For the purposes of this discussion, I am putting aside the less frequent situation in which a company's general counsel is a partner of a private law firm. That particular situation can have its place in certain circumstances, but much of the examination of that role is better addressed when discussing the role of an outside corporate counsel.

8. For all you armchair mathematicians out there (of which I am not one), Pierre de Fermat wrote a simple equation in 1637 within the margins of a copy of *Arithmetica* (an ancient Greek text by Diophantus). The equation was $xn + yn = zn$. Fermat claimed that he had a mathematical proof for the equation but that there was not enough room in the margin to write it down. The enigma of solving its general proof defied mathematical efforts for over 350 years.

9. There are always exceptions, such as companies with multiple divisions and subsidiaries, just as there are some exceptions for each of the upside advantages I have listed, but if the observation ceiling is raised a bit higher, then even the exceptions can characterize themselves within the simplicity hypothesis.

10. Conversely, the intrigue of private practice for many lawyers is that, on any given day, their universe of practice may radically expand or contract—the number of open files and limitlessly diverse issues might be many or few. In fact, when a private practice lawyer has only *one* client, it can create quite a bit of heartburn. The uncertainty of not knowing when the billable hours' gravy train will end can be disconcerting.

11. DeMott, *supra* note 4.

12. Plato, *Parmenides*.

13. Susanna M. Kim, *Dual Identities and Dueling Obligations: Preserving Independence in Corporate Representation*, 68 Tenn. L. Rev. 179, 200 (2001).

14. We will discuss this role more thoroughly in Section 5.4.

15. Model Rules of Prof'l Conduct R. 2.1 (1983).

16. The president & CEO of H&R Block pinpointed two key reasons for H&R Block's announcement that it was hiring Tom Gerke as its general counsel and senior vice president: "Tom has guided Fortune 500 companies through a variety of legal and regulatory challenges. He's also great at helping companies build on opportunities." Julie Beck, *H&R Block Appoints New GC*, InsideCounsel, Jan. 5, 2012, *available at* http://www.insidecounsel.com/2012/01/05/hr-block-appoints-new-gc. In 2011, H&R Block had been prohibited by the Justice Department from buying TaxAct, an online service. The antitrust lawsuit went to trial in late 2011.

17. JPMorgan Chase & Co. investment bank hired Jonathan Schwartz as its new senior lawyer in the spring of 2010. Mr. Schwartz's experience included stints as general counsel of Napster and deputy general counsel at TimeWarner, two companies that had participated in trench warfare with government regulators. Before taking up arms for private corporations, Mr. Schwartz had studied at Cambridge University as a Fulbright scholar, clerked for United States Supreme Court Justice Thurgood Marshall, worked as a federal prosecutor in Manhattan, and risen to the level of a principal associate deputy attorney general in the Department of Justice. Mr. Schwartz's hiring went hand in hand with in-depth SEC investigations and legal actions concerning JPMorgan's role in, and investment advice about, collateralized debt obligations.

18. In January 2012, Gerson Zweifach, a partner at Williams & Connolly, was named as the general counsel and a senior executive vice president of News Corp., Rupert Murdoch's broadcast and journalism behemoth, after the company had endured the ignominy of a massive phone-hacking scandal. The announcement release specifically noted Mr. Zweifach's experience as "one of the nations' [*sic*] leading litigators and a staunch protector of the First Amendment." The strategy of cherry-picking a high-profile First Amendment lawyer for News Corp.'s senior legal officer was directly tied to the company's interest in its bottom line. Mr. Zweifach fittingly said, "I look forward to working in concert with Rupert and News Corporation's businesses to help ensure the best possible return to all of the company's stakeholders." Alex Vorro, *News Corp. Officially Names Zweifach GC*, InsideCounsel, Jan. 10, 2012, *available at* http://www.insidecounsel.com/2012/01/10/news-corp-officially -names-zweifach-gc?t=careers. Eight days after it was announced that Mr. Zweifach had been hired as GC, News International, Inc., the British newspaper unit of News Corp., agreed to a range of settlement payments during a hearing in London. The first of the civil trials was about a month away at the time. Alex Vorro, *News Corp. Settles Hacking Claims with 36 Victims*, InsideCounsel, Jan. 19, 2012, *available at* http:// www.insidecounsel.com/2012/01/19/news-corp-settles-hacking-claims -with-36-victims?ref=hp. One of Mr. Zweifach's more engaging tasks is sure to be dealing with—both internally and externally—the revelation that senior employees and directors of News Group Newspapers (which published some of News International's newspapers) knew about the phone hacking and attempted to conceal it by destroying evidence and deliberately deceiving investigators.

19. Such is the case of David W. Healy, the former co-chair of Fenwick & West LLP's Mergers and Acquisitions Group. Mr. Healy was tapped by Hewlett-Packard to fill the general counsel spot on an interim basis after Michael Holston's departure was announced in December 2011. Mr. Healy had a deep background of corporate representation of technology companies in the practice areas of mergers and acquisitions, joint ventures, strategic partnering transactions, spin-offs, venture capital financing, public offering, and licensing matters.

20. This situation comes from the archives of my own experiences. A $1.8 billion financial institution's audit committee had hired counsel to conduct internal investigations of several of its senior management and board members. I was on the legal team acting for the interim transitional counsel as we investigated, interviewed, and "showed the door" to several high-level officers—the first of which was the institution's general counsel. My main roles were to advise on governance and regulatory issues, as well as to generally oversee the revitalization of the nearly paralytic legal department. As brutal as the process was in some ways, it was also very successful, notably because it provided the real opportunity for radical improvements in management and on the board without causing a single adverse hiccup in the institution's marketing, public image, or profits. Pathetically though, when the smoke had almost cleared, the newly installed senior executive vice president delivered a coup d'état to protect herself from her own eventual demise by strong-arming the still-weakened board into firing all of us. She knew she would probably be let go for her own past indiscretions, so she seized a brief window of power (and board exhaustion) to protect her own skin. The institution had no definitive replacement, and thereafter it seemed foolishly averse to selecting any corporate law attorney as its company lawyer. Mark Twain once said, "A man who carries a cat by the tail learns something he can learn in no other way." I still carry a few claw marks.

21. The Enron debacle should always remain a cautionary tale whose events and players merely recast themselves over time into new displays of corporate malfeasance, greed, willful ignorance, apathy, and criminal collusion. Enron's general counsel, James V. Derrick, provides us with a fateful example of a prominent litigator who was ill prepared (and did little to cure that lack of preparedness) to advise his corporate client on *all* aspects of its business. Instead, he blandly deferred to outside counsel or to "associate" general counsel from various Enron divisions. "[Derrick] reviewed the final drafts to look for obvious errors, but otherwise has little involvement with the related party proxy statement disclosures. He said that he relied on his staff, Vinson & Elkins and [Arthur] Andersen to make sure the disclosures were correct and complied with the rules." *In re* Enron Corp., No. MDL-1446, Civ. A. H-01-3624, 2003 WL 21418157, at 15 (S.D. Tex. 2003) (not reported in the Federal Supplement).

22. Reliance on an attempt to firewall blame or responsibility by hiring outside counsel is a dangerous game. *See, e.g.,* Itel Containers Int'l Corp. v. Puerto Rico Marine Mgmt., 108 F.R.D. 96 (D.N.J. 1985) (imposing liability on general counsel even though only local counsel signed pleadings).

23. This is the title of a poem written by Walt Whitman in 1865 as a tribute to a remarkable lawyer and a master administrator, Abraham Lincoln.

24. Anthony Paonita, *2011 Law Department Metrics Benchmarking Survey*, CORPORATE COUNSEL, Nov. 30, 2011.

25. Alex Vorro, *Jacksonville Jaguars Name New GC*, INSIDECOUNSEL, Jan. 11, 2012, *available at* http://www.insidecounsel.com/2012/01/11/jacksonville -jaguars-name-new-gc?t=careers.

26. I also admit to having an overwhelming urge to pause my writing and call Mr. Brown to ask him just that question.
27. *The Corporate Secretary—Duties and Responsibilities: What Does a Corporate Secretary Do?* The Society of Corporate Secretaries and Governance Professionals, http://www.governanceprofessionals.org/society/The _Corporate_Secretary_-_Duties_and_Responsibilit.asp (last visited Feb. 9, 2012).
28. *Id.*
29. *Id.* This article also makes the very good point that this potential dual identity between a corporate secretary and a general counsel (or other lawyer) may broach an interesting question as to whether advice that is given to the board (or management) is privileged: managerial/governance advice is not; legal/governance advice is if given by a lawyer.
30. Byron F. Egan, *Recent Fiduciary Duty Cases Affecting Advice to Directors and Officers of Delaware and Texas Corporations*, 32nd Annual Conference on Securities Regulation and Business Law, Feb. 12, 2010, at 37.
31. *Id.* at 1.
32. We will take a closer look at this lawyer/executive tightrope walk in Section 6.4.5.
33. DeMott, *supra* note 4, at 962–63.
34. Alex Vorro, *Kodak Promotes Its GC to President*, INSIDECOUNSEL, Dec. 23, 2011, *available at* http://www.insidecounsel.com/2011/12/23/kodak -promotes-its-gc-to-president?t=deparment.
35. Ms. Quatela's business acumen was needed more than ever when, a few days after announcing her promotion to president, Kodak filed for Chapter 11 business reorganization in the U.S. Bankruptcy Court for the Southern District of New York.
36. *Reading the Tea Leaves, supra* note 2, at 622.
37. NYDailyNews.com, *Furor over Arizona's controversial new immigration law continues to grow*, April 27, 2010, http://articles.nydailynews.com/2010 -04-27/news/27062891_1_illegal-immigrants-immigration-status-federal -immigration-officers/2 (last visited Feb. 3, 2012).
38. Moonbattery.com, *Stupid Quote of the Day*, April 27, 2010, http://www.moon battery.com/archives/2010/04/stupid-quote-of.html (last visited Feb. 3, 2012).
39. Patrick Buckley, *Letters: Arizona's Immigration Law in Perspective*, ORANGE COUNTY REGISTER, Apr. 28, 2010, *available at* http://www.ocregister.com /opinion/state-246347-states-register.html.
40. Ludwig Wittgenstein—a twentieth-century philosopher of logic, mathematics, language, and the mind.
41. Unless there is a specific reason to not do so, the terms *general counsel* and *in-house counsel* will be used interchangeably throughout the rest of this book and will be equally covered by the term *corporate lawyer*. Please keep in mind the use of one term does not necessarily preclude the application of any other.
42. Eric Esperne, *10 Pieces of Advice from a Seasoned In-House Lawyer*, INSIDECOUNSEL, Dec. 16, 2011, *available at* http://www.insidecounsel .com/2011/12/16/10-pieces-of-advice-from-a-seasoned-in-house -lawye?t=careers&page=2.

43. *Id.* at 5.
44. *Id.* at 4.
45. For instance, Allen Lo, formerly the vice president and deputy general counsel at Juniper Networks, Inc., was hired by Google, Inc., in 2012 as one of Google's newest patent licensing and litigation lawyers. Mr. Lo had built his entire career in the areas of patent and intellectual property law, and he certainly makes a distinguished addition to Google's legal department, but Mr. Lo's limits of practice are an example of how an in-house counsel's experience might limit the broader value he or she could otherwise deliver to his client at large. (Google is obviously an exception to many, many rules, due to its enormous size and global presence. Google, unlike most corporations, can afford to bring many highly specialized issues and lawsuits in house, and Mr. Lo is very likely an excellent fit for his position.)
46. Esperne, *supra* note 42, at 2.
47. Omari S. Simmons, *The Under-Examination of In-House Counsel*, 11 Transactions: Tenn. J. Bus. L. 145, 147 (Fall 2009).
48. Steven L. Schwarcz, *To Make or to Buy: In-House Lawyering and Value Creation*, 33 J. Corp. L. 497, 498 (2008).
49. As a rudimentary example, performing a search for books on Amazon.com that respond to the query "being a team player" results in approximately 4,000 hits. Performing a search for books on Amazon.com that respond to the query "successful management" results in approximately 28,000 hits, nearly seven times as many possible books for the manager as there are for the team player.
50. Cameron Stracher, Double Billing: A Young Lawyer's Tale of Greed, Sex, Lies, and the Pursuit of a Swivel Chair (William Morrow & Company, Inc. 1998). This is an entertaining, sardonic, and cautionary tale for any lawyer. Michael Lewis drew back the same veil on financial powerhouses in *Liar's Poker*.
51. Because the principles are sound, and because they address the attributes of a successful in-house lawyer, I highly recommend expanding the tools of your value-contribution role by reading John C. Maxwell, The 17 Essential Qualities of a Team Player (Maxwell Motivation, Inc. 2002). You will probably notice some parallel principles to Mr. Maxwell's essential qualities.
52. Take a look at, if not a thorough read of, Stephen R. Covey, The Seven Habits of Highly Effective People (Free Press 2004). Mr. Covey's close kin to the Marine Corps' leadership objective is his second habit: "begin with the end in mind."
53. Shannon Green, *Who Reps 2011: Like Minds*, Corporate Counsel, Oct. 1, 2011, *available at* http://law.com/jsp/cc/PubArticleFriendlyCC.jsp?id=1202513984816.
54. Why not use the term *solution oriented*? How is a remedy different than a solution? I will confess the difference is subtle, but it can be important—important enough for an in-house lawyer to mentally sharpen. *Remedy* is a word that most lawyers are more accustomed to hearing and using. It is the word used in litigation to redress a wrong or to enforce a right. A

remedy suggests an actor-oriented *process of action* that leads to a better resolution of a problematic situation. *Solution*, on the other hand, suggests clinical minimalism—simply an answer. As discussed in this section, an in-house lawyer will probably need a more scrappy approach, perhaps even arriving at the lesser of two evils instead of a neat answer.

55. Janice Block, *Problem-Solving Activities Strengthen Legal Departments: Lawyers Must Prioritize Organized, Creative Thinking Processes*, INSIDECOUNSEL, Aug. 2011, *available at* http://www.insidecounsel .com/2011/08/01/problem-solving-activities-strengthen-legal-depart.

56. *Id.* This article refers to Future Problem Solving Program International (FPSPI), formerly known as the Future Problem Solving Program, which was founded by Dr. Ellis Paul Torrance, an American psychologist who specialized in creative thinking. "FPSPI engages students in creative problem solving within the curriculum and provides competitive opportunities." (*See also* Future Problem Solving International, Inc., http://www.fpspi.org (last visited on February 20, 2012).)

57. Carl D. Liggio, Sr., *A Look at the Role of Corporate Counsel: Back to the Future—or Is It the Past?*, 44 ARIZ. L. REV. 621, Fall/Winter 2002, at 622. Mr. Liggio's article gives a good description of the historical "second-class citizenship" perception of in-house counsel.

58. *See* MICHAEL BASIL, CAROLINE SCHOOLER & BYRON REEVES, POSITIVE AND NEGATIVE POLITICAL ADVERTISING: EFFECTIVENESS OF ADS AND PERCEPTIONS OF CANDIDATES 245–62 (Frank Biocca ed., Hillsdale: Lawrence Erlbaum 1991).

59. Sue Reisinger, *Who Reps 2011: Blood Brothers*, CORPORATE COUNSEL, Oct. 1, 2011, *available at* http://www.law.com/jsp/cc/Pub/ArticleFriendlyCC .jsp?id=1202513986542.

60. Etsy Press, http://www.etsy.com/press (last visited Feb. 21, 2012).

61. Sarah Feingold, *Inside Experts: How to Lose a Client in One Minute*, INSIDECOUNSEL, July 29, 2011, *available at* http://www.insidecounsel .com/2011/07/29/inside-experts-how-to-lose-a-client-in-one-minute.

62. *Id.*

63. *Id.*

64. Egan, *supra* note 30, at 7.

65. *E.g., see* John S. Dzienkowski and Robert J. Peroni, *The Decline in Lawyer Independence: Lawyer Equity Investment in Clients*, 81 TEX. L. REV. 405 (2002). Corporate stock is many times a feature of employee retirement plans.

66. *See* MODEL RULES OF PROF'L CONDUCT R. 2.1 (1983).

67. *In re* Enron Corp., No. MDL-1446, Civ.A. H-01-3624, 2003 WL 21418157, at 15 (S.D. Tex. 2003) (not reported in the Federal Supplement). Recall the unfortunate reliance of Enron General Counsel James V. Derrick on the "independent" judgment and advice of Vinson & Elks. When a steady roll of lucrative fees is involved, everyone's position is susceptible to bias or mixed motivation.

68. My colleagues have too often heard me say, "The practice of law *is* psychology." If you can pin down Maslow's Hierarchy of Needs (which will be utilized in Chapter 4), then you will be masterful at your job.

69. The Financial Accounting Standards Board (FASB) is the organization that provides practice pronouncements under the Generally Accepted Accounting Principles (GAAP), used for domestic compilation of financial statements.
70. Keith H. Hammonds, *Michael Porter's Big Ideas*, Fast Company, February 28, 2001, *available at* http://www.fastcompany.com/42485/michael-porters-big-ideas.
71. Julie Beck, *5 Notable GCs in the News*, INSIDECOUNSEL, Jan. 6, 2012, *available at* http://www.insidecounsel.com/2012/01/06/5-notable-gcs-in-the-news?t=careers&page=4.
72. A paraphrase of a saying made by the fictional character Kai Lung, a literary creation of the English author Ernest Bramah.
73. Lisa Holton, *MIPS Technologies' GC Does Big Work with a Small In-House Team*, CORPORATE COUNSEL, Jan. 4, 2012, *available at* http://www.law.com/jsp/article.jsp?id=1202537255822&slreturn=1.
74. *Id.*
75. For purposes of this section, I will momentarily leave aside legal-services contracts for outside counsel. Legal-services contracts are, obviously, not employment contracts in the traditional sense, and legal-services contracts contain different core issues. Interestingly, legal-services contracts have been replacing the age-old engagement letter for outside counsel lawyers, who are being contractually recategorized as vendors. I encourage this practice with corporate clients, and in today's regulatory environment, it draws brighter, more predictable lines for all concerned parties.
76. CAROLE BASRI AND IRVING KAGAN, CORPORATE LEGAL DEPARTMENTS § 2:2 (4th ed., Practicing Law Institute 2011). "In all cases, the general counsel should reserve the right to report directly to the company's board of directors and CEO on significant legal issues and the operation of the law department (assuming there is no direct reporting relationship to the CEO)."
77. Be cautious of participating in pro bono activities, however. Unfortunately, many states disallow corporate lawyers from providing pro bono services when those corporate lawyers do not hold a law license in their client-company's state.
78. *See* MODEL RULES OF PROF'L CONDUCT R. 1.8(a) (1983).
79. *Id.*
80. *See* Holly Gregory et al., Weil, Gotshal & Manges, LLP, Alert: SEC Disclosure and Corporate Governance, Nov. 22, 2011, *available at* http://www.weil.com/files/upload/NY_Briefing_11_NOV_22_SEC_Disc_Corp_Gov.pdf. As of its November 2011 policy updates, the Institutional Shareholder Service, Inc. (ISS) will not focus on the alignment (in at least three different ways) between a CEO's pay and a company's total shareholder return (TSR defined as an increase in the share price and the value of the dividends).
81. *See* Keith L. Johnson, *Say-on-Pay Lawsuits—Is This Time Different?*, The Harvard Law School Forum on Corporate Governance and Financial Regulation (Feb. 5, 2012, 7:55 AM), http://blogs.law.harvard.edu/corpgov/2012/02/05/say-on-pay-lawsuits-is-this-time-different/#more-25330.

Mr. Johnson, who heads the ISS team at Reinhart Boerner Van Deuren s.c., notes that "boards would be ill advised to take too much comfort in the belief that the business judgment rule will always be held to immunize compensation decisions from shareholder attack in the face of a substantial negative say-on-pay vote."

82. Esperne, *supra* note 42.

83. *Profile of In-House Counsel, supra* note 1. *See also* Shannon Green, *The 2011 GC Compensation Survey*, CORPORATE COUNSEL, Jul. 19, 2011, *available at* http://law.com/jsp/cc/PubArticleFriendlyCC.jsp?id=1202500716658; Association of Corporate Counsel, Southern California Chapter, The 2011 In House Counsel Compensation Survey (2011).

84. *Id.*

85. However, remember the conflict limitations and caveats of MODEL RULES OF PROF'L CONDUCT R. 1.8(a) (1983).

86. You probably need to visit with your CPA too. Section 280G of the Internal Revenue Code provides for penalties on excess parachute payments to executives of target companies. Inevitably, your employment contract should have a provision addressing this issue as necessary.

87. This concept will pop up again later on in Sections 6.4.1.4 and 6.4.4.

88. *See, e.g., In re* Nature's Sunshine, 486 F. Supp. 2d 1301 (D. Utah 2007). The United States District Court of Utah, Central Division, found that the plaintiffs had adequately met the pleading requirement under the Securities Exchange Act to hold a CFO liable even without the CFO's direct involvement or other *scienter.* "[L]iability may be imposed where a defendant possesses the power, directly or indirectly, to direct or cause the direction of management and policies of the primary violator." *Id.* at 1313–14.

89. *E.g., see* Howard v. Babcock, 25 Cal. Rptr. 2d 80, 863 P.2d 150 (1993) and Feamow v. Ridenour, Swenson, Cleere & Evans, PC, 138 P.3d 723 (Ariz. 2006).

90. *E.g., see* Daniel D. Quick, *Noncompete Agreements for Attorneys: Are We Now Fair Game?*, 87 MICH. BAR J. 12, 29–32 (Dec. 2008).

91. *See* Mary L. Mikva, *Drafting Confidentiality, Non-Compete & Non-Solicitation Agreements: The Employee's Wish List,* ABA REGIONAL INSTITUTE, LABOR AND EMPLOYMENT LAW: THE BASICS (based on a paper the author prepared for an August, 2003, seminar sponsored by the ABA's Labor and Employment Law Section).

92. Melissa Maleske, *Judge Says KPMG Defense Counsel Cannot Resign from Case,* INSIDECOUNSEL, Jul. 25, 2007, *available at* http://www.insidecounsel .com/2007/07/25/judge-says-kpmg-defense-counsel-cannot-resign-from -case.

CHAPTER 2
CORE UNDERPINNINGS— YOUR ID, EGO, AND SUPEREGO AT WORK

TABLE OF SECTIONS

In 1923, an aging Sigmund Freud published a paper entitled "The Ego and the Id," attempting to explain various, or all, psychological conditions faced by every human, whether pathological or nonpathological. Many scholars, practitioners, and critics have since pushed most Freudian theories further away from psychology (and rightfully so in my humble and inexpert opinion) and closer to studies in the humanities, but corporate lawyers can borrow the premises of Freud's neat little tome (indecorously perhaps) to provide a triangular view of the foundational subjects of practicing corporate law.[1]

Freud's *ego* is our organized, realistic perspective, which is constantly caught in a tug-of-war conflict between the *id* and the *superego*. Freud's *id* is our uncoordinated instincts, and Freud's *superego* is our criticizing, moral sensibility. Amazingly, without receiving any kind of degree in anything resembling psychology, the dynamic interplay between all three perspectives provides lawyers a ready-made tool for assessing any kind of crisis situation. The law, as every lawyer knows, only gives a set of regulated parameters at best, but its usefulness can rapidly deteriorate when an executive walks in the door and utters the ominous phrase, "I have a problem." At that moment, a good corporate lawyer—one who is concerned with his or her credibility—needs a simple assessment tool to provide a basic decision matrix from which to work.

For instance, there are situations in which a corporate lawyer faces the sober reality of needing to disclose privileged information to a regulatory agency. The dilemma is that the lawyer knows in the real world, he or she must find a way, if at all possible, to disclose what is required (or necessary) without waiving the client-company's privileges. His or her ideals and moral ethos may argue that disclosure is the right thing to do, and cooperation could stave off a stringent enforcement action. On the other hand, there is an almost irrepressible knee-jerk instinct screaming that privilege should *never* risk being waived. The ego is being pummeled by the id and the superego all at once. As is the case within our own psyches, this three-dimensional tug-of-war rarely yields a succinct sense of how a difficult situation should ultimately be handled, but the benefits of being able to analyze a situation, using each unique perspective to arrive at a purposeful, reasoned answer, are priceless.

This is not to suggest that every crisis should be met with a time-consuming pseudo-Freudian analysis. On the contrary, it is better to be preemptive: apply the analysis to the core touchstones of corporate

Core Underpinnings

practice *before* an emergency situation pops up. Once these foundational perspectives are in place, distinctively circumstantial situations will be much easier to address. A corporate lawyer should strive to find the balanced middle ground in every crisis situation by using (or already having a predisposition toward) a three-part analysis of the underlying core touchstones we will be discussing in the next few sections. The ego-id-superego assessment of these core subjects gives a corporate lawyer an anchor—a pivot foot—from which he or she can move in 360 degrees to face almost any new challenge that walks in the door.

So where do we begin?

§ 2.1 Laying a Foundation of Value

To answer this question, we will look at the core touchstones found in nearly every area of corporate practice and day-to-day operations performed on behalf of a client-company. They can spell success or failure without a lawyer ever having rendered a single piece of legal advice. They are not mysterious, nor are they impossible to learn or to keep in mind. Frankly, these touchstones can consist of such common-sense elements that a corporate lawyer can easily overlook their operational significance, global application, and impact on a long-term client relationship.

For example, when most of us attended law school, our conscious thoughts were of becoming a lawyer, and we were immersed in the learning of the law. Interestingly though, there was a more fundamental, common-sense activity driving all of those ambitions and daily efforts: *we were students.* There were core touchstones to our relationships with our academic institutions, almost regardless of what subject matter we studied. These touchstones were: understanding and abiding within a school's academic structure (that is, where and how you fit in); understanding essential duties (that is, to learn and let others learn); understanding the milieu of the academic society in which to study (that is, the overall campus/institutional attitude); understanding what the school expected of its students (that is, class attendance, respect for your peers and the faculty, and so forth); and recognizing and using the tools available to a student (that is, libraries, study groups, academic societies). These relational touchstones shadowed each of us through our legal studies, and, outside of an individual work habit or a native level of intelligence, they largely determined our academic success or failure even though they had nothing to do with the degree we were pursuing. The same types of touchstones—the basic elements of function—apply to a corporate lawyer who steps onto a company's "campus," ready and willing to practice law. What are these touchstones?

Shaping a corporate lawyer's relationship with his or her client-company into a valuable and effective element of business is entirely formulated by:

1. identifying the client-company's structure,
2. identifying (and never forgetting) *who* the actual client is,
3. identifying and juggling issues of privilege,

4. working within (and sometimes changing) a client-company's culture, and

5. shaping and meeting a client-company's expectations.

These five subjects—the fundamentals of corporate practice—will be threaded into everything you say and do as a corporate lawyer on behalf of your client-company.

The understandable and natural rush to get the job done every day can subtly cause you to skip over these relational elements, but you do so at your peril. (For instance, diligently reading a casebook but blowing off class attendance would have ultimately done little to advance your law school career.) The good news is, because these five touchstones will be manifest in everything you do, you will deliver *real business value* to your client-company if you take the time (and an iterative attitude) to use the three-part ego-id-superego decision matrix to influence your perspective of each of the five subjects. Like a predetermined anchor, or the pivot-foot example used above, you will be able to move more nimbly through each fresh problem or situation with a balanced point of view. Instead of an issue catching you off balance, you will have already established a thoughtful baseline for your assessment and action processes.

Corporate lawyers have unique relationships with corporate clients, arising from very unique roles. Defining those roles, as we did in Chapter 1, is the supportive bedrock of those relationships. The fundamental precepts, or touchstones, of those relationships have to be tempered through a weighted but balanced analysis of reality (the pragmatic ego), emotion (the id's sense of advocacy), and critical ethos (the superego's sense of what is right). With these precepts in mind, keep asking this reflective question: How does this develop a foundation of value for the client-company?

§ 2.1.1 Corporate Structure and Corporate Counsel

Corporations are natural creatures of organizational composition. Though we may like the excitement of surprise, and even a bit of chaos,[2] balanced with the familiarity of habits, we human beings and our societies seem to flourish best when we implement organization and reliable uniformity. For our governmental structure, Americans count on an organization of legislatures, executives, and judiciaries. For our macrosocial organization, we have systems of cities, counties, and states.

For our scholastic arrangement, we attend elementary schools, middle schools, high schools, and universities. For business, we also rely upon the consistency of organization, regardless of how relaxed an ambience we may try to create. As laissez-faire as the passenger boarding and seating methods of Southwest Airlines seem to be, with the bourgeois assignments of Group A, Group B, and Group C, as well as the aristocratic assignment (for just a few dollars more) of Business Select, passengers are still given a sense of when they can board and where they are likely to sit. There is a predictable semblance of arrangement and configuration. As nouveau a culture as the one innovated and encouraged by the Internet search giant Google Inc.—where run-of-the-mill employees can question top executives[3]—may be, there is still an order to its corporate world: there *are* executives, and there *are* front-line employees.

Organizational structure "provides guidance to all employees by laying out the official reporting relationships that govern the workflow of the company."[4] Reporting relationships define and assign obligations, responsibilities, liabilities, and etiquette. In flat organizations, employees are empowered to make decisions with few layers of mid-management supervision. The stream of power and communication between employees and top management creates a more compact and directly vertical organization chart (the idiomatic "org chart")—information flows from the bottom to the top and from the top to the bottom. In tall organizations, there are numerous layers of management, wherein managers make most of the decisions after obtaining authority from higher layers of management. This creates a more bloated and graduated organization chart—information typically flows from top to bottom.

When attempting to unravel a client-company's organizational structure, a seemingly apparent question would be, who has power over whom? Its org charts—and its theories of corporate organization—should provide answers to that question. However, strictly looking at a chart and attempting to pinpoint where you geographically fit in and how others fit in around you does not usually provide tangible information about how a corporation is operationally run on a day-to-day basis.

An in-house lawyer who is evaluating in what way his or her role will plug in, or best bring value, to a client-company, should ask: How is the power structure of this corporation constructed, resisted, and subverted within organizational relationships?[5] This is not so much a

Power Structure

question about an org chart as it is a question about finding out how a corporate lawyer's role will work among a corporation's idiosyncratic internal relationships.

> We not only are interested in whether inside lawyers have power in the corporation but also of what kind, under what circumstances, and with what implications for the role of law in corporate governance.... Businesspeople are in continuing relationships with inside counsel and can mobilize for or against lawyers on a range of organizational policies.[6]

All corporate lawyers, regardless of rank or grade, generally find one of three hats to wear within a client-company's organizational structure. It is critical for a corporate lawyer to find the hat that best fits his or her head—his or her style and approach to lawyering and to management—but in reality, the company controls the employee: the hat should be, and ultimately will be, chosen by the *client* through the company's culture of organization. In this, a corporate lawyer must exercise the same restraint or willingness a lawyer in private practice needs to exercise when a client insists on litigating a case with a particular strategic posture. For instance, an aggressive litigator must decide if he or she can compatibly work with a client who wants to take a conciliatory approach to a lawsuit. In the same way, a corporate lawyer must take an honest look at how the role of law—a lawyer's role—will fit within the working construct of a client-company's organization.

Business First

In Section 1.1.1, when discussing the role of a general counsel—and because the concept is applicable to all other corporate lawyers—we talked about the nature of a corporate lawyer who is also a business executive. Acting as, and fulfilling the role of, an executive is a critical function of every corporate lawyer who carries an officer's title. Even when the executive title merely indicates the org-chart level of a corporate lawyer, such as Vice President and General Counsel or General Counsel and Chief Compliance Officer, the executive designation denotes certain obligations, expectations, and potential liabilities that stand apart from the core functions of acting as legal counsel, by virtue of the level of authority, control, and influence the executive-officer role possesses.[7] There are many corporate cultures of organization that expect an executive-lawyer to be an executive first and a lawyer second—business first, law second. (This does not de-emphasize the importance of law; it simply places it as a constructive servant to the overarching goal of business.)

Many executives come to their positions in the same way a corporate lawyer might find him- or herself with an *executive* title. A salesperson who "grew up" making customer calls, bringing home commissions, and living out of a car might eventually find his or her way into the position of Vice President of Marketing, where few if any customer calls are made, the salary is nice (with bonuses), and most of the time is spent in an office. A person's stock-in-trade background may lay the career foundation for his or her advancement, but when he or she assumes the role of an executive, the trappings of that stock-in-trade will, many times, fade into the background. The new obligations and responsibilities of running a department and participating in the running of the corporation as a whole replace the obligations and responsibilities of working as a frontline employee. This same phenomenon can occur to executive-attorneys.

In this environment, the business value of a corporate lawyer's position trumps the legal value of his or her position. Providing legal advice and guidance is still a fundamental contribution, but it is a means to an end. The legal department is not merely a good business investment for purposes of compliance and protectionism. This kind of corporate organizational culture views the legal department as a profit center too.[8] A corporate lawyer is expected to offer advice on matters of law *and* on matters of business. In these organizational environments, a lawyer who moves up from a more law-oriented background, such as litigation, might fare worse than a corporate lawyer whose background has been more business oriented, such as governance. In these organizational circumstances, where power is driven by profit and business deals, a corporate lawyer who insists on acting primarily as a legal gatekeeper, or primarily as a legal advisor, might constantly be battling the tide of an adverse power structure. If swimming with the tide, then the power of a corporate lawyer in these circumstances—the implication of his or her role as a lawyer—is foremost a function of strategic business planning and execution. Law contributes to business and furthers profits. The order of the roles is executive first, lawyer second.

Legal Gatekeepers

In Section 1.1.2, we discussed being remedy oriented as one of the traits of a good in-house lawyer. An effective corporate lawyer is going to look for solutions, not just bark out *No!* every time anyone walks into his or her office. However, certain organizational structures rely on polarization among their leaders in order to find a workable middle ground.

In some organizational cultures, power and effectiveness come from an executive's willingness to pull against other executives. This tug-of-war, when evenly performed and applied, reassures a client-company that it is moving down the center of the road, where relationships are constructed more out of resistance than collaboration. In these circumstances, a client-company most relies on the value of a corporate lawyer's *no*. Legal advice is effectuated by using it as a gatekeeper. When strategies, deals, and decisions are vetted throughout management's ranks, a corporate lawyer's contribution acts best as a bulkhead, setting a hardline channel beyond which the froth and waves of a company's ambition and projects cannot go. There is not as much a sense of corporate lawyers acting as part of the management team in these environments as there is a sense that corporate lawyers act as one of the checks and balances for what the team wants to do. Like a resident regulator, a corporate lawyer in this kind of organization culture must understand his or her value—the implication of his or her role and the power of his or her role—lies in "policing the conduct of their business clients."[9] Corporate counsel keeps the company car in the middle of the lane.

Counselors

There are, however, organizational environments that call for a corporate lawyer to mix the gatekeeper and the business-first roles into a single amalgamation. This composite role is what we have discussed, and touted, in the preceding sections. This role is the one most often fulfilled by corporate counsel, and in fulfilling it, such lawyers arguably deliver the greatest value to their client-companies. This "affords counsel an opportunity to make suggestions based on business, ethical, and situational concerns."[10] This is the consigliere role,[11] in which practicing law, in a strict sense, is one of several activities met by a corporate lawyer, but in which *the* law, and legal training and thinking, is the backdrop for everything he or she does. Corporate lawyers, who act as counselors, relate to management and to the company as lawyers (first) who fulfill their employment obligations and participate and collaborate from a starting point of legal expertise. Legal risks and solutions are presented so the rest of the management team can make informed decisions.

This organizational climate usually means power bases are constructed, interfaced, and challenged in a meaningful, less partisan way. The corporate lawyer's goal is not just growth, nor is it just setting limitations. The goal within this organizational culture is to accommodate and assist in growth while identifying and addressing limitations. This requires a constant balance of concerns and the application of those concerns to each issue and project.

The practical reality of corporate structure (remember the ego?) is that its ultimate goal is to drive and grow a successful and ever-evolving business. This pragmatic does not, however, run free of emotion (the id) or critical morality (the superego). A corporate lawyer's place in a client-company's structure can run the gamut from business first to law first to the balance of acting as a consigliere. Take a look at your geography and influence within your client-company using our method of ego-id-superego triangular analysis. Where and how do you bring the best business value?

Do your homework. Observe and objectively consider *how* your client-company is operationally run on a day-to-day basis. Evaluate how your role will be most effective—how it will bring influential value—to your client-company. Begin by looking at the practical power structure of the corporation in order to characterize how you, as a lawyer, are going to complement and work within that structure. The org chart is a good map, but true reconnaissance requires you to physically observe the landscape.[12] Ask questions (always being careful whom you ask).

Observe interactions between other members of management. Look at the history of the company—its initiatives and its failures—to find out how it arrived where it currently is. Pay attention to the non-policy customs and practices of how internal memorandums flow, who typically participates in what meetings, how responsibility (or blame) is usually shared or hoarded, who goes to lunch with whom, and what role your job position has played in the past. This is not just office politics, and it should not be. This is a value-oriented assessment of structure—structure related to relationships and power—and it is an indispensable tool when determining how legal counsel truly fits within a corporation's daily operational organization.

§ 2.1.2 Who *Is Your Client?*

After introducing our discussion of the roles of general counsel and in-house lawyers as defined by the imperative of working for a single client, and after emphasizing the importance of uncovering how a corporate lawyer fits into the organizational composition of a client-company, we cannot talk about much of anything else unless we can satisfactorily settle on *who* the single client is. *Whom do you work for?*

Like insurance defense litigators, who represent an individual or entity but who are paid by the carrier, corporate lawyers must clarify, and diligently continue to keep clear, *who* the client is in order to understand *who* is really being represented. If we as lawyers literally cannot identify the client, the sacrosanct element within all of our professional rules and obligations, then we cannot proceed a step further.

The *Model Rules of Professional Conduct* provide us with what seem to be the simplest observation of entity representation: "A lawyer employed or retained by an organization represents the organization acting through its duly authorized constituents."[13] The first part of that statement is vanilla plain and very clear. It is in the second part—"acting through its authorized constituents"—wherein the rub lies. Acting as legal counsel for almost any company—especially a company bulging with shareholders (members or multiple partners), directors, and nice-sized cadres of upper-level managers—can make the task of identifying the client notoriously difficult, because pinning down which authorized constituents make up the heart of the organization can be very subjective and dynamic. Perhaps it is this ironic recommendation that might provide the best guidance: accept the fact that the people who represent the heart of the organization—the best interests of the organization—are constantly subject to change.

This is a big leap for the trained, intellectual habit of most lawyers. Most lawyers identify representation with a *person*. Even outside counsel, though representing a corporate entity, very often take direction from a single person, a corporate representative. For in-house lawyers especially, accepting a professional situation in which persons are the fickle variable is a difficult, conscious task, especially when it is still *people*, after all, with whom in-house lawyers interact every day. Lines can blur, and focus on the entity-client can subtly shift to interpersonal relationships and fixations on who has power over whom. Indeed, it is so difficult to consistently maintain an inclusive sense of who the client-company really is that the *Model Rules* chose to frame the definition by using exclusive language—instruction marked by negative guideposts.

> If a lawyer for an organization knows that an officer, employee or other person associated with the organization is engaged in action, intends to act or refuses to act in a matter related to the representation that is a violation of a legal obligation to the organization, or a violation of law that reasonably might be imputed to the organization, and that is likely to result in substantial injury to the organization, then the lawyer shall proceed as is reasonably necessary in the best interest of the organization. Unless the lawyer reasonably believes that it is not necessary in the best interest of the organization to do so, the lawyer shall refer the matter to higher authority in the organization, including, if warranted by the circumstances to the highest authority that can act on behalf of the organization as determined by applicable law.[14]

To stay within the bounds of this rule, a lawyer must strive to define the client by applying the following general formula: (1) Does a constituent's action (intentions and so forth) violate a legal obligation to the company? If yes, then: (2) Is the constituent's action likely to result in substantial harm to the company? If yes, then: (3) You must do what is "reasonably necessary" in the "best interests" of the company to prevent the harm.[15] Though there are subjective cracks in the first two legs of the stool, it is the third leg that is the toughest to keep from breaking. The third leg requires, unless there is a good reason not to, a lawyer to take the matter to a higher authority within a client-company, and if that is not sufficient, then to the highest authority that can legally protect the company.

Wow! This is where the rubber meets the road in a personally challenging way. Professionally, it is expected of a corporate lawyer to evaluate a constituent's actions, and if the lawyer reasonably believes that those actions are likely to result in substantial harm to the client-company, the lawyer is compelled to act—compelled to walk into a likely buzz saw of backlash and corporate politics at its most base level, the level of survival. Granted, there are several very subjective conclusions that need to be drawn, but if an in-house lawyer (or an outside counsel who might face the predicament of challenging his or her assigned corporate representative by going to a higher authority within the company) values the tenets of his or her fiduciary duties and his or her law license, then it is better to err on the side of caution than it is to ignore what might otherwise damage the client-company.

Just be sure to err wisely and with thoughtful objectivity.

Necessary Objectivity

How many times can a general counsel go past the CEO and directly to the board?

Once.

This familiar joke brings a wry smile to most in-house lawyers' faces. In it lies the suggestion of martyrdom: one might have to pay the ultimate price if one is truly dedicated to the cause.[16] In private practice, the ultimate price is almost always characterized by firing the client, which might eliminate a large revenue stream. But as a vacuum is created, other work is likely to quickly fill the void.[17] However, in the world of in-house representation, firing the client, or having the client fire *you*, means your single source of income and employment can come to a sudden, emotionally jarring halt.

Mentally, professionally, and financially prepare yourself in advance for this possibility and you will find the clouds surrounding *who the client is* will also tend to dissipate. Your resolve to stick with the right thing—perhaps where the morality of the superego may outdo the dispassion of the ego and the sentiment of the id—will increase objectivity when ferreting out who the client is when faced with hard decisions and competing interests. Instead of making excuses for a constituent's actions, or presuming their authority trumps their accountability, a corporate lawyer must be braced to keep the interests of the company as a whole in the king's seat. Easier said than done, but absolutely imperative. The earlier a corporate lawyer makes a rule of distinction about who the client is, the less catastrophic the outcome might be when needing to confront a domestic threat to the company. Taking umbrage with a constituent's harmful actions on behalf of the client-company is part of the value a corporate lawyer can deliver.

When reading the title query of this section, an answer might have (should have) popped immediately into your head: *Who is your client? Insert the name of your company here.* As simple as the question might be, the answer is in fact a great place to start and a great memory aid to keep in mind at all times. The client *is* the *organization*.

A corporate lawyer's awareness of a company's history, marketplace, goals, image and culture, and corporate liabilities is a very useful tool for seeing the client as the whole organization, greater than any one constituent or group of constituents. These factors can and should be your reference points. They have the necessary objectivity of distance from and disenfranchisement with most day-to-day operations in order to supply a corporate lawyer with the mantel of being an honest broker when addressing organizational client issues.

Just as is the case in a courtroom, the most prized asset for a corporate lawyer is his or her ability to maintain credibility. When a person or an organization loses the sense that a lawyer is trustworthy, it does not matter if the lawyer's advice or argument is as true as a carpenter's plumb line; no one is going to give it much importance. Being an honest broker means employees, management, board members, and other stakeholders will be able to accept a corporate lawyer's advice at face value without fear of prejudiced subterfuge or scheming. They may not like it, especially if the advice or admonition is to say no to something they want to do or are doing, but they will understand the advice comes out of an organization-wide interest. (If they don't, then there is a deeper problem you will be facing or need to deal with.) The broader horizon of an organization-wide interest can help elevate a corporate lawyer's opinion, advice, and actions above most internal partisanship, and the identity of the client-company should remain a clearer focal point.

Investigations and Prosecutions
Whether you like it or not, if you spend enough time in the employ of a corporate client, the day will come when an internal investigation, and/or some kind of enforcement or prosecutorial action, takes place. An objective sense of client-identity is absolutely crucial when a situation develops into an internal investigatory matter or a prosecutorial action (that is, the specter of a criminal prosecution or a regulatory enforcement action). Whether the issue happens to be anticipatory, as you work to head off pending disaster, or is the result of a trigger event such as a lawsuit or an internal or regulatory complaint, a corporate lawyer must approach each interview, document, conversation, and strategic decision with a deliberate, predisposed view of who the client is.

Corporate investigations can portend some of the most stressful and company-altering situations a corporate lawyer will ever face.[18] Aside from those fearful (and hopefully rare) situations in which you might actually be an involved (and therefore tainted) party, every stakeholder needs to know the company's legal counsel is proceeding from, and evaluating everything according to, the client-company's interests at large. The *Model Rules*, in fact, require a corporate lawyer to be able to literally "explain the identity of the [organizational] client" whenever a corporate lawyer knows that his or her company's interests "are adverse to those of the constituents with whom the lawyer is dealing."[19] Candid (even if gently delivered) conversations, many times introduced by necessary "Upjohn" warnings,[20] with other employees and management should be freely used to put all affected persons on notice that you represent the company, not any constituent.

The Client

A corporate lawyer's judgment and advice will need to be able to ride atop choppy flotsam of innuendo, rumor, and bias, while still recognizing that such debris is what courses along the riverbed of every organization, whether or not it is ill intended. You cannot entirely separate the wheat from the chaff; every business consists of its organic parts as much as it consists of its mechanical parts. A corporate lawyer's job is to process both without losing sight of the true client—the *organization*. In Geoffrey C. Hazard Jr.'s article on ethical dilemmas faced by corporate lawyers, he shares an anecdote demonstrating this reality.

> I recall an observation by a high-ranking executive of a leading company to a university official concerning the significance of office rumors. In this case, the rumors were about a decision made by a university department. The university official protested that one could not operate a university paying attention to rumors. The executive responded that he could not run his company without paying attention to rumors.[21]

A corporate lawyer must heed the ebbs and flows of back-channel information—in fact, it is *required* that a corporate lawyer gather such information and be as fully informed as possible—but without succumbing to its siren call.

Many in-house lawyers elect to engage outside counsel, who may not be typical members of a client-company's legal bullpen, when internal investigations or prosecutorial actions crop up. This is not just another exercise in obtaining specialized or properly qualified counsel. In times of crisis (large or small), good corporate counsel is looking for a positive analysis of a client-company's wisest strategy, based on materially demonstrable observations, instead of normative analysis, which is based on subjective opinions, beliefs, and desires. Engaging outside counsel who may not be on a client-company's routine list of law firms is an effort to make sure if the legal team handling an investigation or a prosecutorial situation is at an arm's length from a client-company's normal party politics and can approach information without the contamination of prior perspective. This will help obtain the objectivity needed to vigorously protect and represent the organizational client with the likelihood there will be less of an inclination to capitulate to personal relationships, biased opinions, and vested interests. The cacophony of a client-company's interested or affected constituency can risk drowning out the muted appeal of the single, overarching organizational client's best interests.

Joint Representation

And yet it is the constituency that *constitutes* the client. Every corporate lawyer will find him- or herself dealing with people who make up the organization. It will be some of these people—sometimes all of them—in their respective corporate capacities for whom a corporate lawyer typically provides legal representation and advice. The *Model Rules* state that a corporate lawyer will take his or her direction from "duly authorized constituents[,]"[22] but the legal interest(s) being represented may be much broader than that.[23]

William H. Simon's law review article, published in 2003, provides an excellent side-by-side comparison and contrast of joint-representation situations in which multiple individuals are clients, versus situations involving the constituent multiplicity of representing organizations.[24] The fact is, a lawyer's duties, limitations, and risks in the two situations can be uniquely different, even though they appear to be similar on the surface.[25] For our purposes, we have already addressed the general nuances of representing an organizational whole—as superseding its individual constituents—so the practical application of the term *joint representation* lies in a situation in which a corporate lawyer is representing a client-company *and* individual constituents at the same time.

Although an infinite number of examples could be used, suppose a corporate lawyer receives an internal complaint from a person in the accounting department who is claiming certain executives are using company credit cards for unauthorized entertainment expenses. The in-house lawyer interviews the complainant (after telling the complainant that the lawyer represents the *company* in this matter, not the complainant). Then, the lawyer interviews the executives (also after telling the executives the lawyer represents the company in this matter, not the executives or the complainant). So far, the corporate lawyer has followed the precept of clearly representing the organization instead of any constituent individuals. The corporate lawyer determines the executives have, in fact, been spending money appropriately. In spite of a follow-up conversation with the employee from accounting, the disgruntled employee still chooses to "whistle-blow" the supposed discrepancy to an oversight regulator. The regulatory agency (hopefully) sends notice to the corporate lawyer and (laying aside issues about privilege for the moment) instructs the corporate lawyer to provide a response with supporting (that is, advocating) documentation. In this situation, the corporate lawyer now represents the organization—in that the organization has not violated accounting principles or compliance—*and* the employee-executive individuals—in that their actions as corporate officers have not impugned the organization with noncompliant conduct. The corporate lawyer is *jointly* representing the organization and individual constituents of the organization: multiple interests that are, at least temporarily, aligned and mutually supportive.

Economies of finance, which are the soft underbelly of the business world, can be oblivious to the apprehensions of legal strategy. It might simply be an issue of funding that brings about a situation of joint representation for a corporate lawyer. It is for this reason a defense counsel who is hired by an insurance company to represent an insured business is many times called upon also to provide a joint defense for the business's employees, who may be named as individual defendants. A litigator may find him- or herself representing a business and individuals in the same matter, even when the interests or strategies of multiple clients could, at some point, diverge. This challenge, as illustrated above, is many times true within a corporate, joint representation setting, and the same concerns apparent in a joint defense situation also hold true in a corporate, joint representation setting. A client-company has a substantial interest in keeping everyone within the circle, with rifles facing outboard for as long as possible. The opportunity to use a corporate lawyer as the epicenter for strategy, communication, and information can be very tempting and sometimes useful.

In such situations, when the choice to hire outside counsel for individual constituents is not made or is delayed, a corporate lawyer must take extra care to make sure his or her ability, and paramount obligation, to continue representing the organization is not impaired or effectively conflicted out by representing one or more individuals. Care must be taken to identify potential and real conflicts as early as possible. Waivers of conflict might need to be executed between all of the mutually aligned parties, with the corporate lawyer's election of surviving representation on behalf of the client-company. Given the severity of the situation, well-drafted joint representation/defense agreements (with clawback provisions for privilege) should be considered and should be in writing.

Joint representation can in fact be a part of everyday life for a corporate lawyer who, for example, drafts employment agreements, advises on retirement plans, or advises on the exercise of stock options. Diligent precautions and careful thought ought to be taken at every turn.[26] When a corporate lawyer's client is both an organization and certain individual constituents, the lawyer must remain aware of the potentially disparate consequences of dispensing broadside legal advice. Most important, a corporate lawyer must stay completely alert to saying something, doing something, or not doing something that would create a professional conflict or that would create a privilege issue, thus precluding the lawyer from effectively representing the long-term client: the company.

You might, as you read this section, have the sinking feeling you are currently facing a client-identity crisis in your own situation. Perhaps someone (or a group of someones) who otherwise has the authority to act on behalf of your client-company has done something, or is doing something, that could substantially threaten your client-company in some way. Or perhaps you have started down a path of jointly representing your client-company and one or more of its constituents without applying too much thought to the possibility of conflicts of interest.

What do I do? you ask. Where do I begin?

The answer is not easily canned, although there is one thing that is almost always a fail-safe when facing a very difficult and probably complex situation: *seek advice.* No matter how long a person has been doing what he or she is doing, everyone needs the benefit of a fresh (and knowledgeable) opinion when tackling circumstances that could have a profound professional impact. When your job is on the line, you need objective guidance. When an issue could substantially affect your client-company's health, you need objective guidance. When you need to make choices, exercising your fiduciary duties and implicating the duties of other stakeholders, you need objective guidance.

Identifying who the client is should never be overlooked or treated indelicately by a corporate lawyer. This subject is a core touchstone of corporate law, and if compromised, a corporate lawyer's value to his or her client-company will be diminished or entirely lost. The practical reality (the ego) is that a corporate lawyer interacts with people every day—the constituents—while being bound to represent the greater whole. Emotional sentiment (the id) may entice a corporate lawyer, or the individual constituency, to inadvertently create or interpret a *personal* representation. Conversely, critical scruples (the superego) might tempt a corporate lawyer to alienate the constituency by constantly announcing to any and all who will hear that he or she represents only the company, and other employees would do better not to speak confidentially about any concerns or grievances they might have. Obviously, a balance must be struck. Each situation will tilt the scale slightly further in one direction or another, but a good corporate lawyer will be able to deliver maximum value to the client-company by consistently clarifying representation and keeping an unwavering eye on who the client is.

§ 2.1.3 Perplexing Privilege Problems

Though the question of identifying who the client is may seem a bit esoteric (albeit necessary), the question of privilege should feel as instinctive as English common law and as sacrosanct as Westminster Abbey. Rightfully so. Privilege—confidentiality—is the confessional booth of law. Indeed, on a topic as revered and ageless as legal privilege, it is fitting to listen to the eloquence of an English court.

> [Privilege] exists for the purpose of ensuring that there shall be complete and unqualified confidence in the mind of a client when he goes to his solicitor, or when he goes to his counsel, that that which he there divulges will never be disclosed to anybody else. It is only if the client feels safe in making a clean breast of his troubles to his advisers that litigation and the business of the law can be carried on satisfactorily[.][27]

Privilege is another core touchstone of corporate law, yet it has the irksome vulnerability of evaporating in a moment of recklessness or imprudence. Increasingly, our society does not often champion secrecy in public business or in the capital markets, and courts are not quick to return what has been given up, even if a privilege has been waived in error. Having spent parts of previous sections intoning the sacredness of the single-client creed, we must now face one of the central problems with that utopian concept: What does corporate counsel do about the vagaries of privilege?

Certainly, the identity of a client drives the threshold boundaries of establishing privilege. Ascertaining a client's identity raises the question of who is safely within the fold and who is without, as well as who seems to straddle the fence. Yet privilege, though elemental, is not neatly packaged. It is common law and rule based, and when it comes to privilege issues for an organizational client, it can be like using a herd of cats to herd a herd of cats.

> [W]henever corporations are involved, there are numerous agents, masses of documents, and frequent discussions with attorneys in order to understand the complex laws and regulations with which these legal entities are expected to comply. These situations and many other conceptual difficulties in defining the [attorney-client] privilege and its scope plague the American courts.[28]

Truer words were never spoken. And yet a corporate lawyer cannot simply shrug his or her shoulders and abandon the lawyerly duty to create, identify, and preserve privileged information on behalf of his or her client-company. Privilege is the castle-keep of modern corporations, and too much is at risk to desert the walls (even if they are as riddled with holes as Swiss cheese). From trade secrets to litigation risk to regulatory risk to the dreaded specter of a falling stock price, corporations and their legal counsel need to be able to communicate freely without the nagging anxiety their communiqués will end up as fodder for the public domain, or worse, as arrows in an adversary's quiver. Now perhaps more than ever, in a time of "open books," transparency, disclosure filings, and a social obligation to the greater good, corporations need their legal counsel to robustly monitor and defend privilege in order to pinpoint problems, manage risk, address oversights, correct inefficiencies, interact with regulators, and handle litigation. Once more, a corporate lawyer can use the 360-degree tool of the ego-id-superego analysis when facing issues of privilege creation and preservation. Such issues are never as easy or as compact as pointing your finger, identifying privilege, and then pouring permanent concrete around it. Establishing privilege creation can be maddeningly tough, and maintaining privilege preservation can be maddeningly maddening.

Yet the importance of privilege surpasses its difficulties. Here again, corporate lawyers can borrow a principle from my fellow leathernecks and remain vigilant when courts, legislatures, regulators, and misplaced public opinion look to jeopardize a client-company's ability to seek and preserve legal advice in confidence.[29] As the Honorable Susan Davis, congresswoman for California's 53rd Congressional District, said of the U.S. Marines, "I'm relieved that the state of the Marines' readiness will remain high."[30]

Privilege

The Privileges

Without question, corporate lawyers should look closely at those laws and regulations that monitor and govern their respective industries for information their client-companies are required to keep confidential.[31] That brand of privilege—statutory or regulatory privilege—is critical in its own right and requires corporate organizations to impose strict policies for countless documents, data identifiers, and reports. The ability to render advice on those regulated issues of privacy and confidentiality is an essential subject for many corporate lawyers; however, a client-company essentially keeps such confidences as a bailee for the benefit of another person or entity. Though important, many of these privilege issues are (or should be) maintained by rote policies and procedures because they make up part of the white-paper extravaganza (whether basic or incidental) of running a business.

We will leave alone these regulated categories of privilege (with the expectation that you are familiar with, or are familiarizing yourself with, all of the privilege bailments required in your client-company's industry). They are simply too numerous and too industry specific, and are outside the scope of this book. Instead, for our purposes, we will take a close look at the load-bearing pillars of every corporation's castle-keep of its own privileges. These are the well-worn twin doctrines of work-product privilege and attorney-client privilege.

Work Product

Perhaps because the attorney-client privilege provides deeper moats and higher walls of protection (in most instances), the work-product privilege is the undervalued frontline defense, with extraordinarily broad application, that is not always given its proper due.

As stock-in-trade as it might seem now, the work-product privilege was first recognized by the U.S. Supreme Court in 1947.[32] Because the attorney-client privilege was more narrow, it failed to meet the needs of the high court when it finally decided to protect "the production of written statements and mental impressions contained in the files and the mind of the attorney Fortenbaugh without any showing of necessity or any indication or claim that denial of such production would unduly prejudice" the requesting party.[33] As a lasting result, work product that has been created in "anticipation of litigation" enjoys privilege from discovery.

But even as the Supreme Court set the stage for the work-product privilege, it also defined the limits of its protections: if a party in litigation can show undue hardship and prejudice, and if it is unable to obtain the requested documents in any other way, then the other party must open its fist and provide the information. This privilege has since been memorialized in the Federal Rules of Civil Procedure (Rule 26(b)(3)) and is echoed in many states' rules of procedure. Even though the scope of the work-product privilege has customarily covered those documents created "in anticipation of [traditional] litigation," some courts have begun to expand the concept, recognizing the temporal ambiguity of the phrase "in anticipation" might include regulatory investigations and some indeterminate period of time in advance of an actual lawsuit for as long as litigation could be "expected."[34]

What does the work-product privilege mean for a corporate lawyer? The expansion given to the work-product privilege, especially in the Second Circuit's *United States v. Adlman*[35] decision, threw its protective covering wide enough to encompass documents that may have been created with dual purposes: in the anticipation of litigation *and* in an effort to inform a business decision. The *Adlman* court gave the interesting example of a company generating "preparatory litigation studies undertaken . . . before [a company] begins to trade under [a] contested mark or publishes [a] book."[36]

Whenever possible, either directly or through an implemented policy or procedure, a corporate lawyer should forecast the purposes of a document *before* its creation. Whereas a simple set of reports or studies generated by a human resources department might have only been intended to better inform a company's procedure for granting discretionary leave, a close initial look could direct the reports or studies to include a section on potential litigation risks if such procedures were implemented or discarded. The litigation-risks section might be an especially persuasive part of a work-product privilege argument if it cites past cases of the company or other companies facing discrimination claims when implementing or discarding similar programs.

Always keep in mind that ideas and conversations are many times reduced to documentation. Thinking ahead, by framing the eventual creation of a document as a tool "preparatory to litigation," may make all the difference in the world later. Written statements created during internal investigations, or meeting agendas between third-party vendors and in-house counsel, are examples of documentation that, if properly directed at the outset, should enjoy the protections of work-product privilege, even if those documents are also heavily slanted toward imparting business advice. Of course, magic doesn't happen simply because it crosses the desk of a client-company's lawyer; the documentation itself, and its reason(s) for existence, have to establish the basis for its protection from an adversary's eyes.

Attorney-Client

Now to the deeper moats and higher walls.

Like a team of carpenters, masons, quarrymen, diggers, and black-smiths, working under the direction of a master builder, building and maintaining a protective wall of attorney-client privilege is the result of every member of a client-company's team's efforts and attention.[37] Care must be taken by everyone to understand what constitutes the privilege, how to create the privilege, and how to preserve the privilege.

"[A] basic element of the privilege is that the attorney be acting in the capacity of legal counsel during communications with the client."[38] This simple sentence lays out the basic elements of the attorney-client privilege. The privilege hinges on the presence or participation of an *attorney* in a communication with the attorney's *client* while providing *legal advice* (or more amorphous "services"). As simple as those elements may sound, a corporate lawyer often has a hand in communication processes that involve a number of different persons and players, most of whom do not constitute the client and which may not involve rendering legal advice or services to the client-company.

For instance, during the due diligence process for a stock offering, when a spreadsheet is circulated to the underwriter and to the client-company's corporate counsel for input or advice, is it protected? Maybe. If the desk of the client-company's legal counsel was the *last stop* before the spreadsheet went back to the client-company, and if the legal counsel provided some kind of legal advice concerning the spreadsheet, then a stronger argument can be made that the communication (and the spreadsheet, hopefully) is protected. What if the communication does not involve a spreadsheet? What if, instead, it involves a conference call? Other privileges may apply (trade secrets, perhaps), but it is unlikely the attorney-client privilege will apply—at least not until the portion of the call when everyone else hangs up *except* the client-company and its lawyer. What if the communication is only between the client-company and its corporate lawyer, but the lawyer's only input is to provide a few comments about whether a particular business unit has exceeded its quarterly legal budget allotment? Is the conversation privileged? Probably not, unless discussing budgets, even if they are legal budgets, can be considered rendering legal advice. Adding some additional complication, the definition of a *client* for purposes of privilege may include (though not automatically) agents of the client-company, such as insurance carriers, consultants, or relatives, who are integrally necessary for the purpose of the communication and the rendering of legal advice. Although the elements of the attorney-client privilege are straightforward, their application is not.

Riddles of privilege are infinite, so here is the takeaway: a client-company and all of its constituents, as well as all the members of a client-company's legal team, must understand how to create the attorney-client privilege and how not to let it slip away in each situation, whenever possible. Exclude superfluous or nonessential parties from communications with legal counsel. Do not copy every single person in the entire information chain unless it is necessary, and understand that by doing so, privilege may be waived. Ask for (or provide, if you are the lawyer) legal advice. Business advice can be in the mix, but there must be some substantive legal guidance that is also part of the communication. If the water is apt to get too muddy, then break the communication into distinct parts: clearly business related versus clearly legal-advice related. Make sure involved persons in a communication *know* the communication is intended to be privileged. Make sure everyone knows the client-company has no intention of waiving privilege.

Truly, the attorney-client privilege is an exercise in complication out of a statement of simplicity. But that doesn't mean a corporate lawyer, or a client-company, should give up the ghost too easily or too quickly.

Defensive Measures
There is no need to "go gentle into that good night."[39] For both privileges—work product and attorney client—there are at least a few principled defenses when you are tiptoeing through minefields of waiver or nonexistence. In truth, aside from a handful of doctrinal defenses, such as common defense and selective waiver, or a rare statutory defense, a corporate lawyer's preparation and imagination are his or her greatest advantages. As we have already discussed, keeping your senses perked for the possibility of privilege situations and taking clear (or as clear as possible) steps to establish privilege are preemptive defensive measures that will pay off in astounding dividends if and when a challenge to your client-company's privilege arises. It is far better to seal a boat while it is in dry dock than it is to plug holes with fingers and toes while far out at sea in a maelstrom.

Selective waiver is a unique privilege concept whereby a corporation may voluntarily disclose otherwise privileged information to a governmental agency while retaining its privilege "vis-à-vis other litigants."[40] The public policy idea is to encourage self-policing and a working relationship with overseeing regulatory or law-enforcement agencies. From a corporation's point of view, the idea is also appealing because it has the potential of stimulating leniency in a world of hard-bitten compliance enforcement.[41] Unfortunately, a variety of federal circuits have whittled the doctrine down to mere shadowboxing practice, but some doors remain open, and a client-company's litigation team should do some case law homework (and apply the imaginative zeal of an advocate) before passing by the opportunity to use selective waiver as a sword, if not a foil.

Common defense or *common interest* is another unique privilege concept, typically more robust in a criminal-defense environment but just as applicable in the right kind of civil environment as well, where privileged information is shared between parties or persons in order to adequately prepare a defense.[42] In a criminal context or civil-litigation context (when a lawsuit is filed and pending), this brand of preserving privilege can have some identifiable lines to it and better sustainability. But what about when a client-company wants to argue the nonwaiver of its attorney-client privilege because it shares a common interest with another company that it is in the middle of vertically integrating? Litigation, it might be argued, is anticipated because a block of shareholders will inevitably voice their displeasure at the acquisition. But is there really a common interest? Numerous issues from a range of opinions could throw some unwanted monkey wrenches into that kind of scenario. Before exchanging confidential paperwork back and forth willy-nilly with a friendly company, person, or party outside of your client-company, and before casually conferencing that company into a call during which legal advice might be provided to your client-company, take a moment and pause. It might not be the best strategy to preserve privilege by assuming a court will agree with your notion of common interest. Even though confidentiality agreements are not always successful at defending against waiver of privilege, they can help to establish a client-company's intent to retain its privilege, and if accompanied at the outset by a memorandum or statement of common interest (which is narrow and carefully adhered to), a reviewing court may later find firmer footing for supporting this distinctive defense of privilege.

Another tactic might be to use a "waiver basket" to preserve privileged materials or communications, especially in light of the gauzy reliability of the selective-waiver doctrine. This concept, typically employed during internal investigations, is designed to anticipate litigation (work-product privilege) for certain informational issues while distinctively segregating confidential communications (attorney-client privilege). As an example, if a corporate lawyer is interviewing an employee, the lawyer explicitly tells the employee the client-company's intention is to provide the substance of the interview information to a regulatory agency; that is, the client-company is gathering information because it anticipates the possibility of litigation or enforcement activity. At that point, even if the information is not ultimately provided to the agency, the client-company is free to selectively disclose the information because it has been developed in anticipation of litigation or in preparation for litigation. Such information—such as that particular interview—is then segregated from other employee communications, the corporate lawyer explicitly explains, that are intended to be protected by the attorney-client privilege and are not to be disclosed at all. This technique can be challenging, and it requires careful handling. Do not get too cute.

Employees
"The professional relationship for purposes of the privilege hinges upon the belief that one is consulting a lawyer and his intention is to seek legal advice."[43] Nowhere are the nuances of who the client is, and how difficult the elements of establishing privilege can be, more potentially calamitous than when they are analyzed in the context of a client-company's employees. When it came to matters of privilege (and other matters as well), employees represented an irascible problem for courts in times past. This is because a corporation is not a physical person but instead solicits and receives legal advice through its employees and agents. Because of this practical reality, courts have historically faced the following problem: if privilege is extended to all of a corporation's employees, then this would create a veritable "zone of silence" nearly impervious to most discovery requests made by outside parties.[44]

Almost predictably, two schools of thought developed two different ways of dealing with this one problem: one school looked to the "person," whereas the other looked to the "subject matter." As for the first approach, the United States District Court for the Eastern District of

Pennsylvania created the control-group test.[45] This test attacked the person element of the problem by stating that "only those communications from employees in a position to control the operations of the corporation" were privileged.[46] Though the Third, Sixth, and Tenth circuits followed the control-group test, the Seventh Circuit struck out on its own, establishing the subject-matter test, which allowed privilege when any employee communicated with a lawyer about the "performance by the employee of the duties of his employment."[47] Despite the fact the United States Supreme Court had affirmed the Seventh Circuit's decision, the Supremes revisited the entire ball of wax ten years later in the *Upjohn* opinion in 1981.[48] From this Supreme Court case sprang the Upjohn warnings mentioned in the previous section, which will appear again in Chapter 5. Using the unpleasant backdrop of SEC disclosures and an IRS criminal investigation, the Supreme Court formally approved the concept of the attorney-client privilege for corporations. It discussed the limitations of the control-group test and declined to apply it, but then the Supreme Court took the nearly useless step of also declining to adopt a bright-line standard. Heralding in a fresh wave of inevitable and resultant confusion in the lower courts, the Supreme Court unremarkably stated that corporate attorney-client privilege should evolve on a case-by-case basis.[49]

The Supreme Court's decision in *Upjohn* left corporate lawyers with the following perception regarding corporate attorney-client privilege:

> [T]he privilege extends to all communications with counsel by corporate employees made under a superior's orders and for the known corporate purpose of obtaining legal advice. To be protected, however, information communicated must be related to matters within the scope of the employee's corporate duties.[50]

The takeaway point is, as before, to be careful. When a corporate lawyer is speaking with a client-company's employee, the lawyer must know why the communication is taking place and that the substance has to do with the employee's job. Additionally, the employee must be initiating or receiving the communication for the purpose of obtaining legal advice (even if, as discussed above, the communication is mixed with business advice). Whereas privilege issues can create the fragility of a china-shop environment, employees live inside the china shop, unlearned in the ways of privilege creation and retention, whereby it would not take the wild exertions of a loose bull to smash everything to pieces.

The reality of privilege for a corporate client (the ego angle) is that corporations, and their constituencies and agents, must be able to produce confidential material and communicate confidential information to their legal counsel, as well as receive such production and communication from their legal counsel. Because that is reality, and because corporate lawyers are ardent champions of their corporate clients, the emotional reaction (the id) is to claim *everything* as privileged. Such a reaction is not necessarily mistaken, but it risks credibility (never risk credibility if you can help it) and ignores the equally tactile reality of waiver (the superego). A balance between protectionism and reactionism is best achieved by preparation and awareness. Keep your client-company and its constituents alert to privilege issues whenever possible (hold an in-house seminar), and work as a team to preserve privilege as situations unfold. Look at each privilege issue globally: its conception, its preservation, its usefulness, its basis, and its effectiveness.

Undoubtedly, matters of privilege are core touchstones of every corporate lawyer's relationship with his or her client-company, and it isn't just a legal term of art. Privilege preserved or lost will be a near and dear part of your client-company's corporate reality. It can be sustaining or devastating. Few things are stronger than privilege, and few things are more fragile, so be discerning and be vigilant.

To quote Monsieur Hugo, "La prudence est l'aîné des enfants de la sagesse" (Caution is the eldest child of wisdom).[51]

§ 2.1.4 Understanding Your Company's Culture

The natural culture of human beings is social, not reclusive. We are, almost without exception, social creatures (even if introverted). We do not work as efficiently or as happily when one of our members tries to become a solitary island. We are uncomfortable with disunity. If we find ourselves in the middle of a cohesive group of people, most of us will find ourselves more quickly chanting a crowd's mantra rather than questioning, much less opposing, its conviction.

When put together for survival, education, pleasure, travel, entertainment, or health, we intermingle and begin to create a culture. The corporate world is no different; it too is another facet of our societal tendencies. A company's employees and constituents unify to exchange, share, advance, or lose values and common practices. Boards will guide their companies in models of environmental sustainability and eco-friendly business practices.[52] Management will develop entire budgets to spend exclusively on corporate social responsibility.[53] Employees will hop onto slides in order to move between floors in corporate offices.[54] Ethically minded investors will buy stock because they like a company's *Don't Be Evil* slogan.[55] In many ways, a company's business plan, operations, and successful existence rise and fall on a company's cultural premise.

"An acceptable observation," you might say. "But what, pray tell, does a corporation's culture really have to do with its corporate lawyers?"

Everything.

Broadly speaking, the presence and participation of corporate lawyers within the culture of their client-companies is akin to the ancient, symbolic use of a Roman fasces, a bundle of birch rods and an ax, carried by a Roman magistrate, signifying the resoluteness and rule of Roman law. Though the greater part of our society thinks of the Scales of Justice as the iconic symbol of our legal system, a corporation's more blinkered view has less to do with balanced scales and more to do with the austerity of rules, regulations, and lurking risks. Corporate lawyers—pointedly, in-house lawyers—should work (and *do* work) against the brutal edges of a Roman fasces, but the image has some reality to it, and that reality is not necessarily a bad thing.

Because corporations germinate, grow, and develop their own idiosyncratic societies, the presence of a corporate lawyer—again, pointedly, an in-house lawyer—acts as the equivalent of the fasces: corporations and their constituents have a reminder to keep within the law or face the consequences. We discussed this role in Chapter 1, and it is, in part, why some in-house lawyers, especially those breaking new ground with fledgling law departments and unreceptive corporate environments, may encounter other employees (managers or board members included) who seem awkward around them, or worse, hostile. A corporate culture unaccustomed to having a proctor in its presence is naturally suspicious, particularly when a legitimate function of that proctor can be to say no and to mete out discipline—the unbundling of the birch rods and axe.

Lest we stray too far into such unpleasant weeds, we can extract a few very useful points from this practical reality that can help us determine why a client-company's culture is such a core touchstone for a corporate lawyer and how a corporate lawyer can bring value to these microsocieties. Because a corporate lawyer works within a client-company's culture, and because a corporate lawyer is a physical symbol of the law, a corporate lawyer has the opportunity to fundamentally affect and change a client-company's culture.

For the lawyer's part, this should be a motivating prospect. After all, it is the client-company's culture—the shaping of its ethos and decisions and demographics—that its corporate lawyers will be destined to defend, overcome, ameliorate, and justify. While in litigation, a lawyer has only the facts that he or she is given to work with; a corporate lawyer's ability to affect a client-company's culture can actually *sculpt* the facts *before* anything happens. That sculpting effort will then resound in litigation, compliance, risk, personnel issues, public relations, market perception, governance practices, operational policies, and ultimately the bottom line.

Culture

Companies with adaptive cultures aligned with their business goals routinely outperform their competitors. Healthy corporate cultures encourage transparency, responsibility, accountability, and compliance. Employee productivity increases, customer satisfaction improves, talent is retained, public relations benefits, and (all else being equal) stock prices can rise. However, regardless of what C-suite executives might secretly wish, corporate cultures cannot be dictated; false veneers will simply ride atop candid emotions until embarrassing cracks form on the surface. Nor can corporate cultures be successfully left to run amok without any direction, control, or consequence; we are, after all, also creatures of gossip, unnecessary drama, and Romanesque mobs. Instead, successful corporate cultures must be shepherded, constantly cultivated and tended, and formed in the wake of sound leadership.

Such an unwieldy chore is, of course, equally shared by other company executives (or at least it should be), and these other executives might even have had the benefit of attending seminars where they learned how to nurture wholesome corporate cultures, promote team building, and embolden all kinds of rah-rah-rah programs. Excellent. Follow their lead (hopefully, a genuine and constructive lead). On the other hand, riding coattails does not diminish a corporate lawyer's own responsibility for making sure his or her client-company has healthy internals. The disciplinarian perception can be important, but it is one dimensional and not very good at the equally important tasks of growing, cultivating, and encouraging. A corporate lawyer must assess, be forward thinking, and engage.

A Culture Audit

Whether you are experiencing your first week in your new digs as a corporate lawyer or whether you have survived twenty-plus years in the business, it is never too late to conduct your own culture audit. In Meghan Biro's smartly done blog for Glassdoor.com,[56] she hits upon a short list of some very practical benchmarks for assessing a company's cultural environment. A few have to do with employee satisfaction, compensation, benefits, and training. The measure of how a company treats (and views) its workforce is a huge bellwether of its long-term success and a significant portion of its risk exposure. One or two of Ms. Biro's suggestions are aimed at management: open-door policies, lines of communication, and making employees feel challenged. Perhaps most important, she asks, "Do your values match those of the company?"

This is not just another qualitative, feel-good exercise (from which the vast majority of corporate lawyers, myself included, would take quick flight). Answers to these questions are actual harbingers of fortune or misfortune. These seemingly vague and reflective questions eventually translate into hard bricks of reality, bricks that a corporate lawyer will have suddenly dropped onto his or her desk to build with or to get rid of as rubble.

Take, for instance, a recent misfortune of PepsiCo. In 2006, the Equal Employment Opportunity Commission brought a vexing issue to PepsiCo's attention: the company's "practice of screening out applicants" who had been arrested but who had not actually been convicted.[57] PepsiCo explained that it had "always applied the background checks neutrally[.]"[58] The policy, on its face, did not smack of malfeasance or ill intent. In fact, it still sounds like a policy designed to foster a healthier, safer corporate environment—a corporate culture of social responsibility and good citizenship. Not bad. Inevitably though, the best-laid plans go awry,[59] and an honest culture audit would have had a good chance of spotting PepsiCo's eventual collision course with federal law. Title VII of the Civil Rights Act of 1964 prohibits the denial of employment based on a person's criminal background, unless the crime is relevant to the job being sought.[60] Not only did PepsiCo's arguably upstanding cultural policy violate Title VII, it also had a disproportionate impact on the number of African American applicants who were turned away.[61] From a culture audit perspective, a corporate lawyer should have been able to see that the company's hiring demographics were imbalanced in spite of an overtly laudable part of PepsiCo's culture—to maintain an employee pool without an apparent proclivity for criminal activity. A swiftly acting PepsiCo lawyer may have called in the prevailing executive powers and discussed preserving the cultural objective while at the same time ending that particular hiring practice.[62]

Good cultural initiatives can have unintended bad consequences. Just as we have to find balance in our society at large, a corporate lawyer brings an enormous value benefit to his or her client-company when cultural positions are objectively evaluated.

The Assessment

Simplicity is beauty. A culture audit does not need to be complicated or involve re-tasking personnel or writing voluminous reports (although it can if that is what is needed). Take a common sense route; develop what seems best to you, given your particular client-company's structure, objectives, and capacity for change. Be repetitive and disciple other attorneys in your department, as well as other willing managers and executives, to perform the same kind of informal assessments. As one of the primary risk assessors of your client-company, this is a great way to generate timely, critical information about the successes, failures, or potential traps within your client-company's cultural initiatives and environment. It can lead to important discussions and changes that may head off investor backlash, compliance problems, regulatory enforcement, customer service issues, and employee discontent. It is not enough for your company to have a particular culture or to promote a culture. Culture is more systemic than the gloss of a neat slogan or fun idea. Your client-company must critique, evaluate, and constantly develop its cultural trends and phenomena. But how?

First, assess. Look and listen for common behaviors. How do managers act? How do employees act? What are the complaints? What are the commendations? Are there any visible signs of problems, or are there visible signs things are working properly? Take a quick look at news pieces, blogs, listservs, and online comment boards. Are there common themes about your client-company's workplace environment, advertising campaigns, level of social responsibility, workforce retention, spending habits, or attitude toward customers, communities, or local economies?

Second, determine what your client-company needs to do and can do to change, improve, or discard its cultural elements. These determinations also need to be simplistic and practical. Buzzwords are not substitutes for real processes, so pie-in-the-sky declarations about "eco-innovations over the next five years" may not be too helpful when trying to define where your client-company should be headed. Clarify (at least in your mind) the overall mission of your client-company. Identify which effective leadership examples or methods to use. Decide how communication of your client-company's cultural changes can be implemented and how a system of constructive feedback can blend with those change efforts. Determine the standards and benchmarks of accountability and accomplishment as change takes place. Recruit the right people to share in your brainstorming and emphasize that change (and constructive criticism) begins and survives *only* because of leadership—leadership from the *front*. If changes, improvements, or new directions need to be pursued, then resolve yourself to the fact that you—and other key personnel—will have to lead by example, with encouragement and patience.

Third, develop a specific action plan (or be ready to provide helpful advice as it is developed). Examine how anticipated cultural changes might impact current policies, programs, or other obligations (such as employment or vendor contracts). As necessary, assist with communicating cultural realignments to employees, vendors, shareholders, and the media. Be ready for feedback (good and bad), and have in place processes for handling resistance, concerns, and unexpected results (no one can ever predict exactly how things will go). Remain consistent. The shine and polish of new initiatives, policies, and procedures will quickly rub off and fade. Change and realignment require long-term, step-by-step formulae and commitment.

Lead from the front, and start within your own department or division.

"If you're a chief executive today, odds are your mind is on talent and corporate culture."[63] At the risk of oversimplifying, that observation is a window into your boss's mindset. If that mindset is an overarching concern for CEOs of most companies, then a company's legal counsel must recognize the global effect corporate culture has on the life of his or her client-company. As the fasces and as the consigliere, a corporate lawyer has far more influence than he or she thinks, even when such a lawyer feels consigned to a very narrow, operational function.[64]

For a corporate lawyer, simply ignoring a company's culture, or treating it as a secondary concern, creates a coming-and-going risk. If the approach is hands-off disinterest, then cultural elements and consequences can propagate and mature into full-blown, bet-the-company problems. Conversely, if the approach is to act as a killjoy, stamping out cultural flourishes and intentions for fear that they will grow into unintended risks, then corporate creativity, productivity, and support structures will suffer. A corporate lawyer must brave whatever awkwardness (or repulsion) might arise when addressing "touchy-feely" cultural sensibilities and be willing to become a good gardener, weeding out bad habits at the roots and nurturing helpful activities into fundamental strengths.

A culture audit, done often if possible and made a part of a legal department's support responsibilities, is an essential tool for addressing a core touchstone of a corporate lawyer's relationship with a client-company. The reality is that every company has its own cultural features. *Your* reality (the ego) is that you play a significant and active role in your client-company's culture. Emotionally (the id), you may see the need for immediate change, and you may want to stalk the hallways foretelling doom if things are not done differently; or maybe you are comfortable letting someone else assess and guide your client-company's cultural environment. It must be the constructive critique of your own role (the superego) that tempers and brings together the other two perspectives. Because you play an active and important role in your client-company's culture, you must accept your responsibility to audit its culture, assess its successes and shortcomings, and lead the efforts to improve its social health.

§ 2.2 EDUCATING THE CLIENT—REVISING AND IMPROVING EXPECTATIONS

We began this chapter by stating a corporate lawyer "needs a simple assessment tool to provide a basic decision matrix from which to work." I proposed the ego-id-superego approach as a means to balance reality with emotion and critical principles when dealing with any of the basic touchstones of every corporate lawyer's relationship with a client-company: corporate structure, the client's identity, privileges, and corporate culture. In the spirit of that 360-degree-style model, it is fitting to close this chapter by discussing how a corporate lawyer can deliver value to his or her client-company by helping the company to assess the touchstones of its relationship with its legal counsel. Lawyers can talk all day (and some do) about their roles and the fundamentals of a value-based client relationship, but all that talk is for naught if a client-company's expectations, or education about the benefits of legal counsel (beyond handling lawsuits), are not in rhythm with its corporate lawyer's purposes and capabilities.

Above and beyond legal-practice issues, this is where the rubber meets the road. If a corporate lawyer truly wants to deliver a valuable service to his or her client-company, then the lawyer must be able to (unpretentiously) educate the client-company about the scope and rationale for its legal services. When personal computers were gathering momentum as a routine part of every family's home throughout the

1980s and 1990s, most people used their computers as glorified type-writers. Though word processing was an essential component in every personal computer, it represented only a fraction of what a computer was capable of doing. As consumers and designers opened their eyes wider and wider to the potential of programming, graphics, microchips, keyboards, and monitors (now flat screens), other software programs multiplied overnight. The consumer side and the provider side simply had to educate each other about capabilities, desires, and needs.

The upside is that, once educated, a corporate lawyer's relation-ship with and value to a client-company will exponentially improve and increase. Identifying a client-company's needs and expectations, and educating a client-company as to the capabilities, benefits, and appropri-ate work quality of its legal counsel, will produce a better relationship, employment experience, and business value, as well as better overall results. Oliver Wendell Holmes Jr. is credited with saying, "A mind that is stretched by a new experience can never go back to its old dimensions."

With that in mind, sit back and ask yourself these questions: Does my client-company understand what all I can offer? Does it understand how I can participate in its business with maximum benefit? Does it understand what my limitations are? How should my services be evalu-ated? My value?

If able to speak, a client-company might echo a turn of phrase uttered by Prime Minister Winston Churchill: "I am easily satisfied with the very best."

When it comes to hiring or retaining legal counsel, corporations hold such a maxim near and dear to their hearts, knowingly or not. Aside from the vast number of small companies, which need superior legal counsel but are only occasionally able to acquire it because of smaller budgets, corporations are usually able to pick and choose at their leisure the lawyers and law firms who provide them with advice and representa-tion. Their pocketbooks allow them this luxury, although irony enters in: without professional guidance on how to evaluate whether they are truly receiving good advice or representation, corporations may be pay-ing a portion, or all, of their legal bills for less-than-great legal counsel.

A corporate lawyer should be as zealously interested in the quality of legal counsel his or her client-company receives as said lawyer is in a vendor's performance, a compliance program's success, or a securities filing's precision. Corporate clients rely on their corporate lawyers to let them know what kind of counsel they should be receiving as well as the quality of that counsel. A fundamental touchstone of a corporate lawyer's relationship with his or her client-company is to understand and assist with a client-company's expectations and a legal provider's capacities to meet those expectations (even when the legal provider is also the same corporate lawyer who is acting as the agent of this balancing act).

In Chapter 1, we discussed the roles of general counsel, in-house lawyers, and outside counsel. Those are roles we can perhaps easily understand, even if we are only giving them some honest thought for the first time. Corporations, however, have historically reached out for lawyers—have only understood them to be useful—when litigation rears its ugly head, a deal or contract needs to be struck, or some kind of investigation, enforcement action, or compliance or regulatory issue requires an attorney's expertise. Like the public at large, corporations have not traditionally seen lawyers as integral members of their business operations and, again like the public at large, corporations can misperceive the limits of a lawyer's or a law firm's knowledge base or skill set.

Generalists

In-house lawyers (and other generalist corporate lawyers) must deliberately be wide-ranging students of a variety of legal disciplines. Just as we have already discussed the assortment of roles necessary to act as a corporate lawyer, Chapter 3 expands on this model by presenting the challenges of different corporate contexts faced by generalist corporate lawyers; contexts that can dynamically shift on short notice, placing a generalist into a whole new universe within which he or she must still function at full effectiveness. Chapter 4 examines the management role and employee role of generalist corporate lawyers. The universal practice areas discussed in Chapter 5 give a good idea of the unadorned need corporations have for well-read and well-practiced multidisciplinarians. Indeed, practicing as a generalist is a specialty in itself, and one that is both exciting and exhausting all at once.[65]

Clients need to know this. A client-company needs to understand the enormous benefit a sharp, knowledgeable generalist corporate lawyer brings to the table. Board members, executives, managers, employees, and shareholders will be able to walk through a generalist's door and expect sound legal advice and strategic thinking from their corporate lawyer. The global perspective of a generalist—usually an in-house lawyer—advantageously ties together all the facets of running a company, instead of risking one discipline's outcome for the sake of another discipline's problem.[66] Strategy and risk-avoidance advice is the result of an overall point of view. It is part of the job of a generalist corporate lawyer to put these benefits into action and to educate the client-company concerning the critical importance of this kind of legal resource.

Specialists

Likewise, a corporate specialist is an archetype of an outside lawyer. This brand of corporate lawyer possesses two or three well-honed, well-studied, and specialized focuses of practice.[67] Historically, it was the outside counsel who acted as corporate America's "company lawyers," as if corporations were the same as individuals, with limited or only a few specialized legal needs. As we took note of in Chapter 1, those circumstances have changed dramatically over the past twenty to thirty years. But even as outside counsel have moved away from their long-time role of acting as senior legal counsel (general counsel) to their corporate clients, they have stepped into the much-needed roles of specialists. Whereas in jolly old England the practice of law has presented a natural slant toward specialization by placing barristers before the bar of the courts and solicitors across the desk from clients, the American legal system has used the term *lawyer* as an all-encompassing sobriquet, which has long left the impression, in corporate and individual clients' minds, that a lawyer should be able to handle every general legal problem *and* highly specialized legal problems. Borrowing an observation from the First Earl of Beaconsfield, an English statesman, parliamentarian, and former British prime minister, Benjamin Disraeli,

> A man may speak very well in the House of Commons, and fail very completely in the House of Lords. There are two distinct styles requisite: I intend, in the course of my career, if I have time, to give a specimen of both.

That is a memorable way to convey the concept of *specialty*.

Clients need to know this. It is the duty of outside counsel (and their in-house counterparts) to educate client-companies about the limits of a particular area of practice,[68] the complexity of a particular area of practice, and when there is the need to engage a specialist whose experience has focused on that particular area of practice.[69] The depth of understanding and the necessary level of proficiency possessed by a specialist corporate lawyer can sometimes be indispensable, such as in corporate bankruptcy, securities laws and regulations, patent (or other IP) filing and litigation, maritime law, corporate criminal defense, financial regulatory law, international employment laws, and a myriad of other demanding practice areas. Many times a generalist can get the ball rolling, oversee progress and benchmarks, provide general evaluations of quality, and tie in other areas of affected concern, but a specialist is the drill-down, go-to, bet-the-company legal resource. A securities lawyer will not be able to spend too much time (if any) conversing about the basic application of the Family Medical Leave Act, but he or she would shut the house down when talking about all the requirements and aspects of a corporation's annual Form 10-K filing with the Securities Exchange Commission. I recall a frustrating conversation I had with a banking executive of a regional bank who was insisting his bank's lawyer meets his bank's legal-counsel needs. Of course, he was referring to a local litigation firm whose practice consisted mainly of collections, foreclosures, and loan workouts—all necessary parts of retail and commercial lending but *not* banking law.

It is a disservice to a client-company not to educate the company—to fail to realign its expectations and its anticipation of value—concerning the benefits of engaging, hiring, or retaining the appropriate and mutually exclusive kind of generalist and/or specialist. Corporate lawyers in both camps need to diligently take up this task (and to be reminded their mutual exclusivity results in complementary financial opportunity).[70]

Your Toolbox
It would seem discomfiting to write a book about lawyers, to lawyers, without at least mentioning Sun Tzu, the oft-quoted ancient Chinese military strategist who is reputed to have written the treatise *The Art of War* sometime between the second and fourth centuries B.C. Here then is a contribution from Mr. Tzu: "He who knows when he can fight and when he cannot, will be victorious."

Educating a client-company about the value you bring to its organization can only be an honest effort when it begins with a healthy sense of self-awareness. As you were reading the previous remarks concerning generalists and specialists, you were undoubtedly identifying yourself with one of the two camps (or both in some ways), and in so doing you were exercising self-awareness. You were looking inside of your mental toolbox and inventorying the capabilities, experiences, resources, and proficiencies you have accumulated: the tools you can bring to bear on behalf of a client-company. With the passage of time, a corporate lawyer's number of tools grows, and he or she possesses a greater skill set, able to meet the needs of a client-company, whether horizontally for generalist in-house lawyers or vertically for specialized outside lawyers.

Expectations

Though most of us enjoy new challenges, we also recognize the wisdom in knowing our limitations. Most corporate lawyers do not like saying, "I'm not sure; let me consult another lawyer about that," when speaking with a client-company, but if a client's expectations have been properly managed, then it will *appreciate* the self-awareness and the prudence the lawyer is displaying. That perceptive erudition is valuable to a client-company, and it should know it. No educated patient would want a pediatrician performing his or her open-heart surgery, even if the pediatrician is brilliant at pediatrics. Hippos just do not wear zebra stripes very well.

Clients need to know this. Take your toolbox inventory seriously and emphasize for your client-company how and when your particular set of tools will help. Remember, a client-company's business *is* its business. Accent the education of your client-company with that kind of focus: how and when your tools will help its *business*, not just when your tools can be used to address a finite legal problem. If a client-company does not have ears for why a certain provision must be included in a particular software licensing agreement, it *will* have ears for how that provision can ultimately affect its profit margin or indirectly affect its compliance requirements. Your understanding of software licensing agreements will have then become an indispensable tool to your client-company's business.

A corporate lawyer *is* a resource for a corporation. Every corporate resource—corporate lawyers included—should be able to meet a qualitative analysis: your value will lie in the contents (and use) of your toolbox. Unfortunately, I have sat next to lawyers in continuing legal education conferences who spend the entire time on their phones or computers, ignoring the panelists or speaker and missing out on a chance to add one more skill to their inventory or to sharpen an often-used and well-worn knowledge base. I have wondered if their corporate clients know how seemingly unimportant it is to their legal counsel to improve upon their value to the company.

It is the ongoing obligation of every corporate lawyer to make sure his or her client-company is, and remains, educated about the distinctive values legal counsel can and should be able to deliver. Corporate dollars are better spent, problems are more wisely addressed, and relationships are more enduring when each party—the corporate lawyer and the client-company—have appropriate and educated expectations. Generalists and specialists alike ought to be pointing to each other *out of value it brings to the client*. And client-companies ought to become well educated enough to understand the benefit of each. Corporate lawyers ought to be able to assess, and should never cease to develop, their own toolboxes of experience and resources.

With the improvement in the quality of legal departments, the ever-increasing complexities of corporate-law practice, the unique intricacies of various industries, and the infinite diversity of client-companies, corporate lawyers must possess an understanding of the fundamental touchstones of their relationships with their corporate clients while educating those same clients about the distinctive benefits different brands of corporate lawyers can bring to their businesses. Corporate structure, client identity, privilege issues, corporate culture, and client expectations are relational touchstones shared by all corporate lawyers and all client-companies. A methodology of analysis—whether or not it is the ego-id-superego approach of balancing reality with emotion and ethical critique—is paramount to understanding, addressing, and resolving those five underpinnings of a corporate legal relationship. The corporate lawyer, as the presumptive subject-matter expert, must take the lead in identifying and demonstrating the value these elements bring to a client-company's business.

Meet with your client-company's constituents, board members, executives, managers, and employees. Sponsor law-department luncheons or law-day breakfasts and educate, educate, educate. Talk about these core issues and how they relate strategically to overall business concerns and objectives. Attend *other departments'* meetings whenever possible. Do not make the mistake of saying, "Oh that just involves a restructuring issue. It's a management decision. I'll only participate if asked." Offer your help; involve yourself in a supportive (nonthreatening) way. Be earnest. By never forgetting the core touchstones of your relationship with your client-company, you, in return, will earn the greatest commodity a lawyer can possess: credibility.

Lizanne Thomas, a partner at Jones Day, related the following anecdote during an interview about predicting success as a corporate lawyer:

> A general counsel of a major company I work with describes her role as having moved far beyond the legal issues. Her legal department has gained such credibility that it is the *hard* issues— irrespective of whether they carry legal implications—that are referred to it. I think this is an extraordinary compliment to her department[.][71]

Those hard issues, and the credibility to deal with them, define your ability and willingness to convey your value to your client-company through the relationship you have with it and the touchstones that form that relationship.

NOTES

1. If the mention of Freud caused a slight brain freeze, stick with me. I'm no personal fan either.
2. The Theory of Chaos, or Chaos Theory, surveys the seemingly unpredictable behavior of dynamic systems that are highly sensitive to initial conditions: that is, the butterfly effect. I am sure, somewhere, a butterfly beat its wings, and I wrote this book. Chaos.

3. Google was named by *Fortune* magazine as the best place to work in America in January 2012. CNNMoney, *100 Best Companies to Work For*, *available at* http://money.cnn.com/magazines/fortune/best-companies/2012 /snapshots/1.html (last visited Apr. 3, 2012). The hype had a lot to do with all the company's everyday perks, but there is a method to the madness. For example, Google found a better retention rate among female employees who requested maternity leave when the company increased maternity leave to eighteen weeks at a 100 percent pay rate.

4. David Ingram, Demand Media, *Why Is Organizational Structure Important?* CHRON.COM, http://smallbusiness.chron.com/organizational -structure-important-3793.html (last visited Mar. 15, 2012).

5. Robert L. Nelson and Laura B. Nielson, *Cops, Counsel, and Entrepreneurs: Constructing the Role of Inside Counsel in Large Corporations*, 34 LAW & SOC'Y REV. 457, 460 (2000). Robert L. Nelson is the director of the American Bar Foundation and a professor of sociology and law at Northwestern University. Laura B. Nielson is a research professor at the American Bar Foundation and an associate professor of sociology and the director of legal studies at Northwestern University.

6. *Id.* I could not have said it better myself. And so I did not.

7. Byron F. Egan, *Recent Fiduciary Duty Cases Affecting Advice to Directors and Officers of Delaware and Texas Corporations*, 32nd Annual Conference on Securities Regulation and Business Law, Feb. 12, 2010. "Good governance practices" in the wake of Sarbanes-Oxley, as well as the fiduciary duties of executive officers, are all duties that extend to every executive's position, regardless of whatever department or division he or she may lead.

8. Alex Vorro, *Jacksonville Jaguars Name New GC*, INSIDECOUNSEL, Jan. 11, 2012, *available at* http://www.insidecounsel.com/2012/01/11/jacksonville -jaguars-name-new-gc?t=careers. Recall that before taking the reins as president of Eastman Kodak Co., Ms. Quatela oversaw the generation of hundreds of millions of dollars in profit revenue through the monetization of Kodak's intellectual-property patent licensing.

9. *See* Nelson and Nielson, *supra* note 5, at 463. This is the cop role of a corporate lawyer.

10. *Id.* at 464.

11. *Reading the Tea Leaves: What's the Current Thinking on How Many Lawyers a Company Should Have?*, Sender Legal Search 634–35 (January 29, 2010), http://www.senderlegalsearch.com/archives/62.

12. Arguably, one of the deciding factors of the Battle of Waterloo was Wellington's personal and careful reconnaissance of the low ridge of Mont-Saint-Jean, south of the village of Waterloo and the Sonian Forest, a year *before* the battle was actually fought. Wellington's knowledge of the terrain helped to trump Napoleon's army's experience and tactical abilities. Never underestimate the advantage of careful observation and preparation.

13. *See* MODEL RULES OF PROF'L CONDUCT R. 1.13(a) (1983).

14. *Id.* at 1.13(b).

15. The Model Rules are not, of course, the be-all and end-all, and the intellectual difficulty of the client-identity problem is not easily solved

by simply applying the rules. There are subtleties that add to the problem's complexity. As William H. Simon points out in his article on organizational clients, the Model Rules adopt an "Authority Structure" in which a constituent's authority is the touchstone to being a corporate agent. William H. Simon, *Whom (or What) Does the Organization's Lawyer Represent?: An Anatomy of Intraclient Conflict*, 91 Cal. L. Rev. 57, 80 (Jan. 2003). Another educating read (that is shorter than Mr. Simon's article) is Geoffrey C. Hazard Jr., *Ethical Dilemmas of Corporate Counsel*, 46 Emory L.J. 1011 (Summer 1997).

16. Catherine Dunn calls out some very on-point remarks concerning a general counsel's role as the "guardian of corporate integrity" from a book by E. Norman Veasey and Christine Di Guglielmo. Catherine Dunn, *What Makes Corporate America's Indispensable Counsel Tick?*, Corporate Counsel, Mar. 7, 2012, *available at* http://www.law.com/jsp /cc/PubArticleCC.jsp?id=1202544609676&What_Makes_Corporate _Americas_emIndispensable_Counselem_Tick. The book is an excellent read. E. Norman Veasey & Christine Di Guglielmo, Indispensable Counsel: The Chief Legal Officer in the New Reality (Oxford University Press 2012).

17. Admittedly, firing a client under any circumstances is difficult. For corporate lawyers in private practice, firing a well-paying, large, corporate client can be exquisitely painful, and it can follow a similar path to the one that might need to be taken by an in-house lawyer. For example, the policy for outside counsel who perform work for Starbucks, Inc., is they are assigned *one* in-house liaison attorney. They are prohibited from dealing with any other constituent of Starbucks (unless under the management of that one liaison attorney). If, however, the assigned liaison attorney is engaged in some kind of activity (or gives some kind of direction) the outside counsel believes could result in substantial harm to Starbucks, then the outside counsel faces the same unenviable task of an in-house lawyer: break with policy and go to a higher authority to deal with the matter.

18. We will discuss corporate investigations in Chapter 5 and risk-management issues in Chapter 6.

19. *See* Model Rules of Prof'l Conduct R. 1.13(f) (1983).

20. Upjohn warnings and other investigatory issues will appear later in this section and in Chapter 5.

21. Geoffrey C. Hazard Jr., *Ethical Dilemmas of Corporate Counsel*, 46 Emory L.J. 1011, 1018 (Summer 1997). In fact, Mr. Hazard describes this exposure to "back-channel information" as the "most significant difference between corporate counsel and lawyers in independent practice." *Id.* at 1019.

22. *See* Model Rules of Prof'l Conduct R. 1.13(b) (1983).

23. By the way, never give *personal* legal advice on a nonbusiness matter to an employee or other constituent. Gently but firmly suggest the employee look for a personal lawyer. It might be a tough bit of advice, but it's the *only* advice you should give as a corporate lawyer.

24. Simon, *supra* note 15, at 65–67.

25. *Id.* at 66.

26. Nancy J. Moore, *Conflicts of Interest for In-house Counsel: Issues Emerging from the Expanding Role of the Attorney-Employee*, 39 S. Tex. L. Rev. 497 (Mar. 1998). Professor Nancy Moore, the Nancy Barton Scholar Professor of Law at Boston University School of Law, does an excellent job in her article of discussing the variety of situations in which conflicts of interest may arise, inadvertently or not, for in-house counsel, including in the area of joint representation.

27. R v. Derby Magistrates' Court, ex p B [1996] A.C. 487, *quoted with approval in* R (on the application of Morgan Grenfell & Co Ltd) v. Special Comm'r of Income Tax, para 10, *quoting* Hobbs v. Hobbs and Cousens [1960], p.112, 116–17, Stevenson, J.

28. Scott R. Flucke, *The Attorney-Client Privilege in the Corporate Setting: Counsel's Dual Role as Attorney and Executive*, 62 UMKC L. Rev. 549, 552 (spring 1994).

29. As an example, my hat is off to William M. Anderson, senior counsel for Wells Fargo Law Department, and all of his attorney compatriots who drafted the ABA's position letter to United States Senate Committee on Banking, Housing, and Urban Affairs, regarding the passage of S.2009 in February 2012. The ABA voiced its support for the Senate bill (and H.R. 4014) and other legislation "that would create a single, consistent standard for the treatment of privileged information submitted to all Federal agencies that supervise banks, including the newly created Consumer Financial Protection Bureau[.]" Letter from Wm. T. Robinson III to the Honorable Tim Johnson, Chairman Committee on Banking, Housing and Urban Affairs, and the Honorable Richard Shelby, Ranking Member Committee on Banking, Housing and Urban Affairs (Feb. 21, 2012) (on file with the author).

30. SanDiegoSource, The Daily Transcript, *San Diego leaders pleased with BRAC report*, May 13, 2005, *available at* http://www.sddt.com/government/article.cfm?SourceCode=20050513cza (last visited Feb. 11, 2012).

31. For instance, a person's health information is protected by HIPAA. A person's financial information is protected by the Graham-Leach-Bliley Act. Business trade secrets are protected from competitors by the Uniform Trade Secrets Act. The government's interest in discovering and prosecuting money laundering (among other things) is protected by the Bank Secrecy Act.

32. Hickman v. Taylor, 329 U.S. 495, 510 (1947).

33. *Id.* at 509.

34. *E.g., see* United States v. Adlman, 68 F.3d 1495 (2d Cir. 1995); Martin v. Bally's Park Place Hotel & Casino, 983 F.2d 1252 (3rd Cir. 1993); Martin v. Monfort, 150 F.R.D. 172 (D. Colo. 1993).

35. *Adlman*, 68 F.3d at 1501.

36. *Id.*

37. Whereas the work-product privilege finds a firm date as late as the last century, the attorney-client privilege is able to work its genealogy back to Elizabethan times or even earlier. Although I will admit that castle-building predated the Elizabethan era, it *sounds* old, and I'll willingly bear the brunt of assault of castle historians for the sake of a very usable metaphor.

38. Flucke, *supra* note 28, at 559.
39. Reference to the first line of a poem by Welsh poet Dylan Thomas, originally published in the journal *Botteghe Oscure* in 1951.
40. Andrew J. McNally, *Revitalizing Selective Waiver: Encouraging Voluntary Disclosure of Corporate Wrongdoing by Restricting Third Party Access to Disclosed Materials*, 35 SETON HALL L. REV. 823, 837 (2005).
41. *Id.* at 837–40. (These pages discuss *Diversified Industries, Inc. v. Meredith*, 572 F.2d 596 (8th Cir. 1977) (en banc).)
42. *E.g., see* Haines v. Liggett Grp. Inc., 975 F.2d 81, 94 (3d Cir. 1992).
43. Wylie v. Marley Co., 891 F.2d 1463, 1471 (10th Cir. 1989).
44. *See* Note, *Attorney-Client Privilege for Corporate Clients: The Control Group Test*, 84 HARV. L. REV. 424, 427–28 (1970).
45. City of Phila. v. Westinghouse Electric Corp., 210 F. Supp. 483 (E.D. Pa. 1962).
46. Flucke, *supra* note 28, at 554–55.
47. Harper & Row Publishers, Inc. v. Decker, 423 F.2d 487, 491 (7th Cir. 1970), *aff'd*, 400 U.S. 348 (1971).
48. Upjohn Co. v. United States, 449 U.S. 383 (1981).
49. *Id.* at 396–97.
50. Flucke, *supra* note 28, at 556.
51. Victor Marie Hugo, the great French poet, playwright, essayist, novelist, and exporter of much-needed Romanticism.
52. In 2003, after a hard-fought, ten-year process of change, DuPont won the EPA's Presidential Green Chemistry Award. Environmental Protection Agency, 2003 Award Recipients, http://www.epa.gov/greenchemistry /pubs/pgcc/past.html#2003 (last visited Mar. 2, 2012).
53. Molson Coors Canada spent over $120,000 in 2009 "to help raise awareness and support communities across the country in their efforts to encourage responsible drinking[.]" Molson Coors, Investor News, *Molson Coors Celebrates Responsibility with Rides Home for the Holiday Season*, http:// phx.corporate-ir.net/phoenix.zhtml?c=101929&p=irol-newsArticle _Print&ID=1369246&highlight= (last visited Mar. 3, 2012).
54. At Dixon Schwabl, a full-service ad agency, the fun side of corporate culture involves a slide built between two office floors. After I am finished writing this book, I am applying for a job at Dixon Schwabl. Democrat and Chronicle, *Dixon Schwabl focuses on having fun at its office playground*, May 9, 2010, *available at* http://www.democratandchronicle.com /article/20100509/BUSINESS/5090323/Dixon-Schwabl-focuses-having -fun-its-office-playground.
55. This is the first sentence to the Preface of Google's Code of Conduct. For those who are wondering, there is no carve-out provision, allowing Google employees to be evil to Yahoo! Google, Investor Relations, *Code of Conduct*, http://investor.google.com/corporate/code-of-conduct.html (last visited Mar. 3, 2010).
56. Meghan M. Biro, *Seven Company Culture Questions You Must Ask Before Accepting a Job Offer*, GLASSDOOR BLOG (Feb. 8, 2011), http://www.glassdoor .com/blog/company-culture-questions-accepting-job-offer. Although Ms. Biro's blog is focused on a cultural assessment as part of evaluating

a person's job opportunity, the advice remains solid for any stage of a person's career.

57. Cathleen Flahardy, *PepsiCo Settles Charges of Racial Bias in Hiring Practices*, InsideCounsel, Jan. 13, 2012, *available at* http://www.insidecounsel .com/2012/01/13/pepsico-settles-charges-of-racial-bias-in-hiring-p.

58. *Id.*

59. An often-quoted adaptation of a stanza in a poem written by the Scotsman Robert Burns in 1785: "But little Mouse, you are not alone, / In proving foresight may be vain: / The best laid schemes of mice and men / Go often awry, / And leave us nothing but grief and pain, / For promised joy!"

60. *Editor's Note*, Title VII of the Civil Rights Act of 1964, Pub. L. No. 88-352, 42 U.S.C. §§ 2000e–2000e-17, *available at* http://www.eeoc.gov/laws /statutes/titlevii.cfm. "Title VII prohibits employment discrimination based on race, color, religion, sex and national origin. The Civil Rights Act of 1991 (Pub. L. 102-166) (CRA) and the Lily Ledbetter Fair Pay Act of 2009 (Pub. L. 111-2) amend several sections of Title VII. In addition, section 102 of the CRA . . . amends the Revised Statutes by adding a new section following section 1977 (42 U.S.C. 1981), to provide for the recovery of compensatory and punitive damages in cases of intentional violations of Title VII, the Americans with Disabilities Act of 1990, and section 501 of the Rehabilitation Act of 1973."

61. Flahardy, *supra* note 57. PepsiCo ultimately agreed to pay $3.13 million to settle federal discrimination charges.

62. My Monday-morning quarterbacking is only meant to discuss the virtues of keeping one's eyes open. I cannot put myself into the difficult shoes of PepsiCo's counsel, and I do not mean my comments to be an unfair critique of them.

63. Barbara T. Armstrong, *At America's Best Workplaces, Good Design Reigns Supreme*, Forbes.com (Jul. 15, 2011, 10:32 AM), http://www.forbes.com /sites/forbesleadershipforum/2011/07/15/at-americas-best-workplaces -good-design-reigns-supreme/.

64. General counsel for nearly all larger and medium-sized law departments "are expected to participate in executive management reviews of corporate strategies and comprehensive business plans, as well as regular operational review sessions." *See* Carole Basri and Irving Kagan, Corporate Legal Departments § 2:2 (4th ed., Practicing Law Institute 2011), at 2–3 (citing to a Price Waterhouse, LLP, survey).

65. The generalist can be industry specific, such as a generalist who works for banks, hospitals, automobile manufacturers, or software companies. Industry, by its nature, is specialized, even though almost all industry possesses common, or general, legal needs—hence, a "banking generalist."

66. For example, think of a transactional lawyer allowing a physician's lease with a hospital to lapse while negotiating a new lease which, unwittingly, could automatically expose several of the hospital executives to the criminal liability arising from the "corporate responsible officer" doctrine used by healthcare regulators.

67. Certain states allow lawyers to include the word *specialization*, or some variation thereof, on their advertising, letterhead, and business cards. The

various state bar rules about using that kind of designation, or telling a client or a potential client that you specialize in a specific area of practice, can be very restrictive. Any lawyer wishing to promote him- or herself in this way is urged to consult the relevant jurisdictional rules and guidelines before doing so.

68. For example, a litigator does not necessarily know how to advise a banking client on potential regulatory (i.e., balance-sheet) risks that may arise as the result of a particular litigation strategy. *See* Steven L. Lovett, *How Banking-Reform Laws Affect a Bank's Approach to Litigation Strategies*, 12 COMMERCIAL & BUSINESS LITIGATION 3 (Spring 2011).

69. For example, Lizanne Thomas, a partner at Jones Day who has extensive experience in mergers and acquisitions and in corporate governance, has found herself engaged by boards looking for specialized counsel other than their in-house counsel or regular outside counsel. Ms. Thomas points to the example of needing "truly independent advice . . . in investigations where senior level conduct is at issue or where there are true conflicting interests." Interview of Lizanne Thomas, *Today's General Counsel: Some Key Factors in Predicting Success*, METROPOLITAN CORPORATE COUNSEL, July 2007, at 47.

70. Although we have been talking in terms of archetypes, it is equally important to remember that generalists also have their own specialties, and specialists are still high-quality lawyers with enough experience to have touched upon and worked through other areas outside their usual concentrations.

71. Thomas, *supra* note 69.

CHAPTER 3

STARTING YOUR JOB— "WHAT DID I JUST JUMP INTO?"

You wake up early, the celebratory drinks and warm congratulations still lingering from the night before. It is your own D-Day. Today, you will be walking into your new office, or assuming a new title, or a new set of responsibilities, expectations, and roles.

A friend's thoughtful question of what this new job or assignment means to you—the essentials of your new *role*—is no longer on your mind. Some personal reflection, mixed with wine (or whiskey), and eventually the first two chapters of this book were able to take care of that query. Instead, it is another friend's comment which casts a long shadow from the evening before, haunting your early-morning shower, and causing you to stare nervously at the morning's paper without actually focusing on it. The comment, quipped on the heels of your excited descriptions about your new office and title, and the impressive sound of your first major project—developing a corporate intellectual-property program—went something along the lines of: "Wow! I'd have no idea where to start!" Unintentionally, your friend's comment made everything in you freeze for a moment.

He's right, you think to yourself: developing and instituting a corporate IP program *is* a lot of work. Where do you start? The uneasy thought is causing you to unconsciously wince with anxiety as you make your way out the front door. Descriptive expletives aside, your heart starts beating fast as you try to think of everything you will be expected to do—everything you will be expected to know how to do or direct someone else to do. You wonder, What did I just jump into? You finally, privately, admit (with sickening despair) that you have never *really* developed or implemented a corporate IP program before. You feel like you have no idea what to do or where to begin.

Take heart. Whether you are riding the initial waves of a new business venture, plunging mid-stream into a vigorous ongoing business, or stepping into an operating-room-like environment where some kind of transition must be carefully (surgically) handled, the feeling of having no idea where to begin or what to do has been shared by the best of the best. You are in good company. Every corporate lawyer worth his or her salt has felt the same sense of untethered apprehension about some looming and uncertain horizon.

The last section of Chapter 2 provided some practical advice on how you could bring this kind of personal panic attack into perspective for yourself and for your client-company. You have to know your limits, be honest with yourself, identify resources, and educate your client-company along the way, while making sure it still receives top-flight legal counsel, even when you are facing the distinctive challenge of developing and implementing an impossible-sounding IP program. You have a firm grasp of your role (Chapter 1), and you have your analytical methodology to address the clutch of fundamental touchstones that arise in every corporate law situation: the client-company's structure, *who* constitutes the client, what the privilege challenges might be, and how the corporate culture will drive all of that (Chapter 2). You have a foundation: you know your roles, and your command of those fundamentals will affect everything you do as a corporate lawyer on behalf of your client-company.

For the moment (hopefully before you are in the middle of your commute to your first morning on the job), put aside any disturbing thoughts about developing a world-class IP program (we will get to that later), and realize, as a first step, that no matter what project you are facing, its constraints, materials, and goals will be prescribed by your client-company's particular stage of business. Its stage of business is the context, the organizational situation, within which you will be practicing corporate law. A corporate IP program for a new venture will, and should, look (and manage) much differently than a corporate IP program for a thriving, ongoing business concern. Sometimes, the stage of business is easy to ascertain, but many times, corporations, or their divisions or business lines, are straddling two or more possibilities. I like how Eric Esperne frames an inevitable condition found in any stage of a company's business: "Accept that all companies suffer from dysfunction. Business rarely happens in some precise, methodical kind of way (unlike the law). It took me years to figure that out."[1] Me too.

Identifying a client-company's stage of business is a critical part of assessing its legal needs, risk exposures, and strategic plans, but it does not need to be hyperprecise or static. It is a business, after all—unpredictably growing, contracting, speeding up, slowing down, and turning left when you were completely convinced it was about to turn right. Even so, the chief questions you will need to ask to determine on what business stage your immediate drama will unfold do not have to be complicated. Here are a few:

- Is your client-company a new venture? Does it have new subsidiaries or divisions, or is it incubating new investment entities?

- Is your client-company an ongoing business concern with years under its collective corporate belt? Is it an industry stronghold, or is it an industry rebel?
- Is your client-company in the middle of a critical merger, a much-anticipated acquisition, a bankruptcy, an emergence from bankruptcy, or a large restructuring?
- Or is your client-company a convoluted triple-helix[2] of business stages, composed of several of these situations all at once?

Do not just read them; really *ask* them. Get yourself comfortable with where you think the majority of your client-company's business activities are situated: beginning, middle, or some nebulous end. Where and how are you most needed? Your client-company's business context answers that core question.

"We learn to protect through our training and experience. To serve is far more complicated. It is facile to presume that any one person is an expert in this regard[.]"[3] Stephen Kaplan's[4] observation and his following comment, "one size fits one," are healthy ways to approach this chapter and your new job. Do not feel overwhelmed, thinking you have to have it all figured out in the first ten minutes, the first ten days, or even the first ten months. Like flying into an as-yet-unvisited city, the best way to orient yourself—to identify areas of high priority versus areas that can wait—is to look out the window as you are on the approach. Your greatest asset will be a bird's-eye view before you hit the ground running.

That is our goal for this chapter: to view your client-company's situation—its stage of business—from a 50,000-foot view to identify where your skills, input, advice, and advocacy are most needed.

Far too often, corporate lawyers are caught flat-footed, at ground level, with an unintentionally myopic view of how they are supposed to fit in and where their toolbox is needed. (Sometimes, they do not even realize that this should matter to them.) Like other professionals it hires, your client-company is going to depend on your ability to look at the overall picture (even when your practical function appears limited) to determine how your role should synthesize with the principal business objective and the client-company's stage of business. Figuring out how to serve a client-company in the way it needs to be served is the real nut to crack for most corporate lawyers. Use your client-company's stage of business as your contextual framework—understand its parameters and goals—and you will have a respectable sense of your surroundings and how best to serve its interests as its lawyer.

§ 3.1 NEW VENTURES

The nascent stage of a business can be one of the most exhilarating times for everyone involved. Plank owners and investors might busy their calculators with infinite numbers of ways their stake might eventually lead to huge dividends or übervaluable equity shares. Top managers—usually those who spawned the idea that led to the new business's creation—are flush with a sense of accomplishment and potential, both mixed into the same heady stew. Employees seem bright and shiny; they feel like they are part of something that has energy and vision. Amazingly, they might not even mind too much when certain benefits are not yet available or are further away than anticipated. Leasing companies are in a good mood, eager to lock in new operating contracts their bookkeepers can quickly input as new income-producing assets. Vendors might hedge with restricted account credit limits, but overall, they are just as excited about the promise of bigger orders as the new business is about placing them. Advertising or marketing salespeople are rapping on the front door, ready to present the perfect marketing plan and to rake in those advertising dollars. Bankers might even roll out a line of credit or two. It really can be a thrilling, if exhausting, time.

And a corporate lawyer can be—should be, or should be ready to be—involved in every area of the business's burgeoning existence.

So how does a corporate lawyer—a lawyer who needs to represent this fledgling enterprise as a whole—get his or her arms around such a lively but disorganized and untried client-company?

Think like a long-term investor. Even if you are terrible at actually investing.

A good investor is going to have a healthy sense of how to make sense of a new business venture. A good investor is going to look at a new business—its leaders, employees, operations, obligations, market—for capital needs (and allocations), assets (be they ideas or widgets), viability (its ability to *do* business and for how long), and human capital. Very simply, a good investor is going to "learn the structure through which the dollars are earned."[5]

Everything that goes into acting as legal counsel for a new venture should carry this reason for existence: *to develop a sound business structure through which the dollars will be earned.* If you can satisfy yourself that each of your undertakings on behalf of your newly formed (or forming) client-company is intended to develop its structure—to advance its ability to make money through a sustainable enterprise—then you will have the right kind of focus, and the appropriate litmus test, for everything you need to do.

Keeping this in mind, we will take a look at five universal spokes that emanate from this hub: formation issues, funding issues, initial intellectual-property issues, regulatory and licensing issues, and employment issues. With those spokes in place, from a legal perspective, a client-company's operations, sales, and services ought to begin to gather and produce their own motion, even better than one of Orffyreus's Wheels.[6]

§ 3.1.1 Basic Formation Issues

> *"But I don't want to go among mad people," said Alice.*
> *"Oh, you can't help that," said the cat. "We're all mad here."*

In all honesty, any commentary written about formation and ownership issues (and the inevitable struggles) of most new companies could be summed up with this one quote from *Alice's Adventures in Wonderland,*[7] written by the brilliant, partially deaf, Oxford-educated Charles Lutwidge Dodgson, also known by the less weighty pen name of Lewis Carroll. The maddening matter of ownership and management is critical, arguably above all else, when it comes to a new business venture. As any corporate lawyer who has had a hand in an initial company's formation and its first era of management will attest, the challenges of dealing with ownership, and delineating ownership from the rightful role of daily management, have little to do with the amount of money involved and more to do with the size (and goals) of the personalities involved.

Here, perhaps more than at any other business stage, it is critical for a corporate lawyer to keep sight of *who the client is* (see Chapter 2). If you represent a board member, the board as a whole, an officer, or any variation of an association of stakeholders, then you do *not* represent the client-company. This can be a hard reality to keep in mind, especially when you are approached by, engaged by, and work closely with only one or two in the client-company's aristocracy—usually the chief officers, inventors, the guys-who-started-this-thing-in-their-garage, or the guy-who-has-put-in-the-most-money-and-feels-the-need-to-oversee-everything. Maybe they need their own private counsel, but if you are tapped to be the *company's* lawyer, you *must* steer clear of playing both sides of the fence. You have to be the first to establish the integrity, objectivity, and fair-mindedness of the client-company's corporate lawyer's position.[8] You also can have a significant shepherding role in leading each of the company's apex personalities into their rightful—and rightfully limited—roles. Take care to be careful.

The best time for this kind of clarity is when you are first approached—regardless of who approaches you—to provide legal services. Find out right then and there in what capacity you are being hired. If you are being hired in an employment sense, it is the perfect opportunity to discuss with the client-company's representative(s) what that means: you will be the *company's* lawyer, and not anyone's personal lawyer. If you are being engaged as outside counsel but as the company's corporate counsel, establish right away who it is you will answer to, who will monitor or oversee your services, and what the scope of your engagement will be (probably something you will have to educate the client about).

New Ventures

From there, you have to begin to amass information—no easy task when centralized departments are in their infancy or simply do not exist yet. (This, by the way, will never stop; you will *always* need to be gathering as much information as possible before you provide legal advice to your client-company.) This first wave of information—comprising, among other things, who the plank owners will be; the size and type of their investments; the nature of the business (product, service, or blend); the proprietary nature of the product or service; the initial lender relations and nature of nonequity funding resources; working budgets and forecasts; anticipated auditing categories and plans; the style of management; the number and category of initial employees; the physical location(s) of the business; regulatory requirements; the business's anticipated marketplace (and the jurisdictions where sales and routine business contacts are expected to take place); tax concerns; anticipated or working risk management plans; and the types (and/or existence) of licensing necessary to do business—is going to help direct what kind of business entity needs to be formed and/or how an existing entity needs to be reformed.

Many times, the temptation is to deliver a prepackaged entity—a kit corporation—or you find yourself inheriting a prepackaged entity formation. After all, there are, realistically speaking, a finite number of types of business formations which are available in most jurisdictions (although you have to keep an eye out for hybrids or new variations on old formations). There is nothing inherently wrong with the economy of a kit approach, but tread carefully. Check diligently for the pros and cons of different entity structures, depending on your client-company's products and/or services, as well as likely ownership, funding sources, possible liabilities, and regulatory and licensing needs. Look for statutory provisions that might affect pass-through or carry-forward liability—especially when you need to reform an existing organization into its second-generation entity structure. Do not forego the homework.

Discuss all this with the client. Do something I have unfortunately seen many otherwise good corporate lawyers fail to do: *make sure the client-company has a good handle on why it is a partnership, a limited liability company, a corporation, or some other novel formation.* A client-company needs to understand why it is formed the way it is formed. Entity formation is not just a legal conception, though we lawyers tend to treat it that way, filling in the blanks for a client-company and not taking a comprehensive look at typical, boilerplate language. Entity formation affects taxes, liability, how a company is managed (or how unmanageable it can become), what it can do and what it cannot do, who owns what and why, when and how it can morph and change as its needs and business change, where it can do business, and ultimately how it makes its money—its gross, then net, revenues. A client-company's entity formation is going to be the scaffolding for all of those elements. Too many times, a new venture has blinders on about everything but tax consequences or liability, and other equally critical implications are left unanalyzed or undiscussed.

Choice of entity formation is a fantastic way to open the floor to robust discussions about all of those core elements, and it is a great foil for discussing, settling on, and implementing ownership and management roles and issues. Choice of entity formation gives the context, and can dictate, many issues with ownership and management. It can be that your most important role is to teach a client-company's tier-one players about their current and long-term roles, obligations, and limitations. A single person many times wears multiple hats in the first era of a new company, and it can make it difficult for anyone to distinguish between proper activities or limitations of owners and management.

§ 3.1.2 Funding Issues—Let the Games Begin!

The chief difficulty Alice found at first was in managing her flamingo.[9]

The unwieldiness of Alice's flamingo easily mimics the sometimes absurd circus of funding and cash-flow management in many a new venture's convulsive beginnings. With an eye toward best viewing a budding client-company through the lens of an investor, a corporate lawyer can approach his or her involvement with the funding flamingo by looking to answer a basic question. Putting aside fancy-schmancy performance metrics, stock ratios, debt ratios, industry ratings, and valuations, a good investor is going to ask "a more basic question: how does the company actually make money?"[10]

This question is answered, says Ben McClure—the director of Bay of Thermi Limited, an independent research and consulting firm—by evaluating a company's business model. The business model is a company's Rosetta Stone,[11] and it is a disservice to the client-company when its corporate lawyer fails to really understand the business at its fundamental, first-language core. Nine times out of ten, the soundness of a client-company's business model is going to be the single greatest portent of how a client-company's business growth, and its risks, will unfold. A business model will give an investor the best forecast for the viability and sustainability of a company. Conversely, an unworkable model can foretell eventual doom: "When business models don't work, it's because they don't make sense and/or the numbers just don't add up to profits."[12] And making a profit is the business of a business.

Even if your client-company does not have a hard-and-fast business model (which it should), there are signposts you can borrow from a typical business model that will help to get your head around funding issues. Although the details of all business models vary with the industry, size, and scope of a company's business, each business model should supply the same vital information: how the company sustainably makes its money. Here are the essentials:[13]

- *Uniqueness*—What separates the client-company's product/service from everyone else's?
- *Start-up costs*—Where is the client-company going to get its seed money?
- *Customers*—To whom is the client-company going to sell its product/service?
- *Competition*—Who are the direct and indirect competitors?
- *Economic mood*—How will the state of the economy (macro or micro) affect the client-company's business launch?
- *Timing*—What is the timing of the client-company's business launch?
- *Marketing*—What is the client-company's marketing plan (campaign, budget, resources, and the like)?
- *Cash flow*—How does the client-company expect to meet its operational and productivity financial demands? (This is the heart of the client-company's financial plan.)

With these categories of information assessed and gathered, you (along with your client-company) will be able to best identify funding needs, timelines, equity resources, debt resources, and financial tolerances.

Equity—*ownership*—means inviting someone to join the party. In some way, shape, or form, a person or an investment entity such as a venture capital firm will be "buying in." Usually, an equity infusion means instant cash (a tough thing to say no to for many start-ups) with no repayment obligation. Equity, like debt, can be nuanced in an almost infinite number of ways: it can be as simple as uncle so-and-so writing a check for membership or some shares, or as complex (and as regulated) as gleaning new investors through a private placement-offering memo-randum, a reverse merger, a direct public offering, or the much-vaunted initial public offering, in which securities laws and arm's-length trans-actions are involved. Regardless of the method, ask your five *w*'s. The who, what, where, when, and why, as well as the how, will give you and your client-company the information needed to weigh its decision about whether to invite equity in the door.

The same fundamental approach applies to financing through debt, where someone will not be joining the party but *will* expect the party to pay him or her back. Usually, debt financing also means instant cash—or access to some kind of a line of credit—but with a preprogrammed schedule of repayment or pay-downs. Again, it can come in a myriad of forms: a loan from uncle so-and-so, a line of credit from a local bank, or a multi-million-dollar bond offering involving an underwriter and institutional bond investors. The same rule applies: ask your five *w*'s.

As the corporate lawyer managing the funding-flamingo madness, you will not be expected to be (nor are you likely to be) the most learned financial counsel at the table, able to draft and fully discourse on the distinctions of convertible notes (a hybrid way of investing that converts a debt into equity). Instead, your basic job is to provide close oversight, ask questions, provide your opinion about the tangential viewpoints on each potential financing option, and assess the impact (legal, risk, com-pliance, and viability) on your client-company as new money and new obligations roll in the door.[14]

§ 3.1.3 Initial Intellectual-Property Issues

> *Alice laughed. "There's no use trying," she said: "one can't believe impossible things."*

> *"I daresay you haven't had much practice," said the Queen. "When I was your age, I always did it for half-an-hour a day. Why, sometimes I've believed as many as six impossible things before breakfast."*[15]

For every person who imagines having invented a never-before-seen newfangled product or process, there is a fairly good chance someone else has also thought of the same "impossible" creation, or there is a good chance that, as soon as the never-before-seen newfangled product or process hits the open market, it will be purloined by an enterprising and less-than-ethical competitor. The race to protect a client-company's proprietary creation—to establish legal ownership—can be a bet-the-company proposition for many new ventures. For those companies that do not centrally rely on the ownership and development of their own unique products, there will still be inevitable issues of licensure, trademarks, copyrights, and trade secrets.

Intellectual property (IP) is, as most lawyers know, a singularly specialized area of law. Companies whose core business lives and dies on the creation and retention of intellectual property—everything from software to medical devices to pharmaceuticals to automobile manufacturers to electronics to photography to book publishing to music, to name just a few—have large armies of employees, consultants, private firms, and lobbyists all trained toward developing, enhancing, and protecting their IP rights. Intellectual property itself, standing apart from the marketable end product, can be a very demanding division of business. In 2010, for instance, IBM was awarded an average of twenty-three patents *every day* by the U.S. Patent and Trademark Office. That is almost at a rate of one patent *every hour.*

Whether your new venture client-company is aiming at attaining 5,000+ patent awards a year or only one for all time, that piece of corporate property—intellectual property—can mean everything to the success or failure of the business, and it must be approached in that light. Generally speaking, a corporate lawyer's chief role in this area will be to identify the mission-critical IP issues, guide the client-company's growing IP matters in the right developmental direction, engage the right human assets (internally or externally), have a dynamic program in place to absorb new benchmarks and multiplying IP assets, create and implement safeguards[16] for specific IP assets, and keep a mindful watch over everyone and every department involved in IP matters. Additionally, you will need to keep your client-company cognizant of its obligations to the requirements of third parties from whom it has obtained licensing rights. Defending against a software audit by Microsoft, as an example, will go more smoothly if you have prepared in advance with a licensing consultant who is up to speed on your client-company's soft and hard inventories, which use licensed programs, processes, and components, or are provided by a technology vendor agreement or other kind of licensing agreement. Corporate lawyers who routinely work in this field are able to grasp its complexity and its breadth. If IP is not part of your native toolbox, then make sure you liaison with a law firm (and/or consultant) that has the depth of experience and the right culture to match your client-company's needs.[17]

Patents, trademarks, copyrights, and trade secrets are *assets*. Tangibly, these life-blood assets may be lost, overlooked, used without permission (that is, without authorized licensure), pirated, sold, bought, or licensed. These assets can be extraordinarily simple or astonishingly complex. Beyond the obvious—such as your client-company's first beta-tested, revolutionary verbal-recognition software platform—look around. *Unrecognized* corporate assets are guaranteed to be staring back at you in a new company's first stages. IP can be found in unconventional places, but the guiding rule of thumb is that intellectual property enhances, markets, preserves, or *is* the product that makes money for the business. Perhaps the bright-red wax seal[18] on a whiskey bottle is just as valuable as the whiskey inside the bottle.[19] Keep in mind that as complex, obscure, or even simple as an IP asset can be, its valuation can be even more complex, and even more critical. After all, what is an asset without a positive value? The valuation (and depreciation) component[20] of your company's IP program should be part of its backbone, along with inventory, maintenance, protection, and revenue-generation strategies.

So what about the razzle-dazzle corporate IP program which I suggested as a hypothetical Gordian knot at the beginning of this chapter? At this point, I will humbly defer an answer to my betters. Edward de Bono, a Maltese author, physician, and inventor, opined that an expert is someone who has succeeded in making decisions and judgments simpler through knowing what to pay attention to and what to ignore.[21] Because I am not an expert on IP matters, I will heed Mr. de Bono's advice and give you what I think is an excellent format—borrowed from the esteemed Intellectual Property Department at Fox Rothschild, LLP—for developing the framework for a sound corporate IP program.[22]

Your client-company should develop a program, even if only in policy form at first, with six components, as needed: (1) evaluation, (2) patents, (3) trademarks, (4) copyrights, (5) trade secrets, and (6) physical security, including internal security and external security. As early as possible, create a standing IP Committee within your client-company using management personnel with decision-making authority and employee representatives to govern the program; review all IP activity, strategies, and portfolios; conduct IP audits; gather competitive intelligence about competitors' IP assets; and establish companywide policies and procedures for all IP work, including origination, development, rights preservation, and transactional work. Meet with outside counsel or other consultants to review the efficacy of your IP program at least annually (depending on your client-company's volume of IP activity), and constantly tailor the program to your client-company's evolving needs and capabilities. Stay abreast of industrywide innovations and relevant litigation, as well as competitors' products and processes. Engage (consistently) with an IP expert.

And above all, let vigilance be your watchword when it comes to intellectual property.

§ 3.1.4 Regulatory, Certification, Licensing, and Insurance Concerns

When it comes to identifying, and satisfying, your client-company's regulatory, certification, and/or licensing concerns, all bets are off. Hopefully, I have not misled you by lumping this plague of topics into a single section—one that is only long enough to suggest a threshold for what may eventually be a labyrinth of issues—thereby implying these are easy topics for a fledgling business. They are not. But they are also not impossible topics to deal with and, much like intellectual-property issues, the more time you spend at the beginning, identifying and addressing your client-company's obligations, needs, and liabilities in each of these areas, the better off you and your client-company will be as the days and months race by.

Here, almost more than anywhere else, our 50,000-foot bird's-eye view is a very handy tool to use. The best advice for taking each of these topics in manageable stride is to look at industry-specific examples. Do not reinvent the wheel. Look at what competitive or similarly situated companies have done. This is most easily accomplished by asking questions. Many times, lawyers have a hard time with this concept because we believe part of our value is in what we know (true to some extent), and to ask a question might reveal that we do not know what we are

Dear Sir,

Congratulations! Your company is now certified to apply for its sales' license pursuant to the regulatory licensure program offered only to those companies that hold a certification to become licensed according to the applicable regulations.

Please let us know how you would like to proceed.

WILBUR IS FAIRLY CERTAIN HE SHOULD BE HAPPY, BUT HE'S NOT SURE WHY

Licensing

paid to know. As Albert Einstein said, "The only thing that interferes with my learning is my education." The greater truth is that a client-company cares more about having the correct answer than it does about what you know or do not know on any given day. So get on the phone, use the Internet, read chat boards and blogs, and take people to lunch. Most of the time, you will be able to access very focused information in a short amount of time, and you will find regulators, insurance brokers and agents, and certifying or licensing agencies to be fairly helpful. As you develop your silo of information about each topic, you will find yourself much more capable of winnowing out what is irrelevant to your new venture client-company versus what needs to be done, and the steps to take, for your own specific circumstances. Your client-company will be ecstatic (and relieved) as you gather it around a conference table, or as you send out a memorandum, to inform it of exactly what steps it needs to take for relevant regulatory issues, certification issues, licensure issues, and insurance matters.

Each industry's and each company's individual needs, obligations, and options in each of these areas is so unique, and so potentially extensive, that a single section, or chapter, could not adequately review or address the necessary particulars. However, there are books (and series of books), as well as reporters, trade magazines, journals, and databases, that provide the kind of comprehensive resources a corporate lawyer will need to take on any number of complex industries. Our purpose in this section is to provide a common springboard from which you can more efficiently go looking for, and begin utilizing, those situation-specific resources.

Regulations

Regulations are an administrative body of laws and rules, usually promulgated by an agency (whether federal, state, or local), that constrain a client-company's rights, mandate obligations and standards, and, to some extent, dictate operations. Some regulations are self-imposed by an industry or trade organization, and some are imposed by markets or social norms and expectations. The better you understand your client-company's business, operational processes, product, manufacturing, third-party vendor relationships, market, and by-products, the better you will be able to zero in on bodies of regulations that will regulate its existence.

For instance, if your new venture client-company is planning on manufacturing molds for dental prosthetics (such as dentures), which it will sell as prefabrication kits in the United States, you will quickly find that these are considered "medical devices," and the federal Food and Drug Administration's (FDA) Center for Devices and Radiological Health (CDRH) is responsible for regulating firms that manufacture, repackage, relabel, and/or import medical devices sold in the United States. Regulatory requirements may include registration of establishment, listing of devices, manufacturing in accordance with the quality system regulation, medical device reporting of adverse events, and "Premarket Notification" or "Premarket Approval." Aside from the helpful advice found on the FDA's Web site, you will find specific regulations for your client-company's product in Title 21 of the Code of Federal Regulations, Volume 8 (21 C.F.R. § 872).[23]

As a corporate lawyer, you do not have to approach the issue of regulations as a lawyer. You do not need to wear your lawyer hat until you have the applicable regulations in hand and there is a need to interpret them for compliance and liability. Instead, think like an investor, as we discussed in Section 3.1, and this will give you your baseline for exploring what regulatory agencies and regulations will govern how your client-company goes about its business. After that, you can distill the import of each regulation as it affects your client-company's formation, ownership, management, operational practices, marketing, risk exposures, and protections.

Certifications

Certifications are those documents or designations that confirm to regulators, inspectors, examiners, trade organizations, investors, creditors, or the public at large that your client-company and/or its business operations possess certain characteristics. Certifications may be elective—usually, then, for marketing purposes—such as an Underwriters Laboratories (UL) safety certification,[24] or certifications may be mandatory—usually compelled by an oversight agency—such as a Clean Air Act Certificate of Conformity issued by the federal Environmental Protection Agency (EPA). Personnel within a client-company can also be certified, such as a Certified Regulatory Compliance Manager at a banking institution.[25]

Mandatory certifications are typically embedded in the body of agency-promulgated regulations, which govern your client-company's overall business operations and/or specific products or personnel within your client-company's business, or they are embedded in the body of self-regulations, which dictate your client-company's participation within a specific industry. Most certifications, however, are elective and should be used to enhance your client-company's standards, performance, quality, and marketing.

Licenses

Licenses give permission. A license can either demarcate permission your client-company *holds* to conduct its business or permission your client-company *gives* for an end user, or another entity, to use or possess a product or service your client-company has provided.

Licensure generally takes the form of some kind of registration process, through which a *licensor* (the entity issuing the license) records the *licensee* (the entity receiving the license) and/or issues an actually documented license. As with certifications, licenses may be held by a company, such as a license to collect sales tax, or by personnel within a company, such as a licensed obstetrician within a medical practice association. A license is by nature *mandatory* in order to accomplish the activity for which a license is issued. A corporate lawyer does well to create a repetitively auditable list and/or license program, which identifies and keeps track of all licensure components within his or her client-company. Most licenses are subject to some kind of renewal process, fee, or reapplication, and if a license expires, liabilities and/or loss of income and rights can be an immediate and sometimes dire result.

Categorically, licensing issues tend to occur at the local and state level for administrative purposes of conducting business, at the federal level for the handling or manufacturing of certain products, and at the intercompany level for the use of licensed components, parts, software, or merchandise.

Insurance

Though insurance is not an oft-mandated part of running a business—although certain trades and practices require malpractice coverage to be maintained—insurance is an extremely important hedge against catastrophe. Mature businesses, to say nothing of new ventures, can struggle to absorb a sizeable loss without it disrupting or crippling operations, budget projections, and investor or creditor confidence. The right kind of insurance policies and coverage limits characteristically allow a company a much better chance to weather unfolding liabilities almost financially unimpeded, while better dedicating resources to public relations, operational recovery, implementation of better practices (as necessary), and talent retention. For a new venture client-company, a lawsuit, accident, or business interruption can quickly prove fatal. Insurance may seem like a too-soon expenditure, but there are few calamities that are kind enough to let anyone know they are coming far enough in advance to avoid.

The trick for a corporate lawyer is to be able to help a client-company identify the right types of policies, at the right coverage limits, with the right riders, at the right time (in balance with other needs and cash-flow capacities). It is no easy trick. There is certainly not a one-size-fits-all solution for various industries, or even various businesses within the same industry. We will cover insurance more thoroughly in Section 5.7.1, but again, when your mind is in start-up mode, think like an investor: understand your client-company's business because it will give you the right framework when you get on the phone with brokers, use the Internet, read chat boards and blogs, and take people to lunch to discuss insurance needs.

§ 3.1.5 Employment Issues

Presumably by this time your mind is in full swing with formation/ operational issues, managing the funding flamingo, identifying and addressing IP issues, and getting your client-company's head around its regulatory, certification, licensing, and insurance needs. One last stick on the camel's back for a new venture: employment issues. Few new ventures begin with hundreds, or even tens, of employees, but the moment a company has its first employee (usually one or more of the inception/ creator personas who morph into a company's "chief something-or-other"), a client-company has employment issues.

At the outset of a new venture company, it is unlikely there will be a human resources department or an officer to act as the vanguard when identifying, handling, and monitoring employment issues. Therefore, there are numerous factors a corporate lawyer will face when advising a new client-company on the topic of employment: contracts, hiring procedures, disciplinary procedures, performance monitoring, regulatory obligations, classifications, compensation, benefits, and termination procedures (to name a few). Section 5.1 will take the bull by the base of its horns, but for purposes of a new venture's context, there are some points to keep in your line of sight as you watch your client-company begin to fill its ranks.

Establish basic procedures at the outset. While attending a corporate-counsel continuing-legal-education seminar a few years ago, I recall hearing the general counsel of a Fortune 500 company say (only half joking) that if your employee manual is more than three pages long, it is four pages too long. That was a voice from the trenches, and there is value in the advice. Our tendency as lawyers to be exceedingly, sometimes exhaustingly, comprehensive can also cause unintended problems. Protracted procedures, which govern the life of an employee, have more of a chance for ambivalent enforcement—leniency may be given to good employees, stringency may be applied to bad employees—which leads to disparate application, or entirely overlooked or unused provisions. In the world of employment issues, disparate treatment, or unnecessarily drawn-out measures (ironically intended to be methodical and fair), can quickly create a rat's nest of thorny problems and potential liabilities. A "three-page manual" concept keeps things clear, easy to forecast, easy to follow, and a cinch to implement.[26] It will be easier for you and your client-company to establish basic procedures at the outset if they are unpretentious and simple. Eventually, those basic procedures will create tradition, and even if a growing number of employees—and therefore a growing number of unique employment situations—necessitates more layers of procedure, they will be built upon a solid core of employer-employee relationship principles. Simplicity at first also allows flexibility to create as your client-company grows. Later on, its mature collection of employment procedures and practices will reflect the character, culture, and business of your client-company.

Employment Law

Aside from a procedural/policy approach, begin to train your client-company to be culturally preventive with employment issues. (Inanimate procedures are almost always reactive. Ultimately, the better practice is to prevent liability instead of to react to liability.) How so? By paying attention to employee workload, workplace conditions, and emotional investment, your growing client-company will take vast strides toward immunizing itself against many employment risks and liabilities.[27] Though an employee's emotional investment—his or her feeling of substantive contribution—might come more easily in smaller, more compact, and newer business environments, workloads can typically be much higher simply because there are fewer warm bodies to accomplish everything that needs to be done. Frequent communications with employees about *their* perspective of their workload, and taking steps to flexibly adjust responsibilities and expectations, will help to stay a step ahead of feelings of burnout, resentment, and bitterness. Similarly, workplace conditions can many times be less than ideal, such as the proverbial case of Steve Wozniak piecing together computer prototypes in Steve Jobs's bedroom, and then garage, when they needed more space to work.[28] Again, frequent communications with employees about their safety, work needs, and comfort level will help to prevent accidents (far more than a mandatory safety poster on a break-room wall) and to improve productivity.

The employment condition is the condition that dominates and underlies, grows and retards, directs and follows, and sustains and collapses every enterprise. Indeed, there are countless prudent sayings about employees, employers, and employment in general, precisely because a person, working for an organization, is the epitome of a capitalistic economy and society (and what has now become our global economy). The value of the employee cuts both ways. Thomas John Watson Sr., who, as chairman and CEO, conducted the growth of International Business Machines (IBM) into a global force from 1914 through 1956, made this wry and well-known remark: "Recently, I was asked if I was going to fire an employee who made a mistake that cost the company $600,000. No, I replied, I just spent $600,000 training him. Why would I want somebody to hire his experience?"

Business formation, new funding, intellectual property, and all of the exciting ins and outs of launching and sustaining a new venture may be areas where a corporate lawyer feels more comfortable with flexing his or her mental muscle and making practical contributions, but without a workforce—even a workforce of one—a company is not going anywhere. *Omnia unum*: all things make one thing.

§ 3.2 ONGOING BUSINESS CONCERNS

Even if a greater process is infinite, any new element added to an infinite process has its own beginning. At any point past its embryonic stage, a business is an "ongoing concern."

The less philosophically affected question for a corporate lawyer who leaps into a client-company in full swing is: Where do I begin? The question begs a practical answer.

> *The White Rabbit put on his spectacles. "Where shall I begin, please your Majesty?" he asked.*

> *"Begin at the beginning," the King said gravely, "and go on till you come to the end: then stop."*[29]

The unique situation of every company is, of course, *unique*, and the initial priorities of a corporate lawyer new to the scene will be dictated by a client-company's current events. However, just as is the case with a new venture, there are particular areas of involvement every corporate lawyer ought to spend time and energy evaluating and addressing.

Thankfully, plunging into an ongoing business concern—where core business operations do not have any apparent end horizon—is probably, in many ways, a fairly natural adjustment for a corporate lawyer, whether in-house or outside counsel. Because the client-company is an existing, working business, a corporate lawyer's 50,000-foot view of the client-company's strengths, shortcomings, future expectations, historical struggles, and likely (or realized) risks and liabilities is apt to be much clearer than the view might be for a new venture. A corporate lawyer can (for the most part) rely on existing divisions and departments—sometimes including an existing legal department—as well as data, both historical and present, to develop a fairly good picture of a client-company's business in its entirety. There might be less imaginative conjuring involved than is the case with a new venture, and a corporate lawyer, coming into an ongoing business concern, can quickly direct his or her efforts to daily, repetitive business matters.

So what more does a corporate lawyer—a lawyer adjusting to an ongoing business concern—need to focus on to acclimate and bring immediate value to a client-company?

There are a few fundamentals an effective corporate lawyer should pay attention to as soon as possible after coming on board, regardless of the situation-specific needs of a client-company (which are most likely already waiting for you, piled high on your desk). In spite of the natural tendency to become fixated by pressing day-to-day matters,[30] time spent on each of the following areas will greatly advance your efforts on company-specific matters and will ensure a more seamless integration between yourself, a legal department, your client-company, and its many constituents.

§ 3.2.1 Identifying Issues, Goals, and Competitors

"One of the benefits of the growth of inside counsel or corporate lawyering is that lawyers are now intimately involved in the business decision-making process at many corporations."[31] We discussed a corporate lawyer's role in regard to this involvement in Chapter 1, but fulfilling such a role in an ongoing business concern requires a corporate lawyer to have a solid grasp of a client-company's issues, goals, and competitors.

Issues are those activities or topics that, aside from the workings of the core business enterprise, dominate a client-company's time, efforts, and resources. Some of the most illuminating data for a corporate lawyer to take in are the issues faced by the client-company historically, in the present, and as anticipated in the future (based on past and present events). For instance, if a client-company has struggled in the past with compliance issues, or if compliance is a current concern, then a corporate lawyer—regardless of whether he or she is tasked at the present to work on compliance—does well to do some homework: some light research into the handy five *w*'s of the client-company's compliance program, the key personnel involved in the policy- and procedure-making stages, the consultants or persons responsible for auditing the compliance program, the key regulations influencing or mandating compliance policy, and methods of identifying and correcting compliance problems and/or program updates.

An eye toward diplomacy (and sometimes discretion) will keep you from stepping on toes or appearing threatening. In fact, be candid as you speak to your client-company's constituents about relevant issues for the company. Let them know you are on an "educational safari" to help position yourself with essential information, when or if needed, to be able to help with preventive measures and/or crisis management. Ask for opinions. Different people—different divisions and departments— have distinct opinions about what issues they believe affect your client-company. They also, usually, have distinct opinions about how those issues might be handled or redressed. All of this will give you the advantage of identifying critical issues with the depth and scope of the company at large. As a result, your strategic legal advice to your client-company will be all the more prepared and useful.

Goals is a term meant to be more broadly applied than a client-company's self-evident goal of making more money.[32] That can certainly be a paramount long-term objective, but it is underpinned by a multitude of other support goals, some of which, such as expanding production or avoiding bankruptcy reorganization, may momentarily usurp the moneymaking goal. In the area of litigation, a lawyer must understand what the goal of the client is—short term and big picture—in order to provide effective representation. The same concept applies to providing legal counsel as a corporate lawyer: pertinent advice takes into account the support goals of a client-company. When a departmental manager from procurement calls you with a concern about changes that need to be made to a vendor-management program, you need to be able to have that discussion while keeping an eye toward the procurement department's (not just the compliance department's or the legal department's) goals when managing vendors. A corporate lawyer, ignorant of procurement's goals to develop vendor relations in the Midwest, brings little value to the discussion by insisting on standard purchasing-contract provisions originally drafted for vendors located in Louisiana.

An interesting phenomenon to remain aware of, especially the larger a corporation becomes, is that support goals are not necessarily shared between departments or executives. Even though departments are quick to talk about their goals among their own personnel, or to discuss them vertically with their immediate, executive hierarchy, little reason usually exists for support goals to climb over territorial walls and be shared throughout the company horizontally. A customer-satisfaction department is unlikely to share its quarterly performance goals with the IT department. Whether that is a good thing or a bad thing is largely irrelevant for purposes of our present discussion. As is the case with identifying a client-company's issues, a corporate lawyer should spend time with department heads and other executives discussing the historical, present, and future goals of the client-company. Distinct patterns will likely emerge. There may be goals driven by audits, reviews, or regulatory examinations. Goals may be driven by performance directives.

Goals may be the result of litigation risks. They may be result of, or the cause of, expansion or downsizing.

The takeaway point is, a corporate lawyer—professionally tasked with knowing the direction a client-company and its parts have taken and are taking—has to be willing to go around those walls proactively. Goals sometimes have to be ferreted out. Ask, and ask *why*. Explain to people that if you know where they are headed, you can be there to help, just in case. Know your client-company's goals and why those goals are in place. Your advice on any given day, on any given topic, must be informed by the direction in which your client-company and its constituent parts are intent on going.

Learning about the competition—the wolves at the gate—can seem somewhat disconnected from the topic of a corporate lawyer's acclimation process, but it is an important step to take. For many corporate lawyers, learning about competitors may come in tandem with litigation (either adversely or as a common party). Occasionally, competitors also join forces with a client-company in order to present a united lobbying front, or, in the interests of the industry at large, for purposes of public relations or direct competition with another industry (such as the sugar industry going toe to toe with the artificial-sweetener industry). These acquainting events are a critical part of the role a corporate lawyer plays on behalf of his or her client-company, but it can be a mistake to wait until one of these kinds of events occurs to learn about the companies competing with your client-company, either directly or indirectly.[33]

We have given an earlier nod to Sun Tzu,[34] and an abridged idiom from Chapter 3 of the *Art of War* fits nicely here: "Know thy enemy." A corporate lawyer should possess up-to-date information about his or her client-company's competitors so he or she is always able to knowledgeably contribute sound advice or provide a warning about possible adverse actions or infringements (either by, or against, the client-company). For close-to-home purposes, studying how competitors integrate their legal departments and outside counsel into their operations might model a more efficient or effective way for you to do the same thing. If you pick up the phone, you will likely be surprised to find that a competitor's legal counsel is quite willing to discuss his or her own experiences and share information (even if obliquely) about the common hazards encountered when dealing with shareholders/owners, board members, executives, department heads, vendors, and consumers.

Additionally, the competition is a great source of supply for a wealth of timely information about the industry at large, the marketplace, new products or services, regulations, and litigation trends. Competitors are not just "the competition," they are a fantastic resource for corporate lawyers to use. As easy as it is (and as fun as it may be) to begrudge a competing business, savvy executives know that competitors are close-to-perfect doppelgängers[35] in business. They can also help inform a corporate lawyer about what a client-company should be doing, and what it should not be doing. You do not want to be—and should not be—the last person to know about a class-action lawsuit against a competitor involving a product or service your client-company manufactures or provides. You do not want to be the last person to know about a regulatory enforcement action against a competitor involving an operational or accounting methodology used by your client-company. You do not want to be the last person to know about a derivative-shareholder lawsuit against a competitor involving a price-per-share change similar to a price-per-share valuation pattern closely mirroring your client-company's. Instead, you should be relishing how much more helpful you are to your client-company, and how much more well-rounded your advice and admonitions are, when you take the time to stay abreast of the competition.

§ 3.2.2 The Industry—Taking the Temperature

"Who did you pass on the road?" the King went on, holding out his hand to the Messenger for some more hay.

"Nobody," said the Messenger.

"Quite right," said the King; "this young lady saw him too. So of course Nobody walks slower than you."

"I do my best," the Messenger said in a sullen tone. "I'm sure nobody walks much faster than I do!"

"He can't do that," said the King, "or else he'd have been here first."[36]

In business, the Nobody passed on the road is Industry. Each industry is shapeless yet real. Each industry has regulatory agencies, trade associations, trade publications, standards or performance awards for its members, licensing bodies, conferences, litigation trends, and lobbyists. Each industry also remains fluid to some extent as changes over time affect its laws, market, technology, financing, and makeup of its company constituents. Each industry acts as the shapeless force of gravity that can, without warning or input, alter your client-company's business model, affect its stock price, impact its workforce, or impose a public relations crisis.[37] And it is this overarching nobody that an effective corporate lawyer must be able to understand, describe, and keep an ever-watchful eye on.

Polson Enterprises, a small but innovative market-research firm located in Stillwater, Oklahoma, utilizes a twenty-two-step process for clients who are interested in researching a particular industry. Although all twenty-two steps would not necessarily apply to every corporate lawyer's need for information, it is intriguing to see how many of Polson Enterprises's recommended steps hit upon topics and issues that constantly provide the backdrop context for a corporate lawyer's work.[38] Some of these more practical and informative steps include the following:

- Identify trade organizations, publications, and trade shows (Step 3).
- Learn about the consumers of the product or service (Step 4).
- Examine the patent and trademark situation in the industry (Step 5).
- Determine the legal issues in the industry (Step 6).
- Examine the regulatory issues of the industry (Step 7).
- Define the type of competition in the industry (Step 8).
- Search the history of the industry (Step 9).
- Learn about government and/or military implications (Step 15).
- Interview people from the industry (Step 18).

Every corporate lawyer should be able to look at this relatively short list and easily identify with how important an education about a client-company's industry can be.

Taking the temperature of a client-company's industry—whether it is currently running hot or cold—on any of the above-described points of the compass will contribute critical information to a corporate lawyer's assessment of all manner of operational, financial, regulatory, IP, workforce, and risk issues. When it comes time to address a variety of matters, such as collective-bargaining agreements, lobbying activities, proposed regulatory changes, or revised governance standards for the board, a corporate lawyer will need to have the industry's position as part of his or her mental repertoire as the client-company looks for assistance and counsel. A corporate lawyer must do so while managing the client-company's policies and reactions, whether it is echoing the industry's party line or going against the grain. Good corporate lawyers want to make sure their advice and strategic assistance are imbued with a global view of the business environment in which their client-companies exist. Making a consistent effort to stay in touch with that environment—the Industry—will ensure that Nobody never passes you by.

§ 3.2.3 Introductions—After the Party Has Already Started

"Who are YOU?" said the Caterpillar.

This was not an encouraging opening for a conversation. Alice replied, rather shyly, "I—I hardly know, sir, just at present—at least I know who I WAS when I got up this morning, but I think I must have been changed several times since then."[39]

Believe me, if a caterpillar smoking a hookah has the temerity to ask such a question of a young girl, then it should be a given that the question will be asked when a new corporate lawyer is introduced to an ongoing business concern's constituents. Even if you are the tenth lawyer everyone has seen pass through a client-company's halls, *you* are new to the party, and *you* are an unknown quantity. Doubt it? Reverse the roles.

If a new chief financial officer is hired by your client-company, you and other constituents may draw the reasonable assumption that the new executive is knowledgeable in subject-matter areas of financial risk management, planning, reporting, recordkeeping, and data analysis. Depending on how well known the new executive's previous employment (or reputation) is, you might also make reasonable assumptions about his or her leadership style, temperament, performance expectations, and work ethic. The fact is, however, you don't *really* know *who* the person is, what he or she is like, or what value he or she will be able to deliver on behalf of the company. True, much of that information reveals itself over time, but if a company is an ongoing business concern—expanding operations, capturing new business, deepening lender relationships, attracting new investments or shareholders—it is in the company's best interest to do everything it can to educate its constituency, and many times the public, about its new CFO. The company will want to instill a sense of confidence in the change of a leadership position, and the new CFO will likely take the opportunity to vocally echo his or her excitement about the opportunity to join the company and his or her commitment to improve, excel, and deliver the goods.

Fitting In

When a new corporate lawyer is hired—or new outside counsel is engaged—there is likely to be an even greater void in what is known about the new legal counsel than there would be about a new CFO. Even when a new general counsel is hired, the nature of the position is probably less visible than other senior executive-level positions and, by the very nature of what corporate lawyers do (so much of which is behind the scenes), the majority of the company would probably sum up who you are with the uncertain observation, "Um . . . a company lawyer," and not much beyond that. That lack of knowledge about who you are—what you are there to do for the client-business and its constituents—can present an enormous hurdle to effectively and efficiently getting your job done.

Lawyers—whether we want to be or not—are viewed through fairly simple but alien lenses by most of the public. Though most people do not actually have a good idea of what lawyers—especially corporate lawyers—do every day, if you ask almost anyone, they seem to have an implacable opinion about who lawyers are. Those implacable opinions are usually unkind. A corporate lawyer arriving at the offices of a new client-company needs to work to change those stereotypical views, or (sometimes) to undo the damage done by a previous lawyer, and introduce how he or she can bring value to a client-company's operations. Unfortunately, just as lawyers are not typically trained in business, we are also not typically trained in how to adapt ourselves to a business environment. Many of us stay cocooned in our law firms and courts, but for corporate lawyers—significantly those who act as in-house counsel—the business world is where they work, live, eat, and breathe.

Sam Grobart, a former senior editor of *Money* magazine, wrote a great piece advising readers about how to make the right impression and how to introduce themselves to a new business environment.[40] I have met more than a few crusty, unpopular corporate lawyers who would have done well to heed Mr. Grobart's warning to his audience: "You have a critical window of opportunity when you start a new position; botch it and you can wind up paying (in loss of effectiveness, resentful co-workers and no lunch buddies) for months, maybe years." So what can be done? What *should* be done? Mr. Grobart offers four sensible means of introducing yourself to your new client-company:

1. Tone down the star quality—"Get a couple of minor accomplishments under your belt, and you'll earn your office's trust. After that, your ideas will be judged on their merits, not on who's proposing them."
2. Don't be Mr. (or Ms.) Personality—"Be pleasant, be polite—but check your ebullience at the door. You don't get to make jokes for a while or spout off at meetings[.]"
3. Get the inside scoop—"You want to learn . . . how things are supposed to work and how they really work because of the idiosyncrasies of co-workers . . . but don't come across as prying."[41]
4. Give 'em something to talk about—"Determine who the influential people are [*not* always other executives] . . . , and find a reason to work with them. . . . Get on their good side (by being competent, pleasant and professional), and you may find that a whole lot more people have started to warm to your presence."

Remember, a client-company that is already established and in its prime years will immediately look to you for relevant, digestible legal advice, as well as strategic business advice that fits (seamlessly, one would hope) into an existing corporate culture. This is heavy stuff to deal with almost before your shadow even has the chance to darken the doorway, but in order for a client-company to be culturally, emotionally, and strategically willing to accept your advice, it must *trust* you; it has to respect you, even if it does not always like you. The relationship is going to be almost entirely dependent on how you conduct yourself—how you introduce yourself and work to integrate yourself into a client-company's business environment. A new corporate lawyer is not, and should not be seen as, just another punch-the-clock cog in the wheel. Good, effective legal counsel is truly mission-critical for a healthy, ongoing business concern. The delivery and acceptance of that counsel—the heart of a corporate lawyer's value to a client-company—is largely determined by a corporate lawyer's ability and effort to let a company's constituency know *who* he or she is and *what* he or she can do, and that he or she intends to be a *complement* to all of the hard work a client-company has already accomplished.

Lord Chesterfield, a British statesman who, in 1730, was awarded the Order of the Garter, the highest order of chivalry in England, once advised, "Never seem more learned than the people you are with. Wear your learning like a pocket watch and keep it hidden. Do not pull it out to count the hours, but give the time when you are asked." As a professional service provider—and a profit center whenever possible—a corporate lawyer must always be able to "give the time when asked" and must be equally able to establish a relationship that will allow him or her to "give the time" when it is needed *without* being asked. Such is diplomacy.

§ 3.2.4 Incremental Adjustments—Forming a Plan

"Would you tell me, please, which way I ought to go from here?"

"That depends a good deal on where you want to get to," said the Cat.

"I don't much care where—" said Alice.

"Then it doesn't matter which way you go," said the Cat.

"—so long as I get SOMEWHERE," Alice added as an explanation.

"Oh, you're sure to do that," said the Cat, "if you only walk long enough."[42]

The die has been cast. Your client-company is an established enterprise. Its divisions, departments, owners, management, and rank and file all have customary ways of getting the job done. So once you have joined the party and are working on assimilating yourself, where do you, as a corporate lawyer, take it from there?

Granted, you will most likely have a stack of tasks to work on the moment you walk in the door. Those tasks will lead to other tasks, and they will begin to give you a picture of what work elements are likely to fill your daily universe as time marches on. But what is *your* plan? Where do *you* intend to go? What do *you* intend to accomplish—short term and long term—on behalf of your client-company and, frankly, on behalf of your own career?

Some or part of the answers to these questions might already have been predetermined by the law department in which you work, another supervising lawyer, or the "motivating event"—usually a crisis or other significant event the client-company believed needed your particular set of skills or expertise—that got you there in the first place. However, those hat pegs all have a downward slant; inevitably, they have too limited a focus to sustain every moment of every work day. Even if the project for which you have ostensibly been hired seems all consuming, an effective corporate lawyer—a client-company's legal counsel—always remembers the standards by which a corporate lawyer plies his or her trade require a lawyer to have a global, competent perspective.

> In representing a client, a lawyer shall exercise independent professional judgment and render candid advice. In rendering advice, a lawyer may refer not only to law but to other considerations such as moral, economic, social and political factors, that may be relevant to the client's situation.[43]

Burying one's head into the sand of a single project, however large it may be, invites disaster. Just as a corporate lawyer new to an ongoing business venture should have a plan to identify issues, goals, and competitors—and to learn his or her client-company's industry and use thoughtful, diplomatic efforts to integrate into his or her client-company's cultural and operational world—a good corporate lawyer should also have a personal plan, designed to create and maintain proper perspective, assist the client-company in achieving its overall goals (such as advancing its core business), and keep his or her eyes up through the grind of each workday. "Great idea," you might say, "and I want to offer the best, most competent service I can to my client-company, but what kind of a plan will get all of that done?"

A simple one.

Every plan designed for progressive application takes into account three fundamental points of view: (1) Where are you now? (2) Where do you intend to go? And (3) how do you intend to get there? None of these questions require knotty answers. They are, and should remain, as simple as they appear. The key is to answer them honestly and knowledgeably, and, most important of all, to revisit them often. This, in fact, is exactly what a healthy, forward-thinking business is constantly doing: assessing its situation, goals, and methodologies. Be your own business.

Where are you now?

Think of this question in concentric rings, beginning with the inner, most personal ring. Self-assess. Where are you professionally? How comfortable are you with your area of practice (that is, the greater part of what you have typically done)? How comfortable are you with stepping into a corporate lawyer role? What areas of practice do you anticipate needing more work and more effort from you? What is currently in your professional toolbox?

After expending some thought on each of those questions, step into the next concentric ring. What is the current condition of your position/office/department? What is the scope of its responsibilities? Where is it positioned in relation to the client-company's other legal resources, operational resources, managerial resources, and strategic resources? How effectively does it meet those responsibilities? Is it adequately resourced to meet the client-company's needs and demands? With whom does it typically interact? Is that interaction efficient and effective? Are there other persons/areas/departments within the client-company that have legal-counsel needs which remain unaddressed?

Finally, the third ring should cast a wider net, asking questions of the client-company as a whole—its competition, its industry, and other factors (such as regulators, market shares, market conditions, litigation trends, liability trends and exposures, labor issues, vendor issues, and public sentiment). All these ground-floor questions—each of these three rings—need not take more than fifteen or twenty minutes of your time. Asking them will quickly point out strengths, deficiencies, and gaps of knowledge. Instantly, you will have a realistic idea of where you and the world around you stand. Just as most insurance companies require regular case status reports from assigned litigation counsel, these questions will give you a reliable status report from which you can plan and work.

Where do you intend to go?
The answer(s) to this question should be self-evident if you have spent an honest amount of time assessing where you presently are. *Where do you intend to go?* should flow from the answers to *Where are you presently?* Again, tackle the process one concentric ring at a time. Set reasonable benchmarks by which you will be able to evaluate your progress, your department's progress, and your client-company's progress. Many times, these benchmarks are set periods of time (just as a classic business plan uses one-year, three-year, and five-year projections), but they can just as easily be set against project deadlines, departmental goals, or company events. The point is to realistically determine where you (your position, department, company) should be—where you want to be. Naturally, these forecasts will have some elasticity, but like a crack team of Tamaskan sled dogs, your objectives will pull each day in a focused, iterative direction. At the end of any given day, week, or month, you will be able to look at where things now stand in relation to where they were, and gauge whether they are on track for where you believe they should be.

How do you intend to get there?
This most practical component of your planning should be saved until last. After all, if you do not know where you are or where you are intending to go, it is more than a little difficult to identify how you plan on getting there.

Use those concentric rings, and be practical. For instance, if you have realized you are weak on corporate debt repurchase or restructuring strategies, and you want to have a better handle on those techniques and practices before your client-company's next round of refinancing occurs in six months, then set objectives for yourself to look for subject-specific CLEs, take other attorneys to lunch (or get online) and listen to their experiences and advice, find a well-respected bookshelf resource to read and have handy, read a few cases (preferably from your company's jurisdiction) that illuminate some of the risks of debt financing gone wrong, and thoroughly acquaint yourself (if you have not already) with your client-company's last round of bond issuance or refinancing structures. If you have realized the legal department is struggling to provide timely contract reviews for your client-company's sales department, and you intend to reduce the wait time from one week to two days, then set objectives for your department (and discuss all this with your peers and staff) to trial-test new procedures for receiving, reviewing, redlining, submitting for comment, re-reviewing, and finalizing each contract. Focus on changing the areas of inefficiency (once identified) and on preserving and improving the areas of productivity. You get the idea: be practical, be hands on, and have your how-tos relate directly to your present observations and your future goals.

Why, blame it all, we've GOT to do it. Don't I tell you it's in the books?
Do you want to go to doing different from what's in the books, and get things
all muddled up?

Tom Sawyer's indignant question, put to his fellow conspirators who were quizzical about Tom's explanation of how to "ransom" someone,[44] is a fitting question to ask of a corporate lawyer as he or she leaps onto the swiftly moving treadmill of an ongoing business venture. The last thing a lawyer wants to do in such a situation is to "get things all muddled up." By identifying issues, goals, and competitors of the client-company, learning the industry, working to introduce yourself to the constituency of the client-company as a valuable, adaptive quantity, and implementing a practical plan for constant assessment and improvement, you will find yourself quickly settled, able to competently participate and give advice, and contributive to the progression of yourself, your department, and your client-company as a whole.

§ 3.3 TRANSITIONS AND THINGS THAT GO BUMP IN THE NIGHT

In January of 2008, Bear Stearns Companies, Inc., an eighty-five-year-old investment bank and securities and brokerage firm with significant international business, had a market capitalization worth approximately $20 billion. Within roughly seventy-five days, by March 16, 2008, Bear Stearns had lost almost ninety-nine percent of its value. It was worth only $236 million—a paltry $2 per share—and it was being sold—swallowed with virtually no effort—by JPMorgan Chase. Michael S. Solender, Bear

Stearns' general counsel, who would later (ironically) join Washington Mutual (WaMu), led the team of attorneys who oversaw this almost unreal fire sale; also involved were some of the crème de la crème of mergers and acquisitions lawyers, such as Henry Rodgin Cohen, then chairman of Sullivan & Cromwell, LLP.[45] When market dynamics shift, catastrophe strikes, or lawsuits roll in, the fortunes of any company can precipitously change overnight even when the best and the brightest are involved.

For the uninitiated, the violent velocity at which the circumstances of a client-company can change may cause a bit of shock when it happens. In life, as with most things, we are only tepidly aware of change unless it drops into the middle of our egocentric universe. We can read a newspaper, watch the news, and casually speak with a colleague about circumstances forcefully altering the state of another person's life, another company's fortunes, or another country's stability, but we do not often have a visceral sense of how change feels unless the earthquake is occurring beneath our feet.

Every business goes through transitions. Employees and management come and go; products and services are developed, marketed, sold, and retired, or morph into newer versions; owners buy equity and sell equity; customers and clients emerge and recede; laws are passed, implemented, changed, or repealed; regulators are at one point lax and then become stringent. Most transitions—moving from one circumstance to the next—are relatively uneventful and swiftly fade into the intricate tapestry of a business's long history.

There are, however, those transitional events that are momentous, that change the entire direction of a company, alter the public perception of a company, or bring about a company's ultimate failure. In recent memory, there are more than a few examples of such significant transitional events: the run on Washington Mutual in 2008, the largest bank failure in American history; the British Petroleum oil spill (aka Deepwater Horizon oil spill) in the Gulf of Mexico in 2010; the death of Steve Jobs, the iconic face of Apple, in 2011; the $2 billion trading loss reported by the previously conservative JPMorgan Chase at the beginning of 2012; among many, many others. The nature of these events can deliver a breaking-point test of pass or fail for even the largest, best-resourced corporate behemoths.

Businesses face issues of succession, litigation, public relations, dissolution, bankruptcy, takeover attempts, and operational disaster every day. Every situation requires all hands on deck, working at full speed, hopefully in unison, with as much alacrity and intelligence as can be mustered to keep operations running, products and services selling, investors investing, regulators at bay, employees at their desks, and creditors appeased (even if exasperated). Even when a major transition is welcome, and has been planned, a corporate lawyer's role—both as legal advisor and strategic counselor—is a critical, if not central, component to seeing the transition through from beginning to end.

So what does a corporate lawyer—a lawyer facing a substantial transition of his or her client-company—need to know in order to skillfully deliver valuable advice and guidance?

Most major events in a business's existence are likely going to require very specific and involved skill sets and levels of adept proficiency. Corporate lawyers who are generalists will quickly find themselves in dark forests of law from which others have carved their entire careers: such areas as bankruptcy, mergers and acquisitions, corporate dissolutions, and management (turnaround) of distressed enterprises. However, there are fundamentals that belie all of these events of change, and at a time when his or her client-company needs to be able to rely on sage legal counsel and guidance the most, its corporate lawyer must (as calmly as possible) be able to also keep the concept of business as usual in mind, instead of succumbing to the quicksand of a particular—especially if decisive—event.

Transitions

Therefore, in this section, our attention will be directed toward those useful tools and practices a corporate lawyer can take advantage of in order to guide, help, and sustain his or her client-company through tense, or dark, moments of precarious change, regardless of how the change might manifest itself.

§ 3.3.1 The Five Ws of Initial Assessment

"It seems very pretty," she said when she had finished it, "but it's rather hard to understand!" (You see she didn't like to confess, even to herself, that she couldn't make it out at all.) "Somehow it seems to fill my head with ideas— only I don't exactly know what they are! However, somebody killed something: that's clear, at any rate."[46]

In any evaluation of a transitional event, begin with the obvious. Then, just as we have previously discussed for a variety of other situations, it portends well for a corporate lawyer, whose client-company is now facing a grave circumstance, to use the five *w*'s of assessment to determine the client-company's current position, as well as how it got into that position. This is ground level, and it will begin to dictate what the possible solutions are, if any; how to arrive at those solutions, if possible; and how to prevent reoccurrences. An effective corporate lawyer will not settle for superficial conclusions and then rush to judgment; be prepared to dig below the surface. That is where the roots live. Though an "event," almost by definition, is singular in its scope, a business, also by definition, is multifaceted in its present state and in its time horizon of existence. A corporate lawyer's assessment must account for those contrasts, where the roots will ultimately be just as important as the thorn bush.

These investigative tools will give you a working context for curative measures and/or strategic decisions that will need to be made. Use them. Draw diagrams to make sense of complicated relationships or transactions. Create timelines. Discuss them with other members of your team, select members of management, and your outside (or in-house, if you are on the outside looking in) counsel. Understand them to the best of your ability.

- Why has this event occurred and, if applicable, why didn't someone, anyone, see it coming?

- When did it begin, how long will it likely last, and when should it be finished?
- Where and how will it affect operations within the client-company, and where and how will it affect core businesses?
- Who or what has caused it, and who or what is responsible for its resolution?
- What is the known universe of solutions, regardless (at this point) of how unlikely, unworkable, or ineffective they may be? What favors, or disfavors, each possible solution?

The bottom line: you have to know what your client-company is dealing with to be able to shepherd its resources and efforts to the other side. Incomplete information is dangerous. *Due diligence* is a term of art that comes as second nature to deal lawyers—those who regularly work with transactional events, usually mergers, acquisitions, sales, bond issuances, workouts, and offerings. Due diligence, in fact, should be the hallmark device of *every* major corporate transition. It means to thoroughly investigate, review, and be able to opine on every aspect of a situation.

Question, question, question. Review, review, review. Research, research, research. As much as possible—as much as time will allow (which is not always a lot)—engross yourself in the underlying factual information.

§ 3.3.2 *Adapt and Overcome*

For a corporate lawyer who is facing a momentous, potentially terminal, bet-the-company circumstance, there are few reliable comforts. A major corporate transition—whether innocuously planned, deliberately instigated, or adversely caused—has the real, and likely, potential to become frustratingly unpredictable and risky at a moment's notice. Legal counsel must be ready to adapt and overcome as crisis situations, for better or worse, roll through the door. To that end, an adage used by U.S. Marines, "adapt and overcome," has two premises: (1) remain flexible, and (2) realize that, regardless of obstacles, you have to figure out a way around them, under them, over them, or through them.

We all like to think of ourselves as being flexible, until reality catches us flatfooted and trapped in the narrow sluice of a particular activity or strategy that, moment before, seemed a steady and certain way to go. With any time spent in the saddle, this unsettling experience happens to everyone. The solution—the key to flexibility and the key to accomplishing the end goal—is more of a philosophical approach than it is a practical or methodological approach: do your best, but never "own" what you are doing. When a person finds him- or herself resistant to change in a transitioning business environment—even when the need to be flexible is apparent—it almost always is the result of that person feeling too strong a sense of ownership, a sense of identity, with what was happening before the change was necessary, and being obstinately protective of that ownership/identity.

For instance, let us suppose an internal investigation is underway. Unexpectedly, a regulator telephones and suggests his or her agency "needs to be involved." Putting aside issues about confidentiality and privilege for the moment, most corporate lawyers would feel an instinctive resistance to including an outside agency in what had been an internal, privately handled investigation. There is a sense of ownership and control over the investigation, which instantly slips when the regulator calls. However, because excluding an interested regulatory agency from an investigation would probably be a losing prospect in the long run, a savvy corporate lawyer will promptly change strategic gears. He or she will be flexible. He or she will realize, though there may now be some new goals (such as avoiding oversight disciplinary action) added to the mix, the original goal of conducting the investigation and arriving at a well-informed conclusion must still be met. He or she will work with the regulator to negotiate a way to include the outside agency without compromising the investigation at hand and without exposing the client-company to undue liability or risk. Flexibility may change the dance step, but the dance must still continue.

Lawyers, by trade, have an instilled sense of advocating: defending or advancing a particular position. A fixation on advocacy can, however, imperceptibly mutate into unhelpful rigidity. We make a living by our advice—our counsel—and when forces out of our control change the strategies and plans we have so carefully recommended and implemented, we can have a very hard time adapting. Knowing this, a corporate lawyer should remain mindful of his or her tendency toward inflexibility—a trait that can, at other times, be an honorable convention.

Understand that most major corporate transitional events thrive on contingency and variance. An effective corporate lawyer has to be willing and able to adapt and overcome unforeseen hurdles as the transitional event takes place. Inflexibility—whether strategic or emotional—can cause crippling delays and avoidable complications to an already unstable situation.

Be prepared to be flexible: strategically, emotionally, intellectually, and even physically. A storm has a far less likely chance of snapping a tree in half when the tree bends with the wind.

§ 3.3.3 Know the Players, Know the Game

"I like the Walrus best," said Alice, "because you see he was a little sorry for the poor oysters."

"He ate more than the Carpenter, though," said Tweedledee. "You see he held his handkerchief in front, so that the Carpenter couldn't count how many he took: contrariwise."

"That was mean!" Alice said indignantly. "Then I like the Carpenter best—if he didn't eat so many as the Walrus."

"But he ate as many as he could get," said Tweedledum.

This was a puzzler. After a pause, Alice began, "Well! They were both very unpleasant characters—"[47]

Figuring out who the players are in any given transitional event can many times be a challenge, and initially, it might seem to be a secondary concern to the actual event taking place. However, if a corporate lawyer can identify the cast of characters who are involved in or affected by a transitional event, that information will disclose volumes of data about causes, impacts, solutions, obstacles, timelines, and resources. Taking the time to identify and assess the players will, as a result, unveil for a corporate lawyer the parameters, options, and consequences of the "game."

As an illustration, let us imagine you meet with your CEO, who somberly informs you that a stock-owning hedge fund has initiated a shareholder proxy fight in order to dislodge certain members of your client-company's board and management.[48] The guess is the hedge fund is prompting the proxy fight because it is ultimately interested in a takeover, and the fund wants to put in place more compliant board members and managers to relax the current takeover defense strategies. A flood of thoughts courses through your mind: recalling the latest stock ownership percentages, whatever you might know or have heard about the hedge fund and its investment strategies, the defensive tactics set by your client-company's policies or bylaws, the specialist takeover defense firms with whom you have relationships, the date of the next shareholder meeting, and so on.

But what is really going on here? What rudder is deep enough to guide the strategy that will need to be taken? The answer is going to come down to *who* the players are.

As you make your way through the assessment questions we set out in Section 3.3.1, you will realize that at least three of the questions directly involve *people*:

- Why has this event occurred and, if applicable, why didn't someone, anyone, see it coming?
- Where and how will it affect operations within the client-company, and where and how will it affect core businesses?
- Who or what has caused it, and who or what is responsible for its resolution?

Ultimately, people—the players—are going to be *the* variable that drives the answers to all these questions, as well as the variable that eventually reveals the best way around, over, under, or through the threat, and perhaps reality, of the proxy fight. Why? Because understanding the players who comprise the hedge fund, different shareholder factions, the board, and current management will tell you almost everything you need to know about motives, tolerances, vulnerabilities, strengths, resources, unanimity, and discord.

It is this kind of information that might illuminate a way to head off the proxy fight before it gains momentum or substance—to arrange negotiations between different players to exhaust alternative solutions. Perhaps, if presented with the right compromises and guarantees, the hedge fund's takeover motivation can transform into a friendly merger or integration. Or, the player information can act as the proverbial rudder, guiding you and your team through the shoals of whichever takeover defense(s) best suits the situation, given what you have learned about the involved parties—the Nancy Reagan defense, the lobster trap, the targeted repurchase, the Crown Jewel defense, or leveraged recapitalization, to name a few.

The Wits & Wagers[49] of a corporate transitional event revolve around identifying and understanding the people who are involved in, affected by, or responsible for the event. This information defines the central premise behind a corporate lawyer's ability to knowledgeably, efficiently, and skillfully advise and guide his or her client-company through a challenging transitional event, whether friendly, hostile, anticipated, or unexpected.

Spend time learning faces, names, backgrounds, positions, roles, and personal stakes. One of the fundamental tenets of an effective cross-examination is to never ask a question for which you do not already have the answer. In much the same way, a fundamental tenet of dealing with a major transitional event is to never proceed without accounting for the players. At the end of the day, it will be people, not the actual event, who will determine what happens, when it happens, and why it happens.

§ 3.3.4 *Transition Plans*

Transitions, as we have been using the term throughout Section 3.3, are "those transitional events that are momentous, that change the entire direction of a company, alter the public perception of a company, or can bring about a company's ultimate failure." Later on, in Chapter 6, we will deal with several of the issues surrounding crisis, or risk, preparedness, as well as a more practical focus on some of the key areas from which a crisis or risk can arise. Here though, we want to take a brief look at what a corporate lawyer can do before, during, and after a transitional event.

We already have in place the concepts of assessment, flexibility, and identification of the players in each transitional event. The next arrow in the quiver is to have a framework for a transitional plan. Categorically, there are a number of "plans"[50] a corporate lawyer may encounter, become familiar with, draft, and/or need to review: succession plans, bankruptcy plans (à la a debtor's reorganization plan), litigation plans, business plans, merger plans (such as the more formal plan of merger), dissolution plans, marketing plans, and risk-management plans. Each of these event-specific plans has its own unique features, applications, limits, and expected results. A transitional plan, therefore, is an umbrella concept, which should give a corporate lawyer key elements to consider during any transition of magnitude for his or her client-company. A thorough, event-specific plan should have its own interpretation of each key element, and a corporate lawyer can use them as planning evaluation measurements.

Goals

This key element is no more complex than it appears. For a transitional plan to be efficient and effective, it must have clear goals. Its goals should not merely be defined by end results, but should also include benchmark accomplishments to gauge its progress and regularly evaluate its likely overall success. Simple goals typically lead to clearer, more realistic plans, but goals must also be articulate enough to define a plan's scope and to be able to determine when the plan, as formulated, is no longer working.

For example, the goal of a typical succession plan is to provide for the smooth transition from a current executive or senior manager to a future executive or senior manager. That goal, though necessarily a simple one, ought also to be stated specifically enough for a client-company and its constituents (and the investing public, perhaps) to be able to understand its scope and general process: when it will be implemented, who will be in charge of its implementation, what its criteria are, how long it will take, what it will accomplish, what it is not designed to accomplish, what resources it will require, and what contingency will take place if the plan is unsuccessful. A sample goal for a general counsel's succession plan might be:

> To initiate and complete a qualified candidate search for a successor general counsel, no later than two years prior to the current general counsel's retirement, to identify no fewer than three candidates, who shall be vetted and then presented to the executive hiring committee no later than three months prior to the current general counsel's retirement, and if no such qualified candidates are identified, then to engage (X law firm) to perform general counsel services for the company until such time as qualified candidates may be identified.

Such a goal (though a bit wordy) spells out the core requirements around which the succession plan's processes, necessary resources, and progressive benchmarks can be formed. Every event-specific plan's goals will have their own hallmarks—even similar plans within the same client-company will not inevitably have identical goals—but it is a mistake when little thought is given to properly developing a transition plan's goal. When you find yourself involved in the task of defining a transition plan's goal, understand it is the *goal*, not the process, that is the backbone for what needs to be done. Take your time; analyze its efficacy; troubleshoot its shortcomings; and invite feedback.

Regardless of the size or power of the train, it will not go anywhere without two flat-bottom steel rails.

Needs

Like a transition plan's goal, this key element is also as simple as it appears to be. And, like a plan's goal, it is also a critical element. A transition plan—whether prepared in advance or on the fly as a major transitional event unfolds—must address, in some measure, the needs of *all* concerned parties, or the plan will fall short of succeeding every time. An unresolved need will compromise the plan's effectiveness and the permanence of its success (even if the plan itself is only meant to succeed for a limited period of time, such as a plan of merger). Overlooking a license application, required regulatory filing, public relations announcement, electronic data backup, or confidentiality agreement are only a few examples of neglected needs that could derail a smoothly functioning transition plan.

Transition plans, as a whole and in their component processes, are motivated by a wide variety of needs. These may consist of financial needs, IP needs, strategic needs, operational needs, regulatory needs, management needs, or ownership needs. A perceptive corporate lawyer will identify those needs—usually aligned directly with the identification and assessment of visibly involved parties—and develop processes and goals calculated to meet those needs.

Make lists of affected employees, departments, owners, vendors, divisions, creditors, and regulatory agencies. Identify those parties' needs before, during, and after the transition. Ascertain whether those needs are administrative, financial, operational, logistical, or regulatory, as well as whether they are direct or indirect, required or optional, and pragmatic or emotional/psychological/reputational. (Do not underestimate the sheer staying power of a party's emotional need when a major change is taking place.) Draw schematics to illustrate how those parties' needs may correspond or contradict with each other, and how those needs may need to be sequenced. Flag those needs that might create, or do create, risks, and decide whether those risks are manageable and how they will be managed if necessary. If a need cannot be met, develop a strategy for any fallout; however unpleasant it might be, remain proactive and address this kind of issue head on whenever possible.

Once you have the transition plan's goals well defined, and once you have identified and characterized the motivations (needs) within the plan's processes and stages, you need to make sure the plan has anticipated any barriers to its success.

Change

Barriers to Success

A transition plan is a *positive* activity, meaning it is moving a situation forward, even when the eventual outcome appears dismal. For example, if a client-company has finally admitted it is financially distressed—its income cannot meet its operational and debt obligations—and the decision has been made to prepare for Chapter 11 reorganization relief under the U.S. Bankruptcy Code (or, even more desperate, if a creditor has filed an involuntary petition of bankruptcy against your client-company), then a transition plan must be developed, complete with preparations for operations during bankruptcy, as well as post-bankruptcy recovery and eventual growth. Moving toward bankruptcy, or through bankruptcy, hardly seems like a positive activity, but it can and should be. It should mean that a business, even if temporarily in financial straits, is planning to cut the fat and come back leaner and stronger than before. If, then, a transitional plan is a positive activity by definition, a wary corporate lawyer must look for those untoward pitfalls that may hinder its progress or entirely wreck its processes.

Barriers to the success of a transitional plan should be identified and addressed in much the same way the needs behind a transitional plan are identified and addressed. Make lists of possible hazards and potential liabilities if the plan should move forward. Identify parties associated with those hazards, whether directly or indirectly, and determine if or how they can be neutralized; or if they are friendly, determine if or how they can be engaged to help minimize those hazards. Ascertain whether hazards are administrative, financial, operational, logistical, or regulatory, and whether they are pragmatic or emotional/psychological/reputational. Draw another set of schematics to illustrate how the anticipated hazards may correspond to a particular process or goal within the plan. Develop contingencies in case the anticipated hazards materialize, and if possible, develop alternative processes within the plan in case the anticipated hazards become impassable barriers. (*Adapt and overcome.*)

Occasionally, a potential barrier is identified that is, from the outset, insurmountable. The proposed transition plan is scrapped. The upside to this scenario, even when it is disheartening, is that your client-company can be kept from uselessly expending resources and time, as well as building up pointless expectations, when the planned transition would have ultimately faltered.

As we have previously discussed, there are several different categories of seminal transitional events, which may be encountered by almost any business at almost any time. The idea thus far has been to better equip you, the corporate lawyer, with basic tools to deploy on almost any transitional front: assess, remain flexible, know the players to know the game, and make sure your client-company's transition plan is well formed.

Though certain pivotal events, such as successions, investigations, or litigation, certainly can create fissures wide and deep enough to swallow an entire company, they also come in a variety of shapes, sizes, and scales. They require close attention and professional expertise, but for the purposes of the rest of our discussion about transitions, we will leave them alone. Instead, there are two particular bogeymen of the business world that almost always cast long shadows at the far end of the street.

We will spend a few minutes discussing them: events of financial and/or operational distress and mergers and acquisitions.

§ 3.3.4.1 Distressed Companies, Dissolution, and Bankruptcy

Before briefly ruminating on such potentially distasteful things as dissolution, financial and/or operational distress, or bankruptcy, a parable is in order.

> Long ago, near the ancient city of Uruk, a Master instructed his Servant to go to the marketplace in the city and buy food for the evening meal. The Servant did as he was instructed, but less than an hour had passed when the Servant burst back into the Master's home, and begged his Master to lend his fastest horse to him.
>
> "Why?" demanded the Master, "What has happened?"
>
> The Servant, distraught and pleading, replied, "I saw Death in the marketplace. He stared at me with a dreadful look on his face. I must get away tonight, or Death will find me."
>
> The Master agreed, commenting how lucky his Servant was to have seen Death before Death was able to take him. The Master told his Servant to take the fastest horse from his stable and to flee to the neighboring city of Lagash. Quickly, the Servant ran to the stable, bridled the swiftest horse, and fled into the night for the city of Lagash.
>
> The Master, having been left without anything to eat that evening, rode out to the marketplace himself. As he approached the city, he saw Death leaving on a pale horse.
>
> "Halt!" cried out the Master to Death. "How dare you scare away my Servant."
>
> Death turned to the Master and said, "I did not intend to scare your Servant. I was only surprised to see him in the marketplace in Uruk, since I have an appointment with him tonight in Lagash."[51]

The moral? If your client-company is in trouble, it can only avoid it for so long before Trouble catches up.

I often say the reason most people have a sour taste in their mouths about lawyers is because engaging a lawyer is something that is done only when some kind of catastrophe has taken place, such as a car accident, being served with a lawsuit, being fired from a job, having a loan go into default, receiving notice of a tax lien, or going through a divorce. Lawyers, generally speaking, are identified with anxiety, physical trauma, financial distress, loss, and adversity. Though it should be a priority for every member of the bar to change those impressions or misconceptions, it is true that a great portion of a lawyer's enterprise is to deal with, and work through, the muck and mess of life.

Practicing corporate law is not—as some might naively expect—an exemption from the messiness or angst of catastrophe. Practicing corporate law just means catastrophe comes in the context of business-related events, which can be no less emotional, uneasy, threatening, or bellicose than when it occurs to an individual. Businesses in distress—*distress* meaning bet-the-company situations—are usually facing limited options and grim consequences. Their need for sharp, competent legal counsel is never greater. As was mentioned at the beginning of Section 3.3, a good corporate lawyer is going to make room for whatever calamitous elephant just shouldered its way in, while never forgetting that the *business*, if and wherever and however possible, must continue to operate. In this way, working for, or with, a distressed client-company is the loose equivalent of brain surgery while using a local anesthetic: the patient is awake, aware, and able to autonomously function even as the cranial cavity is opened and instruments are flicking in and out of the gray matter inside.

Grotesque? Client-companies in distress are messy, messy affairs.

The distress elephant can come in many different shades of gray. Fundamentally though, it will mean a great portion of a client-company's creative resources and financial resources are anxiously distracted. Two shades of that gray—dissolution and/or bankruptcy—are worth a few special remarks, but for the moment, our discussion will apply to almost all other transitional events that ominously may lead to those two definitive outcomes.

Corporate problems that lead to the client-company functioning under distress typically involve mistakes in financial statements, relying on too few customers, losing key customers, failing to understand costs, failing to clearly assign responsibilities, failing to control expenses, or failing to conserve cash reserves. These missteps may lead to lawsuits, collection actions, loss of vendors, loss of lending relationships and credit, regulatory discipline, loss of investor confidence, and an inability to retain talent or a broader employment base. If a corporate lawyer finds him- or herself dealing with any of these symptoms on a systemic level (versus the occasionally passing storm cloud), then curative measures— legal advice and strategic counseling—will need to reach further back than the symptoms and address root causes. Symptomatic events are the visible consequences, and they can be disastrous as stand-alone events.

An effective corporate lawyer will deliver the most value to his or her client-company by dedicating resources and ingenuity to making sure the client-company does not perish from the symptoms, but a corporate lawyer must also begin a treatment of the source of the problem as soon as possible; this, most likely, will require a separate set of resources and skill sets. Management, in whole or in part, may need to change. Core business operations or business models may need to be restructured or revised. Financial reporting and control methodologies may need to be overhauled and corrected. Technology may need to be updated. Information streams may need to be combined.

There will likely be a lot of stepping on toes and some hurt feelings, but if a corporate lawyer turns a blind eye to the source of a client-company's distress—if a corporate lawyer is not asking, What led to this, and how can it be resolved?—then he or she simply is not doing the job they need to do. To advocate for a client-company—to act on behalf of its constituency—also means to challenge and address internal dilemmas, as much as it means to protect against and confront external threats.

Dissolution

The *dissolution* of a business is when it closes its doors forever. Bankruptcy may involve reorganization—life after death—but dissolution is when a business breathes its last. The manner and methodology of any given business's dissolution will depend almost entirely on its size, industry (regulations can have a lot to do with dissolving a business), ownership structure, liabilities, and distinctive characteristics. Dissolution may take a long time—a few years perhaps—or a very short amount of time—within a week. Regardless, a corporate lawyer's attentiveness, skill, and work product should be no less keen than when his or her services are used at the height of a business's heyday.

Two general components should motivate a corporate lawyer's function in the dissolution of a client-company: (1) ensure compliance with all legal requirements as the business dissolves and (2) manage its dissolution in such a way as to minimize risk to the client-company's constituency, most pointedly, its owners (and/or guarantors). A corporate lawyer needs to be able to answer, or have the client-company answer, the following questions and all derivative questions that any answers may prompt:

- Have alternatives to dissolution been pragmatically vetted and found to be untenable?
- Have proper governance steps been taken in order to decide upon dissolution?
- Has a dissolution plan been developed, and/or is such a plan already in place?
- Have assets been audited and valued? Has an asset liquidation plan been developed?
- Have current insurance policies been evaluated for appropriate coverages?
- Have regulatory and other government agencies and entities been properly informed? Has approval, if needed, been received?
- Have necessary licenses and permits been cancelled?
- Has a public relations plan, if necessary, been developed?
- Have vendors, creditors, and other stakeholders been notified?
- Have taxes and other liabilities been audited and settled?
- Have employee benefits been prepared for transfer, rollover, or cancellation?

Perhaps more than ever before, a corporate lawyer should make every effort to look behind every door, peer under every bed, snoop in every closet, and lift every floorboard to make sure he or she is proceeding—and providing advice based upon—complete information. As one could imagine, it is more than a little difficult to sell a business's assets when one is unaware of all of the assets a business owns. Proper and comprehensive auditing by each department, in each area of responsibility, needs to be performed efficiently and as soon as possible.

The dissolution of a distressed business enterprise can be a sad occasion, but it is also a necessary part of the greater marketplace, and it is a hallmark of mature, responsible ownership and management. If a business is broken beyond repair, or beyond the desire and means to fix it, then the solution is an accountable, transparent-as-needed dissolution process.

Bankruptcy

To be *bankrupt* is to be insolvent in common vernacular. Usually, these terms refer to a situation in which a business has more debt obligations and other unrealized liabilities than it has assets and income to meet when they become due. Bankruptcy, as a jurisprudential process, can be strategic (based upon projected insolvency, such as may arise from lawsuits or future guarantees), or involuntary—or the undesirable but necessary result of current insolvency. Although it has become much less of a stigmatized procedure, to declare bankruptcy still carries enough distaste and rigidity for a business to leave it as an option of last resort. A corporate lawyer—even though sometimes stuck in just a strategic mindset—must be cautious about suggesting bankruptcy. Though its protections and fairly predictable process can be appealing from a risk point of view, bankruptcy can be abhorrent from a marketing, sales, or public relations point of view. Broaching the subject ought to be done with diplomacy and healthy doses of explanation—not necessarily technical information but with a view toward the practical effects on operations, employees, vendor relations, creditor relations, growth plans, customer bases, regulators, investor relations, and bond holders. Remember, as bankruptcy is being initially discussed, you will be seen as a central information fount; your demeanor, concern, attitude, and command of this unique situation (even if not at the level of an expert) will directly influence your management and board. You will be *the* attorney, even when high-dollar bankruptcy counsel is brought in, and like other instances of litigation management, you will need to have a close and knowledgeable handle on what is happening and why it is happening.

Liquidation, a filing under Chapter 7 of the Bankruptcy Code, will not grant a business-debtor a discharge as it would an individual debtor. There are no "exempt" protections from liquidation; a fire sale of assets is a complete liquidation event. Reorganization, a filing under Chapter

11 of the Bankruptcy Code, anticipates that a business will reorganize its debt-obligation payment schedule, typically extending payment schedules and modifying interest liabilities and/or penalties. The idea is for a business to survive its current state of insolvency and develop a plan to reach profitability again in the future.

The filing of a bankruptcy petition under either chapter is usually preceded by weeks, if not months, of preparation. A corporate lawyer should exhaustively glean every scrap of information from a dissolving company; bankruptcy counsel will also need an absolutely comprehensive view of *every* aspect of a client-company. This is not, of course, just a matter of filling out reams of forms (although there is that practical part of it), but a matter of complete disclosure to the bankruptcy court and to the appointed trustee. Any piece of undisclosed information has the potential to strip a client-company of its codified protections and expose it to significant risk.

Once a bankruptcy petition is filed, every creditor of a business is affected. Lawsuits within the purview of the bankruptcy proceeding may be initiated, and there will be a flurry of filings and activities: notices, claims, objections, depositions (known as *2004 exams* after the applicable Bankruptcy Code provision), interpleader actions, quarterly reports, a creditors' meeting (a *341 meeting*), a proposed plan (for reorganization), conversions, and more than enough hearings. Meanwhile, in most cases, *business* must continue, whether by the debtor in possession, or through an appointed receiver, at the approval or behest of the court and/or trustee.

A valuable corporate lawyer will liaison the bankruptcy process on behalf of his or her client-company, closely monitoring the progress, strategy, and efficacy of the bankruptcy counsel while continuing to advise the client-company on all other matters of business operations, risk, and strategic planning.

§ 3.3.4.2 Mergers and/or Acquisitions

Although mergers and/or acquisitions (M&A) can arise from distressed circumstances, M&A is not generally seen as categorically a response or a consequence of a business's distress. In fact, it many times is interpreted as a sign of a business's strength and growth. However, M&A activity is, in most cases, a transitional event that can be fraught with anxiety and potential risks. For this reason, I have characterized it as a subsection of Section 3.3, "Transitions and Things That Go Bump in the Night."

Without a doubt M&A is a specialized area of law. Deal lawyers—sometimes even those who are in house and are working for an especially aggressive, growth-oriented company or division—live, breathe, eat, and sleep M&A. These transactions are where corporate strategy, finance, and management converge to buy, sell, divide, or combine similar entities or entirely different companies. M&A activity—on the absorption side—can help a business to expand its market share, geographic locations, and product or service lines without creating a subsidiary or a joint venture. M&A activity—on the divesting side—is also a method of expansion; expansion achieved by divesting a business of its (usually smaller) autonomous existence. Though subtle differences remain between the terms *mergers* and *acquisitions*, the activities are typically coupled into an overall transaction, and one is not distinguished from the other.

An M&A deal is a transitional (transformative) event, and a client-company should have a firm sense of its motives, capacities, resources, and options before pulling the trigger. Valuable corporate lawyers, even if not deal makers by trade, must educate themselves on the characteristics of M&A activity, weighed against their clients' best interests, strategic goals, and risk exposures and tolerances. Overall, as should be the case with almost every decision and occupation of a client-company, M&A deals are meaningful for their (presumptive) ability to improve financial performance. The following are a few of the tactical motives behind an M&A deal:[52]

- *Economy of Scale*: The combined company can often reduce its fixed costs by removing duplicate departments or operations, which lowers the costs of the company relative to the same revenue stream, which then should increase profit margins.
- *Economy of Scope*: This involves demand-side change efficiencies, such as increasing or decreasing the scope of marketing and distribution of different types of services or products.
- *Increased Market Share*: The buyer will absorb a major competitor and increase its market power to set prices.
- *Cross-Selling*: A company acquires an indirect competitor, so it can now sell its products to the acquired company's customer

base. (For example, a computer manufacturer buys a software company so it could then sell its hardware to a captured market of software consumers. Likewise, the software can be sold to a captured market of computer hardware consumers.)

- *Tax Liabilities*: A profitable company might buy a company with significant losses in order to use the acquired losses to reduce tax liability.
- *Vertical Integration*: This is when upstream and downstream companies merge (or one acquires the other). Vertical integration can be used for a variety of different reasons, such as to set a downstream company's monopoly price to a competitive price, which increases affordability and profitability for the entire product or service stream.

Because it is not a statistically likely consequence that an M&A deal will automatically lead to higher profits, nonfinancial motives, such as diversification, may play a part in a client-company's decision to move forward with a deal.

M&A work—an enormous amount of which is poured into due diligence between the party-companies—is accomplished by each company's "best efforts."[53] Though some asset-purchase agreements leave this phrase mostly undefined, others closely describe exactly what is expected. Of course, even the best contractual description does little to direct a company in practice. Necessary due diligence "includes an evaluation of the target company's financial, legal, and commercial activities (among others), including information technology, to determine points of risk and value prior to the execution of the transaction."[54] A client-company's corporate lawyer and his or her team step in here. M&A specialists might be (and probably should be) engaged in most circumstances, but the steward of the fiefdom is still the corporate lawyer, who is ultimately responsible to his or her client-company for the success, efficiency, progress, or failure of the deal.

In such M&A environments, a corporate lawyer—along with other departments and key management—may need to participate in: (1) establishing information flows (which may need to remain very confidential), (2) updating management for troubleshooting and progress, (3) identifying retention risks, (4) determining a new organizational structure, (5) determining severance costs, (6) eliminating adverse effects of, or quantifying exposure to, "parachute payments," (7) reviewing valuation models and financials,[55] (8) obtaining letters of opinion, and (9) planning and implementing employee communication strategies.[56] There are, in any space of time, a multitude of tasks to accomplish, many of which must be done confidentially and apart from day-to-day operational activities.

M&A work is not for the faint of heart, but it is such a common form of business growth that an effective corporate lawyer should spend the extra time and resources to prudently escort his or her client-company through each step while, as always, making sure all other aspects of an ongoing business concern are properly serviced.

§ 3.3.5 Exit Strategies

Beware the Jabberwock, my son

The jaws that bite, the claws that catch!

Beware the Jubjub bird, and shun

The frumious Bandersnatch![57]

Having discussed the excitement of new business ventures, the vigorous undertakings when jumping into an ongoing business concern, and the challenges of major transitional events, it is fitting to close this chapter with a word about exit strategies.

Exit strategies should be a natural part of every corporate lawyer's repertory, regardless of the stage of business of his or her client-company. Because business almost by definition operates in a constant state of risk—whether expanding, contracting, or simply plodding along, and whether it is new, mature, or aged—a client-company's legal counsel should always be thinking about exit strategies.

If things do not work out, how do we get back to good?

There is nothing inherently magical about an exit strategy. It is simply a forethought, planned (even if loosely) method for extricating a client-company from a chosen course of action. William James, the brother of American novelist Henry James and a psychologist and philosopher in his own right, said, "Acceptance of what has happened is the first step to overcoming the consequences of any misfortune." Therefore, *anticipate* that a chosen course of action will become a misfortune, and begin forming an exit strategy from that point. Several contingencies may come to mind, or only one or two.

Discuss these contingencies with other members of the corporate-counsel team, and once a strategy (or two) has distilled into something you feel is workable, discuss it with the client-company's management. Identify what resources and personnel would be needed in order to take advantage of the strategy, and put into place whatever might be needed as a preliminary matter. Call up whichever subject-matter specialists may be needed, and discuss the strategy with them. If necessary, depending on the circumstances, pay a retainer, and have them on standby.

As an example, a corporate client was facing several serious lawsuits. The company was in the middle of expanding part of its operations, and it was in a very solid financial position. However, as the lawsuits progressed, the potential collective-liability exposure became enormous. After failed mediation attempts, and an early litmus-test trial of one of the cases, the decision was made to file for bankruptcy and reorganize. The filing was relatively harmless to most of the company's creditors because bankruptcy had not been a result of any immediate solvency issues, but it threw the right kind of monkey wrench in the lawsuits. Filing for bankruptcy protection at the right strategic time was only possible because our team had been preparing for it for months, just in case.

Every room should have two doors: the one you walk in and the one you know you can run through. Establish exit strategies as part of your normal planning processes, and whatever Jabberwock your client-company may encounter, it should be able to extricate itself smoothly and with minimal damage.

We opened this chapter by discussing the importance of identifying a client-company's stage of business as a critical part of assessing its legal needs, risk exposures, and strategic plans. The context of every stage of business should tell a corporate lawyer where the maximum value of his or her services will lie. Every situation will be different and have its own challenges, but if you remember the fundamental concepts, tasks, and strategies applicable to almost all stages and events of business, then your client-company will be all the better for it.

During a panel discussion of the vagaries of in-house lawyers also acting as compliance officers, Jason Romrell, who is the president & chief legal officer of Budget Van Lines, said simply but emphatically, "I always try to do the *right* thing."[58] Though Mr. Romrell poked fun at himself good-naturedly for the near futility of better defining this simple goal, his observation was precisely on point. A corporate lawyer must struggle, endeavor, make every effort, and go all out to do the *right thing*. Whatever difficulty there may be in ascertaining what that right thing is in highly complex and ever-gray situations, it is worth the fight, worthy of a corporate client's expectations, and worthy of our own professional obligations to fight that fight, to be able to say to one and all you did your utmost to do the right thing.

Notes

1. Eric Esperne, *10 Pieces of Advice from a Seasoned In-House Lawyer*, InsideCounsel, Dec. 16, 2011, *available at* http://www.insidecounsel .com/2011/12/16/10-pieces-of-advice-from-a-seasoned-in-house -lawye?t=careers&page=2.

2. Why not make the second endnote of this chapter a definition of something that is well beyond the feeble grasp of my scientifically challenged brain? A triple-stranded deoxyribonucleic acid (DNA) is a structure of DNA in which three oligonucleotides wind around each other and form a triple helix. Watson, J.D. and Crick, F.H.C., *Molecular structure of nucleic acids: A structure for deoxyribose nucleic acid*, Nature, Apr. 25, 1953, No. 4356, p. 737.

3. Stephen Kaplan, *In-House Counsel Must Tailor Their Work to Best Serve Their Clients: One Size of Service Does Not Fit All*, InsideCounsel, Jan. 2012, *available at* http://www.insidecounsel.com/2012/01/01/in-house- counsel-must-tailor-their-work-to-best-se.

4. Senior vice president and general counsel of Connextions, Inc.

5. Ben McClure, *Getting to Know Business Models*, Investopedia, Jan. 28, 2011, *available at* http://www.investopedia.com/articles/fundamental/04033104.asp.

6. *Orffyreus* was the alias of Johann Bessler, a German entrepreneur who, in 1712, appeared in the town of Gera in the province of Reuss with his first "self-moving wheel." Good Mr. Bessler's wheels seemed to work—to perpetually keep moving under their own power—but, alas, because perpetual motion violates the law (the first two laws of thermodynamics), "Orffyreus's Wheels" were probably powered by fraud, which, unfortunately, can sometimes be the darker side of a business venture.

7. First entitled *Alice's Adventures Underground* as an illustrated, handwritten manuscript in late 1864.

8. This will also be the time when you begin developing the law department, but for our purposes, we will save that topic for Chapter 4.

9. Again, a borrowed aphorism from *Alice's Adventures in Wonderland*.

10. Ben McClure, *Getting to Know Business Models*, Investopedia, Jan. 28, 2011, *available at* http://www.investopedia.com/articles/fundamental/04033104.asp.

11. The Rosetta Stone is a stele engraved with a decree issued by Egyptian king Ptolemy V at Memphis in 196 B.C., just in case you were wondering.

12. Ben McClure, *Getting to Know Business Models*, INVESTOPEDIA, Jan. 28, 2011, *available at* http://www.investopedia.com/articles/fundamental /04033104.asp.

13. Claire Bradley, *Is Your Business Model Viable: An 8-Point Test*, INVESTOPEDIA, July 7, 2010, *available at* http://www.investopedia.com /financial-edge/0710/Is-Your-Business-Model-Viable-An-8-Point-Test .aspx#axzz1sojAXpm0.

14. I highly recommend getting a copy of KENNETH MARKS ET AL., THE HANDBOOK OF FINANCING GROWTH: STRATEGIES, CAPITAL STRUCTURE, AND M&A TRANSACTIONS (John Wiley & Sons, Inc. 2009), which is part of the Wiley Finance Series. It covers just about everything you need to know about financing and is a very readable, accessible resource.

15. Taken from Mr. Carroll's fantastic sequel, *Through the Looking-Glass, and What Alice Found There*, first published in December 1871.

16. Be careful of overly zealous protectionism. For instance, "copyright traps" themselves cannot actually be copyrighted. *See* Nester's Map and Guide Corp. v. Hagstrom Map Co., 796 F. Supp. 729, 733 (E.D.N.Y. 1992). In the *Nester's Map* opinion, the district court stated: "[t]o treat 'false' facts interspersed among actual facts and represented as actual facts as fiction would mean that no one could ever reproduce or copy actual facts without risk of reproducing a false fact and thereby violating a copyright. . . . If such were the law, information could never be reproduced or widely disseminated." *Id.* at 733.

17. I can't leave you without a very reliable shelf reference (which I have and use) for non-IP types. ALEXANDER POLTORAK & PAUL LERNER, ESSENTIALS OF INTELLECTUAL PROPERTY (2d ed., John Wiley & Sons, Inc. 2011).

18. Something that could be categorized as a "protectable trade dress right."

19. On May 9, 2012, the Sixth Circuit Court of Appeals ruled that the red dripping-wax seal appearing on bottles of Maker's Mark bourbon since 1958 is an "extremely strong" trademark deserving trademark protection. Ashley Post, *Maker's Mark Wax Seal Gets Trademark Protection*, INSIDECOUNSEL, May 10, 2012, *available at* http://www.insidecounsel .com/2012/05/10/makers-mark-wax-seal-gets-trademark-protection?t=ip.

20. For some "light" reading on this subject, take a look at Damien Geradin & Anne Layne-Ferrar, *Patent Value Apportionment Rules for Complex, Multi-Patent Products*, 27 SANTA CLARA COMPUTER & HIGH TECH. L.J. 763 (2011).

21. The illustrious Mr. de Bono has been a proponent of the deliberate teaching of *thinking*, which, in my estimation, we need more of. His advocacy of sideways, or lateral, thinking, challenges the traditional linear, or logical, model adapted from Aristotle, Plato, and Socrates. His book, *Six Thinking Hats*, is definitely worth the read. EDWARD DE BONO, SIX THINKING HATS (2d ed., Back Bay Books 1999).

22. Fox Rothschild, LLP's, Practical Advice from the Intellectual Property Department, *Does Your Company Have an Effective Corporate IP Program*, http://www.foxrothschild.com/uploadedFiles/practiceareas /intelPropGuidebook_doesYourCoHaveEffectiveProg.pdf (last visited Apr. 14, 2012).

23. 21 C.F.R. § 872.3600 will actually give you this product's specific description, classification, the International Organization for Standardization standard (ISO 10993), and the applicable federal register publication (52 Fed. Reg. 30,097).

24. Underwriters Laboratories (UL) currently offers certification on 67,798 manufactured products and components, meaning that UL has tested and evaluated representative samples of that product and determined that they meet UL requirements. *See* UNDERWRITERS LABORATORIES, www.ul.com (last visited Apr. 14, 2012). A UL mark can be a very powerful marketing tool for safety and quality.

25. Certified by the Institute of Certified Bankers, a subsidiary of the American Bankers Association.

26. Having said that, make sure your manual and policies are thoughtful and strategic. Simplicity as a result of naivety is a ticking time bomb.

27. I have borrowed these three key concerns from a great, accessible resource for small or start-up businesses: SmallBusinessBible.org. It is an online resource "intended to guide budding and experienced entrepreneurs who plan to start a new home based business or a small business firm[,]" but I have found its practical advice to be just as sound and rational when applied to larger, more developed business ventures. You can find it at SMALL BUSINESS BIBLE, www.smallbusinessbible.org (last visited Apr. 17, 2012).

28. STEVE WOZNIAK & GINA SMITH, iWOZ: FROM COMPUTER GEEK TO CULT ICON (W. W. Norton & Company 2006).

29. If only monarchs were as sage in real life as they are in *Alice's Adventures in Wonderland*.

30. As you will recall, we discussed the hurdles to providing *comprehensive* legal counsel when a client-company hires a situation-specific corporate lawyer (whether a general counsel or not) in Chapter 1, Section 1.1.1. It is a typical scenario, but one that an effective corporate lawyer must work to overcome as the legal advisor to the company as a whole.

31. CAROLE BASRI AND IRVING KAGAN, CORPORATE LEGAL DEPARTMENTS § 5:1 (4th ed., Practicing Law Institute 2011).

32. For non-profit organizations, or governmental agencies, making more money is unlikely to be a "self-evident" goal. The self-evident goal may be a particular service, mission, or mandate. For those corporate lawyers who labor on behalf of these clients, our discussion of "support goals" remains relatively the same.

33. Direct competitors are those businesses that manufacture the same kinds of products or market the same kinds of services as your client-company to the same, or part of the same, marketplace. Toyota is a direct competitor with Ford Motor Company. Indirect competitors are those businesses that manufacture different products or provide different services than your client-company, but do so in order to satisfy the same market needs. Amtrak is an indirect competitor with American Airlines: one provides passenger rail service, whereas the other provides passenger airline service, but they both compete for people who need to travel.

34. *See* Section 2.2.
35. German for "double walker," used in folklore as a living person's paranormal twin, which typically represents some kind of evil or doom.
36. Usurped (furtively) from *Through the Looking-Glass, and What Alice Found There.*
37. As an example, after domestic, economic markets began to crash in 2007, JPMorgan Chase & Co., was seen as one of the few major banks to be able to weather the ensuing financial crisis relatively unscathed. Regardless, the crisis, whose epicenter was the banking *industry*, caused regulatory reforms to take place, lending standards and habits to change, borrowing to grind almost to a halt, real estate and related asset values to drop precipitously, and downsizing to occur. All of these aftershocks to the banking industry directly affected JPMorgan, for better or for worse, in spite of the strength of its own position. No business is ever autonomous from its industry.
38. Polson Enterprises has, in fact, made this kind of research supremely easy on all of us technological ne'er-do-wells. You can use any of their twenty-two steps online at http://www.virtualpet.com/industry/howto/search.htm.
39. Commandeered from *Alice's Adventures in Wonderland.*
40. Sam Grobart, *Allow Me to Introduce Myself (Properly)*, MONEY, Dec. 27, 2006, *available at* http://money.cnn.com/2006/12/27/magazines/money mag/newguy.moneymag/index.htm.
41. This echoes the understanding-the-corporate-culture advice from Section 2.1.4.
42. Borrowed (to be put back later) from *Alice's Adventures in Wonderland.*
43. *See* MODEL RULES OF PROF'L CONDUCT R. 2.1 (1983).
44. From Chapter 2 of Mark Twain's marvelous novel, *The Adventures of Huckleberry Finn.* Tom Sawyer is convinced that to "ransom" a person means to capture that person and to keep him or her captive until their death.
45. *See* Heidi N. Moore, *Here We Go Again: Washington Mutual's Chief Lawyer Is Bear Stearns Alum*, WSJ BLOGS (Sept. 19, 2008, 3:33 PM), http://blogs .wsj.com/deals/2008/09/19/where-is-bear-stearns-top-lawyer-at-wamu/. *See also* Dan Slater, *The Bear Stearns Meltdown: A Spotlight on S&C's Rodgin Cohen*, WSJ BLOGS (Mar. 28, 2008, 9:07 AM), http://blogs.wsj.com /law/2008/05/28/the-bear-stearns-meltdown-a-spotlight-on-scs-rodgin -cohen/.
46. Poor Alice. I would be equally befuddled trying to come to grips with the inscrutable nonsense of the poem "Jabberwocky," another gem from Mr. Carroll's *Through the Looking-Glass, and What Alice Found There.*
47. Appropriated from "The Walrus and the Carpenter," a narrative poem by Mr. Carroll, unearthed from *Through the Looking-Glass, and What Alice Found There.*
48. Although most proxy fights against incumbent management and directors are not successful, studies have shown that proxy fights initiated by hedge funds succeed up to 60 percent of the time. *See* April Klein & Emmanuel Zur, *Entrepreneurial Shareholder Activism: Hedge Funds and Other Private Investors*, 64 J. FINANCE 187–229 (Feb. 2009).

49. Wits & Wagers is a board game published by North Star Games, requiring healthy doses of guesstimated risks. The game has won over twenty awards, including the Mensa Select award.

50. This section's discussion of plans is, practically speaking, a discussion involving plans of action, versus plans that tend to define programs, such as insurance plans or deferred-benefits plans.

51. I have made slight changes to the retelling of a story that appears as the epigraph to John O'Hara's 1934 novel, *Appointment in Samarra*. JOHN O'HARA, APPOINTMENT IN SAMARRA (Random House 1934). In the foreword to the 1952 reprint of the novel, O'Hara describes having come up with the title after his friend Dorothy Parker showed him the story in a play written by W. Somerset Maugham, entitled *Sheppey* (1933). The ancient version of the parable can be found in the Babylonian *Talmud*, tractate *Sukkah*, p. 53a.

52. We will see considerations taken of these same concepts, such as *economy of scale* and *economy of scope*, when we look at variables for the use of outside counsel, versus in-house counsel, in Chapter 4.

53. *Model Asset Purchase Agreement with Commentary* (ABA Publishing 2001), § 1.1. "Best efforts" are defined as "the efforts that a prudent Person desirous of achieving a result would use in similar circumstances to achieve that result as expeditiously as possible, *provided, however,* that a Person required to use Best Efforts under this Agreement will not be thereby required to take actions that would result in a material adverse change in the benefits to such Person of this Agreement and the Contemplated Transactions, or to dispose of or make any change to its business, expend any material funds or incur any other material burden."

54. Chris Ruggeri & Bart Siegel, *Reducing the Risk of Post-Merger Discovery Surprises in M&A*, CORPORATE COUNSEL, Mar. 28, 2012.

55. There are five common valuation models: asset valuation, historical earnings valuation, future maintainable earnings valuation, relative valuation (based on comparable companies and transactions), and discounted cash-flow valuation.

56. These nine items are not, of necessity, sequential, nor is this list meant to be exhaustive, versus demonstrative.

57. We have pilfered our last verse from the kind Mr. Carroll's *Through the Looking-Glass, and What Alice Found There*.

58. Jason Romrell, *Should In-House Counsel Be Navigating in the Choppy Waters of Corporate Compliance?*, A.B.A. SEC. BUS. L., ANNUAL BUSINESS LAW SECTION MEETING, Las Vegas, Nev., Mar. 22, 2012. This quote is taken directly from the author's memory as an audience member of the live panel on which Mr. Romrell sat. The author takes full responsibility for any unintended mischaracterization or misquotation.

CHAPTER 4

THE LEGAL DEPARTMENT— "WHERE IS MY OFFICE?"

We have spent the past three chapters largely discussing the individual features of what it means to wear the spurs of a corporate lawyer on a daily basis. But even if a client-company is small enough (or, in some unfortunate cases, shortsighted enough) to hire only a single corporate lawyer as its legal counsel, that lawyer constitutes a collective reality: *the legal department*, what should be an essential support and business unit of every client-company.

A brief study of what a legal department entails is as basic to an understanding of what it means to be a corporate lawyer as it is to find out where your new office is located. It is not an easy undertaking to do one's job if one is marooned in a hallway. Legal departments, like offices, are part of the natural geography of most businesses and the natural homes of corporate lawyers. Therefore, we now advance into that demanding terrain, "half a league, half a league, half a league onward[.]"[1]

As wildly different as every corporation is from its next-door neighbor, so too is the universe of variation when comparing different corporations' legal departments. Though the term *legal* can be applied in most situations, the term *department* is truly fluid. Some corporations' legal departments are entirely external, wholly dependent on outside counsel or legal-service firms[2] to act as their chief legal officer, or general counsel, and to handle all their day-to-day legal needs. Some corporations hire a single lawyer, sometimes on just a part-time basis, to handle their in-house legal needs and act as their default legal counsel. Some corporations have in-house legal departments composed of a single lawyer and only one or two staff members. Other corporations—an increasing number—have in-house legal departments that run the gamut from a few lawyers and staff to several hundred lawyers, trained paralegals, and hundreds of staff personnel.

The differences in structure and utility are also just as varied as the size and placement. Some corporations' legal departments are almost exclusively concentrated into single areas of law, such as intellectual property (from filing to licensing to litigation), mergers and acquisitions, or compliance. Some legal departments handle just a few areas of practice and focus on providing substantial support services to other departments and divisions. Some legal departments are akin to full-blown law firms, with their own internal sub-departments, practice groups, and business models. A few legal departments cannot rightly be called *departments* at all. They are too big, positioned throughout various divisions or subsidiary corporations owned or controlled by massive, international parent companies.

One size does *not* fit all.

One Size

One's inclination might be to say, "Someone else runs the department," or "I work for an outside law firm," or "I only have one staff member," or "I don't have anything to do with the pens and pencils of our department; just patent filings." Those statements may be accurate on a surface level, but they are all limited—and potentially risky points of view.

When a lawyer works for a corporate client as its legal counsel (not just its litigation counsel, patent counsel, or collective-bargaining counsel), his or her responsibility is not restricted by his or her own perception; it is governed by the *client's* perception. No employee in any company truly works in isolation. Business geography is not an archipelago of independent isles. It is a single, linked landmass, even when some departments or persons seem to crest more prominently than others. A corporate lawyer, whose general job description (or letter of engagement description) is to "provide legal services," or some variation of that, is just as responsible for the "services" part of that obligation as he or she is for the "legal" part. Regardless of one's particular, external role, a successful corporate lawyer will retain a sense of (if not have direct involvement in) the characteristics, responsibilities, processes, and resources of maintaining a legal *department.*

What affects the one affects the many. If a law department's metrics reveal inefficiencies, a task goes unattended, or a paralegal blows the whistle on an unethical company practice, then a responsible corporate lawyer—one who puts the interests of a client-company above his or her own personal or professional interests—is going to acknowledge his or her connection to those events, even if subordinate or supplementary, and work as a departmental member to resolve problems, curb wastefulness, and cure discord. As we will discuss later, corporate executives will ultimately have little interest in individual achievements. Their bottom line is *the* bottom line—cost and results—and their evaluation of a company's corporate counsel is a department-wide concern. A corporate lawyer who believes his or her visible duty is the limit of his or her participation in, or responsibility to, a legal department, is ill suited to be part of a corporate—a community-driven—enterprise.

Lawyers, as individually licensed professionals, may see themselves first as independent actors, but in many circumstances—prosecuting offices, public defender offices, military JAG units, special interest organizations, and, of course, corporate legal departments—good lawyers realize their own success is mutually dependent on the success of their peers and coworkers, and on the overall success of the greater, non-legal entity. Because this is the case, corporate lawyers at every level of an organization should take the time to ask, and reflect on, the following questions:

- In order to effectively contribute to a client-company's business, what does running or being a part of a legal department mean?

- What plank work leads to an adaptable, proficient, well-administered, and tailored business unit for a client-company's legal counsel?

§ 4.1 WHAT *IS* A LEGAL DEPARTMENT?

There are at least two things all legal departments share, regardless of their location, size, personnel, or utility.

First, a company's corporate lawyers are viewed by their client-companies as *the* legal department. They are (or should be) seen as a repository of answers for otherwise unresolvable questions. Psychologically, for a client-company's constituency, its corporate lawyers are melded into a single, departmental noun: *Go ask legal. Check with legal. Has anyone checked with legal on this issue?* A legal department, at a fundamental level, as well as a practical level, is expected to be the legal brain trust of a client-company, even if its day-to-day tasks are largely confined to a single practice area of law. Why? Because, realistically speaking, *people expect every lawyer to know the law.*[3] This is the eyeglass through which supportive aspects of a legal department are assessed, observed, and anticipated by the rest of the client-company.

Second, a legal department is, and should act as, a *department*, however few or great its number of members. A client-company's legal department—when it is seen as such by its own participants, even if the department is an outside law firm—has its own need for resources, personnel, administration, and management. There should be predictable task assignments, accountability, reporting requirements, budgeting, periodic training, auditing, and personnel management. All these concerns can exist at a macro level or at a minimal, one-person level, but for a department of corporate lawyers (even just *one* corporate lawyer) to efficiently and successfully support and augment a company's business enterprise, these concerns must be a part of *every* corporate lawyer's field of view. The entire rationale behind a legal department's existence is for it to be a contributing unit to a client-company's business, whether on the expense side or on the profit side. This is the lens through which the value-augmenting aspects of a legal department are assessed, observed, and anticipated by the rest of the client-company.

If a legal department, regardless of its location, size, personnel, or utility, is unable to handle the legal needs of its client-company in whatever ways they may arise, *and* if a legal department is unable to administer itself resourcefully and effectively for the greater good of a client-company's core businesses, then it should hang up its spurs and leave the rodeo before anyone gets hurt.

Because a successful legal department must deliver results, it must be viewed and managed as a business within a business. Strategic planning—in complement to the needs of other departments and the specific projects or responsibilities assigned to a legal department—should translate into a departmental business plan. If you plan it, it will get done, and over time, it will get done in the most productive and efficient way possible. Departments without a fluidly managed and faithfully followed plan are doomed to eventual disorganization, shortfalls, and recurring failures.

A legal department's plan does not need to be complicated; anything superfluous—detail just for the sake of beefing up a plan—will most likely cause it to become unwieldy and inflexible. Instead, a departmental plan should be built from the staples necessary to get the job done. Providing top-flight legal counsel is the objective; organization and administration are the processes. ("Pluck up thy spirits."[4] You will still be able to practice law.)

Topically, a legal department's plan should address the following components:

- *Resources*—everything from hardware to software to pens and pencils
- *Personnel*—lawyers, administrators, paralegals, other staff, and consultants
- *Tasks and Responsibilities*—areas of practice, projects (repetitive and anomalous), organizational structure, reporting, lines of authority, and administration/management
- *Access (Procedures and Expectations)*—departmental expectations, streams of information, and systems for interdepartmental support

In addition to assessments, budgets (where applicable), procedures, and projections for each component, a legal department's plan may also incorporate a mission statement (plural, if the legal department is composed of different units), long-range planning methods, support systems (such as document construction, review, retention, and security and communications), training expectations, and audit/performance procedures. Make sure a plan's expectations and methodologies are designed to mesh with the activities, resources, and demands of other departments, keeping in mind that each plan, as well as every aspect of a legal department, should be thoughtfully tailored to a client-company's distinctive needs, budget, structure, and expectations. Be quick to change things that are not working, but make sure each correction is directed first to genuine inefficiencies, instead of adjusting goals and projections to match less-than-proficient procedures.

§ 4.1.1 Resources—"What's in the Pantry?"

When most of us think of resources, we usually think in terms of *things*: computers, office furniture, copy machines, cell phones, yellow pads, highlighters, and paperclips. Reviewing physical supplies is a great place to start before turning to other, less tangible departmental assets, such as support from other departments (IT, HR, and whoever is willing to spiral-bind your reports); research tools; consultants; software platforms (budgeting, scheduling, data sharing and storage, document production); and litigation support services (as well as other specialized or outside counsel). You should be able to develop a working inventory and an inventory-of-use database for everything your legal department has, needs, wants, and (frankly) does not need but has.

Applying a few simple questions to every object, device, gadget, contraption, and thingamajig in your department will quickly tell you what lines the pantry's shelves.

- What is it?
- Where does it come from (that is, how do I procure more of it when needed)?
- What does it cost?
- Is its cost fixed or variable?
- Where is it stored or officed, and is it on-site or off-site?
- How, why, and when is it used?
- Who uses it?
- Is it up to date?
- Does it require licensing?
- How many users can access it at one time?

- How is it protected, firewalled, backed up, and shared?
- Does it require contracting or per-project engagement?
- Who orders or procures more of it?
- How long does it take to obtain more of it?
- Who monitors its supply level, storage space, or budget allotment?
- Is it depreciable?
- Does it have or does it require a company-wide inventory identifier as a depreciating asset?

The point is to evaluate and understand what resources your department has at its disposal and which resources it lacks, needs to upgrade, or needs to outsource. This inventory evaluation can then provide a basis for budgeting, resource-access management, license and contract calendaring, depreciation tables, and realistic projections.

After the rough inventorying is over, you will also have a good idea about how to improve your legal department's access to needed resources, both hard and soft. Improving and maintaining departmental resources is not just a matter of cracking open a purchasing catalog, downloading new software, or calling up your favorite specialized counsel or consultant. Departmental resources represent a *cost* in some way, shape, or form. A cost someone has to pay, directly or indirectly. In that sense, part of the energy and creativity involved in improving and maintaining resources is to mitigate, manage, and justify cost.

Mitigating cost is fairly straightforward: only spend—in time, effort, and/or money—what is necessary to get the job done. Offset costs when and where you can. For instance, having offices requires having office furniture. You do not need to requisition the cheapest furniture (which usually costs more in the long run because it falls apart more quickly than quality-built furniture), but you also do not need top-of-the-line, name-brand furniture to grace every office. From a budgeting perspective, this kind of thinking not only mitigates the cost of purchasing furniture, but it might help to ease the cost of necessarily expensive software platforms or important travel expenditures. Pay attention to your department's real needs and be creatively stingy when you can be.

Managing cost is an ongoing effort: make sure resources are consistently used at their optimal levels of productivity, relative to their cost. For instance, outside counsel should not use a partner to pen a simple status report when a less expensive associate can do just as good a job.

Time-management software should not be used simply for intra-office meetings and appointments; spend time rummaging around in the software manual and using its helpdesk features, because it can likely manage (and account for) every crumb of time spent by every person during every day, whether they are members of the department or are engaged by the department for specific projects or periods of time. More than just the top twenty pages of each yellow pad should be used. (I will ashamedly admit that a stack of half-used pads habitually clutters my own desk. This is a personal confession of my struggles with optimal resource management.) Money spent should be money *well* spent.

Justifying costs is the mission-critical element to justifying the contributing value of the legal department as a whole: understand and identify which resources are necessary for, and are used by, which specific projects, personnel, and tasks. Justifying costs is impossible to do unless you can tie resources to results. For instance, determine what physical resources (or what percentage of physical resources), personnel resources, and consulting or licensed resources are necessary for the research, drafting, and filing of a single utility-patent project. Do the means justify the ends?[5]

What are a few other ways to wisely shepherd a legal department's—and a client-company's—resources?

Aside from taking and monitoring inventory, mitigating costs, optimizing assets, and justifying resource usage, here are a few informal ways to make sure your legal department is running as efficiently and as capably as possible.

- Cultivate a good rapport and collaborative relationships with other departments. When you are shorthanded or in need of someone else's extra elbow grease or high-production copiers, those relationships will become priceless.
- Share resources when convenient, without compromising productivity. Offer idle or unused resources to others who might need them. This fosters those collaborative relationships, but it also optimizes, and therefore further justifies, your department's resources.
- Get involved in and familiar with all of your department's activities and how those activities are accomplished. This is a casual, ongoing audit process to identify inefficient or improper uses of resources, whether intentional or unintentional.

Resources are the beans and bullets of every legal department. Be inquisitive, practical, imaginative, and honest, and move your legal department's beans and bullets to the front lines as cost effectively and as expeditiously as possible.

§ 4.1.2 Personnel—Diplomacy at Work

Effective as of January 1, 2012, five partners from the law firm of Willkie Farr & Gallagher joined Bloomberg's legal department, including Dick DeScherer, who was named Bloomberg's chief legal officer.[6] The integration of these new hands was most likely a harmonious event: Mr. DeScherer had worked with Bloomberg for years and had served on Bloomberg's board of directors for more than twenty-five years. Willkie Farr & Gallagher had been retained by Bloomberg as its primary outside counsel since 1987. Instant camaraderie and previous relationships can make a significant difference. After all, diplomacy is needed less when one is among friends.

And yet, to state the obvious but routinely forgotten: dealing with people, even friends, is not a one-off occasion. Diplomacy and human psychology lie at the heart of building and managing a legal department's personnel team.

> Building a strong legal team starts with hiring people with the ideal mix of legal expertise and people skills, and then retaining those who best adapt to the collaborative culture. . . . [I]t's important to hire those who have a psychological predisposition to be happy in that environment.[7]

Even if your proprietary intellectual-property portfolio software seems to be the most complicated asset in your legal department, it is not. The most complicated assets, and the most valuable resources, are your department's personnel. A legal department's personnel may consist of departmental lawyers, paralegals, secretarial support, consultants, administrators, and outside or specialized counsel. Each category and each person will have his or her own responsibilities, expectations, goals, strengths, shortcomings, personality quirks, and tolerances.

Legal departments and a multitude of print and online resources expend great amounts of energy thinking about and addressing issues involving e-discovery, intellectual property, employment trends, litigation trends, technology, regulatory developments, and compliance, as well as benchmarking management techniques, surveys, and metrics. As well they should. These are all important and indispensable elements to successfully navigating the field of corporate law. However, the human element is as much a challenge for legal departments to understand and successfully address as every other issue in the corporate-law universe, and yet it is the human element that habitually slips through the fingers of most commentaries, and through the fingers of far too many supervising lawyers and administrators.

Interacting with humans requires more than just management. Typically, advice and information about supervising and working with employees is directed toward practical—and frequently very good—external methods to increase productivity, decrease tension and stress, improve efficiency, and foster creativity. We will discuss a few of these useful ideas in Section 4.3, but because the concept of this book is to give some earthy, basic perspectives to corporate lawyers, it is better to begin by suggesting a ground-level matrix through which legal departments—corporate lawyers—can come to grips with *people*.

Personnel Are People

Most lawyers, almost by natural design, have a short supply of the X-factor for managing and coping with other people in a teamwork-supportive fashion. Lawyers are not generally creatures of group hugs, motivational meetings, employee-of-the-month certificates, or copious amounts of sympathy. Indeed, the law acts as an enabler, as a comfortable arbiter of orderly measurements and unemotional—unpsychological—choices and determinations. It is comfortably *un*personal. Other personnel—other *people*—and the need to work with them, manage them, or answer to them, can give many lawyers hives.

I have a colleague, a fantastic lawyer whom I greatly respect, who believes office birthday parties are a complete waste of everyone's time.[8] He hates leaving his desk and heading down to the kitchen area to stand around in an instant-but-odd cocktail-party-like atmosphere, where everyone is eating cake, cracking bad jokes about getting older, and blurting out mental memos (such as, "Oh, Bob, I forgot to tell you I need an extra day to finish that memo") which mean nothing to everyone else who is listening. My friend is convinced people would prefer being handed a twenty-dollar bill on their birthday, with a few extra hours off work, than to munch on their choice of dessert and listen to their coworkers make a fatal wreck out of the melody to "Happy Birthday." For a few individuals (such as himself), he is absolutely right. For most people, however, an extra twenty bucks and a few hours off would be nice, but being the center of attention—even briefly—of peers, supervisors, and other staff members, somehow carries a lot more weight and significance. Why? Personnel are *people*, not automatons, and as social creatures (by an even deeper, natural design), humans crave recognition and belonging.

Note 68 of Chapter 1 promised that if you could pin down Abraham Maslow's Hierarchy of Needs,[9] then you would be masterful at your job. Although the footnote came during a look at the role of outside counsel, the suggestion is applicable to every corporate lawyer's job and almost every area of law. With a basic understanding of human needs and desires—and a conscious effort to use those needs and desires as prismatic lenses—a corporate lawyer, and a legal department, can go a long way toward unlocking motivations, settling disputes, avoiding unnecessary conflicts, forecasting reactions, and developing well-cut strategies. This is not subterfuge. This is simply paying attention to a person's "true north."

Abraham Maslow presumed human needs come from an individualistic perspective, and for corporate lawyers, who practice their craft in the legal departments of American corporations, that presumption makes perfect sense. An individualistic perspective means needs and desires tend to be more egocentric—self-centered—than collectivist. Though individuals will make personal sacrifices (such as staying late to make sure a task is finished) for the good of the whole, they will only do so if the collective whole—the legal department—has met, or is meeting, their own needs first. At first, this may sound tacky and ignoble, but for the moment, set aside any moral or principled judgments about this perspective's premise. This perspective relies on deducing a person's instinctive motivations, information that is priceless in any context where the collective whole (such as a legal department) depends on the smooth and peak functioning of its many individual members.

Roll up a pair of imaginary sleeves and consider the value of each of the following questions as they may apply to the personnel in your law department:

- Are they eating well? Sleeping well? Being given enough time to stay healthy? (Physiological level)

- Do they feel secure about their employment? Are they satisfied with their income and benefits? Are they having problems at home? (Safety level)
- Do they have a sense of departmental camaraderie (not clique-ish isolationism)? Would they consider anyone else in the department a friend (more than a coworker)? (Belonging level)
- Do they have a good sense of self-esteem? Do they have the respect of coworkers and supervisors? What are they proud of (in typical work product, awards, and accomplishments)? (Esteem level)
- Are they realizing their full potential? Do they understand where their greatest potential lies? (Self-actualization level)

Imagine how much better you would understand how each person functions, thinks, makes decisions, and handles a crisis with answers to these questions. By using these questions to approach your legal-department personnel—to approach everyone, as much as possible—you will find yourself with a far more content, mutually supportive, and productive *people-resource*.[10]

If, however, Abraham Maslow's theorizing provides only partial authority on its own, consider this minimalist, direct observation of those circumstances in which people operate in a high-stress, rigorously demanding, and sometimes antagonistic environment: "In war, morale is everything."[11]

Practical Points for Productivity

Because a legal department's most vital resource is its personnel, managing and justifying the costs of human assets requires a corporate lawyer to be watchful for the many ways in which the productivity of the department's personnel can be leached away: illness, vacations, computer downtime, lack of supplies, too many emails, excessive time on the Internet, time spent gossiping, and so on. The list of pitfalls can be endless, and there are many, many good suggestions and methods that have been developed to combat your personnel's attrition of time, focus, and productivity.

Most of these issues can be resolved through policy revisions and policy enforcement, or the application of old-fashioned common sense.[12] However, legal departments (and law offices) are just as susceptible to these pitfalls, and sometimes just as notorious for their lack of proficient workflow as entrenched bureaucracies. Just as the legal field struggled (and in some ways, still struggles) to exit the dark ages of ditto machines, carbon paper, handwritten briefs, note cards, and typewriters, so too has the legal field struggled to come to grips with the conscious realization that law is a business as much as it is a profession. With some rumblings and bumblings, it has increasingly begun to recognize its need for business-management consultants, marketing and advertising agencies, data-management companies, and other nonlawyer, business resources.

A legal department, as a business within a business, is an ideal environment for these kinds of administrative and productivity resources to come into play. They, not lawyers (with a few enviable exceptions), are the experts in running well-organized, efficient workplaces. Many legal departments start down this more productive path by installing a department administrator. An administrator usually performs in the same way a business manager does, and for legal-field-specific purposes, acts as liaison between lawyers and paralegals as well as the administrative staff. An administrator *runs* a legal department. An administrator's reporting relationship depends upon the structure and organization of the legal department, but he or she is most effective as the administrative right hand of the most senior lawyer (such as general counsel or chief legal officer). This way, an administrator has enough clout to get things done but defers to the ultimate decision of the department head.

For those legal departments that cannot afford an administrator, or are not big enough for an administrator or the assistance of other business-management resources, it is strongly recommended that you doff your barrister's wig and replace it with a manager's hat for as long as it takes to make sure your department's personnel are working efficiently and effectively.

"Bah, humbug!" you might say. "We're doing fine as we are." If some refrain of that nature crossed your mind as you were reading, or if you think you do not have the time to dedicate to optimizing the workflow and performance of your human assets, then I will leave you with a common, and deceptively benign, example of arch-inefficiency. An example of what most of us have been seduced into thinking is a "management thing" when, in fact, it is a wasteful, unproductive thing: *holding meetings.*

Carol Tice, a blogger for Entrepreneur.com, wrote an article attacking one of the all-time greatest offenders of wasted personnel resources: meetings.

> Unnecessary meetings cost the U.S. economy $37 billion a year, the U.S. Bureau of Labor Statistics once estimated.... The basic fact is that while workers are in meetings, they are not accomplishing their work. Still, we can't kick the meeting habit. Despite all the statistics that show meetings are a colossal waste of time, they continue to be scheduled—some three billion of them annually, by some estimates. And yet sometimes we need teams of people to coordinate what they're doing, or to plan something that needs to happen.[13]

In case you broke into a cold sweat as you realized how many meetings you have held, or been a participant of, in the past year, Ms. Tice provides seven excellent suggestions to slay the meetings dragon. Here are four of the seven, which should make immediate sense and be immediately applicable.

- Have a limited, focused agenda (suggestion one)
- Reconsider regularly scheduled meetings (suggestion two)
- Cut the attendee list (suggestion three)
- Send a memo (suggestion six)[14]

Meetings be gone! (Except for a few important ones, of course.)

Sharpen your management skills and maximize the potential of your personnel: bring some expertise to the table.

Personnel—the people you live with in the trenches every day—are the most critical elements to your legal department. Without their efforts and productivity, all the computers and software, and desks and swivel chairs, amount to nothing. Successful personnel management—optimizing effectiveness, work product, and corporate effort—begins with seeing them as individuals and balances that point of view with smart business administration.

At the fulcrum of those two objectives lives *diplomacy.*

Diplomacy

§ 4.1.3 Tasks—"Get 'Er Done"

The wise assignment of tasks and delegation of duties is essential to good management, effective oversight, accountability, and measurements of progress. Like a symphony's conductor, the person at the top must know how everything is done but must then step back and orchestrate the doing.

How does a corporate lawyer conduct a legal department's symphony?

Procedures

An efficient legal department should have orderly, predictable procedures for receiving requests (such as contract review), being notified of events (such as a subpoena), initiating projects (such as the filing of a lawsuit), and handling communications (such as requests for interviews). These procedures should schematically trigger assignments of tasks and oversight to appropriate personnel, detail a reporting structure, define benchmarks and deadlines for progress (or reports on progress) and individual roles, allocate resources (as necessary), and describe expectations for results (such as what the end product should be). These procedures need to be proactively oriented, anticipating the typical needs and requests of other departments, regulators, consultants, auditors, media groups, outside counsel, senior management, and board members.

As a rule, assignment procedures should be as simple as possible while remaining aware that sometimes being simple means not being thorough enough. Procedures for assignment of tasks should be tailored to the terrain of a legal department—its available assets and resources. Measurements and monitoring of progress should be cognizant of reasonable workloads and the diversity of tasks needing to be accomplished. End-result work product should reflect the expectations of the recipient and the reasonable capabilities of the legal department.

Exceptions will invariably occur, but as often as possible (even when it seems toilsome to staff members), stick with the department's procedures. When the moment comes—and it *will* come—that some higher power is demanding to know what happened to project X, request Y, or contract Z, or if they want to know its status *right now*, you and your department should be able to follow a formulaic diagram of assignment and progress from the moment the task was initiated to each of its points of progress to its final result. Smartly developed procedures—which are far too often the neglected, ignored, or clumsy cut-and-paste tools of many corporate departments—propagate streamlined workflows, timely communications, appropriate oversight, and, best of all for the client-company, high-quality legal services.

What are the key concepts to follow when creating and maintaining a legal department's routine processes for assignment, monitoring, and completion of its tasks and projects?

- Assign by strengths (but allow for cross-training to mitigate weaknesses and enhance departmental capabilities).
- Assign by resources.
- Distinguish tasks and projects by priority levels.
- Describe scope.
- Use predictable, preset deadlines for benchmark progression and completion.
- Use preset reporting patterns for decision making, progress, and completion.
- Use preset matrices for communications to be sent and received by the appropriate personnel.
- Identify and describe expectations for the final work product.
- Incorporate contingencies in case of absent personnel, higher-priority tasks or projects, resource unavailability, and general work interruptions.

Take every opportunity to spot-check tasks and projects for effective workflow. Welcome feedback from involved personnel. Constantly evaluate and be willing to correct procedures, depending on inefficiencies and changes in department resources and/or priorities. Communicate with other departments about timelines and expectations.

A Cautionary Tale

As of June 2012, the Ohio-based power-management company Eaton Corp. lost two of its in-house counsel over an eyebrow-raising gaffe during an eight-year-old ongoing lawsuit between Eaton and six of its former engineers and an aerospace manufacturer, Triumph Actuation Systems. Vic Leo, vice president and chief litigation counsel, and Sharon O'Flaherty, another member of Eaton's in-house litigation team, were reportedly fired, although Eaton did not officially comment on the circumstances of Mr. Leo's or Ms. O'Flaherty's exits from the company.[15] Apparently, new emails were discovered that somehow had not been timely disclosed to opposing counsel years earlier. Who exactly had been originally tasked with gathering, reviewing, and producing the undisclosed emails[16] (almost always an interdepartmental project between an IT department and a legal department and whoever else might have a decentralized email storage capability) may forever be lost in the gray mist of years-old litigation turmoil, but several of Eaton's senior personages were called upon to answer for the foul-up.

> On May 10, a judge ordered both lawyers [Leo and O'Flaherty]—along with CEO Alexander Cutler, general counsel Mark McGuire, chief in-house counsel Taras Szmagala Jr., and outside counsel Michael Schaalman of the Milwaukee law firm Quarles & Brady—to produce sworn affidavits explaining in detail why the emails weren't originally produced and who was responsible for their withholding.[17]

One of the greatest, and earliest, American writers of the personal-success genre, Napoleon Hill, said, "Big pay and little responsibility are circumstances seldom found together."

Task delegation is critical to efficient management, but efficiency means nothing without proper results, and proper results involve responsibility. Everyone, unofficially, and specific personnel, officially, need to understand and insist upon the need for accuracy, integrity, timeliness, thoroughness, and accountability throughout the course of every assignment and project. No one is immune from responsibility: support personnel, secretaries, legal assistants, paralegals, administrators, or lawyers. Corporate law is a multifaceted, high-stakes, demanding area of practice. Missteps can instantly and adversely affect an enormous number of people, their careers, and their livelihoods. Every task and project is embedded within the greater context of a larger business concern, and a lawyer's professional obligation to provide responsible, honest, reliable legal services is never more vital than it is when he or she is serving as legal counsel for a client-company.

Ultimately, your legal department's success in managing its task and project assignments as well as their progress and oversight, and the quality of the end-result services and products will come down to the department's ability to clearly communicate, and adhere to, its workflow procedures.

§ 4.1.4 Access—How Far Open Is Your Door?

Carole Basri and Irving Kagan[18] have provided a very direct and erudite observation of the two-part effect of a legal department's management and function.

> Few would dispute the fact that effectively managing the corporate law department enhances productivity, teamwork, efficiencies, timeliness, and quality of legal work. Full-time attention to the management of a law department is essential in providing the client with the finest legal services possible.[19]

This two-part effect is all about being present for duty.

Most of us believe we are accessible. We carry around our cell phones—which are virtual offices these days—and keep them on 24/7. We share calendars. We are constantly staring at our desktops or laptops. And many times we even offer the come-one, come-all suggestion to "call me any time, even if it's 5:00 a.m." And if you are like me, corporate clients will take you up on your brash invitation, and they will expect you to be wide awake and functioning at full steam. Somehow, though, all of that does not necessarily equal being present for duty— being *accessible*.

True accessibility is actually a *proactive* task, whether for an individual or for an entire department. Client-companies and other departments are really passive consumers, and if a legal department, or a corporate lawyer, does not remain proactively accessible, then communication can begin to break down, and important tasks, requests, or issues might begin to be overlooked or neglected. As Ms. Basri and Mr. Irving put it, managing (and participating in) a legal department requires "[f]ull-time attention[.]"[20]

Imagine your client-company and its different departments and constituents as being much like a baby. A baby is certainly capable of asking for things, usually by crying, spastically reaching out and grabbing, or incoherently gurgling. Client-companies can "communicate" in much the same way. Issues are emergencies by the time they make it to the legal department, or client-companies insist their issues get priority attention without any sense of what else is going on, or they are unclear and plagued with incomplete information. Corporations, however, are not cute, and problems can rarely be resolved by changing a diaper, babyproofing file drawers, spoon-feeding mashed carrots, or buying a sturdy plastic toy.[21] Corporations need expedient, thoughtful answers, and they need their corporate lawyers to anticipate their questions and needs in order to have those answers ready.

For legal departments and corporate lawyers, accessibility comes in the guise of preparedness. For a parent, it means having milk bottles ready, having diaper bags (and a keen nose) in good order, making sure fresh batteries are in the baby monitor, and putting the phone number for poison control on speed dial. For a corporate lawyer and a legal department, accessibility means more than just hanging a sign on the legal department's front door that says, "open for business." It means more than carrying around a cell phone 24/7 or saying, "You can reach me by email." Accessibility includes those things, but fundamentally, it means for a corporate lawyer and a client-company's legal department to instigate communication, anticipate questions and needs, and encourage routine interactions between legal staff and the rest of the client-company.

Access, from a client-company's perspective, should mean the legal department has actively involved itself in supporting other departments, executives, and other constituents. The legal department does not merely sit at idle until a situation or issue emerges. Access does not equal passivity. The affably favored open-door policy pitched by most managers and support departments should be a door-opens-both-ways policy for a legal department. Its resources—lawyers and staff—are walking *out* the door and into other departments as much as other departments can walk in through the door whenever the need arises.

Client-companies that become accustomed to their legal departments and their corporate lawyers preemptively asking, "How are things going?" and "Can we help with anything?" are going to be much more likely to raise questions *before* grass fires start and before anything has exploded, and they are going to have a better sense of how to incorporate and make use of a legal department's resources effectively and routinely in their own business and support activities.

"Wait a second!" you might be thinking. "My legal department already has too much work to do. How can it possibly become 'more accessible' by traipsing around, deliberately eating up time, while asking if anyone needs anything?"

Good question.

An initial answer comes from a counterintuitive fact: when a legal department begins to access its client-company, instead of leaving the question of accessibility to the client-company, tasks and projects become more orderly and predictable and less desperate (in timelines and/or priorities), and more issues are dealt with before they become problems. Lawyers are generally trained to think in terms of disaster. This pre-programming gives corporate lawyers a distinctive way of approaching almost every issue: presume the issue will eventually become a problem. This perspective results in effort and creativity being expended on developing hedges against possible future problems. Very few other employees, or client-company constituents, will be trained to think that way. Nor does a doomsday mentality play a necessary part in their daily work assignments.

When a legal department and its lawyers "access" a client-company, the result is one of the best preventive law strategies: troubleshoot before there is trouble. Ironically, when accessibility is left to the client-company—waiting for other departments to walk through your open door—trouble has, many times, already begun to bloom. Proactivity eventually creates less work, or work that is less involved, less urgent, and less stressful.

Another answer lies in creating an ideal organizational structure for a legal department, taking into account the department's intent to be proactively accessible. Legal departments, as microcosm businesses, have the same need for organization that a greater client-company has. There must be descriptive lines of authority, areas of responsibility, and established channels of communication. Personnel, and the rest of the client-company, need to know who makes what kinds of decisions and who is responsible for getting what done.

The need for workable organization should be a no-brainer (although I have been unpleasantly surprised, sometimes, by the haphazard, unpredictable, and nebulous structure I have found in some departments).[22] We discussed corporate structure to some extent in Section 2.1.1, so we will not re-till the same soil here, but recall there are several ways to become organized, each with its own pros and cons and power bases. When a legal department's organization and decision-making structure include its intent to actively engage its resources with other departments, workflows become more streamlined, communication becomes more efficient, and every task and project becomes more fluid, less disruptive, and easier to accomplish.

Running a legal department—being a contributing part of a legal department—takes full-time attention. Being accessible to a client-company is the means by which a legal department meets its objective: to be a valuable support element for a client-company's core business, even at 5:00 a.m.

Accessibility

A successful, efficient legal department is always the sum of its parts. It houses the legal brain trust of a client-company, providing well-managed resources, proficient personnel, efficient workflow management, and proactive contributions to the rest of a client-company's departments and constituency. A thriving legal department is a business within a business, with its own plan and a collective sense of its supportive purpose and tailored methodologies.

§ 4.2 PLANNING AND BUDGETS

Jonathan Oviatt, chief legal officer of the Mayo Clinic, has observed:

> Legal departments are increasingly held to exactly the same standard as all other service areas. We're expected to be continuously improving our value proposition, the quality of our services, the turnaround time of our delivery.[23]

Strategic planning and budgeting create the framework for a legal department's ultimate valuation by its client-company. Those departments without deliberate planning, and without a reliable accounting of costs (and what drives costs), will eventually fall apart under the glare of a client-company's cost-benefit analysis. This is the hard and fast fact about corporate legal departments of the present day: their support services had better contribute to a company's bottom line. "Whether or not business worsens, one thing is near-certain, however: Corporations are going to pay even closer attention than before to the performance of shared services, such as the legal department."[24]

A legal department's performance measurements and benchmarks will be predicated upon the usefulness of its planning and budgeting processes and internal evaluation. When the time comes (quarterly, semiannually, or annually) for a general counsel to face his or her CEO and talk turkey about the economic efficiency of the legal department, it will be the department's planning and budgetary management that will make the long-term difference.

How, then, should a legal department deal with the Sword of Damocles[25] that is economic justification?

How should strategic planning and budgeting be approached?

For the most part, unless a lawyer has previously acted as defense counsel for an insurance company, has had to put together a business plan to take out a line of credit or a traditional business loan, is regularly involved in investment banking or mergers and acquisitions, or has been involved in a law firm's finance committee and has become accustomed to reviewing balance sheets and business valuation models, the word *budget* can strike insecurity and trepidation into the stoutest of hearts. *Planning ahead*—except for routine demands of normal litigation—and *budgeting*—except for uncommon circumstances (especially budgeting for a department)—are relatively foreign concepts for lawyers. Legal departments, without the benefit of an experienced administrator, can fall prey to that state of unfamiliarity, and legal departments can find themselves struggling to make business sense of their existence and ongoing survival.

Budgeting (such as annual budgeting) is a form of planning, so we will first discuss how to approach, and get your legal department's arms around, its atlas: strategic planning.

§ 4.2.1 Assess, Acclimate, and Aspire

Corporate planning for almost every other business department (most of which are likely permeated with MBAs or other business-trained personnel) can actually become ponderous, ungainly, and a hindrance. Ironically, planning—when imbibed with too many layers and needless redundancy—can slowly choke a department into inefficiencies and waste. Planning, of its own accord, can deviously become the brass ring, replacing a department's real purpose: to make, or support the making of, money. Legal departments need to be aware of this risk, but for corporate lawyers, who are not naturally schooled to "plan, plan, plan," it is far more likely that a good notion of strategic planning will *help*, not hinder, the survival and efficiency of the department.

At the risk of sounding trite, if your legal department (or your unit) does not have a plan, then how does it know where it's going, where it should go, or how it will get where it needs to be?

There are a variety of corporate planning techniques. I have been largely referring to one technique, *strategic planning*, as the interchangeable pseudonym for planning at large. For our purposes, strategic planning, as opposed to long-term planning, for instance, is a better fit.[26] Strategic planning typically spans a single year, or it can be project specific. Planning strategically for a legal department can help keep the immediate horizon in focus while clearly describing where the department intends to be productively, financially, and organizationally at a later date.

Strategic planning is normally based upon some very simple, clear components any group of lawyers should be able to get their heads around and which should set the rhythm for your legal department's budget, and *justify* that budget.

- *Forecast*—This is commonly referred to as describing a *vision* for your department, but that word smacks of indefiniteness in my mind. However, if you *forecast* an event, or any view of future circumstances, you are closer to predicting than merely having an opinion (a vision) about where you anticipate things will be. Prediction requires commitment. Be realistic; keep it simple.
  - *Where does your department stand right now?*
    - "It takes our legal department two weeks to complete a due-diligence analysis for a proposed acquisition."
  - *What is the forecast for the legal department?*
    - "To reduce the time it takes for due-diligence analysis for proposed acquisitions from two weeks to one week."
- *Purpose*—This is commonly referred to as the *mission statement.* Nothing wrong with that phrase, but having a purpose makes it more personal: everyone onboard, everyone at the oars, everyone pulling in rhythm. The legal department's purpose is how it actualizes its forecast.
  - *What is your department's purpose (over the next year)?*
    - "To provide high-quality legal counsel to the client-company by instituting preventive measures into all support functions, providing prompt and accessible communications with other departments, efficiently managing outside legal counsel, and economically managing workflows for optimal proficiency and work product."
- *Culture*—This is commonly referred to as describing *values*, but merely stating values can be too cliché and short-winded. Your legal department's description of its culture should reflect its purpose and the makeup of its personnel, but it should also reflect the broader culture of the client-company. The culture of the legal department suggests its priorities.
  - *What are your department's cultural values?*
    - "To insist upon, and consistently audit for, the provision and delivery of first-rate legal services through our attention to detail, concern for others, personal initiative, accessibility to the client, professionalism, and reliable work ethic."

- *Strategy*—Here is the meat on the bone. These are the descriptions of various goals and objectives and the means, policies, and procedures intended to accomplish those goals. Usually, strategy development will follow one of two widely used methods: a *situation-target-proposal* method or a *draw-see-think-plan* method. Both methods are, generally speaking, facsimiles of each other; the former method uses statements (such as "situation: evaluate the present situation"), whereas the latter method uses questions (such as "see: What is today's situation?"). Here is a simple example of the situation-target-proposal method:
  - *Situation:*
    - "Commercial loan contract review process requires one week."
  - *Target:*
    - "To reduce the commercial loan contract review process time to three days."
  - *Proposal:*
    - "Assign staff member to audit commercial loan contracts for standard compliance parameters and policy controls. Assign staff lawyer to audit commercial loan contracts for substantive and loan-specific risks and parameters. Procure document sharing platform with simultaneous editorial capabilities."

Developing a strategic plan for your legal department that addresses all of these key components comes down to three simple verbs: *assess*, *acclimate*, and *aspire*. First, *assess* the current condition of the department, how it currently manages and accomplishes its tasks and projects, what its capabilities and resources are able to absorb, and how flexible management and the use of those resources can be if needed. Next, envisage how your legal department can *acclimate*—adjust and adapt—to increases in efficiency, more goals or more-complex goals, and greater demands (in time and results) on its services. Finally, conceive of how to reasonably and methodically *aspire* to achieve benchmarks of change and improvement.[27] Out of these three approaches, a workable, well-formed, and realistic strategic plan can easily be created.

Most Importantly . . .

Of all the topics to scrutinize when you are launching into your planning, *workflow*—the sequence of events and persons through which a task or project flows from beginning to end—is the most important in terms of identifying room for improvement and budget validation.

Experts say the most effective way to reduce costs is to conduct workflow analyses, which essentially study how tasks are distributed within and outside of the law department. The goal of such analyses is to help in-house teams logically redistribute work to maximize its value, implement the correct processes so they can effectively manage their work portfolios on an ongoing basis, and better estimate and plan for their projected legal spending.[28]

Workflow analyses will expose everything else necessary for well-developed strategic planning. Begin there, and you will begin well.

Workflow

§ 4.2.2 The Balance Sheet—Pens, Pencils, and Legal Pads

"There's no getting away from it: numbers rule our professional lives. Even the legal department cannot avoid a razor-sharp focus on quantifying its operations."[29]

Over the past fifteen to twenty years, corporate legal departments have begun experiencing greater involvement in their client-companies' budgeting processes, as well as the direct responsibility to develop their own departmental budgets. Business—including the business of providing corporate legal services—is quantified by numbers. Numbers squeezed out of assets and liabilities. Numbers originating in line-item budget descriptions. Numbers that eventually tell a tale of whether a corporation is liquid, successful, growing, or headed for a cliff.

Budgets and the budgeting process can take on all manner of manifestations and formats. Conceptually, budgets are a component of microeconomics: the study of the behavior of an entity's decisions regarding the allocation of limited resources. In other words, a budget is the financial way—the *numbers* way—of describing the cost constraints of a task or project, the forecast of revenues and expenditures, and the way to measure actual operations against that forecasting. For legal departments as service departments, where it is unusual to be able to demonstrate direct revenue streams, the greater concentration gives way to the dark side: expenditures.

So how does a legal department develop a defensible budget?

"[S]taff numbers and expenses—both relative to total corporate revenue[,]"[30] are the bellwether measurements of a positive cost-benefit analysis or a negative cost-benefit analysis by a client-company. The ugly fact is, a chief financial officer may really be concerned only about expenses when it comes time to assess the economic efficiency of a legal department.[31] Because this is the case (or at least a good presumption with which to begin), a legal department should craft its budget against the backdrop of a departmental balance sheet.

A *balance sheet*, simply put, lines up assets and liabilities. In one column, list all of your department's assets—this goes back to the resources analysis we discussed in Section 4.1.1—and the value (if known), minus depreciation, of each asset. Do not forget to include nonmonetary assets, such as your personnel. In a column mirrored to your assets, list all your department's liabilities. These are expenses that should correspond to assets. Some assets, such as your personnel, will not have a specific monetary positive value; their value lies in the service they provide. This correlative value is what will eventually need to be tied (directly or indirectly) to your client-company's net revenues in order to demonstrate economic efficiency.[32]

Once your balance sheet is drawn up, you can develop a budget. You should know what you have, what it costs, and what you will need in the future. This budget exhibits how your legal department will operate on the resources it has, or will have, and what those resources will cost. Those costs will be counted against your client-company's revenue, but when that happens (as you stare across the table at the CEO or the CFO), you will be able to justify the costs by discussing how the legal department's support services indirectly (or directly) offset those costs, contribute to decreasing the client-company's other costs (such as "preventive risk management led to a 10 percent decrease in workers' compensation payments"), or contribute to increasing the client-company's revenue (such as "this past year's successful patent infringement lawsuit added an additional $2 million to licensing revenues").

Legal departments are almost always "cost centers" for a corporation. However, the benefits of their services as they contribute to and influence better governance, better risk management, better employment practices, more efficient litigation management, better intellectual-property programs and protections, and improved compliance can be measureable advantages. These can be monetized with the right approach to a legal department's balance sheet and budget.

There is no reason a well-run legal department's numbers should not demonstrate an actualized financial benefit to a client-company. Therein lies a department's economic efficiency.

§ 4.2.3 Reporting

Reports seem to represent one of the necessary evils in the corporate world. At its most fundamental expression, a report should provide a summary designed to convey progress, digression, or a result. In such a context, reports have real value. They are the means by which to communicate benchmarks, achieved or unachieved. This information is useful to almost every level of a corporate organization. Companies report to shareholders, lenders, regulators, consumers, and the public. Boards report to shareholders. Executives report to each other and to boards. Management reports to executives. Departmental personnel or units report to management. By staying abreast of progress, or digression, recipients are able to make timely and informed decisions. Reporting is an essential part of good governance practices and effective management.

Periodic reporting is a fairly routine part of corporate life, and a legal department should take its reporting requirements seriously. If no reporting requirements are in place, or if the only reporting requirement is an annual report, then a legal department should give serious consideration to self-imposing reporting requirements, or more frequent reporting requirements, such as quarterly or semiannually. A by-product of reporting is feedback. The more often you let a decision maker know what is going on, the more often you will have the opportunity to take corrective action before it is too late, or the more often you receive confirmation that what is going on is working.

Reports by a legal department, or internally within a legal department, are fantastic occasions to communicate with a client-company and its decision makers in a comprehensive format.[33] Reporting comes in all kinds of layouts and presentations. For example, there are financial reports, auditor's reports, census reports, scientific reports, investigative reports, budget reports, appraisal reports, and progress reports.

A legal department's reports should be customized to its activities and to the information needs and expectations of the reports' recipients. For less frequent, more comprehensive reports, I have found *checkpoint* reports to be useful. These are really nothing more than progress reports. Generally, a legal department's periodic reports should consider including discussions and information on the following topics:

- An executive summary
- A list of accomplishments and how they relate to previously stated objectives
- A budget and budget analysis
- A discussion of the department's strategic, or long-term, plan
- A review of human resource issues and training
- A review of litigation issues (new, pending, closed) and litigation counsel

The less frequently a report is generated, the more comprehensive it should be. Conversely, more-recurrent reports should be focused and, perhaps, driven by specific projects, lawsuits, or tasks, instead of attempting global repetitions of topics that may experience little to no change in shorter periods of time. "When words are scarce, they are seldom spent in vain."[34]

How can a legal department communicate its progress, externally and internally, without counterproductively wasting too much time on reporting or ineffective reporting?

Especially in flattened hierarchies, where there is increased autonomy and responsibility spread out among several decision makers (a frequent environment for legal departments in which lawyers exercise a great amount of independent authority and control over specific projects and tasks), accurate and timely communication about progress is critical. However, the need to communicate—to report—can create its own difficulties and inefficiencies, unless the reporting process, and style, is well managed.

In this instance, low tech beats high tech.

5/15 Reporting

Yvon Chouinard, the founder and former CEO of Patagonia, Inc., a manufacturer of clothing, accessories, and luggage designed for the outdoors, is credited with inventing the *5/15* reporting method. The idea is that a report should take no more than fifteen minutes to write and no more than five minutes to read.[35] By imposing those two time requirements, frequent reports can stay very predictable and very streamlined.

Within a legal department, a 5/15-style report can be modeled on person-to-person reporting, project-driven reporting, unit reporting, or topic reporting. Choose the right method to provide the information needed at the time, and change the method as necessary. Assign reporting responsibilities to each person: describe the method, the frequency of the report, and the recipient. Each 5/15 report should include a simple three-part description:

- What has happened in the past week (or the prescribed reporting time period)?
- Is the activity on track to meet its benchmarks, or has its progress has been interrupted? If so, why?
- What, if anything, will improve efficiency and progress (that is, troubleshoot)?

If this method does not work for your department, take the concept of shortened, focused reporting and develop a method that does work. Noncommunication is not an option, and "reporting" that is consists of "stopping by for a second to talk about X" is unreliable, too limited, untraceable, and far too vulnerable to all kinds of mistakes and missed or deficient information.

Reporting is a vital part of well-informed planning, and strategic planning is, along with budgeting and cost justification, a vital part of running and validating a legal department's existence and activities to a client-company. No one needs to run out the door and earn a master's in business administration or a degree in accounting to make these things happen.

Be realistic. Assess.

Keep it simple. Acclimate.

Be deliberate. Aspire.

§ 4.3 Managing Others: The World's __?__ Boss

David Hechler wrote an article entitled "Best Legal Department 2011 Winner: Google," in which he observed the following about Google's in-house legal team's environment:

> There are no offices. The renovation of their building that [Kent] Walker [Google's general counsel] ordered last year for the law department was part of an "open style" in hierarchy and architecture. "We don't have an open-door policy," he explains. "We have a no-door policy."
>
> And they reach decisions by consensus, abetted by a multitude of inviting spaces where lawyers are encouraged to congregate—including a library reading room with a virtual fireplace.[36]

Granted, with the explosive growth of Google over the past decade, "It's hard to know even the whole legal department"[37] (numbering over 200 lawyers worldwide). But in spite of any inconvenience, it appears Google's legal department, and the department's senior management, have got a good thing going.

That is no easy task.

In Mr. Hechler's brief description, the emphasis and importance Google's legal department attaches to its people assets are easy to spot: communication flows freely (remember *accessibility?*), hierarchy is flattened, morale is valued, and the use of consensus brings together department-wide talent and knowledge. This endorses what we discussed in Section 4.1.2: the most valuable asset for any legal department is going to be its personnel. "Interacting with humans requires more than just management." Having addressed the baseline context of how to *understand* and *approach* a legal department's personnel as a first, broader step, we can now turn our attention to some of the more practical ways to *manage* people assets.

A corporate lawyer, whether he or she is in charge of a single staff member or the entire legal department, will discover that success in management—overseeing a respective area of responsibility—has a direct correlation to success with people. Successful management of people assets takes the right amount of poise, decisiveness, and tractability. Success with people—the underpinning to successful management—is the result of balance: empathy, active listening, and firmness, all in the right measure, resolved to lead to the best result for the client-company.

Management

Importantly, keep in mind such a notion calls for even-handedness too. Empathy, active listening, and firmness cannot be fickle or selective. They must be uniformly applied—not mechanically or thoughtlessly, but with rational consistency. Security, and a willingness to work for the greater good of the whole, comes out of a sense of belonging, and belonging comes out of a sense of being treated equally, whether in reward, recognition, or punishment.

A fair-minded iron hand in a kid glove.

Legal departments are uniquely situated communities within the legal profession. They possess the distinct characteristic of having every member working for the same client.[38] Everyone's common goal is the business success of a client-company, not the result of a single lawsuit, a single project, or a billable hour's goal. Departmental personnel can more readily identify with the greater whole, instead of their own individual circumstances.

A legal department's ethos and procedures are better able to change or shift in communal cadence. Even when one unit, such as the intellectual-property unit, can boast of an important success while another unit, the mergers and acquisitions unit, is struggling with a disintegrating deal, a legal department's value to a client-company is evaluated and felt *en masse*. This characteristic—working for a single, shared client—is a fantastic way to establish a sense of long-term teamwork. Moreover, successfully and uniformly managing a legal department's personnel can then become an easier job when that standard of collectivism is emphasized.

Google-esque work environments may be popular (and enviable), but most legal departments deal with walls, cubicles, intercoms, and doors that can click shut. That is OK. These environments can work just as well. Offices without doors may help foster teamwork and collaboration, but those dynamics have more to do with how you manage *people* than how many virtual fireplaces populate your office spaces. Having an understanding of personnel as people, applying supervision in an even-handed way, and accentuating the collective awareness of everyone pulling for the same, larger goal are the real-world ways most legal departments are able to unhinge their doors, cultivate fellowship, and inspire solidarity and enthusiasm.

Therefore, our challenge at this point is to decipher some of the more specific techniques for managing different personnel demographics: a legal department's lawyers, paralegals, and staff, consultants, and out-side counsel.

§ 4.3.1 Lawyers

Managing begins with hiring.

Nowhere is this more evident than in a legal department's efforts to recruit lawyers. A novel but amazingly sensible approach to hiring the right kind of legal counsel has as much to do with what—or *who*—the legal department represents as it does with the quality of a potential new candidate-for-hire: "You want the legal department to look like the stakeholders you deal with."[39] This piece of advice, shared by Cameron Findlay, the general counsel of Medtronic, makes perfect sense in other ways too. "There are also business benefits. Juries are not all 50-year-old white males. Regulators are not all 50-year-old white males. Our customers are not all 50-year-old white males."[40]

With this kind of hiring mindset, a legal department's pen of law-yers should be a much more manageable group. Why? A legal depart-ment serves a distinct, unique client. If a legal department's core people assets—its lawyers—reflect a client's same kind of distinctiveness, then there is a good chance the departmental culture, and the methodologies for approaching and resolving tasks and projects, will also reflect the client-company's values and qualities. The resulting effort to manage—to direct energies and creativity—will not lose precious time dealing with ideals, goals, or attitudes that rarely, if ever, align themselves with the client-company.

Do not worry. Because lawyers are schooled—formed from their shoes up—to work and prosper in an adversarial profession, they only possess a trivial, if existent at all, inclination to become yes-men. Law-yers are bred to have individualistic opinions. Hiring lawyers for shared principles and sensibilities that reflect those of a client-company will not spontaneously quash contrary points of view. But from a management (and corporate culture) perspective, these divergent vantages will most likely replicate the differing interests and ideals that exist within the greater client-company.

A custom-built petri dish of legal talent.

Once the right kind of hiring mentality is in place, and your legal department's lawyers epitomize a scaled-down version of your client-company's stakeholders, how can you capitalize on their talents?

First, make sure your lawyers are working with complete information. (Or as complete as you can make it.)

Allow me to explain.

Lawyers—presumably the ones you have hired—are very good at what they do, but like any intelligence officer, their advice and performance are constrained by the limits of the information they possess about any given task, project, or problem. Poor information leads to poor strategies and poor results, which is a management nightmare. Strangely perhaps, one of the best ways to effectively manage a lawyer is to make sure he or she has the best information possible. Armed with that, lawyers will deliver anticipated, useful results (or reveal an inability to do so); they will deliver the right kind of work product (or reveal a lack of training or experience); and they will deliver thoughtful, well-reasoned advice (or reveal a disposition to be too hasty). From a management perspective, it will be far easier to assign and oversee lawyers when you know their limits, work ethic, methods of reasoning, and styles of delivery. Providing complete information is not only the best way to assign tasks, it is the best "technology" for making sense of, and learning to successfully use, your lawyer assets.

Second, push the limits of their comfort zones. Thomas Lalla, the senior vice president and general counsel of Pernod Ricard USA, makes this suggestion: "[E]ach of us should be a catalyst for change that enhances our own legal skills and those of our attorneys and paralegals."[41] Some of Mr. Lalla's ideas for moving corporate lawyers, and all staff members, beyond their normal borders, are as follows:

- Invite representatives from various business units to address your legal team about their initiatives and business plans.
- Incorporate in-house training conducted by members of your legal team.
- Encourage your team to become involved in professional opportunities outside the department.
- Engage your team in off-site, community-service-related activities.[42]

This builds team confidence, enhances team members' skills, acclimates their interaction with other client-company constituents, keeps them challenged, and helps you to create tactical redundancy in your legal department. At the end of the day, your legal team is going to be far more well-rounded, proficient, and well informed about other perspectives throughout the legal department and the client-company. Most cleverly perhaps, this brings your lawyers to your side of the table. They will share a larger view of what it takes to successfully manage themselves and the rest of the legal department's personnel.

With a staff of lawyers who reflect the client-company's makeup, work with the best information possible, and continuously push their own comfort limits, your efforts to successfully manage this unruly breed of personnel will most certainly bear good fruit.

§ 4.3.2 Paralegals and Support Personnel

There is an Indian proverb that says, "You cannot cut off a man's nose and then hand him a rose to smell."

Because lawyers stereotypically hold such strong opinions about almost everything, they can find it particularly hard to assign a task to another person and let it go. Too bad. Effective management of a legal department's support personnel—its paralegals, legal secretaries, data managers, secretaries, and assistants—requires your ability to *supervise*, not do it yourself. In light of the six steps we will momentarily discuss, good managers will not go about supervising by enforcing a do-it-my-way-or-hit-the-highway set of policies, procedures, and expectations. Be flexible when you can be and open to your staff's suggestions and feedback. This incorporates them into the process, which creates teamwork and pride, without yielding ultimate control. No one wants to work for, or does his or her best when working for, a draconian taskmaster.

You can tell your staff how to smell, when to smell, what to smell, and what it should smell like, but the first rule of effective management is to let them keep their noses.

As with managing lawyers, management begins with the hiring process. Make sure your staff has the emotional stamina and the wits to get the job done. Frankly, if they do not, get rid of them. Look beyond their résumés and make sure they are a good fit. You have to be able to trust them, work with them, correct them, depend on them, and (notably) make them feel good about their jobs. It is a work relationship, but it *is* a relationship. Be selective.

With the right kind of support personnel in place, there are a few key concerns to which you must always pay attention. If you do, then managing will (mostly) be a snap.

- *Clarify duties*—Beyond written procedures and job descriptions, take the time to think about, and verbally communicate to each member of your support staff, what is expected of them. This is critical. You will be mildly surprised to realize how different it is to talk about day-to-day expectations versus what is written in a job description or set out in a procedural manual. This is also an ongoing process. As often as is needed, check with your staff to make sure they understand what is expected, and be ready to discuss those duties that are infrequent but important, hard to accomplish, or have been neglected.
- *Clarify reporting, supervision, and performance review*—This is where the rubber meets the road. Clarifying reporting, supervision, and performance reviews with each staff member sets out the expectation of benchmarks and oversight. This embeds personal accountability into everything they do. They will *expect* to be evaluated, corrected, and rewarded. Ultimately, this gives them a measurable sense of accomplishment.
- *Assign duties and tasks according to professional training and personal characteristics*—A *paralegal* is a paralegal by training *and* by personality (hopefully), or he or she should not be a paralegal. A hammer has very little use when it comes time to change a light bulb. Routinely (informally and formally) assess your support staff for skill sets and the ability to accomplish assigned duties and tasks.
- *Encourage training*—Or require it. Training sharpens a person's proficiency level, but it is also a source of encouragement and satisfaction. The better trained your staff is, the more manageable they are.
- *Coordinate workflows*—The way a task or project flows through a legal department arguably has the single greatest impact on efficiency and quality work product. Staff members need to be a part of those work schematics. They will not only have some excellent input, they will also have a sense of ownership over each work stream and will work to resolve inefficiencies.

- *Establish policies and procedures for interaction with other departments and managers*—A large part of the communication from a legal department, and the rest of a client-company, flows through the support staff. Make sure they are communicating with a uniform perspective and with the appropriate personnel from other departments.

When a legal department suffers from poor performance or the disjointed efforts of its support personnel, it is almost a foregone conclusion that one or more of these six steps have been overlooked or inadequately implemented. In short, here is the takeaway point:

> Surround yourself with the best people you can find, delegate authority, and don't interfere as long as the policy you've decided upon is being carried out.

Whether or not you like his brand of politics, this quote from former president Ronald Reagan hits upon the finest reflection of successful management—specifically, *the management of legal department personnel*, even if his remark did not anticipate that.

§ 4.3.3 Consultants

Except for large legal departments, it is not common for a legal department, or corporate lawyers, to think about working with a *consultant*—any person, entity, or agency engaged by a legal department or client-company to provide expert advice or services. But one of the primary functions, if not *the* primary function, of a legal department is to work with consultants: outside counsel.

Because of this primary function, there is a growing library of commentary on how to manage outside counsel (typically, litigation counsel and associated costs). We will jump into that particular puddle in the next section, but legal departments of almost any size will, at one time or another, find themselves dealing with or directly managing consultants other than outside counsel for a wide variety of purposes: technology, e-discovery, budgeting/auditing, compliance, public relations, workflow analyses, lobbying, and financing. Thankfully, managing a consultant, irrespective of the consultant's area of expertise, does not need to be an uncomfortably foreign or complicated undertaking. Concepts for managing consultants of any stripe have an all-purpose application and use common-sense principles.

- *Establish expectations*—As with support personnel, a legal department needs to establish very clear expectations with a consultant, preferably through a contractual agreement. Everyone should know *who* is expected to do what, *when* it is expected, *where* (and *how*) it will be performed, and *in what manner* it is expected. Clearly spell out what will constitute a satisfactory job, who will perform maintenance and periodic oversight, and what constraints are on information, access, use, personnel, and time. Be thorough and consciously ask (repeatedly) if anything is unclear or needs further explaining.
- *Assign a point person*—This is straightforward but critical. Assign one person to be the conduit between the legal department and the consultant. This centralizes information, promotes efficiency, and clarifies accountability and oversight. Just make sure to properly supervise your point person.
- *Communicate regularly*—Emphasizing what we said regarding establishing expectations, make sure that regular communications, both formal reports and informal conversations, are taking place between the legal department and the consultant (largely through the point person). Consistent communication will increase productivity, proactively avoid most problems, and leave little room for lackluster results.
- *Keep staff informed*—Although you should have a single point person in place, make sure other members of the legal department know who the consultant is, what the consultant will be doing, why the consultant will be doing it, and what part, if any, a staff member may need to play in the process. This leads to better planning, avoids confusion (or feelings of insecurity), and creates an indirect group of eyes and ears to monitor the consultant's activities and progress.
- *Give yourself an out*—Again, this should be a contractual provision. Be careful to give yourself, the legal department, and the client-company a safe exit strategy, available at any point in the consulting process, if benchmarks are not being met, the consultant is not properly staffing the project, reporting is inconsistent or useless, billing (and any work) is superfluous or outside the scope of the project, or the consultant is simply not a good fit. Follow your exit protocols and obligations closely to minimize

liability, but do not hesitate to be adamant about the need to end the relationship if it is not working out.

This, then, leads us to the question of managing the peculiarities of the number-one consultant hired by, or engaged by, a legal department: outside counsel.[43]

§ 4.3.4 Outside Counsel—The Other Lawyers

Though many legal departments have begun to incorporate more concentrated areas of law into their own range of capabilities, legal departments have traditionally looked to outside counsel for augmented, specialized legal resources, such as litigation, securities filings, bankruptcy, mergers and acquisitions, intellectual property filings, internal investigations, bond issuance, and securities placement and offerings. As with other consultant resources, however, legal departments remain responsible to their client-companies for the performance, value, and results of outside counsel. For these reasons, "CLOs are looking for increased value from their outside law firms—expecting their firms to provide the 'appropriate lawyer-to-task' and are looking for 'improved budget and matter management.'"[44]

Good outside-counsel relationships are hard won over time. Law firms are not accustomed to being managed by lawyers outside the firm. Certain areas of practice, such as insurance defense, are similar to this kind of situation, but usually, those other areas involve nonlawyer administrators. Engagement with a legal department means an outside firm is acting as the department's surrogate on behalf of the client-company. Numerous legal departments—especially over the past ten to fifteen years—approach this as a master/agent relationship, and in many technical respects, it is. But for effective management purposes, a too-vertical arrangement breeds tension and stymies open communication. The preferable approach is to encourage the idea that the outside counsel is "one of the team."[45] As that awareness takes hold, outside counsel is more likely to proactively take cost-saving measures, promptly and timely communicate, be more open and supportive to strategic direction, and be more eager to deliver work product in the way it is expected.

Practical elements of management then fall into place.

Guidelines, budgets, and other aspects of an outside counsel program are meaningless if they are not managed. Formal processes are necessary to efficiently manage outside counsel, to enforce outside counsel guidelines, and to manage budget compliance.[46]

Bret Baccus and Matthew Schuetz, both directors of Huron Consulting Group, Inc., and consultants who spend their days working with law firms and corporate clients to enhance their operational and strategic efficiency, suggest ten steps to successfully manage outside counsel:[47]

1. Choose the right firm for the work and desired outcome.
2. Establish a baseline budget.
3. Leverage resources efficiently.
4. Pay the right price for the services provided.
5. Validate pricing using benchmarks.
6. Review historic and current billing data for trends in pricing.
7. Establish an appropriate (alternative?) fee arrangement.[48]
8. Manage outside-counsel expenses.
9. Update and strengthen all outside-counsel guidelines.
10. Regularly review and measure the effectiveness of your outside-counsel management program.

Several of Mr. Baccus and Mr. Schuetz's recommendations could migrate back and forth between our discussions of consultants at large and outside counsel, specifically. The contrast comes from the exceptionality of a legal department's relationship with outside counsel. Within the scope of their assignment, outside counsel is interchangeable with a legal department—something that does not happen with any other kind of consultant. Greater scrutiny, greater demands, and greater expectations naturally follow.

A parting thought about managing people assets: If you ever happen to travel to Japan, you will notice you never refill your own glass while eating a meal. Whoever you are eating with fills it for you. In turn, you keep his or her glass filled. No one has to ask for more water (水), tea (茶), sake (酒), or beer (ビール). Everyone is looking out for everyone else's needs, and in that way, everyone receives everything they need.

Set an example for the people you manage and work with. Refill someone else's glass.

There are few things more meaningful, more magnanimous, or more effective than genuine humbleness. People *respond* to a leader who has the dignity and the sincerity to admit when he or she is wrong, needs help, or is not the smartest person in the room. Be self-assured enough to apologize when it is needed. Be deferential enough to be the first to recognize someone else's talent or contribution. Be modest enough to refrain from reminding everyone of your own accolades (even if well deserved).

Managing other people is a balance of empathy, active listening, firmness, and being humble enough to lead.

§ 4.4 MULTIPLE DIVISIONS

Sticking with our momentary Japanese theme . . .

Japanese mythology tells of the Shinto storm god, Susanoo, being expelled from heaven for tricking his sister, Amaterasu, the sun goddess. After his expulsion, Susanoo encounters two earthly deities who are weeping because they have been forced to give up one of their daughters every year for the past seven years to Yamato no Orochi, an eight-headed snake. Before they are forced to sacrifice their eighth daughter, Kushi-inada-hime, Susanoo transforms her into a comb, which he sticks into his hair for safekeeping. When the serpent shows up, Susanoo tricks it into becoming drunk and chops off its heads.[49]

Yamato no Orochi, loosely translated, means "legal department with multiple divisions."[50]

There are those legal departments—such as the one at Google—that consist of several departments, units, and groups, sometimes containing hundreds or thousands of personnel at a number of different physical offices. These departments are small (or not-so-small) corporations unto themselves, and the challenges in managing them and their personnel are exponentially greater than managing smaller legal departments. However, just as breathing is essential for a human being, regardless of size, shape, age, or ethnicity, the fundamental concerns and solutions for successful management remain the same regardless of the size of the department.

Resources, personnel, tasks, and access are all issues requiring the same essential context and approaches. Planning and budgets have the same fundamental challenges and the same fundamental value to the department and to the client-company. Management issues, for lawyers, support staff, consultants, and outside counsel, need the same attention to quality, structure, and oversight. Size can be intimidating, but you swim in the ocean the same way you swim in a pool.

Dr. David Javitch, Ph.D.,[51] an organization psychologist with significant corporate experience working on key management and leadership issues, suggests the following in order to successfully manage a multisite organization—suggestions that are perfectly applicable to a multidivision legal department:[52]

1. Create a structure. It can be informal or formal—just make sure it clearly points out the reporting relationships.
2. Specify formal and informal power relationships and lines of authority.
3. State whether flexible, rigid, or semi-rigid hours are in effect.
4. Decide on mutually acceptable end points, productivity levels, or outcomes.
5. Identify clear, mutually owned goals, milestones, and deadlines.
6. Create both scheduled and impromptu onsite visits, videoconferencing, or conference calls.
7. Develop an atmosphere that allows offsite employees to communicate as soon and as often as possible with corporate.
8. Communicate, communicate, communicate. Seek out opportunities for newsletters, phone calls, pictures, joint meetings, get-togethers, and celebrations to encourage a positive atmosphere of camaraderie, cooperation, and collaboration.

Legal departments of all shapes and sizes are the home port of every corporate lawyer, whether in-house or outside counsel. They are the center of activity for a corporation's legal needs, humming with endless tasks and projects, using limited resources, surviving on superior personnel, and relying on the constancy of accessibility and exchange.

Administration and management are full-time preoccupations in the midst of a full-time corporate legal practice. This is where a legal department's value and economic efficiency meet and struggle to coexist.

"Without a struggle, there can be no progress."[53]

NOTES

1. A respectful nod to Alfred Lord Tennyson's poem, "The Charge of the Light Brigade," published December 9, 1854.
2. A legal-service firm is a relatively new kind of service provider: a third option to the traditional in-house counsel or outside-counsel choice.

Generally, these firms provide general counsel and legal department services on a contract basis, such as providing a set number of hours or days every week at a set price.

3. This underscores the importance of our toolbox discussion in Chapter Two and helping to educate the client-company about your strengths and those areas where other counsel needs to become involved.

4. Mr. Shakespeare's *The Taming of the Shrew*, act 4, scene 3.

5. This is not to suggest that quantifying the means, much less the intended result, is an easy task. For example, drafting an Internet-usage policy can be a legitimate project for a legal department. Identifying and quantifying the resources required to generate the policy may prove easier than quantifying the policy's perceived or actual benefit to the client-company. Justifying resources in a strictly fiscal sense can become a challenge when quantifying a result that is more accurately measured in terms of risk management.

6. Alex Vorro, *Bloomberg Blows Out Its Legal Department*, INSIDECOUNSEL, Oct. 2011, *available at* http://www.insidecounsel.com/2011/10/31/bloomberg-blows-out-its-legal-department?t=d.

7. Mary Swanton, *Best Practices for Building Strong Legal Departments*, INSIDECOUNSEL, June 2011, *available at* http://www.insidecounsel.com/2011/06/01/best-practices-for-building-strong-legal-departmen.

8. He will forgive me if I pick on him. He is a former Marine, like myself, and eating cake with a plastic fork while making small talk is not his version of a good time. Besides, he argues, it interferes with perfectly good billable time.

9. Maslow's Hierarchy of Needs has occasionally been maligned as being too ethnocentric or Westernized. Whether or not that is true—and I will leave it to better armchair theorists than myself—it still works well with the general demographic of this book.

10. This approach also works with cross-cultural communications. Motivations drive decisions and actions in all human beings in all cultures. Make it a point to spend time deciphering and addressing motivations, and the end results will fall more easily into line.

11. So said the famous, or infamous, Corsican military leader and once-emperor of France, Napoleon Bonaparte.

12. Chapter Seven will give you a few more resources, but one of my favorites is DAVID ALLEN, GETTING THINGS DONE: THE ART OF STRESS-FREE PRODUCTIVITY (Penguin Group, Inc. 2001). It is very readable and practical, and contains excellent advice.

13. Carol Tice, *Seven Ways to Kill Your Meetings and Unleash Productivity*, ENTREPRENEUR (Feb. 8, 2012), http://www.entrepreneur.com/blog/222759.

14. *Id.*

15. Sue Reising, *In-House Litigation Counsel Dismissed in Ongoing Eaton Corp Legal Saga*, CORPORATE COUNSEL, June 1, 2012, *available at* http://www.law.com/jsp/cc/PubArticleFriendlyCC.jsp?id=1202556700223.

16. Take a quick look back at the assessment questions we discussed in Section 3.3.1.

17. Reising, *supra* note 15. Some shovels seem destined to only dig deeper holes. Eaton's own complaint had been dismissed in December 2010 "for

alleged improprieties by its lawyers[,]" including "hiring a secret outside counsel to influence then-sitting judge in ex parte communications." The countersuit by Triumph Aerospace and the engineers remains pending as of the writing of this book. Also pending is a derivate lawsuit by Eaton shareholders that "claims that Eaton's mishandling of the trade secrets case has cost the company $1 billion in proprietary assets."

18. *See* Carole Basri and Irving Kagan, Corporate Legal Departments § 2:2 (4th ed., Practicing Law Institute 2011).

19. *Id.* § 4-2.

20. *Id.*

21. Even though I have been tempted to try each of these options at different times with a few clients.

22. Do your homework. Examine the strengths and weaknesses of flat reporting structures, tall structures, decentralized organization, centralized organization, and all the different strains and mutations in between. The goal is to institute an organizational structure that complements your resources, is easy to follow, provides appropriate oversight, easily processes routine requests and tasks, creates predictable patterns of communication, and is measureable and flexible over time.

23. Nigel Holloway, *Questions & Answers with Nigel Holloway/Jonathan Oviatt*, Corporate Counsel, Nov. 2011, *available at* http://www.law.com/jsp/cc /PubArticleFriendlyCC.jsp?id=1322410463439. This is a great article by two veteran corporate lawyers: Nigel Holloway, a vice president of research for ALM Properties, Inc., who interviewed Jonathan Oviatt, chief legal officer of the Mayo Clinic.

24. Nigel Holloway, *Taking Your Measure*, Corporate Counsel, Nov. 2011, *available at* http://www.law.com/jsp/cc/PubArticleFriendlyCC .jsp?id=1322410473190.

25. Damocles is a classical Greek figure who (as legend would have it) was a courtier in the court of Dionysius II of Syracuse in the fourth century B.C. After lavishing Dionysius with compliments about his great fortune, Dionysius offered to switch places with Damocles. Damocles jumped at the chance and sat down on Dionysius's throne. In order to convey the sense of possible doom, which is the ever-present fear of great fortune, Dionysius arranged for a sword to be hung above his throne, suspended by a single horse-hair tied to its pommel. Eventually, Damocles could no longer bear the terror of waiting for the hair to snap and the sword to drop, so he begged to be allowed to leave and no longer be "so fortunate." Plato recounted the legend in his Tusculan Disputations, V. 61-2.

26. I have a reference suggestion, but it is not, admittedly, entirely on point. Though there are a lot of blogs, online articles, and white papers about legal-department management (and some on planning), there are few, if any, books. For that reason, I still think the best bookshelf resource is Joseph Bailey et al., Law Firm Accounting and Financial Management (5th ed., Law Journal Press 2012). Though it is geared toward private law firms, it has a wealth of good and understandable information about accounting, budgeting, planning, project management,

structures, and other financial considerations unique to managing lawyers and their staff.

27. This is my adaptation of one of the more popular tools for strategic planning: the SWOT analysis (strengths, weaknesses, opportunities, and threats). There are a number of other good tools, such as balanced scorecards and scenario planning, but in my experience, legal departments have less of a need to overcomplicate the process, and they need a process with enough elasticity to fit a variety of workplace and client situations.

28. Ashley Post, *3 Cost-Cutting Tips for Legal Departments*, INSIDECOUNSEL, Apr. 30, 2012, *available at* http://www.insidecounsel.com/2012/04/30/3 -cost-cutting-tips-for-legal-departments?page=2. Ms. Post's other two tips were to evaluate outside law firms and to prevent extra e-discovery expenses ("the primary driver of cost in litigation").

29. Holloway, *supra* note 24.

30. *Id.*

31. *Id.*

32. Holloway, *supra* note 23. The ratio of legal expenses (including litigation) to revenue is, perhaps, the most vaunted metric a legal department should be analyzing.

33. Remember, if a report contains some goal, portion, or intention of conveying legal advice, the report may enjoy the insulation of the attorney client privilege either in whole or in part.

34. John of Gaunt, the uncle of England's King Richard II and a character in William Shakespeare's play *The Life and Death of Richard II*, had a handle on the value found in brevity.

35. Though the original idea was geared toward employees reporting on what they did, their morale, and one idea that would improve their job, their department, or the company, I have modified (or warped) the idea to fit *activities* instead of *people*.

36. David Hechler, *Best Legal Department 2011 Winner: Google*, CORPORATE COUNSEL, May 2011.

37. *Id.* quoting Chris Chin, the fifth lawyer hired by Google.

38. This same shared consciousness can exist in outside firms when several lawyers and/or staff members share a corporate client. This is a "satellite," or outside, legal department mentality.

39. Swanton, *supra* note 7.

40. Swanton, *supra* note 7.

41. Thomas Lalla, *Legal Departments Benefit When In-House Counsel Deviate from the Norm*, INSIDECOUNSEL, Mar. 2012, *available at* http://www.inside counsel.com/2012/03/27/legal-departments-benefit-when-in-house -counsel-deviate-from-the-norm.

42. *Id.*

43. There are even consultants who manage outside counsel. For example, Huron Consulting Group, Inc., a Chicago-headquartered management consulting firm, offers, among many legal services, "Outside Counsel Management," which can include creating and implementing a "preferred provider program" of key law firms for your legal department.

44. Cathleen Flahardy, *CLOs Look for More Value from Outside Counsel*, INSIDE COUNSEL, Oct. 25, 2011, *available at* http://www.insidecounsel.com/2011 /10/25/clos-look-for-more-value-from-outside-counsel.

45. Essentially, this is Maslow's "need" principles as they might be applied to an entity or a group of people.

46. Flahardy, *supra* note 44.

47. Bret Baccus and Matthew Schuetz, *Top Ten Practical Suggestions for Managing Outside Counsel Spending*, ASSOCIATION OF CORPORATE COUNSEL (Mar. 10, 2011), http://www.acc.com/legalresources/publications/topten /Outside-Counsel-Spend.cfm.

48. In April 2012, Alanna Byrne of InsideCounsel gave the following quick breakdown of some of the impact alternative fee arrangements (AFA) have recently had among law firms:

    • 13.4 percent of firms' 2012 revenues projected to come from AFAs
    • 11.8 percent of revenues attributable to AFAs in 2011.
    • 61 percent of firms use AFAs.

    Alanna Byrn, *Facts & Figures: 5 Sets of Newsworthy Data*, INSIDECOUNSEL, Apr. 13, 2012, *available at* http://www.insidecounsel.com/2012/04/13/facts -figures-5-sets-of-newsworthy-data?page=3.

49. I have adapted my short and inelegant retelling of the tale from the *Kojiki*, one of the two ancient texts (circa A.D. 680) that describe the legend.

50. I am, of course, respectfully and light-heartedly joking.

51. Dr. David Javitch is founder and president of Javitch Associates in suburban Boston and is an award-winning faculty member at Harvard University and Boston University.

52. Dr. David Javitch, *Tips for Managing Multiple Locations*, ENTREPRENEUR, Dec. 6, 2004, *available at* http://www.entrepreneur.com/article/74898.

53. Quoth the firebrand, American orator, writer, and statesman Frederick Augustus Washington Bailey, more famously known as Frederick Douglass.

CHAPTER 5

AREAS OF PRACTICE— "IT'S A WONDERFUL LIFE!"

In 2007, the American Bar Association's Section of Business Law compiled and published *The In-House Counsel's Essential Toolkit*, comprising seven volumes of comments, notes, and standard forms for seven major practice areas of corporate law: employment law, general business contracts, corporate compliance and ethics, corporate governance, intellectual property, litigation, and training outside counsel.[1] Its introduction, written by the editors, Jolene Yee, Mari Valenzuela, and David Benson,[2] explains the purpose behind the cooperative endeavor:

> We also recognized that many in the in-house world have specific expertise gleaned from private practice or other experience, but often are expected to become generalists with the ability to competently practice in several different subject matter areas.
>
> ... [W]e decided that the best way to serve the in-house counsel members of our Committee was to collaborate with our colleagues nationwide—both in-house and outside—to create a guidebook filled with annotated forms, general advice, and practical tips.[3]

Close relationships with client-companies are patiently built and carefully maintained, and the reward (or anxiety-riddled reality) is that client-companies look to their lawyer—many times their limited-resource in-house counsel or a small- to medium-sized outside counsel—for almost *all* of their legal needs and issues. True, there are many well-staffed, large private firms and several major in-house legal departments which possess the collective depth to handle a wide variety of practice areas, but this is not the industry norm, and even in those circumstances, it can be a game of hopscotch for a client-company, or its legal counsel, to direct an assignment or task to the right practice group, especially when any given legal issue can be interlaced with multiple disciplines. Corporate lawyers, regardless of their circumstances (whether abundant or scarce) should have a basic working knowledge of each major area of practice, if at all possible. The ability to spot issues in, review the merits of, opine on, and actually participate (even with limits) in most, if not all, of a client-company's legal issues increases the value to a client-company and, in turn, a corporate lawyer's individual value.

Recently, a bank client asked me about a fairly knotty real-estate transactional problem. Because real-estate transactional work is not traditionally my strong suit, I brought in another senior lawyer who concentrates in that area of law. I could instantly see that securitization and regulatory issues were secondary issues to the problem, but because I have developed a rough-hewn working knowledge of real-estate trans-actional work, I was still able to act as a competent intermediary for my client bank and supplied a requested review and second opinion of his work based on what I knew about my client's tolerances and goals. The bank was delighted with the thorough work product.

This kind of experience can be like sitting with your child at a doctor's appointment. You know enough to be able to tell him or her if it will hurt, or to interpret what the pediatrician says, and you give the pediatrician your child's medical history, but you are not the one holding the stethoscope. Your child never loses his or her sense of familiarity or security, and he or she does not have to worry about facing the doctor without you close by. You do not simply hand your child off to an unfamiliar and maybe intimidating stranger. You stay with him or her, and you learn what you need to learn to administer medicine, to be encouraging, and to keep watch for recurrences or other symptoms.

A great part of successfully maintaining a good relationship with a client-company requires the same dedication, whether you are in-house or outside counsel. You do not need to be the expert all the time, but you do need to be on deck, ready to opine, review, and provide informed counsel.

This chapter is not meant, of course, to be an exhaustive resource on each of the highlighted areas of practice, any more than *The In-House Counsel's Essential Toolkit* (the *Toolkit*) was designed to provide an all-inclusive collection of contracts, forms, sample letters, or commentary.[4] Treat this chapter as a set of starting blocks, fixed against the following questions:

- What core principles should I be aware of?
- Who should I anticipate working with (or for) within my client-company?
- What are a few of the major projects, topics, problems, or issues I should expect?

From the answers to these questions, you should have a contextual, working sense of each major practice area encountered by a corporate lawyer, and you will be far less likely to have an absolutely blank, glazed look in your eyes when your client-company asks you—a conventionally trained litigator—to tackle a difficult best-practices governance issue.

Or at least the glazed look in your eyes should quickly subside.

§ 5.1 EMPLOYMENT AND LABOR LAW

Employment, or labor, law is a body of laws, regulations, and industry practices—both at the federal and state level—that govern the relationships, rights, and restrictions between employers and employees. Employment-law issues also bleed into other practice areas, such as workplace safety (health or environmental law), transactional (contract) law, torts, alternative dispute resolution (ADR), tax, immigration, compliance, and mergers and acquisitions. Employment law has spawned its own subset of specialties, such as collective bargaining, litigation, benefits, workers' compensation, and union administration.

Perhaps the most significant hazard for a corporate lawyer to consciously avoid as he or she is facing, and working through, virtually every employment-related issue is the tendency to believe a contract, manual, policy, or procedure will be the end-all, be-all. Employment-related issues—noticeably distinct from other practice areas—arise from, and exist because of, *human relationships*. Think of family law. Your efforts to anticipate, decrypt, and resolve employment-related issues will always have fairly similar perspective of human emotions and psychology.

Stephen Paskoff, the president and CEO of ELI, Inc., which works to transform complex laws and ethics into simple behavioral rules, shared the following opinion in an article he wrote for *Corporate Counsel*:

> Legally compliant workplace training programs tend to deal exclusively with workplace behavior that is easily identified as illegal. However, employee complaints are not always a result of that which is expressly forbidden, nor have our courts and legislatures envisioned every possible workplace scenario that may be found to be illegal under current law.[5]

The takeaway point is to retrain (part of your mind, at least) to think beyond an eventual day-of-reckoning lawsuit, or even typical crisis-prevention steps, when dealing with an employment-related issue. Those viewpoints and preparations can be indispensably important, but the more significant context is that employment-related issues arise from *human* interactions, motivations, and emotions, cloaked in business attire. A savvy corporate lawyer needs to be prepared to discuss these emotive nuances with his or her client-company.

Pinning down the human element in an employment-related problem (or project) has a wonderful way of then directing the subsequent pragmatic steps that may need to be taken. Do this by diving beneath the surface of the apparent problem or project.

What does the employee *really* want? What is *really* bothering him or her? What is the employer *really* trying to accomplish? What creative steps would the employer be willing to take?

Employees

§ 5.1.1 *Who Are Your Internal Connections?*

Unless it is your stock-in-trade, the first thought that should cross your mind when a new assignment lands on your desk is: Who do I need on speed dial in order to get this done?

Corporate lawyers can sometimes forget their greatest resources are the *nonlegal* resources spread throughout their client-companies. The legal aspect of a task, project, or problem probably only represents a fraction of the whole. For instance, drafting an employee manual— a project which may land on the desk of a corporate lawyer—will be threaded through with employment-law-specific provisions, but it also needs to take into account other ingredients, such as a client-company's home-grown policies on earning vacation time, taking sick leave, Internet usage, industry-specific privacy policies,[6] and even gossiping.[7] Employment-related issues have a predictable way of rapidly affecting an entire company, so the entire company's culture needs to be a routine part of any employment calculation.

Because one bad apple can quickly spoil the whole bunch, get out of your office and include the rest of the bunch. Sit down with the human resources director, the chief compliance officer, and other executives and department heads, all of whom will add to your understanding and impression of attitudes, expectations, and historical issues (or problems), and usually will have constructive suggestions. No matter where an employment-related issue arises, your ultimate opinion, document, or position should be the result of a tapestry approach, in which you have a good idea of the broader view of your client-company's decision-making constituency. As often as possible (without inadvertently stirring the pot or stepping on toes), reach out to other parts of your client-company for input and advice.[8]

§ 5.1.2 Hire 'Em, Fire 'Em, and Everything in Between

As an embryonic issue, correctly classifying, and understanding the classification of, your client-company's workforce is a critical task. Generally, this is guided by what particular employees do for the company and how they do it. Before your client-company can determine how to account for payments to a person for his or her services (and/or pay federal or state taxes), an employee must be properly classified.

What does *classification* mean? Is an employee

- *an independent contractor?* "The general rule is that an individual is an independent contractor if the payer has the right to control or direct only the result of the work and not what will be done and how it will be done."[9]
- *a common-law employee?* "Under common-law rules, anyone who performs services for you is your employee if you can control what will be done and how it will be done."[10]
- *a statutory employee?* "If workers are independent contractors under the common law rules, such workers may nevertheless be treated as employees by statute (statutory employees) for certain employment tax purposes if they fall within any one of four

categories and meet the three conditions described under Social Security and Medicare taxes[.]"[11]

Furthermore, your client-company must determine whether an employee is exempt or nonexempt under the Fair Labor Standards Act (FLSA),[12] or whether his or her job is governed by the FLSA at all. If another federal labor law governs a job, then it is generally not covered by the FLSA. Thankfully, for simplicity's sake, "[m]ost jobs are governed by the FLSA."[13] Most employees are nonexempt if they are covered by the FLSA, as long as they do not meet three exemption tests.[14]

Classification and exempt/nonexempt status are baselines that must be addressed and understood before any employee is hired, paid, disciplined, laterally moved, promoted or demoted, laid off, or fired, and before any employee retires. Spend time familiarizing yourself with classification and exempt/nonexempt status under the FLSA to have a basic grasp of what your client-company is required to do, not do, implement, permit, proscribe, or enforce.

What happens if you get it wrong? It can be a costly mistake. In spite of the limelight employee-discrimination lawsuits receive, the threshold issues of tax and wage-and-hour lawsuits are the litigation heavyweights that financially hammer U.S. industries every year. "In the past three years, more than 20,000 wage and hour class-actions have been filed in the U.S.—many of them related to alleged misclassification of workers as exempt from federal and state overtime and other labor laws."[15]

Once these inceptive issues are settled and understood, other concerns and tasks naturally follow in their wake.

Shamelessly, and intended as a compliment, we will take advantage of the united wisdom of the ABA's Business Law Section—their *Toolkit*[16]—by drawing from some of their suggested "employment-related issues," as well as adding a few of our own, to identify employment matters routinely faced by corporate lawyers:

- Hiring applications
- Disclaimers and acknowledgments
- Offer letters
- Background checks
- Nondisclosure/confidentiality agreements
- Employment agreements/contracts

- Separation agreements/contracts/provisions
- Exit interviews
- Whistleblowing
- Equal Employment Opportunity Commission (and individual state agency) complaints, investigations, responses
- Employment policies (such as antidiscrimination, antiharassment, FMLA and USERRA,[17] substance abuse, WARN[18] notices, workplace violence)
- Immigration
- Workers' compensation claims
- Litigation

This list of topics is intended to foster your curiosity and a healthy realization that employment-related issues run deeper than hiring, firing, and litigation. Aside from the *Toolkit*, which I highly recommend, look for a comprehensive resource to help guide you through each of these topics' characteristics, perils, and forms.[19]

§ 5.1.3 The Manual

Usually the employee manual or handbook—the backbone of an employer and employee's relationship—is the responsibility of a human resources department, but the legal department is invariably involved (if not primarily tasked) with its drafting and modification, as well as when it comes time for its enforcement. "Strictly speaking, the remit of law departments is to ensure that corporate policies don't modify the employment-at-will relationship, don't conflict with other laws or rights, and that all compliances are up to date."[20]

Employee manuals come in all different arrays. The ideal manuals incorporate necessary legal and compliance components with well-considered provisions, tailored to a client-company's specific culture, operational needs, industry, and expectations. I have found the following questions, which can be applied to any developing policy, provide excellent guideposts for developing and auditing a sound employee manual.

- Are objectives clearly articulated? Do the objectives make sense within the company's business model, culture, and goals?
- Is the manual based on existing laws and regulations? Is it based on accepted industry standards?

- Can included policies and provisions be expressed in clear, actionable job requirements?
- Can performing the manual's policies and provisions on the job be measured? If not, why not? Are measurements needed?
- Does the manual create potential risks, including wrongful-termination claims? What are they, and how will they be minimized or handled?[21]

Topically, what should an employee manual cover? There are different schools of thought when it comes to the extent of a manual's contents. You may remember an anecdote I related earlier in Chapter 3 in which I mentioned having heard the general counsel of a multibillion-dollar international corporation say that if an employee manual is longer than three pages, then it is four pages too long.[22] The idea, especially in an at-will employment environment, is that too many topics, and too much information, actually incites unnecessary risk and memorializes unnecessary commitments to policies and procedures. The takeaway point is to look at each topic in your client-company's manual from a 360-degree perspective and ask, Is this necessary? and if so, Why?

With that said, here are some common topics:

- Nondisclosure agreements and conflict-of-interest statements
- Antidiscrimination policies
- Compensation
- Work schedules
- Standards of conduct
- Eligibility
- Probationary periods
- Termination and resignation procedures
- Transfers and relocations
- Union information
- Safety and security
- Benefits
- Leave policies[23]

Some might argue otherwise, but an employee manual is not a work of art. It needs to be clear, unmuddied by verbose legalese, consistent, not any thicker than is needed, and routinely audited and updated. Do not include provisions just because "everyone does it," or because they sound authoritative. Keep in mind an employee manual is the playbook for a *relationship* between your client-company and its employees. Too many rules, and it will be crushed and become paralytic under its own weight. Too few rules, and it will be uncertain, insecure, and fickle. The happy middle ground is, well, somewhere in the middle.

§ 5.1.4 Employment Contracts

If an employee manual is a general playbook for an employer-employee relationship, then an employee contract is a specific playbook for a specific relationship between your client-company and an employee. Even if an employer seemingly has all the leverage when forming a contract, flaunting that leverage unnecessarily can sew the wrong kinds of seeds for the future. "The employee and the employee's lawyer should be aware going into the negotiation that [an employee's] leverage is only as strong as the employer's desire to keep the employee happy. The employer is entitled to a take-it-or-leave-it attitude."[24] However, an employer's desire to "keep the employee happy" should be a strong one (or why hire the person in the first place?), and an employment contract should reflect that desire as much as it reflects a client-company's authority. It is rarely a happy employee who causes problems or sues.

In Section 1.1.4 of Chapter 1, we discussed the ins and outs of a corporate lawyer's employment contract—*your* employment contract or engagement letter. Many of those same topical provisions and issues apply to other executive, or management-level, employment contracts. What are the basics?

- The position being offered and accepted
- The compensation that will be paid
- Whether the employment is for a set length of time or at will
- Specifics regarding vacation time and sick leave and whether such time accrues from year to year
- The responsibilities of both parties with regard to the work to be done and the work environment[25]

"First and foremost, the contract should protect promises made by both parties at the time of hiring."[26] The key to all of those provisions, and any others that might be individually applicable, is the need to carefully draft a contract so both parties understand and acknowledge what is expected, not just by countersignatures, but by actual conversation. Too many times, contracts are negotiated at arm's length, and the final product is simply signed—the gross presumption then being everyone supposedly understands its provisions in the same way. Terrible, terrible outcomes can and do occur when an entire relationship is built on a *presumption* of understanding.

On the heels of a $16 million verdict in favor of Donald Drapkin's[27] lawsuit against MacAndrews & Forbes Holdings Inc., David Dunn, a partner at Hogan Lovells and an experienced employment litigator, observed that the multimillion-dollar litigation was the result of Mr. Drapkin's "ambiguously drafted contract clauses. 'It became clear that the parties didn't agree as to what their respective obligations were[.]'"[28] The prickly pear in Mr. Drapkin's separation agreement was not a monetary issue. Instead, it stemmed from whether Mr. Drapkin was clearly obligated "not to induce other employees to quit and to return all company documents."[29] Apparently, all concerned parties did not interpret such an obligation in the same way. Who knew the phrase "not to induce" might be interpreted differently?

Employment law is a daily reality for corporate lawyers. Be mindful of the hazards, as well as where the path is smooth and where it is rocky and unsettled. Human relationships are never strictly the result of a collection of laws, regulations, standards, or contracts.

§ 5.2 CONTRACT AND TRANSACTIONAL LAW

Contracts—agreements—compose the framework of nearly everything we do even when we are not consciously aware of it. In 1762, Jean-Jacques Rousseau[30] wrote *Of the Social Contract, or Principles of Political Right*, which based its premise on a person's decision to enter into a "social contract" with others in order for there to be progress and an equality of rights and obligations. An example of the papered result of Rousseau's theory can be seen in the U.S. Constitution, to which each individual American is a party, possessing rights, obligations, and expectations. The concept of *contracts* defines who we are, what we can do, what we should do, what we should not do, what we cannot do, and how others should and are expected to act in relation to us.

In the world of business, the dirt-floor basics are no different, which makes the competent practice of contract law a vital skill for all corporate lawyers. Of all the processes involved in establishing and running a successful business, where the beat of a butterfly's wings may cause the end of the world,[31] the weak link is many times within the four corners of a not-so-well-drafted contract. Alan Shepard, the second person and the first American to travel into space, best described the crucial importance of how a simple contract can predict the ultimate success or failure of any enterprise: "It's a very sobering feeling to be up in space and realize that one's safety factor was determined by the lowest bidder on a government contract."

Predictably then, contract law is part of the core curriculum for every first-year law student. As though practicing the rote conjugation of a Latin verb, first-year law students drum into their heads the essential components of every contract: an offer, acceptance in compliance with the offer, a stated legal purpose or objective, the mutuality of obligation (the "meeting of the minds"), consideration, and the competency of the parties. Case studies are analyzed and exams are taken in order to ensure that every graduating law student is capable of creating, dissecting, or challenging the legal concept of a binding agreement between parties. But then, like Latin, contract law seems to become a dead language for many practicing lawyers, even for business lawyers. Somewhere between the blackboards of a lecture hall and the confines of an office, many lawyers seem to lose the ability to skillfully draft and/or analyze contracts. This may partly be blamed on the cut-and-paste habit of modern computers and word processing software platforms. Complex and lengthy contracts now take only a fraction of the time to draft they once did, because large sections of boilerplate text can be taken from earlier documents and placed into a new document with only a few clicks of a mouse. Time and money are saved, but quality and accuracy can unwittingly be compromised. Corporate lawyers who routinely draft or review contracts while assuming boilerplate language is correct, or that it satisfies one or more of the basic elements of contract construction, run the risk of embedding the flight of a butterfly into their client-company's universe. Many times, hurricanes later appear on the horizon.

Remember our earlier discussion in Section 1.1.1 of the promotion of Sashi Brown as senior vice president of football operations for the Jacksonville Jaguars? Mr. Brown replaced Paul Vance, who had been with the Jaguars as their general counsel since 1994 and became their senior vice president of football operations. Why was Mr. Vance fired? It may have been the result of a dispute over a contract drafting error between the Jaguars and seven fired coaching assistants—a very costly, $3.5 to $4 million contract drafting error.

> The seven assistants had signed extensions in 2010 and the club believed it was for two years that would expire at the end of the 2011 season. However, the applicable clause in dispute states, "shall terminate on the later of January 31, 2012 or the day after the Jaguars' last football game of the 2012 season and playoffs[.]"[32]

Mr. Vance "called it an incorrect reference and that it 'should have read the 2011 NFL season.'" Indeed, the devil—the beat of a butterfly's wings—is in the details.

Words count. Neither a court, a client, a board, an employee, a shareholder, nor an aggrieved party is going to look the other way simply because an error occurred in a boilerplate provision, or simply because it was inadvertent. When drafting and reviewing contracts, the takeaway core principle for every corporate lawyer is to *sweat the details.* Lou Holtz, the only college football coach to lead six different programs to bowl games and move four different programs into the final top-twenty rankings, said, "In the successful organization, no detail is too small to escape close attention."

§ 5.2.1 *Who Are Your Internal Connections?*

It is the business of a corporate lawyer to know and understand the business of his or her client-company. However, a corporate lawyer's role, whether it manifests as an executive, advisor, or counselor, comes from the contextual framework of *law*. A contract—in its embryonic state—is a creature of the law, but much of the substantive content of a fully drafted contract, and its entire reason for existence, has little or nothing to do with the fundamentals of contract creation. A corporate lawyer needs to take the time and to gently insist upon learning and understanding the core components:

- *Why* a contract is being written
- *What* it is expected/intended to accomplish
- *What* it is intended to protect

- *Whom* it will involve or effect
- *What* actions or omissions would constitute default
- *What* remedies should be available
- *How* expansive it should be
- *When* it should become effective
- *When* it (or certain provisions) should terminate or lapse

A corporate lawyer's primary skill and capacity is to apply the law (statutes, regulations, common-law doctrines, and legal custom) to the creation or review of a legally enforceable agreement, and to anticipate consequences of default and liability exposure; but the *substantive content* typically involves business decisions, corporate objectives, marketing objectives, financial goals, and tolerances unique to a client-company or to cohorts, departments, or divisions within a client-company. Almost every aspect of every business enterprise is predicated upon and sustained by contracts. Therefore, you should *involve the stakeholders.* Department heads, managers, employees, board members, and consultants who specialize in a given area are all facets of information which should be freely utilized and accessed when drafting and reviewing contracts.

Contract issues are evolving issues even when they seem to repeat themselves over and over again. It is unlikely that by attending a single meeting with procurement, compliance, billing, human resources, marketing, product development, or customer service, you could learn and understand everything there is to know about each contract requested by that department or employee. It is also unlikely you would be able to convene a lengthy sit-down every time a contract issue arose; such a tact would be too inefficient and probably unnecessary when only facing minor variations to otherwise "standardized" contracts. The trick is to create a middle ground between the two extremes. The guiding principle is that a good corporate lawyer asks questions, is not hesitant to ask questions, and *thinks* to ask questions, whenever necessary.

§ 5.2.2 The Four Corners of the Document

Every industry has its stock-in-trade contracts, some of which are (occasionally mandatory) forms that may require the approval of a governing regulator or industry association. A corporate lawyer should not only become proficient with these industry-tailored contracts—including all of the humdrum boilerplate print—he or she should also become proficient with his or her own client-company's individual contractual needs. At the end of the day, it will be what words exist or do not exist within the four corners of a sheaf of papers that might cause a client-company to grow, stagnate, or fail. Put another way: "A small leak will sink a great ship."[33]

Many times, contracts are preceded by negotiations and term sheets, which identify the salient terms of a yet-to-be-drafted contract. A term sheet, in fact, can be an excellent tool to use on behalf of a client-company to define key deal requirements before a client-company is locked into a contractual relationship. Developing a term sheet can also focus negotiations, clarify needs and objectives, and make more efficient use of everyone's time, energy, and budget resources. This is the blueprint before a corporate lawyer goes to work on the construction of a contract. Once construction begins, each nail, two-by-four, screw, and joint will not easily yield to too much change, and costs—measured in time and money—may be compounded.

Whether you are able to work from a term sheet or simply a set of notes or instructions (or a template from helpful outside counsel), the fundamentals remain the same for every contract. The fundamentals, in themselves, are not obtuse or complex; instead, it is the *application* of these fundamentals within the bodies of contracts that creates fodder for hornbooks, case studies, lawsuits, and unhappy clients. *Application*, in almost every case, can be tied to a question of *clarity*. Therefore, the overarching concern of a corporate lawyer who is tasked with drafting, or reviewing, something so monstrously long and complex as a ninety-plus-page trust indenture for a new bond issue, or something so routine as a purchase order for goods below $10,000, is to *make sure each contractual element is clearly recognizable and unambiguous.*

As a quick exercise, take a brief trip down memory lane, settle into a seat in your first-year contracts class, and pull out a legal pad. Your professor is passing around a seductively simple-looking three-page contract. You are partially bored (because contracts do not seem nearly as exciting as torts), but you are also a little tense. You are fully aware a trap is being set. You quickly scan through the document and utter a frantic first line of defense, "um," when your professor announces your name and rapid-fires the following questions:

- What is the legal purpose of the contract?
- Who is making the offer?

- What is the offer being made?
- What is the method (and/or terms) of acceptance?
- Has acceptance been made?
- What obligations, covenants, restrictions, privileges, and representations are attributable to which party?
- Is there a fair exchange of value between each party for such obligations, covenants, restrictions, privileges, and representations?
- Is each party competent, and competently/authoritatively represented, to enter into the contract?
- Does the contract comply with applicable laws, regulations, industry standards, and corporate policies?

You, I suspect, were able to deftly parry each question's blow with a precise and cogent answer drawn from your naturally shrewd reading of the professor's sample contract. My own memory lane, however, would reveal more painful recollections of me repeating the fateful "um" several times until putting an end to my misery by involuntarily blurting aloud, "Hail, Emperor, those who are about to die salute you!"[34]

The truth is that without exception, you—and every person, party, arbitrator, court, or other trier of fact—should be able to easily answer those questions when looking at any contract you draft or review. Try it. Grab a contract out of the inbox on your desk and ask those same questions. Do the answers jump off the page? Are they clear? If not, what is missing? Is there too much verbiage? Are there unnecessary or superfluous provisions or terms? How could a provision(s) be made less ambiguous?

A client-company depends on its corporate lawyer to make sure its contracts are not only substantively complete but that they are *clear* and *fundamentally* complete. This is where a corporate lawyer really makes his or her bones. A well-written, well-constructed contract is a client-company's first defense and best defense when, or if, a contractual relationship sours. Read and write every contract as if you were still a first-year law student.

§ 5.2.3 Support, Support, Support

Contract drafting and review is an obvious support function of corporate law. Here, a corporate lawyer's role is very much about creating or affirming a mission-critical tool in order for an employee, department, division, or client-company at large to achieve its business objectives in a safe, predictable, and efficient manner. The contract is *not* the end result. It is

Clear Contracts

the means to the end, and a good corporate lawyer is going to evaluate all of his or her efforts to draft, review, revise, advise, caution, and approve based upon one question: Does this contract help my client-company achieve its business objectives as effectively and efficiently as possible?

In order to answer that question in the affirmative, a contract should be able to meet a simple four-part *support* assessment:

1. The contract uses unambiguous, plain language wherever possible (while utilizing statutory or standard legalese when necessary).
2. The contract addresses and incorporates the protections necessary to limit liability or loss exposure to the client-company while still allowing for a fair and constructive business arrangement between the contract's stakeholders.
3. The contract anticipates and clearly provides a structured accommodation for change, modification, addition, or subtraction without compromising the contract's overall intent, basic protections, or the client-company's business objectives.
4. The contract actually achieves the client-company's business objectives while maximizing efficiency and minimizing costs.

A corporate lawyer should take steps to help keep a client-company's contract issues razor sharp (that is, the four corners of each contract) and supportive (that is, the four-part assessment of support). Here are a few suggestions:

- Establish scheduled review anniversaries for standing or standardized (routine) contracts.
- Organize and track progressive variations/versions.
- Monitor how laws and regulations may effect standardized provisions by using reference indices.
- Routinely reverse the review process—ask nonlawyers to review *your* work and not to take a contract as sacrosanct because it came from legal counsel.
- Alternate review or drafting assignments between different lawyers (if possible and when financially feasible) to keep a fresh set of eyes looking at each contract.

The title of Section 5.2 includes the designation of *transactional* law because it is within a client-company's transactions that contracts exist. Business transactions cover a wide variety of topics, such as commercial real estate, debt financing and restructuring, intellectual property, mergers and acquisitions, negotiated transactions, equity and capital transactions, employment law, and franchise law. Contracts underlie all these areas, and it is ultimately the four corners of a contracting document that perform the heavy lifting during the life of every transaction.

In Greek mythology, Atlas, a primordial Titan, is sentenced by Zeus to stand at the western edge of Gaia (Earth) and hold up Uranus (the Sky) on his shoulders, earning him the title "enduring Atlas."[35] Contracts—binding agreements between parties who need each other but also need to remain distinct and protected—are the enduring Atlases of the business world. They define, contain, and support all the ideas, terms, goals, concerns, and covenants of contracting parties, and in so doing, they oversee and govern the practical, everyday functioning of each business enterprise.

§ 5.3 Regulations, Compliance, and Investigations

If enduring Atlas is the allegory for contracts in the business world, Atlas's brother Prometheus, punished for stealing the miracle of fire for the benefit of humankind, is the allegory of *compliance*. Compliance programs, borne of governmental guidelines, regulations, and statutes, are business's efforts to promote ethical conduct and adherence to the law. But like Prometheus, who paid for the virtuous intention of his theft by being eternally bound to a rock so an eagle (Zeus's symbol) could feed on his liver every day, compliance programs and guidelines pay for their goal of attempting to establish a fair marketplace by having capitalism or a progressing world (or thinly disguised human avarice) pick and nibble at their good intentions.

Indeed, the unintended consequence of endeavoring to regulate an industry's playing field so it is fair and ethical is that it summons the inventions of desire and greed to rise to the occasion. And yet compliance programs, and a corporate lawyer's responsibility to champion their creation, implementation, and improvements, act as the great temperance to industry's excesses and scandals—a process that, in the end, fosters constructive competition, creativity, safety, consumer protections, and investor safeguards. Compliance issues—in both adherence and avoidance—reflect the ethos of our society's marketplace and corporate industry.

> A man does what he must—in spite of personal consequences, in spite of obstacles and dangers and pressures—and that is the basis of all human morality.[36]

In Section 3.1.4, we broached the topic of regulations as they relate to the context of new business ventures. As you may recall, the term *regulations* typically refers to a body of administrative laws designed to implement a primary statute or piece of legislation. Regulations and their shepherds, regulatory agencies, are intended to govern market entries, prices, labor conditions, wages, environmental issues, health and safety concerns, standards of production, the dissemination or protection of information, public disclosures, responsible governance, and financial accountability. Businesses—both domestic and foreign businesses that trade with the United States—are required to comply with the sets of regulations that affect their corporate structure, operations, products, employees, materials, services, and financing. *Compliance* is the business world's parlance for a company's internal programs designed to ensure that its day-to-day operations and management are within the boundaries of the law.

Regulations are nothing new. Historically, however, they tended to direct their applications more toward social concerns and individual citizenry.[37] Business regulation was generally left to some kind of guild system[38] and a policy of self-policing.

In the United States, the distinct shift of business oversight and regulation from industry to government might be said to have occurred in 1906, on the heels of Upton Sinclair's novel *The Jungle*. At the time, social Darwinism—a buyer-beware and survival-of-the-fittest business attitude—best described the American economic landscape. Although Mr. Sinclair meant for his book to champion the plight of immigrants' rough-scrabble lives,[39] its graphic and detailed descriptions of the practices and corruption in the meatpacking industry spawned a public outcry great enough to move the Pure Food and Drug Act[40] and the Meat Inspection Act[41] through Congress. The Pure Food and Drug Act dealt with the correct labeling of certain drugs and products, while the Meat Inspection Act provided for the inspection of the slaughter and processing of meat and meat products. These laws formed the plank work for the Food and Drug Administration and provided additional regulation and enforcement powers to the U.S. Department of Agriculture (created approximately forty years earlier).

As the twentieth century worked its way forward, several more decades saw ethical failures of business result in the growth of government regulations and regulatory bodies. In the 1950s and 1960s, widespread price-fixing by more than thirty electrical-equipment manufacturers resulted in antitrust prosecution by the Justice Department and several self-policing programs. In the late 1960s and into the 1970s, growing concerns about the industrial neglect of the environment—clinched by the 1969 Santa Barbara oil spill[42]—resulted in the National Environmental Policy Act[43] and the emergence of the Environmental Protection Agency.

In the late 1970s, after over 400 U.S. companies admitted to making questionable or illegal payments (that is, bribes) to foreign government officials, politicians, and political parties, Congress enacted the Foreign Corrupt Practices Act[44] (FCPA) to restore faith in American businesses. In the 1980s, as a by-product of the Sentencing Reform Act, which was meant to increase uniformity in federal sentencing, the U.S. Sentencing Commission was established and produced the Federal Sentencing Guidelines (FSG). Because the FSG allowed businesses to earn credits that would reduce criminal penalties if a business had created and maintained an effective compliance program before an alleged crime had occurred, companies began to design and carry out robust compliance programs, following the blueprint of the FSG.

The 1990s and the turn of the century witnessed an economy of bubbles and bursts made up of dot-coms and colossal corporate and accounting scandals, prompting the seminal enactment of the Sarbanes-Oxley Act of 2002[45] (SOX), along with the adoption of dozens of new regulations by the Securities and Exchange Commission. Instead of using the carrot-and-stick routine of the FSG, SOX was a sweeping legislative response, mandating a multitude of changes in corporate America that ranged from additional governance responsibilities to new criminal penalties. In the later part of the first decade of the twenty-first century, the United States grappled with the causes and consequences of the worst economic downturn since the Great Depression. Lawmakers largely found fault with the financial services industry—everything from brokerage firms to mortgage lending companies—and on July 21, 2010, the Dodd-Frank Wall Street Reform and Consumer Protection Act[46] (Dodd-Frank) was signed into law.

For the past 100 years, and particularly the past 40 years, regulations, and each company's need to comply with sector-specific regulations, have become a central component of creating, running, and growing almost every business in the United States (and many foreign businesses as well). Generally speaking, comprehensive compliance programs address the following:

- Antitrust issues
- Employment/labor issues
- Environmental concerns
- Privacy and data/records protection
- Securities
- Intellectual property

Undoubtedly, your client-company is affected by and must comply with a variety of regulatory mandates and guidelines, both at the state and federal levels. At the moment, your client-company's compliance program may consist of only a few outdated posters hanging on a wall in the break room,[47] or it may have a vigorous, dedicated compliance department already in full swing. Regardless of where your client-company's compliance efforts may currently be, "the avoidance of violations of the law is a core part of the mission of a corporate law department."[48] Not only does compliance with governing regulations and guidelines originate from the law, but "many compliance issues revolve around legal issues or the application of legal issues to business problems."[49]

This slice of corporate life may then sound like a natural place for a corporate lawyer to weigh in, perhaps even to take the lead. But as with any ambiguous optical illusion,[50] it is perfectly clear to certain persons that corporate lawyers must stay on the outside of compliance, looking in, while it is equally clear to other persons that corporate lawyers need to be on the inside of compliance efforts, looking out. Even lawyers themselves do not share a unified view of whether a corporate lawyer should be "navigating in the choppy waters of corporate compliance."[51]

So how do you best fit into, or provide support to, your client-company's compliance programs?

WHEN GIVEN THE CHOICE, THEODORE'S MIND PREFERRED THE ILLUSION OF A NECKER CUBE OVER THE IMPOSSIBILITY OF REGULATIONS ...

NECKER CUBE

REGULATIONS

Compliance

§ 5.3.1 Who Are Your Internal Connections?

Ignore for the moment the question of whether you, the corporate lawyer, are or should be leading compliance or standing outside and looking in. Undeniably, you will be involved in compliance at some level, likely a significant level. Therefore, the first, hopefully obvious, step is to determine who, within your client-company, is prone to be your point of contact when it comes to compliance issues and programs. If your client-company boasts its own compliance department, then that department is a great place to start. Plan on meeting with the compliance officer on a regular basis, and work (diplomatically) on establishing a relationship that clearly augments and supports the compliance officer's efforts. Let him or her know (again, diplomatically) you are there, willing to provide legal counsel on any and all compliance matters, policy reviews, legal sufficiency reviews, assistance with program auditing functions, assistance with training programs, and internal corrective actions.

In the interest of being frank, compliance officers are many times akin to accountants: they are detail-oriented, bureaucratic specialists who are nonlawyers, and they can be territorial about their jobs and their work product. Please do not misunderstand. I do not mean these descriptors to be slights against compliance officers. For such a complex area of corporate administration, with ever-changing rules and opinions, it takes a unique character to deal with compliance issues day after day. However, the challenging part for a corporate lawyer, whose feathers naturally ruffle when a *non*lawyer is practicing what appears to be *law*, is to approach the situation thoughtfully and with appropriate patience and corporate etiquette. Remain aware of that; do not let your emotions or opinions lead to a wrestling match or a cavalier decision to ignore compliance and pass the buck. *You* are your client-company's corporate lawyer, and as such, you do not have the option or luxury of inciting turf wars or sticking your head in the sand in an area where your expertise is inevitably needed.

A wonderfully disarming and extremely useful method is to ask questions. Play the attentive audience and allow the compliance officer to explain all of the department's different programs, processes, reviews, concerns, accomplishments, and resources. Over time, this will not only keep you well informed about potential liabilities, shortcomings, and risks of your client-company's compliance efforts, but it will also give you the best insight for where, when, and how your advice and help are needed.

If your client-company does not have a stand-alone compliance department, then the job is likely to fall on you or an outside consultant. Your client-company's board of directors, records department, internal auditor, IT department, and other business units such as finance, human resources, marketing, and engineering[52] can and should all be part of the compliance program. Each of these disparate resources will bring its body of expertise to the table when it comes to developing the subject-matter-specific components of a compliance program, and their assistance and leadership in matters of training, information dissemination, and feedback will prove invaluable. Although we will reserve our discussion on governance matters involving the board of directors for Section 5.4, it bears stating that the relationship, interaction, and access between a client-company's corporate counsel (usually the general counsel) and the board of directors is absolutely crucial to the success of a compliance program. Communication channels must remain open. This sometimes can create a sensitive interplay between a chief executive officer, a board, and a client-company's legal counsel. More than ever, an understanding and professional (and authoritative) acknowledgment of everyone's roles and responsibilities must be clear and supported by the board.

§ 5.3.2 *Know the Law*

> The point of [a regulation] is to start with something so simple as not to seem worth stating, and to end with something so paradoxical that no one will believe it.[53]

> In the U.S. alone, 4,000 new laws and regulations are in the works—and that's in addition to the more than 3,500 federal regulations passed just last year.[54]

These two quotes alone ought to be enough commentary for this section, and enough to keep many corporate lawyers awake at night. It is impossible to know if a client-company is doing wrong (the very thing an organization must avoid according to the FSG) if a client-company's legal counsel does not know what the right thing is. Other than the knowledge base a corporate lawyer might bring to his or her job, this is where interactions with other department heads, the compliance department, and the board will become priceless, because they provide a wealth of education (knowingly or not) on the regulatory agencies, regulations, policies, industry practices, and guidelines governing each of their respective business and administrative operations.

As we discussed earlier in Section 1.1.1, there is often the tendency among client-companies to hire a general counsel (or other in-house or outside counsel) because of a specific corporate crisis, need, or plan. The specific crisis, need, or plan may have to do with a compliance matter, but as often as not, a corporate lawyer is hired for other reasons, and compliance issues—and the behemoth regulatory Krakens[55] that come with them—are not part of the corporate lawyer's universe of experiences. In those situations, the learning curve can be a challenge.

What to do?

Divide and conquer. Meet with each department head and point of contact to identify and discuss what regulatory issues and concerns affect their business units and operations. Go outside your client-company's front door and meet with (or contract with) outside counsel or consultants who can bring specific knowledge or resources to bear on particularly difficult regulatory matters. Putting together a comprehensive compliance program that addresses all the laws, regulations, and guidelines affecting your client-company should not be a matter of reinventing the wheel. Many, if not all, of the highly regulated industries even have the benefit of vendors with products and services focusing exclusively on compliance.[56]

There are fifteen cabinet-level departments in the federal government: state, treasury, defense, justice, interior, agriculture, commerce, labor, health and human services, housing and urban development, transportation, energy, education, veterans affairs, and homeland security.[57] Several of these departments house their own agencies to oversee and regulate particular aspects of their areas of responsibility. Additionally, there are approximately seventy-four "independent" agencies and government corporations not subordinated under the auspices of any executive department. These agencies and corporations range from the Corporation for Public Broadcasting to the Export-Import Bank of the United States to the National Science Foundation to the Farm Credit Administration to the Tennessee Valley Authority to the U.S. Postal Service. The underlying mission of each government agency is to promulgate regulations, guidelines, and opinions to implement federal laws. Regulations then possess the power of federal law, even though they are not voted on by the U.S. Congress.

The Code of Federal Regulations (CFR) is the "codification of the general and permanent rules published in the Federal Registry by the departments and agencies of the Federal Government."[58] As such, the CFR should be a corporate lawyer's sourcebook for all federal regulations. Likewise, the Federal Register is the ground-level resource for the official, daily publication for rules, proposed rules, and notices for federal agencies and organizations.[59] The public's ability to comment on proposed regulations is a unique part of the regulatory process, and it should be an essential component of a well-maintained compliance program (and lobbying efforts) for most businesses.

Executive Order Number 13,563, "Improving Regulation and Regulatory Review," signed by President Barack Obama on January 18, 2011, stressed the need for regulations and regulatory processes to be "accessible, consistent, written in plain language, and easy to understand."[60] Additionally, it resulted in guidance to all federal agencies from the Office of Management and Budget regarding a "retrospective analysis of existing significant regulations."[61] Essentially, this means that government agencies are supposed to review regulations even after regulations are implemented. The idea—an excellent one—is to evaluate the practical consequences of regulatory mandates to see if the darn things actually do what they are supposed to do.[62] Providing comments, and supplying empirical data to agencies after regulations are implemented, allows the public—your client-company—to become part of the brain trust for developing rational and understandable (if not favorable) regulatory controls.[63] When everything is said and done, it is those regulatory controls, mandates, and guidelines that will form the crucible of your client-company's compliance program.

Roll up your sleeves, make the calls, have the meetings, and do your homework, and you will be surprised at how quickly good information and practical systems begin to appear.

§ 5.3.3 Policies and Procedures

> For chief compliance officers, the challenge is how to implement policies, procedures and standards that, in spite of the regulatory complexities, are easily understood by, and transparent to, employees and stakeholders.[64]

The nitty-gritty of a compliance program is its policies and procedures. For the most part, the document drafting for these policies and procedures can benefit from the numerous and easily accessible form policies that have been painstakingly created, drafted, implemented, revised, critiqued, and then revised again a thousand times by a legion of corporate lawyers and compliance departments over the past twenty to thirty years. As we did in Section 5.1.3 for employment-law issues, we can look at the fantastic work contained in volume three of *The In-House Counsel's Essential Toolkit*.[65] Most bread-and-butter compliance policies, along with numerous notes and sample forms, are addressed in the *Toolkit*.

Actual implementation, as with any corporate program, follows policy directives and the pragmatics of how an individual corporate organization works. In this respect, one size does not fit all, so do not be hesitant about creatively implementing an adaptive policy. Just make sure the end result stays true to the policy's intent.

Implementation of an effective program is not a science, nor is it usually an easy or seamless adjustment for most companies. All of a client-company's key players must be on board with the goals and methodologies of the company's compliance program, and open and routine communication must be encouraged to make sure issues are being promptly addressed, questions are being answered (at all levels), procedures are being disseminated and followed, and inconsistencies are being identified and reconciled.

In this respect, the FSG can prove to be a very helpful, practical evaluation medium. The FSG identify seven types of steps to include in an effective compliance program. Even though the FSG are focused on possible criminal conduct, the concept, and the application of each objective, is the same. If you are able to recognize these steps—these benchmarks—in each of your client-company's compliance policies and procedures, then there is a very good chance the program will be a fruitful one.

The seven types of steps are as follows:

1. Organizational implementation of compliance standards and procedures reasonably capable of reducing the prospect of criminal conduct.
2. Assignment of high-level personnel to oversee conformity with standards and procedures.
3. Due care in avoiding delegation to individuals whom the organization knows, or should know, to have a propensity to engage in illegal activities.
4. Effective communication of standards and procedures by requiring participation in training programs or by disseminating publications that explain in a practical manner what is required.

5. Establishing monitoring, auditing, and reporting systems by creating and publicizing a reporting system whereby employees and other agents can report criminal conduct without fear of retribution (that is, a whistleblower system).
6. Enforcing standards through appropriate mechanisms, including, as appropriate, discipline of individuals responsible for the failure to detect an offense.
7. Developing appropriate responses to offenses by taking all reasonable steps to respond appropriately and to prevent further similar offenses, including any necessary modification of programs.[66]

Another resource worth mentioning for its accommodation of almost any organization's needs, structure, and operations is the Open Compliance and Ethics Group (OCEG). The OCEG is a nonprofit organization helping organizations create and maintain "Principled Performance by enhancing corporate culture and integrating governance, risk management, and compliance processes[.]"[67] The OCEG offers a variety of products and services useful for assessing compliance (and ethics) programs, implementing programs, certifications, education, and connecting organizations with other resource providers.

You may now be saying to yourself something like the following: *Even if there are a lot of resources out there, and even if I can sit down with everyone I need to within my client-company, how do I know whether or not I am putting together the right kind of policies and procedures—the right compliance program—to meet my company's needs?*

You are asking the right kind of question, and with an ironic smile, I will cheekily refer to another available resource for an answer. Bryan Cabrera, vice president, general counsel, and secretary of Synopsys, Inc., has done the heavy lifting for you. Mr. Cabrera suggests five essential elements for "compliance best practices . . . that promote the effective understanding and awareness of enterprise risk management, while helping steer clear of ethical, regulatory, and legal issues throughout the global landscape."[68]

They are as follows:

1. *Effective design: straightforward and transparent*—"[T]he substance of the compliance programs must be understood, relevant, and

updated such that employees and business partners can easily comprehend and execute on the principles so important to doing business ethically and legally around the globe."

2. *Efficient communications: more partnering, less policing*—"Without collaborative relationships across the organization, compliance staff may be feared, but they won't be effective."

3. *Proactive training: relevant, relatable, and repeatable*—"Training should be about ensuring employees understand what is expected of them, not simply passing on as much information as possible."

4. *Ongoing monitoring and reporting: extending your reach*—"A company must have mechanisms in place to ensure the security and integrity of these reporting channels, and must ensure that these reports are managed properly."

5. *Effective enforcement: accountability and transparency*—"The compliance organization should be reviewing all significant compliance violations reported to it in order to evaluate the effectiveness of the company's existing compliance programs, policies, and procedures related to the violation."[69]

These five essential elements reflect several of the core "types of steps" recommended in the FSG, but they move past a slant toward implementation and offer a more comprehensive way of assessing your client-company's developing, or already implemented, compliance program.

Between these five elements, the FSG steps, the use of services such as those offered by OCEG, and the form-ready materials in a resource like the *Toolkit*, a corporate lawyer's anxiety over where to begin, how to create a compliance program, how to implement the program, and how to evaluate the program should switch from a full-blown, lights-out migraine to a low-grade, one-aspirin headache. (If not, seek medical attention.)

§ 5.3.4 *Working with the Internal (or External) Auditor*

Now that you have that headache under control, take a deep breath. This is a good time to introduce you to a friend who has been sitting quietly in a shadowy corner taking notes, and whispering in the ears of the Board of Directors' Audit Committee: the internal auditor.[70]

Internal auditing, as a corporate mission, seeks to improve an organization's operations by ensuring a systematic and disciplined approach to the evaluation of the effectiveness of risk management, control, and governance processes.[71] The scope of activity is more wide ranging than mere compliance, but conceptually, the fundamental purposes of compliance and internal auditing are very similar and have significant overlap.

An internal auditor or, in the case of publicly traded corporations, a chief audit executive in charge of the internal auditing department will frequently measure and report on an organization's compliance with policies and procedures across several areas of responsibility, such as operations, financial reporting, the deterrence and investigation of fraud, the safeguarding of assets and records, and compliance. In the truest sense, an internal auditor is strictly an *auditor* and does not possess enforcement authority. He or she acts as the board's, and executive management's, eyes and ears within a corporation to increase efficiency, improve effectiveness, ensure uniformity, manage risk, and identify liabilities.

There are times when the work of an internal auditor does not affect or involve corporate counsel, but internal auditors and corporate lawyers do share many of the same concerns and advisory activities in matters of risk management, internal controls assessment, and governance participation. From the perspective of a corporate lawyer, an internal auditor acts as the trouble-spotter for issues that could result in some level of corporate liability. As an internal auditor goes about his or her work, it is a good practice—a *best* practice—for a corporate lawyer to regularly meet with the auditor, discuss internal liability concerns, and offer assistance if and when it might be needed to supplement the reporting and advisory role of the auditor to the board or to management.

There is a Roman proverb that says, "Beware of a silent dog and still water."

Corporate lawyers will find that the usually taciturn role of an internal auditor does not mean turmoil isn't about to bubble over when illegal actions, malfeasance, or improper conduct result in the need for an internal investigation.

§ 5.3.5 *Conducting the Internal Investigation*

> *The evil that men do lives after them; the good is oft interred with their bones.*[72]

"An internal investigation is an inquiry conducted by, or on behalf of, an organization in an effort to discover salient facts pertaining to acts or omissions that may generate civil or criminal liability."[73] In short, something within a client-company has misfired, and there needs to be an inquiry to determine what, if anything, needs to be done about it. An investigation, by its focus on specific allegations, is not an audit; audits are creatures of review and are generally routine affairs. Audits are checkups. Investigations are surgeries.

Essentially, an investigation acts as a defensive tool, probing and excising the bad out of the good. As regulatory oversight began to encroach upon, and eventually overtake, corporate America during the past thirty to forty years, federal enforcement efforts—whether civil or criminal—began to "delve into realms of activities once perceived solely as internal corporate affairs."[74] Corporate lawyers realized that internal investigations could assist their client-companies by "uncovering problems and staving off prosecution through voluntary disclosure and remedial action."[75]

In a post-FCPA, post-FSG, post-SOX, post-Dodd-Frank world, a corporation simply cannot afford *not* to pay serious attention to internal allegations or evidence of foul play or illegal behavior. The consequences—not the least of which is the possible loss of public confidence—are too great.

Like surgery, investigations are sometimes invasive and traumatic. They are designed to root through statements and records in fixated and potentially unsettling ways, even when the utmost care and tact are used. For privilege reasons, privacy reasons, liability reasons, and strategic reasons, internal investigations are generally conducted as quietly as possible, cordoned off from employees at large, shareholders, the public (including regulatory and law enforcement in many cases), and, occasionally, certain members of management and the board. Ironically, the confidential nature of internal investigations—regardless of the reasons—is also their major challenge and the chief cause of their complexity and difficulty. Secrets, especially those involving the possibility of civil liability, employment termination, negative press, drops in price-per-share value, fines, or criminal offenses, do not sit well with corporate organizations.

Therefore, the overarching concern of every corporate lawyer should be not only to conduct a thorough and appropriate investigation to the extent one is necessary, but to do so with aplomb, efficiency, focus, and calmness. Lawyers—contrary to popular misconception—are people too, and the intrigue and seriousness of internal investigations can stir up feelings of tension, excitement, apprehension, and instability. To the best of your ability, those personal reactions must be controlled. In the midst of an investigation, a client-company needs the reassuring leadership of its corporate counsel more than ever. No patient ever wants to hear an attending surgeon say "uh oh" or "oops," or "I'm just really stressed out," as the scalpel incises a wound.

Proceed methodically, proficiently, and with intelligent caution.

The actual conduct of an internal investigation can be simple or complex, although even simple investigations have the potential of bet-the-company consequences. With that in mind, each investigation should be conducted meticulously and with attention to detail and hard-to-see pitfalls. Thankfully, there are an increasing number of excellent resources available to address almost every conceivable investigatory situation, and one, if not more, should occupy some shelf space in every corporate lawyer's office.[76]

The issue being investigated, and the breadth of its reach within a client-company, most often dictates how involved or complicated an investigation may become. For routine issues, such as a hotline complaint that a mid- or low-level supervisor is practicing some form of illegal discrimination, there might be a standard pattern for an investigation to follow: a certain number of employees to be interviewed, a certain time period of documentation to be reviewed, and a particular hierarchy of management to be notified and advised. For anomalous situations, or situations involving executive-level personnel, or that appear to be pervasive companywide, there might not be any precedential or standardized way to conduct the investigation. Prudence may have to combine itself with creativity.

Regardless of the intricacy or size of an internal investigation, a corporate lawyer should be diligent to follow, or be aware of, these basic elements of progression:

- Determine who the initiating and authoritative person or entity is for purposes of the investigation (such as the CEO, the audit committee, the board of directors, and so forth). A letter, an engagement letter, a committee resolution, or a board resolution should be generated to set the terms of representation, the scope of the investigation, and the expected reporting requirements.

- Determine whether in-house counsel can be, and appears to be, independent and objective when conducting the investigation. If not, engage outside counsel, who would not have any conflicts as a result of previous representation activities of certain personnel or departments.
- Determine the intended scope of the investigation.
- Determine which persons—management, committee members, outside counsel, board members, auditors—need to be included within the fact-gathering and reporting structure.
- Determine what potential litigation actions, and which potential litigants, there might be in order to evaluate possible liabilities and to invoke the work-product privilege.
- Determine the control of information to be gathered during the course of the investigation. Alert necessary departments, such as IT and HR, about specific information needs, requests, and confidentiality concerns.
- Determine which interviews need to be conducted and make sure that each interview conforms with interview requirements (that is, two interviewers present if possible, the giving of clear Upjohn warnings,[77] and the safeguarding of appropriate privileges).

Because employee interviews, informally or taken as sworn statements, are usually the heart of internal investigations, a corporate lawyer must make sure that each interview is carefully approached. At the outset of every interview (even if it has been provided in previous interviews), an Upjohn warning should be clearly given.[78] There is no universally recognized, magic language to an Upjohn warning, but the concepts of identifying who the interviewing represents (that is, the client-company, *not* the employee) and the assertion of privilege should be a part of every warning. Here is an example:

> I am conducting this interview in order to gather facts so I can provide legal advice to the Company. This interview is part of an internal investigation in anticipation of possible civil or criminal action because of circumstances X. I am here to represent the Company and only the Company. I cannot, and do not intend to, act as your lawyer. Because of this, the Company holds the privilege over all communications during this interview and this investigation. You may not disclose the substance of this

interview, or any information exchanged in this interview, with anyone else without the express permission of the Company.[79]

Do you have any questions about anything I've just explained?

Are you willing to proceed?

Though you do not want to alienate or scare your employee witness, it is better to be clear about everyone's roles and duties before proceeding with an interview. If an interview is being conducted along with counsel for another organization or person who has a common interest in the outcome of the investigation, or if the interview is later shared with such counsel, then make sure a Joint Defense Agreement has been executed, and begin every meeting, or include in every cover letter, a statement that the information is being shared subject to the Joint Defense Agreement and subject to joint defense legal principles. Internal investigations lose a significant portion, if not all, of their effectiveness if a client-company's privileges are needlessly lost.

There are many times when the phrase "internal investigation" is spoken in anxiety-riddled whispers, but in reality, a corporation's ability and desire to quietly police itself *before* anyone kicks in the door should be seen as a positive change agent, or as a constructive affirmation that a client-company's policies and procedures are working. Corporate lawyers may have the unpleasant chore of conducting investigations, but doing so with professionalism, composure, reassurance, and a plan in hand will soothe an edgy client-company and allow its focus to turn back to the business of conducting its business.

At this late point, you may notice (if you haven't already) that this chapter separates *compliance*, *audits*, and *investigations* from *ethics*. The reason for this is to draw attention to the fact that *law* is not necessarily *ethos*. Strictly speaking, laws are mandatory restrictions, permissions, or obligations, and by their mandatory nature, they seek to eliminate a moral, or ethical, analysis and bring uniformity to a society's expectations and interactions.

True, the separation between law and ethos may be an academic fiction (the law is far too peppered with principled subjectivity), but the distinction is still important for a corporate lawyer to recognize as he or she goes about advising a client-company in matters of compliance or investigation. There are times when a corporate lawyer may look at his or her client-company and say, "Doing that is legal, *but . . .*" The ellipsis carries the ethical analysis that may need to be superimposed upon the character of whatever legal advice is given.

Successful compliance programs, and certainly internal investigations, will have—must have—a solid, ethical disposition, but where that ethos comes from is found in the *culture* of the company, not just a program. A client-company's ethics grow out of how it is *governed* and operated by those who are in charge. The next section will underscore that reality.

§ 5.4 GOVERNANCE AND CORPORATE ETHICS

Edward Ludwig, chairman and CEO of Becton, Dickinson and Company,[80] delivered an address on November 2, 2011, at the Atlantic Legal Foundation's Annual Award Dinner, during which, Mr. Ludwig remarked,

> More and more leaders are embracing the reality that societal needs—not just conventional economic needs—define markets, and that societal harms and costs can create internal costs and inefficiencies for firms. This is not to be confused with corporate responsibility or pure philanthropy.[81]

This observation goes to the root of how a business decides to run itself. The practicalities of operations, accounting methods, and hierarchical structure directly reflect the governing mindset of an organization. Increasingly, companies have realized their mindsets need to reflect an awareness and an activism toward societal needs and societal harms— the likes and dislikes of a company's demographics and the expectations of our society when addressing those likes and dislikes.

How a business runs itself is ultimately the basis by which it will be judged—by employees, vendors, business partners, management, shareholders, regulatory agencies, the courts, and the public. Governance is a deeper concern than corporate responsibility, mission statements, or public relations campaigns (although they are all derived from how a business is run). *Corporate governance* is literally how a corporation goes about governing—supervising and monitoring—all of its affairs.

How a corporation governs its affairs *is* its ethos.

Governance

§ 5.4.1 Who Are Your Internal Connections?

The governance of a company involves its board of directors, its share-holders, and its officers and managers. These are the decision makers, and it is their responsibility—within distinctive capacities—to determine how a company is run, whether it is being run according to its policies, and what policy changes may need to be made. Their decisions, and their willingness and ability to monitor the effects of their decisions, have a variety of business-related consequences: public-exchange-listing requirements, governance ratings for investors, efficiency and effectiveness of business units' performances, compliance with regulatory requirements and guidelines, risk management, industry certifications, underwriting requirements, and government-program participation eligibility. There are, of course, potential adverse consequences, such as civil lawsuits, regulatory enforcement actions, and criminal penalties.

A corporate lawyer's internal connections—and external relationships—need to reflect attention to all of these business-related and sometimes adverse consequences to the manner in which a client-company is governed. The board of directors is the focal point of the majority of governance issues; therefore, a corporate lawyer should look to and work with those connections which assist and advise the board in its governance activities. These connections will include auditors (internal and external), compliance officers, risk managers, senior executives, consultants, and sometimes independent governance counsel, who may be engaged specifically to advise and represent the board on governance matters.

§ 5.4.2 *Know the Law*

The law of corporate governance involves the policies, goals, actions, and decisions taken by a client-company's decision makers: shareholders, board members, and officers. Understanding the roles and responsibilities of each of these decision makers is critical if a corporate lawyer—who many times is also the corporate secretary[82]—is to understand how, when, and whom he or she should advise on governance matters.

- Shareholders receive financial and operational data (a monitoring role), and they vote on board membership, significant mergers and acquisitions, changes in a company's charter or bylaws, and certain proposals by management or other shareholders (a supervisory role).
- Board members receive financial data, auditing advice, and compliance reports (a monitoring role), and they endorse financial reports, hire and fire management (or at least the CEO), approve policies, maintain oversight committees (such as the Audit Committee), and respond to and authorize lawsuits on behalf of the company (a supervisory role).
- Management receives compliance reports (a monitoring role) and implements decisions by the board, prepares and presents reports to the board and to shareholders, and runs the company's day-to-day operations (a supervisory role).

Each industry will have its own required policies, which a client-company must develop and implement, but there are some laws that generically affect the governance of almost all businesses: SOX and Dodd-Frank (which even affects nonfinancial companies).

The ways that SOX changed public companies, however, are undeniable. SOX led to greater internal control of financial reporting, and increased expertise and independence among more-focused boards, committees and directors. It imposed new reporting, audit, disclosure and ethics requirements, and created internal reporting and whistleblower structures upon which the Dodd-Frank Wall Street Reform and Consumer Protection Act has built.[83]

The roles of governance—both monitoring and supervisory—come with legal and ethical duties a corporate lawyer must become familiar with. To a greater extent, board members have worn the bull's-eye of blame when the duty to properly run a company has come into question, and a corporate lawyer needs to be able to communicate clearly and practically what duties and standards are expected of board members. Because the bulk of governance responsibilities lie with a client-company's board, the placement of the bull's-eye makes sense. "The most prominent change SOX engendered was a shift from a perspective that the board serves management to a perspective that management is working for the board."[84]

The basic consideration for every board member is his or her obligation to apply a duty-of-care standard in dealing with all corporate matters.

> Where a director in fact exercises a good faith effort to be informed and to exercise appropriate judgment, he or she should be deemed to satisfy fully the duty of attention. If the shareholders thought themselves entitled to some other quality of judgment than such a director produces in the good faith exercise of the powers of office, then the shareholders should have elected other directors.[85]

The American Bar Association's Model Business Corporation Act[86] provides an excellent checklist to refer to when assessing whether a director has met the standard of the duty of care:

1. Did the director act in "good faith," in a "manner the director reasonably believes to be in the best interests of the corporation"?
2. Did the director use "the care that a person in a like position would reasonably believe appropriate under similar circumstances"?
3. Did the director "disclose, or cause to be disclosed, to the other board or committee members information not already known by them but known by the director to be material to the discharge of their decision-making or oversight functions"?
4. Did the director "rely on the performance by any of the persons" who has been authorized "to perform one or more of the board's functions that are delegable under applicable law"?

5. Did the director "rely on information, opinions, reports or statements, including financial statements and other financial data, prepared or presented by any of the persons" who has been authorized to provide such information?

If so, then there is a very good chance that a director has met his or her duty of care in the discharge of his or her governance role.

§ 5.4.3 Beyond Compliance—Conducting Business

Corporate governance is, in its truest sense, not about meeting certain compliance standards or nervously wondering whether a duty of care has been met. Corporate governance is about running a business *the right way*. Generally speaking, our society—as capitalistic as we might be—has roughly interpreted this to mean maximizing returns, protecting assets, looking after the share price, increasing efficiency, promoting integrity and fairness, requiring transparent reporting, managing risk and liability exposure, and retaining public trust and confidence.

These concerns manifest themselves in a multitude of tasks and responsibilities, mostly held by a board of directors. Corporate lawyers must become comfortable with the legal tenets of each task and responsibility but must also understand how the discharge and monitoring of each task and responsibility actually affects the progress of the overall business enterprise. To best assist the board members of a client-company, a corporate lawyer needs to be prepared to address and advise upon the following:

- Corporate governance guidelines
- Board committee charters
- Corporate disclosure policies and practices
- Ownership reporting
- Board performance evaluation
- Board meetings, actions, and resolutions
- Shareholder meetings and actions[87]

Keep in mind, governance issues are not merely the formal drafting, approval, and implementation of policies; they are the backbone of how a client-company goes about running itself.

§ 5.4.4 What Is the Ethical Culture?—Defining Risks

> [Policies] encompass not only boards of directors and executive officers, but also general codes of conduct and codes of ethics intended as standards for all employees.[88]

Most corporate lawyers have had to, at some point, deal with situations in which they applied the Best Judgment Rule to ferret out, or defend, whether a board (or management) decision could be second-guessed. The Best Judgment Rule is a presumption that a decision maker has acted in good faith "in the honest belief that the action taken was in the best interests of the company."[89] The three main legs of the rule are all questions of ethos: good faith, honest belief, and a company's best interests (which is *not* merely a question of profit).

In Section 2.1.4, we discussed how a corporate lawyer goes about understanding and working within a client-company's culture. In the world of corporate governance, the rubber meets the road. Cultures of waste, illegality, fraud, self-interest, and apathy create gaping holes of potential liability and inefficiency—all issues that could strip away the protections of the Best Judgment Rule—exposing a corporate ethos of bad faith, ignorance, and egocentric hubris. Cultures of productivity, efficiency, transparency, awareness, and lawfulness create insulation against risk and the promotion of growth.

Corporate culture—the extension of its governance—is not limited to a client-company's top echelon of decision makers. "An employer may be liable for both negligent and intentional torts committed by an employee within the scope of his or her employment."[90] Good corporate governance practices, and a corporate lawyer's diligent encouragement and advice to follow best practices, can bring an entire company's population into line.

Ben Heineman, former general counsel of GE and distinguished senior fellow at Harvard Law School's Program on the Legal Profession, said the following:

> General counsel are responsible at the senior levels of not only asking the first question—is it legal?—but also the last question: Is it right? That means the skills that are required of them go far beyond being a technical lawyer. They have to be wise counselors and leaders. They can't just hide in their offices and wait for someone to ask them a legal question, and then look in their Rolodex and call somebody.[91]

§ 5.5 INTELLECTUAL PROPERTY

> Intellectual property law is increasingly complex. Licensing, joint development, strategic alliances, and mixed media all can involve multiple types of IP. Additionally, transactions or matters involving intellectual property . . . often implicate other areas of law, including corporate, partnership, tax, employment, government procurement, export control, antitrust, and bankruptcy.[92]

Intellectual property (IP), more than ever, can be such a daunting and specialized field of law that many corporate lawyers will shrug their shoulders and admit they do not know much about it. As long as that honest self-assessment does not result in turning a blind eye toward IP issues, it is a great place to start.

We spent some time in Section 3.1.3 identifying IP issues faced by new business ventures, as well as those companies that have spent little time understanding or protecting their IP assets and obligations. Therefore, the purpose of the present section is not to revisit those observations (even though I am often guilty of needlessly repeating myself). Instead, this section is intended to give the ground rules of what you need to know.

Below are some fundamental definitions:

- A *patent* (utility, design, or plant) is a set of exclusive rights awarded by an authorized agency to an applicant (usually the inventor or an assignee) for a certain period of time to protect those exclusive rights after the public disclosure of an invention. The award of a patent usually requires the elements of patentability (that is, meets the legal requirements to be patentable), which are novelty, nonobvious (U.S. law) or involving an inventive step (European law), and usefulness (U.S.) or industrial application (European).

- A *trademark* is a distinctive indicator exclusive to its owner for the purpose of identifying for consumers and the public the unique source of certain products or services and distinguishing those products and services from similar or competitive products or services. An unregistered trademark, [TM], is used to brand or promote goods. An unregistered service mark, [SM], is used to brand or promote services. A registered trademark is indicated by ®. Normally, a trademark is a name, word, logo, design, symbol, image, or a combination of any of these, including nonconventional trademarks, such as those based on color, smell, or sound.

- A *copyright* is a set of exclusive rights awarded to the creator of an original work for a limited time. The copyright holder has the right to receive credit for the work and determine who may adapt the work and in what form, who may perform the work, and who may financially benefit from it. Most copyright laws have been relatively standardized through international copyright agreements, pursuant to the Berne Convention,[93] although some unique characteristics still exist in most countries. The use of a copyright symbol, ©, is optional but recommended in order to avoid the defense of "innocent infringement."

- A *trade secret* is, uniquely, not awarded by any filing. Instead, it is a particular formula, process, methodology, practice, design, pattern, instrument, or compilation used by a company and that is not generally known or reasonably ascertainable. A trade secret is further characterized by its ability to give an economic or competitive advantage to a company. A company's lack of vigilance to protect the confidentiality of a trade secret, or to sue for its disclosure, may lead to the loss of its rights.

§ 5.5.1 *Who Are Your Internal Connections?*

Corporate lawyers do not have any problem accepting that IP issues can be a big deal for a client-company, but a disconnect can begin to occur when a couple of questions are asked:

Who, within a client-company, is affected by IP issues?

Why are they affected by IP issues?

In answer to the first question, a quick survey of different business units and departments should provide a handy list of those who are affected by intellectual property: compliance, finance, operations, sales, public relations, human resources, IT, research and development, customer service, manufacturing, and records. In short, nearly everyone in a company is affected by intellectual property. A corporate lawyer need only poke his or her head out the door to spot a unit or department that deals with IP issues or generates IP issues. (The legal department, in fact, is no exception.)

Each of these users, or originators, should be following the applicable provisions of the corporate IP program, and some of them probably need additional, department-specific programs and policies to handle IP issues unique to their area of responsibility and function. To best understand what works, what is needed, and what needs to be anticipated, a corporate lawyer ought to visit with each department or business-unit head on a regular basis (perhaps once a quarter or biannually) and focus on that department's concerns, questions, and expectations. This kind of "meet-and-confer" should supplement the IP program's inventory and review process. Taking this kind of a step will put a corporate lawyer in a much better position to identify inefficiencies, misuses (intentional or otherwise), potential liabilities, accessibility issues, and changes that might need to be made within the client-company's IP program, or within a department-specific program.

In answer to the second question, the reason business units or departments are affected by IP falls under one of two umbrellas: (1) they use intellectual property in order to get their jobs done; and/or (2) they generate intellectual property as a result of getting their jobs done. Intellectual property can be found in all kinds of media, technologies, formulae, end products, components, methodologies, software, hardware, services, goods, and concepts. When departments and units use something that is the protected work product of a human mind, they are using intellectual property. When departments and units generate or create something that is the protected result of their own minds—their work product as a result of their employment—they are generating intellectual property.

For the most part, business units and departments will be aware of when they are using intellectual property and when they are generating intellectual property, but not always. For instance, licensing agreements may have been signed, but the software is innocently being used by unauthorized users (or an unauthorized number of users). New business methods may have been adopted, but they have already been patented by another organization. Proprietary products may be manufactured in one country and assembled in another, but how those steps affect patent or trademark protections has been overlooked. A corporate lawyer, who is regularly meeting with department heads and who stays abreast of how different business units work, can help shed light on issues that may end up having a critical impact on a client-company's intangible asset value or on its way of doing business.

§ 5.5.2 A Commodity or a Tool?

No surprise here. Identifying what pieces of intellectual property are part of a client-company's business is a first essential step. Take careful inventory. Then, there is one essential question to ask that will determine a path of *permissions* or a path of *protections*:

Is the intellectual property a commodity or a tool?

If your client-company is *using* someone else's protected intellectual property in any way, then you need to address licenses, permissions, and attributions. These IP items are tools.[94] For the *tool* category, you need to pay attention to the following general issues:

- Are the necessary permissions in place?
- Will the permissions need to be renewed or renegotiated? How often? By whom?
- What are the restrictions on use? Are there controls in place?
- What are the restrictions on access? Are there controls in place?
- Does the permission or license require any kind of indemnification? What is the scope? Does this violate any existing insurance agreements?
- Does the use violate any other noncompete agreements?

If your client-company is *generating* its own intellectual property, you need to address filings, renewals, licensing, confidentiality, and litigation. These IP items are commodities. For the *commodity* category, you need to pay attention to the following general issues:

- What kind of protection(s) is needed? When does it need to be obtained? What is necessary in order to obtain it? Who is responsible for obtaining it?
- In what jurisdictions does a protection need to be obtained? When?
- Are controls in place to avoid waiving or losing the protection?
- Are renewals/refilings necessary? When? Who is responsible for obtaining them?
- Has the object of IP protection been altered (that is, made into a new version) since protection was first obtained? If so, is a new protection needed?

- Is a tracking system in place for licensed use or sales?
- Is any end user, licensee, or competitor in violation of a protection? How? Who is responsible for addressing the violation?

§ 5.5.3 *Who Owns What?—The Basics*

Intellectual property comes in all shapes and sizes. There are patents (utility, design, and plant), trademarks, copyrights, trade secrets, databases, domain names, and reputations. The owner of any of these types of protections is the person or entity who is awarded the protection from the appropriate issuing agency. For instance, if the U.S. Patent and Trademark Office (USPTO) awards the utility patent of widget X to your client-company, then your client-company *owns* the intellectual property covered by the utility patent for widget X even if your client-company did not invent widget X.

IP protections grant owners exclusive rights, such as the ability to sue for infringement and to permit the manufacturing and/or distribution of a protected item. The intellectual property can be sold, licensed, or lost if renewals are not timely filed, or if it is determined that the protection was improperly awarded in the first place. Because control over a protected item's usage and financial value is the bread and butter of ownership, a corporate lawyer needs to be aware of several different contractual and policy issues:

- Invention/copyright assignment provisions in employment contracts
- Policies on implied assignments of inventions/copyrights
- Nondisclosure agreements
- Noncompete issues
- Joint-ownership agreements
- Branding agreements
- Licensing agreements (patent, trademark, and software)
- Web site terms and conditions of use[95]

The last situation you want to be facing is when everything is in place for an exciting merger, vertical integration, spin-off, or hefty infringement lawsuit, and someone realizes the client-company's IP assets are not what they thought they were, or that its IP assets have never been properly protected, leaving intangible "assets" worthless.

You might be surprised at the number of companies who only discover during pre-sale due diligence that their registered mark is actually different from the company's current mark.[96]

The passage of the Jumpstart Our Business Startups Act[97] (JOBS),[98] signed into law on April 5, 2012, introduced an intriguing new concern into the field of IP law: crowd-funding. In the past, *crowd-funding* has traditionally been defined as the collective effort of individuals who pool financial resources to support a person or organization, such as disaster-relief efforts, political campaigns, shareware development, and scientific or medical research. The JOBS Act has now taken that funding resource and used it to carve out an exemption from the requirement to register public offerings with the SEC, subject to several conditions.[99] The exemption is intended to open the door to legalizing crowd-funding equity financing. This exemption has initiated some fascinating commentary and debate in the area of securities laws, but it also opened the door to an IP concern.

"In order to engage the crowd [usually via Internet portals], a large quantity of information about the project is shared with the public, either voluntarily in the case of donation-based [Internet] portals or, as will be required by [the JOBS Act], in the case of portals offering crowdfunded securities."[100] The sharing of confidential information (that is, the sharing of "non-obvious" or "novel" information) may trigger certain patent filing deadlines and/or result in the loss of patent eligibility. Because of the mandatory disclosure requirements imposed by the JOBS Act, a company may be compelled to disclose that kind of confidential information and, therefore, "should take special precautions to ensure that they have clear title to their IP rights before they make a crowdfund offering."[101] An article written by Scott Popma, a partner at Finnegan, Henderson, Farabow, Garret & Dunner, and Elizabeth Shah, an associate with the same firm, have coauthored an article (which I have been quoting) that offers five solid "best practices" to consider when faced with this kind of situation.[102]

§ 5.5.4 State, Federal, and International IP

Some states have an office or agency in charge of IP filings and recordings, but these are generally limited to trademarks and may have very limited usefulness in interstate or international commerce.[103]

IP

Federally, the U.S. government maintains the USPTO for issuance of patents and the filing of registered trademarks.[104] Copyrights are filed with the U.S. Copyright Office.[105]

Though most domestic companies with domestically sold products or services may not need to worry about international IP protections and laws, a corporate lawyer would do well to be familiar with the World Intellectual Property Organization (WIPO)[106] and the World Trade Organization's Trade-Related Aspects of Intellectual Property Rights (TRIPS),[107] which "establishes minimum levels of protection that each government has to give to the intellectual property of fellow WTO members."[108]

A final word before leaving the Candy Land© of intellectual property: the most important thing to do when it comes to intellectual property is worth mentioning again—engage an expert.[109]

§ 5.6 LITIGATION

If there is an area of practice that feels like home to most lawyers, it is probably the area of litigation. Researching cases, reading briefs, drafting briefs, answering discovery, propounding discovery, sweating through hearings, sitting through mediations, and preparing for trial are some of the experiences most of us would be able to share at least a few stories about. Indeed, the common experience of law school, whether one attended an Ivy League institution or fought one's way through night courses at a city college, is that the law is mostly taught through the standpoint of litigation, memorialized by case law: plaintiffs versus defendants duking it out until a lofty and learned court tells us lesser mortals why one is right and one is wrong. This is not to say every lawyer, or even most lawyers, are *comfortable* with litigation, but litigation probably feels more like the lingua franca[110] of lawyers than, say, admiralty law.

Corporate lawyers—at least those who were not immediately pigeonholed in mergers and acquisitions, governance, lobbying, or some other customarily nonlitigious pursuit—are surprisingly familiar with litigation. The frock of a litigator might seem like a three-piece, polyester, bright-green suit that doesn't fit too well, but corporate lawyers generally know how to put it on. This familiarity is largely due to the tough reality that litigation is very often a normal cost of business for most organizations. Disgruntled employees, defaulting borrowers, unhappy shareholders, choleric competitors, upset customers, zealous regulators, and uncooperative vendors all represent potential lawsuits—filed either by the client-company or against the client-company. In this day and age, few companies carry on their businesses unscathed.

Familiarity is a good thing. In fact, a good corporate lawyer will make a real effort to understand and actively supervise,[111] or even participate in, each piece of litigation, but here is the trick: a good corporate lawyer's greatest contribution—his or her maximum business value to the client-company—in litigation matters is to *know his or her limits* and to act responsibly within those limits.

If a corporate lawyer recognizes and understands his or her limitations when it comes to a client-company's litigation needs, everything else should fall into place with less effort, lower costs, and better results.

Take a hard look at your experience and your skill set. Take an equally hard look at your law department's capabilities and resources. How big of a case can you handle? What if it is aggressively litigated? Are you capable of thousands (if not tens of thousands) of pages of document reviews? Can your schedule, or any support staff's schedule, absorb the time needed to investigate facts, draft briefs, research issues, attend depositions, attend hearings, prepare for mediation, attend mediation, prepare for trial, and attend trial? Are policies and procedures in place to manage outside counsel? Are policies and procedures in place for e-discovery issues and management? What kinds of cost controls are at your disposal? What company resources, and/or personnel, are available?

Answering these questions—answers that will likely evolve over time and perhaps vary from case to case—will determine the who, what, when, where, why, and how of each lawsuit's management, no matter who ends up wearing the bright-green, polyester suit.

§ 5.6.1 *Who Are Your Internal Connections?*

Lawsuits can spring up at any time and involve virtually any part of an organization, but there are a few consistent connections to keep in mind when your client-company is preparing to file a suit, knows it is about to be sued, or has just been served.

Internet Technology, the mystical IT department, should almost always be your first stop. Over the past fifteen years or so, our world has irreversibly entered an electronic age of emails, texts, electronic files, instant messaging, personal digital assistants (PDAs), smartphones, electronic notepads, digital videos, and social networking. Virtually every kind of data—especially business communications and records data—can be, or is, electronically generated, stored, and tracked, even unwittingly.

Unlike a sheet of paper, which was once wadded up and tossed for three points into the nearest trashcan, an email, for example, may remain in existence long after it was deleted from a user's inbox. Unlike dealing with a sexually suggestive comment once made by a dim-witted executive to a subordinate while in the break room, a corporation may now face the damning, incontrovertible existence of hundreds of "sexting" texts. Unlike the cocktail-induced dance of an impulsive employee during a 1989 company Christmas party, a corporate lawyer may now open an Internet browser in 2012 and watch a viral video of the misconduct along with millions of other entertained people. Suffice to say, corporate lawyers and their client-companies have been running at full throttle over the past decade to come to grips with the dark side of electronic technology. That dark side, and the sheer volume and permanence of electronic records, has brought IT departments to the forefront of corporate litigation issues.

If you haven't already, you will be introduced to words and phrases such as *cloud data, e-discovery, predictive coding, electronically stored information* (ESI), *early data assessment, keyword searches,* and *statistical document-sorting technology.* You will quickly become a student of your client-company's IT capabilities, what data it stores, how it stores it, where it stores it, for what period of time it is stored, who has access to it, and how and in what format any given part of it can be retrieved, segregated, redacted, or mirrored. In return for this education, you will eventually throw the switch that will move the IT department's, and your client-company's, standard information-retention procedures onto an alternate track. The switch is referred to as a *litigation hold* or *document preservation directive,* and it needs to be sent to all departments and department heads from whom you may need to request records (whether paper or electronic) during the course of a lawsuit.

Essentially, a litigation-hold letter is a letter from legal counsel to a client, instructing the client to preserve all records of any type that are within the scope of a lawsuit or an anticipated lawsuit.

> [M]ake sure the litigation hold is in writing, and includes at minimum the date of issue, the recipients and the scope of preservation. Many parties include more in their holds, like reference to the triggering event that made litigation reasonably foreseeable, avenues for recipients to ask questions and advice of others who might be subject to the notice and/or an initial explanation of how the data will be collected.[112]

By itself, a litigation-hold letter is not a complex document,[113] but the practical implementation of its directives can seem unworkable to an IT department (or other departments), which might be caught flat-footed, especially if there is not already in place a well-structured document retention policy.[114] An effective document retention policy[115] sets out procedures for records' generation, access, handling, retention, and destruction to meet industry-specific regulations and the individual needs, capabilities, and goals, both immediate and future, of a client-company.[116] The *consistent* implementation of the policy is critical and must include regular training, periodic reminders and flags for permanent records disposal, and hardware and software system checks.

Because it typically involves regulatory compliance issues, and because it can predetermine how easy, difficult, or costly electronic discovery may be, it is in the best interests of a corporate lawyer to become very familiar with his or her document retention policy (if not help draft it) and the IT department's capabilities. Being proactive will help keep costs low, reduce business interruptions, and prevent the unsavory possibility of sanctions.[117]

Close on the heels of meeting with the IT department and issuing a litigation-hold letter, a corporate lawyer will need to make sure the proper notifications have been sent to a client-company's insurance carrier (that is, meet with the risk manager). Sometimes a corporate lawyer may need to anticipate and explain to management the arrival of a reservation-of-rights (ROR) letter from a client-company's carrier if the carrier has reason to believe the client-company's alleged liability may not ultimately be covered by its policy; that is, the carrier is reserving the right to deny coverage at a later date and/or recover expenses. There might also be the need to issue a tender-of-defense letter to the insurance carrier of another party or potential party, such as a vendor, who might need to foot the bill for litigation costs.

A corporate lawyer will want to meet with the public relations department if the lawsuit is significant enough, or likely, to precipitate public exposure. Senior executives and the finance department need to be made aware of the possibility of sizeable financial exposure and the need to set aside reserves if necessary (either strategically or due to regulatory or underwriting obligations). The compliance department can become part of the conversation too, in those situations where regulatory agencies must be notified of the lawsuit or apprised of its progress.

Without stirring the pot unnecessarily, it is usually the safer bet to at least touch base with as many departments and managers as you think might need to know, for whatever reason. This way, they can anticipate possible scheduling changes, reassignments, or other business interruptions; what additional responsibilities they may have; what departmental records or procedures may be requested; and interviews that may be requested from key personnel.

Make sure the cinches are tight and the wagons are circled.

§ 5.6.2 Evaluating the Case—The Linchpin

Superlative trial attorneys have a sixth sense about lawsuits; this is part of the art of litigation. Based on known facts, likely witnesses, the possible need for experts, verdict trends, possible timetables for trial, recent damages awards, and the personalities and inclinations of judges, experienced trial attorneys are able to arrive at fairly accurate case assessments.

From these initial assessments, decisions can be made whether to actually file the case (if the client is the plaintiff); what causes of action, or which affirmative defenses, will need to be asserted; whether early settlement is an advisable option (and in what price range); what discovery will need to be requested and what documents will need to be reviewed and preserved; who will need to be hired for expert testimony; how much time will almost certainly be needed to conduct discovery; which court the case should be filed in or moved to (if possible); and—above all, perhaps—*what the beast will cost*. In short, early case assessment is as critical to litigation as accurate intelligence is to a military commander.

A corporate lawyer must be able to evaluate a case *before* making decisions that could commit massive amounts of resources and dollars to a lawsuit. However, unless a corporate lawyer has been hired out of a litigation background, the finer points of the art of early case assessment might be harder to divine. But in some way, divine them you must.

If you are lacking a lot of litigation experience, if a lawsuit appears to be uniquely complex, or if it centers on an area of law with which you are unfamiliar, do not hesitate to reach out to someone else who can help. An early case-assessment process represents a fantastic window of time during which to ask outside counsel for its advice on costs, strategies, document production and review, and timetables, even if a decision has not yet been made whether to actually assign the lawsuit to in-house or outside counsel. Or, in this new, glossy age of electronic information specialists, it may be time to bring an e-discovery vendor into the loop to get a realistic handle on what could be just as critical: early data assessment.

> The substantial expense of preservation, collection and review in the e-discovery era and the risk of serious sanctions for any significant error in this process have shifted the focus from case assessment to data assessment, a change that threatens to subvert the essential role of trial counsel in early strategic analysis and planning. In a very real sense, trial counsel are now competing with both e-discovery vendors and specialized e-discovery counsel for the client's time and resources in the early stages of litigation.[118]

The takeaway point is that a corporate lawyer must develop as much reliable information as possible about a lawsuit before it even begins, or very shortly after the first shot is fired. For client-companies that bristle at the costs and liabilities inherent in litigation but also understand that it is an inevitable cost of doing business, their legal counsel must be able to deliver the value of knowing what to expect: what a lawsuit will cost in manpower, hard resources, time, money, and public exposure.

One of the most helpful litigation-preventing tools, and one that can greatly assist a corporate lawyer to develop a better case-assessment skill set, is the litigation audit. The process and elements in most lawsuits are relatively similar, which invites the opportunity to set up an audit process designed to inform "company officials about litigation pitfalls, how certain documents might be misinterpreted if introduced at trial, and the legal exposure that could exist if greater sensitivity is not developed toward potential legal issues."[119] Carol Basri and Irving Kagan's treatise repeats the "essential elements of a litigation audit" originally posed by David Silversteen. The elements are as follows:

1. The recognition of an "evolving legal issue" that may affect the company "long after it becomes embodied in legislation or judicial decisions."
2. The determination of the direction in which the legal issue is evolving and how rapidly.
3. The decision of how best to respond to the issue.[120]

Ms. Basri and Mr. Kagan also offer a solid checklist for a corporate lawyer to use when conducting litigation audits.[121] Armed with *historical data* regarding the nature of lawsuits a client-company has typically faced, a corporate lawyer will have the kind of information needed to help a client-company steer clear of likely litigation exposure, as well as the kind of information necessary to provide a more accurate picture of what any given lawsuit might cost in terms of time, money, hard resources, and personnel, not to mention what may be the most probable outcome.

§ 5.6.3 In-House Capabilities

Some law departments are large enough to house their own litigation team, and going in house with litigation has become a snowballing trend over the past few years. That is perfectly fine, and many in-house teams do quite well. However, most corporate lawyers are not litigators any more than they are architects. Law departments are generally not designed to absorb the exigencies and budgetary demands of litigation, especially when a lawsuit takes on a life (and size) of its own and lasts for unexpectedly long periods of time.

These reflections then leave three obvious options for a corporate lawyer who is facing a fresh lawsuit to choose between:

1. Manage the lawsuit: supervise and monitor outside litigation counsel;
2. Manage the lawsuit AND help to litigate the lawsuit: supervise and select an area of responsibility in which you will directly assist the hired litigation counsel; or
3. Manage AND litigate the lawsuit: supervise and litigate the entire lawsuit on your own.

Each of the three options has pros and cons, which should largely depend on the answers to the series of self-evaluation (and department-evaluation) questions posed at the end of Section 5.6. Predictably, there should be a balancing act between available resources, costs, levels of competency, and the anticipated complexity of a lawsuit. Take the balancing act seriously, and be sure to set aside any shred of vanity that may cloud your judgment.

In bet-the-company lawsuits, or for high-profile legal issues, it is not uncommon for in-house counsel to feel the need (or the pressure) to take the helm, but I disagree with any approach that makes the perceived importance of a lawsuit the final arbiter of which of the three options a corporate lawyer should choose. Corporate law is not football; no glory comes from "wanting the ball" when the game is on the line. Instead, corporate lawyers need to keep a cool-headed, disciplined line of attack when a client-company faces a lawsuit and determine to give the client-company the absolute best value in quality and personnel.

In the late 1990s, TaylorMade Golf Company, Inc., launched an advertising campaign around one phrase: "Find Your Game." As far as golf goes, I am personally still looking for my game and the search has not been pretty, but as a corporate lawyer, I do not entertain the luxury of a hit-and-miss quest in the landscape of litigation. Too much is on the line for the client-company, even in small cases.

Having said that, a corporate lawyer *is* a company's legal counsel. Handling litigation in house can be a perfectly legitimate use of a law department's time and resources. Know ahead of time what you can handle, what your law department can handle, and what your normal stable of outside counsel can handle.

EVEN NOT-SO-SUBTLE ATTEMPTS TO JOKE ABOUT THE NEW IN-HOUSE COUNSEL'S CAPABILITIES SEEMED LOST ON HIM ...

HEY, TOM, LOOK! I REALLY DO THINK THEY BELIEVE I'M THE LITTLE ENGINE WHO COULD! ... WHAT? ... NO, I THINK THEY'RE SERIOUS. THEY BELIEVE IN ME, MAN!

WWW.TOONDOO.COM

slovett524

Capabilities

§ 5.6.4 Outside Specialists—The "Henhouse"

In Section 4.3.4, we discussed the "other" lawyers—the indispensable outside counsel—in the context of law-department management. With the right management policies and procedures in place, it is very likely your client-company will already have at its disposal the right pool of talented and practice-focused outside counsel on whom to call. However, as with any task that requires going outside, it is a threshold mistake to simply presume a particular law firm (or litigation service vendor) is the right one to go with simply because it has been used in the past. Existing relationships are valuable, but in the arena of litigation, where outcomes and public images can swiftly snowball out of control, the process of choosing the right litigation counsel must go further than the reasoning, "but we've always used Bob's firm in the past . . ."

Howard Scher, a co-managing shareholder of Buchanan, Ingersoll, and Rooney's Philadelphia office, made the following observation about choosing the right litigation counsel:

Many factors go into choosing the right trial lawyer, and conflicts and costs can limit your options. Of course experience matters, but it is far from the only measure. After decades in the trenches, I've found that the most effective lawyers don't just lean on their experience. They use it to enhance their five key traits and continually improve their craft.[122]

Mr. Scher's article goes on to discuss the five key traits a corporate lawyer should be looking for when engaging litigation counsel: credibility, civility, confidence, curiosity, and a competitive spirit.[123] Each trait is self-explanatory—and important—but it is worth noting that aggressiveness, which is so often seen as the hallmark of a litigator, is missing, or better yet, *reworked*. Aggressiveness can, of course, be prized in an area of practice that is by definition combative, but most gifted litigators understand that at every moment, at every turn, the best results may also come from an olive branch. Sheer aggressiveness will trample an olive branch underfoot, so I appreciate Mr. Scher's perceptive inclusion of a competitive spirit in the lineup of key traits, instead of aggressiveness—an insight that suggests both graciousness and fierceness.[124]

After identifying which bull in the pen to assign a case to, do not overlook the essential need for a retention letter, or an engagement letter. *Every time* a client-company engages outside counsel, a retention letter should be issued. Even in those instances in which an engagement is a standing assignment, such as in the case of regularly funneling simple contract-review tasks to an outside firm, there should still be a retention letter that sets out the terms of the engagement: its scope, the limits of an outside counsel's authority, the fee arrangement, a work-product evaluation process, and the terms for termination.

In fact, both parties—the client-company and the outside law firm—should want a retention letter in place every time, before representation begins. As with any contract, a retention letter is where both parties will be able to refer for guidance, admonishment, expectations, and procedures. A retention letter should not be pro forma but instead tailored to each circumstance, project, or lawsuit, and it should be closely followed by both parties. Whatever policies, procedures, reporting forms, and timetables that might apply to the engagement should be attached as appendices. Likewise, a clear record of reimbursable expenses, billing methods, payment schedules, assigned persons, a set fee structure, and cost expectations (that is, a partner should not be billing for work that a junior associate could be performing) should be appended to each retention letter.

On to the issue of budgeting . . .

There are few statements that better sum up the significance of establishing and supervising an outside counsel's budget than the one made by Carole Basri and Irving Kagan in their two-volume reference for corporate legal departments: "A budget is not an end in itself, but is rather a translation of the case strategy into financial terms."[125] If you keep that in mind as budgeting policies, procedures, fee arrangements, and evaluations are established and applied, you will do fine.

Though many instances of engagement, such as transaction-oriented tasks like a merger, can have more predictable financial projections, litigation is far less concrete. What looks to be a vastly expensive case could be over with on a motion to dismiss before discovery has even begun. Conversely, what looks like an artless contract dispute could unexpectedly proliferate an insane number of briefs, hearings, depositions, documents, and appeals. Accordingly, it is critical to have reasonable policies, procedures, and fee structures in place for effective budgeting purposes. Expectations should be routinely revisited and modified as needed. Work-product and progress evaluations should be standard, and there should be processes for providing feedback. Budgetary limits and goals cannot be met without the appropriate monitoring mechanisms in position.

Budgets, of course, affect strategic decisions, so financial issues should not be viewed independently of what they mean in terms of how a lawsuit is being conducted. Beyond a corporate lawyer's, or a law department's, own perspective, it will ultimately be necessary to demonstrate to the client-company—a concerned-looking chief executive—what *value* has been purchased and *why* the price is what it is.

> [R]eal legal project management requires a true up-front understanding of a case's likely financial trajectory along with investment in tools and training needed to control costs while providing quality representation. Distinguishing between proposals that really deliver on both value and quality—and those whose sizzle lacks steak—matters to the bottom line.[126]

A true surrogate for an in-house lawyer is his or her outside counsel counterpart. Outside counsel allow in-house generalists to secure top-flight, expert legal services to a client-company. Indeed, the judicious use of outside counsel, and the intelligent management of their efforts, is one of the most critical tasks an in-house lawyer will fulfill.

The importance of this task, therefore, rates a mild warning. Warren G. Harding, the twenty-ninth president of the United States, whose pleasant manner and unwarlike campaign strategy won him the 1920 Republican National Convention, made this erudite remark:

> I have no trouble with my enemies. I can take care of my enemies in a fight. But my friends, . . . they're the ones who keep me walking the floor at nights!

The efficacy of his presidency may be questionable, but his shrewdness is not. Take heed, and make sure your policies, processes, and supervision allow you to sleep undisturbed.

§ 5.7 OTHER SUPPORT SERVICES—"IN CASE YOU ARE NOT BUSY ENOUGH . . ."

We have finally elbowed our way through six major practice areas of corporate law, only to find there is a little more tunnel to clear before there is daylight.

A corporate lawyer's work is never done. There are too many aspects to running a corporation that need the input, guidance, leadership, or caution of a conscientious lawyer. On any given day, a corporate lawyer may find him- or herself drafting legal opinions[127] or conflict-of-waiver letters,[128] or handling responses to subpoenas.[129] Because an organizational client has an almost infinite number of issues and tasks with which to deal at any one time, a corporate lawyer might wake up to a corporate tax concern, eat lunch while scrutinizing the final draft of a shareholder report, and end the day strategizing with a client-company's lobbyist.

By way of adding to our six areas of practice, the following sections raise seven other areas that are, or are likely to be, common to all corporate lawyers. These are not close to being in-depth commentaries, but they should provide just enough commentary to trigger the need for one extra aspirin.

§ 5.7.1 Insurance

Insurance is one of those topics that can slip under the radar for corporate lawyers. As in our private lives, we spend very little time thinking about what kind of coverage we have, and we might even spend very little time shopping around for them. It is only when disaster occurs that we realize we do not have the right policies, riders, or coverage amounts. Insurance issues for businesses can suffer the same cold-water shock. Though insurance matters, as a risk-management tool, may not fall squarely on a corporate lawyer's list of duties, good legal counsel is going to make sure—as the true lookout for liability—that his or her client-company has the right kind of underwriting protection, at a fair price.

Be forewarned: a commercial general-liability insurance policy will not cover all your bases. An errors and omissions policy, directors and officers policy, product-liability policy, or property-liability policy will not either. Instead, a collection of policies, *along with situation-specific riders*, is most likely your best bet. In an article set against a context of physical disasters rather than other liability concerns, Catherine Dunn articulates several excellent points for a corporate lawyer to keep in mind when evaluating all of a client-company's insurance needs and current coverages.[130] Ms. Dunn's recommendations are as follows:

- Evaluate the risks your business is likely to face
- Read the existing policies closely (what is really covered?)
- Negotiate for more coverage
- Protect your books and records
- Give prompt notice (of damage)

If forced to pick the most important one, I would suggest *reading the existing, or proposed, policies closely.* Because so many parts of an insurance policy use standardized language, the temptation, as with any boiler-plate language, is to gloss over those provisions. Big mistake. Keep in mind that every part of the policy is a potential ground for denial of coverage, limitation of coverage, and waiver of coverage.

An insurance policy is Contracts 101. Treat the reasons for entering into an insurance policy, and the assessment of all of its terms, just as scrupulously as you would treat the complexities of a multimillion-dollar trust indenture contract.

§ 5.7.2 *Subsidiary and Franchise Issues*

Isaac Singer, who became the founder of I. M. Singer & Co. in 1851 (which later became Singer Corporation), began one of the first franchising efforts in the United States, having realized the use of franchisees was a much more cost-effective way to distribute his products than building and maintaining proprietary, or company, stores. Franchising took more popular hold as a business model with food service companies in the 1920s and 1930s, and when the interstate system came about in the 1950s, franchises began to sprout up everywhere.

The U.S. Federal Trade Commission (FTC)[131] regulates franchised businesses through the Franchise and Business Opportunities Rule.[132] The most critical components to a franchise operation are its Franchise Disclosure Document and its final agreement. Be aware that there are usually state franchise laws to consider as well, when participating in, or conducting, a franchise business.

A subsidiary is not a franchise, but it shares the characteristic of possessing a degree of independence from the parent company (or a holding company) while still being bound by ownership, decision-making, and/ or operational controls. The core difference between a franchise and a subsidiary is that a subsidiary is partly or wholly owned by a parent company, whereas a franchise is independently owned and only licenses, or franchises, a particular product, concept, or service.

Control of a subsidiary can be practical—that is, actually controlling the composition of a subsidiary's board—or theoretical—that is, possessing the ability to cast more than half the votes but not exercising that power. Tread carefully: ownership and control are the fundamental benchmarks for liability when the actions of a subsidiary are involved.[133]

§ 5.7.3 Legislation and Lobbying

In March 2012, the Association of Corporate Counsel released its 2011 Census Report, which revealed changes in the in-house counsel (or corporate law) profession.

> Compared to the last survey's data, in-house lawyers in 2011 were much more likely to specialize in regulatory matters and government lobbying. In 2006, only 5 percent of in-house counsel focused on government regulatory issues, and none of the surveyed lawyers claimed lobbying as a specialty.[134]

Lobbying and legislative activities may result in make-or-break situations for many companies. For example, with the whirlwind of media focus and public concern regarding the costs of higher education, especially in light of the nation's recent economic recession, for-profit colleges and universities have fought back against accusations of abuse with lawsuits and very active, well-funded lobbying campaigns.[135] Their ability to continue to offer nontraditional classroom experiences, and to be able to charge enough in tuition to make a profit, depends largely on the success of their efforts to convince legislators and regulators that their business models and business activities are fair, reasonable, and legitimate.

Lobbying, of course, can be a legitimate effort by an organization to influence decisions made by legislators and regulators in order to gain more favorable market or labor conditions. Corporate lawyers who are involved in a client-company's lobbying activities, or who provide oversight, management, or advice to a client-company's lobbyists, must understand and adhere to a complex and extensive set of rules and laws at every level of government in which a lobbying effort is undertaken.

§ 5.7.4 Public Relations and the Media

Inevitably, corporate lawyers find themselves involved at some level with a client-company's public relations concerns. Most of the time, the involvement is low key but important, such as reviewing press releases, advertising materials, and public statements or speeches. Lawyers should certainly be prepared to be included in (and politely insist on being included in) public relations issues that might precipitate some kind of liability.[136] Sometimes, the possibility for liability may be difficult for a public relations officer or media consultant to understand; it is up to the corporate lawyer to remain vigilant for possible bear traps. For instance, the announcement that a board member is leaving before the expiration of his or her term—how the announcement is worded, what information it contains, where it is disseminated, and when it is disseminated—may initiate the kind of curiosity, or animosity, that could eventually give rise to a shareholder suit or regulatory inquiry.

Messages—unpleasant ones, pleasant ones, informational ones, marketing ones, mandatory ones—are an inescapable part of every business enterprise. A healthy working relationship with a client-company's media department or public relations officer is imperative. A public relations officer, or a public relations consulting firm, is not the "enemy," despite how it may feel from time to time, and good corporate lawyers understand how to complement a client-company's need to "get the word out."

§ 5.7.5 *Valuations and Securities (More Regulations)*

Business valuation models are a highly specialized area of finance, typically used for leveraged buyouts, mergers and acquisitions, distressed-securities analysis, and financial statement analysis, to name a few. Investment bankers spend their days rolling around in valuation models as financial institutions marry with corporations and municipalities to raise debt or equity capital. Corporate accountants and executives pore over financial statement analysis, based on particular valuation methodologies, for purposes of shareholder reports and public securities filings. Corporate financial planners and strategists fiddle with and tweak different models in order to project and prepare for different business-unit outcomes, potential mergers, potential spin-offs, and new market growth.

Though many corporate lawyers do not need to moonlight as financiers, capable of creating various distressed-security analyses for client-companies, it is a good idea to become acquainted with the different kinds of models and their customary uses. Notably, it is especially important to have a working understanding of the three generally accepted valuation methodologies: discounted cash-flow analysis, trading multiples, and precedent transactions. These methodologies set the groundwork—determine the rules—for developing and interpreting an organization's financial statements.

Securities and securities regulation are broader and even more complex than the topic of valuation models. We often think of securities in terms of national or international markets and regulations, but securities laws and regulations exist at the state level as well, and can be created, bought, and sold in the private marketplace (that is, without any listing). Depending on the size and activities of a client-company, securities matters may rarely or constantly cross the desk of a corporate lawyer. Unavoidably though, securities—as characterized by stock ownership—form the equity basis of the vast majority of private and public incorporated organizations in the United States. Therefore, most corporate lawyers would do well to keep a manageable desk reference nearby[137] and give some time to understanding the implications of The Securities Act of 1933,[138] The Securities Exchange Act of 1934,[139] and SOX.[140]

§ 5.7.6 *Tax*

For the few lawyers who hold an L.L.M. in taxation, or who wear the green shade of an accountant (CPA) over their solicitor's wig, corporate tax issues are part of their daily routine. For most other corporate lawyers, however, tax matters typically have to do with the expected consequences of a particular action, the treatment of a particular taxable event, or the characterization of an employee (or contractor). Corporate lawyers do not need to have a copy of the Internal Revenue Code tucked behind their ear, but softball questions about stock distributions, reorganizations, capital structures, stock redemptions, and penalties might be pitched in their general direction. Moreover, supervising a client-company's tax counsel can be exceedingly difficult, unless one spends some time acclimating oneself to the dizzying warren of corporate tax issues.

Do what I do: grab a decipherable book,[141] get on the Web as often as you need to, and do not hesitate to ask a professional.

§ 5.7.7 *Multinational Companies*

There is a cadre of corporate lawyers who work for multinational corporations[142] or companies heading into multinational operations. Commonly, this means that the client-company produces and/or provides services in more than one country.

Aside from organizational challenges (some of which we addressed in Section 4.4), corporate lawyers working for multinational corporations must have the policies and processes in place to cope with and resolve the inevitable conflict of laws between different jurisdictions. This predicament has been termed *private international law*,[143] in which the ultimate outcome of a dispute will depend upon which law, and upon what authority, the disputants have chosen to apply. A determination of jurisdiction, choice of law, and the ability to recognize and enforce a foreign judgment are key components to the uniquely complex area of conflict of laws, which may require a corporate lawyer to link arms with jurists from foreign jurisdictions and lawyers who concentrate their practices in international dispute resolution.

Tax implications, employment issues, governance requirements, securities regulations, intellectual-property rights, industry-specific regulations, and even *elves* are some of the more critical concerns to keep in mind when working for a multinational corporation. Imagine this: before building a new aluminum-smelting plant in a particular foreign jurisdiction, your client-company assigns you the task of obtaining the proper government certifications to verify that there are *no elves on, or under, the new plant site.* Sound like fiction? Bad fiction? Guess again. Michael Lewis, long celebrated in most MBA programs for having written *Liar's Poker,*[144] recounted this exact scenario, as experienced by Alcoa, the largest aluminum-smelting plant in Iceland, in his 2011 book, *Boomerang: Travels in the New Third World.*[145]

Who said working for a multinational company was boring?

This chapter began with a simple conclusion about the successful practice of corporate law: "You do not need to be the expert all the time, but you do need to be on deck, ready to opine, review, and provide informed counsel." Telling someone you practice corporate law or business law is the equivalent of saying you are a generalist—who needs to be a specialist at the drop of a hat.

There are several core but disparate disciplines that have to be understood, if not mastered, to provide the level of valuable legal counsel your client-company should, and probably does, expect. That is a tall order, but it *is* doable.

Judge Billings Learned Hand, a distinguished federal district-court judge for the Southern District of New York and later a judge on the U.S. Court of Appeals for the Second Circuit, once said,

> Life is made up of constant calls to action, and we seldom have time for more than hastily contrived answers.

Such is the everyday circumstance of a corporate lawyer. All the better then to be as prepared as possible, regardless of what issues come roaring through your office door.

Notes

1. ABA Committee on Corporate Counsel, The In-House Counsel's Essential Toolkit (ABA Publishing 2007).
2. Respectively, Jolene Yee was the former cochair to the Committee on Corporate Counsel and is an assistant general counsel at E. & J. Gallo Winery; Mari Valenzuela was the former ambassador to the Committee on Corporate Counsel and is assistant managing counsel to Microchip Technology, Inc.; David Benson was the chair to the Subcommittee on Privately Held Companies and is a partner in the corporate practice group at Stoel Rives, LLP, in Seattle, WA.
3. ABA Committee on Corporate Counsel, *supra* note 1, *Introduction.*
4. *Id.* "This publication is not intended to be so extensive as to serve as a treatise on any particular subject. Instead, think of the Toolkit as the first place to go . . ."

5. Stephen Paskoff, *Effective Employment Counsel Requires Going Beyond the Law*, CORPORATE COUNSEL, Mar. 14, 2012.

6. Such as privacy requirements under the Gramm-Leach-Bliley Act, also known as the Financial Services Modernization Act of 1999, Pub. L. No. 106-102, 13 Stat. 1338 (Nov. 12, 1999). Financial institutions must have a policy (or policies) in place to protect nonpublic information from foreseeable threats in security and data integrity. Institutional personnel who gather consumers' nonpublic personal information and personal identifiers are an integral component of these policies.

7. "Many employment handbooks contain 'open communication policies' that encourage employees to discuss any issue they might have with a coworker first and then go to a supervisor if they can't resolve the issue. The policy also should remind employees that it's counterproductive to a harmonious workplace to create or repeat corporate rumors or office gossip and it's more constructive to consult a supervisor with any questions." HR Hero, *What Can HR Do About Workplace Gossip?* CUNA, INC. (Sept. 1, 2009), http://www.cunahrcouncil.org/news/3081.html.

8. By the way, there is no need to breach any confidences as you do this. Speak in generalities and hypotheticals; after all, you are really after a sense of other parts of the client-company, not what they think of a particular employee (which, even when informative, could create problems or conflicts).

9. IRS, *Independent Contractor Defined, available at* http://www.irs.gov /businesses/small/article/0,,id=179115,00.html (last visited May 2, 2012).

10. IRS, *Employee (Common-Law Employee), available at* http://www.irs.gov /businesses/small/article/0,,id=179112,00.html (last visited on May 2, 2012).

11. IRS, *Statutory Employees, available at* http://www.irs.gov/businesses /small/article/0,,id=179118,00.html (last visited on May 2, 2012). The four categories are

    - A driver who distributes beverages (other than milk) or meat, vegetable, fruit, or bakery products; or who picks up and delivers laundry or dry cleaning, if the driver is your agent or is paid on commission.
    - A full-time life insurance sales agent whose principal business activity is selling life insurance or annuity contracts, or both, primarily for one life insurance company.
    - An individual who works at home on materials or goods that you supply and that must be returned to you or to a person you name, if you also furnish specifications for the work to be done.
    - A full-time traveling or city salesperson who works on your behalf and turns in orders to you from wholesalers, retailers, contractors, or operators of hotels, restaurants, or other similar establishments. The goods sold must be merchandise for resale or supplies for use in the buyer's business operation. The work performed for you must be the salesperson's principal business activity.

12. The U.S. Department of Labor provides compliance assistance with the FLSA, including several guidance materials (such as a handy reference guide), which are great bookshelf resources for a corporate lawyer. United

States Department of Labor, Wage and Hour Division, *Compliance Assistance—Wages and the Fair Labor Standards Act (FLSA)*, *available at* http://www.dol.gov/whd/flsa/ (last visited May 2, 2012).

13. Chamberlain, Kaufman and Jones, *Coverage under the FLSA* (2003), *available at* http://www.flsa.com/coverage.html (last visited May 2, 2012).

14. These are the salary-level test, the salary-basis test, and the job-duties test.

15. Mary Dollarhide and Haley Morrison, *Employee Classifications: Getting the C-Suite's Ear*, InsideCounsel, Dec. 7, 2011, *available at* http://www .insidecounsel.com/2011/12/07/employee-classifications-getting-the-c -suites-ear.

16. ABA Committee on Corporate Counsel, *supra* note 1.

17. Uniformed Services Employment and Reemployment Rights Act.

18. Worker Adjustment and Retraining Notification Act.

19. There are hundreds of topic-specific texts out there and a few good "global" handbooks. A very comprehensive but accessible bookshelf option is Orrick, Herrington & Sutcliffe LLP, Employment Law Yearbook 2012 (Practicing Law Institute 2012). This reference resource is updated annually and contains recent activity (cases, legislation, and so on), as well as practical steps to minimize risk and ensure compliance.

20. Eric Esperne, *Inside Experts: Corporate Policy Checklist*, InsideCounsel, Jun. 3, 2011, *available at* http://www.insidecounsel.com/2011/06/03/inside -experts-corporate-policy-checklist.

21. *Id.*

22. *Supra* Chapter 3, Section 3.1.5. She, and her company, shall remain nameless. She made the remark as a panelist at a corporate counsel CLE conference in Texas a few years ago. Because the remark was meant to make a point, rather than to commit her client-company to a policy position, the idea, rather than the actual source, is more important.

23. The U.S. Small Business Administration provides a nicely done, basic employee-handbook template, although there are dozens of samples and templates online. U.S. Small Business Administration, *Employee Handbooks*, *available at* http://www.sba.gov/content/employee-handbooks (last visited May 3, 2012).

24. Mary Mikva, *Drafting Confidentiality, Non-Compete & Non-Solicitation Agreements: The Employee's Wish List*, ABA Regional Institute, Labor and Employment Law: The Basics. Ms. Mikva specializes in representing plaintiffs in employment cases in federal and state court, as well as at the Chicago Commission on Human Relations and the Illinois Human Rights Commission.

25. Bernard C. Dietz, *Employment Contracts: Everyone Needs Promise Protection*, Ask the Headhunter, http://www.asktheheadhunter.com/gv050701.htm (last visited May 3, 2012).

26. *Id.*

27. Mr. Drapkin was a long-time business associate of billionaire Ronald Perelman and was the vice chairman at Perelman's MacAndrews & Forbes Holdings, Inc., a holding company with interests in a diversified portfolio

of public and private companies and various of its affiliates from 1987 to 2007.

28. Shannon Green sought out Mr. Dunn's perspective in her article *Employment Law Lessons from the $16M MacAndrews & Forbes Verdict,* Corporate Counsel, Feb. 1, 2012, *available at* http://www.law.com/jsp /cc/PubArticleCC.jsp?id=1202540876819.

29. David Glovin, *Perelman's MacAndrews Faces $18 Million Back-Pay Trial "About Fairness,"* Bloomberg (Jan. 24, 2012, 5:27 P.M.), http://www .bloomberg.com/news/2012-01-24/drapkin-s-lawsuit-against-perelman -begins-with-jury-selection-in-new-york.html.

30. I have always thought it ironic that a philosopher hailing from Switzerland—the symbol of neutrality in war—should have played such a key role in having influenced the bloodbath of the French Revolution.

31. Another appropriate tip of the hat to the butterfly effect, a study within chaos theory that theorizes about how the sensitive dependence on initial conditions, such as a small change at one place (for example, the flight of a butterfly), in a "deterministic nonlinear system" can result in large differences later on (such as a hurricane). Edward Norton Lorenz, an American mathematician and meteorologist, coined the term in 1969.

32. Chris Mortensen and Adam Schefter, *Jags Fire Senior VP Paul Vance,* ESPN.com (Jan. 9, 2012, 5:20 P.M.), http://espn.go.com/nfl/story /_/id/7441572/jacksonville-jaguars-senior-vp-paul-vance-fired.

33. Attributable to the remarkable polymath, Benjamin Franklin.

34. *"Ave, Imperator, morituri te salutant"* is a phrase quoted by Gaius Suetonius Tranquillus (known as Suetonius), a Roman historian, in his biographies of Julius Caesar and the first eleven emperors of the Roman Empire, Lives of the Twelve Caesars. According to Suetonius, the phrase was shouted out by captives and criminals who were slated to die fighting during mock naval encounters during an event in AD 52 in the presence of Emperor Tiberius Claudius Caesar Augustus Germanicus, a member of the Julio-Claudian dynasty. The phrase also seems well suited for any Socratic-method law class.

35. More modern interpretations relate that Atlas was forced to hold the Earth, not the Sky, on his shoulders.

36. Eloquently said by Sir Winston Churchill, two-time British prime minister, Nobel laureate, officer in the British army, historian, and the first person—one of only seven—to be made an Honorary Citizen of the United States.

37. *Sumptuary laws* throughout history are good examples of this kind of regulation. Generally, these were laws intended to reinforce social hierarchies and morals by restricting and regulating clothing, food, and luxury expenditures and uses by those persons of different social rank and privilege. They did, however, affect trade by limiting the consumer market for expensive goods.

38. *Guilds* were essentially confraternities of workers in a particular trade. They usually influenced training, licensing, ownership of tools, the supply of materials, and the flow of trade.

39. Prior to writing The Jungle, Mr. Sinclair had spent about six months investigating the Chicago meatpacking industry on behalf of the socialist newspaper Appeal to Reason. Mr. Sinclair later bemoaned the effect of his book, saying, "I aimed at the public's heart, and by accident, I hit it in the stomach." Cosmopolitan Magazine, Oct. 1906.
40. Pure Food and Drug Act, Pub. L. No. 59-384, 34 Stat. 768 (1906), 21 U.S.C. § 1-15 (1934) (repealed in 1938 by 21 U.S.C. § 329(a)), is also known as the Wiley Act.
41. Meat Inspection Act, 34 Stat. 674 (amended by Pub. L. No. 59-242, 34 Stat. 1260 (1967), 21 U.S.C. § 601 (the Wholesome Meat Act (1967)).
42. The Santa Barbara oil spill occurred in January and February of 1969 in the Santa Barbara Channel in Southern California. Like the Deepwater Horizon disaster of 2010, the Santa Barbara oil spill was the result of a blowout on Union Oil's Platform A in the Dos Cuadras Offshore Oil Field. The Santa Barbara oil spill was the largest of its time and now ranks third, behind the 1989 *Exxon Valdez* spill and the 2010 Deepwater Horizon spill.
43. National Environmental Policy Act, Pub. L. No. 91-190, 42 U.S.C. §§ 4321–4347 (1970) (amended by Pub. L. No. 94-52 (1975), Pub. L. No. 94-83 (1975), and Pub. L. No. 97-258 (1982)).
44. Foreign Corrupt Practices Act, 15 U.S.C. § 78dd-1.
45. Sarbanes-Oxley Act of 2002, Pub. L. No. 107-204, 116 Stat. 745, 5 U.S.C. §§ 552a and 704 (also known as the Public Company Accounting Reform and Investor Protection Act in the Senate (S. 2673) and the Corporate and Auditing Accounting and Responsibility Act in the House (H.R. 3763)).
46. Dodd-Frank Wall Street Reform and Consumer Protection Act, Pub. L. No. 111-203 (2010). The Statutes at Large citations and the U.S. Code citations are simply too numerous to list here. The law can be read, downloaded, and saved at http://www.gpo.gov/fdsys/pkg/PLAW -111publ203/pdf/PLAW-111publ203.pdf.
47. As hard as this is to believe in this age of pervasive regulation, there are many companies that are far behind on their homework. For instance, in 2008, the Wage and Hour Division of the Department of Labor concluded a whopping 28,242 compliance actions and assessed over $9.9 million in civil money penalties. *Available at* http://www.dol.gov/whd /statistics/2008FiscalYear.htm#_ftn1.
48. ABA Committee on Corporate Counsel, *supra* note 1, at 3 *Corporate Compliance and Ethics*, xxiv.
49. *Id.*
50. What better place to throw a little illusion and ambiguity in the mix than when speaking of compliance? In fact, if this section of Chapter 5 were to be reduced to a single artistic rendering, it would be a Necker Cube as illustrated in the cartoon. A Necker Cube shows no depth but appears to. The first Necker Cube was published by Louis Albert Necker in 1832.
51. I have borrowed this turn of phrase from the title of a panel discussion held during the American Bar Association's Business Law Section's Spring Meeting. Annual Business Law Section Meeting, Las Vegas, Nev., Mar. 22, 2012.

52. Several of these are key players for a company's governance information program, as suggested by Mark Diamond. Mark Diamond, *Five Key Players You Need on Your Information Governance Team*, INSIDECOUNSEL, Mar. 7, 2012, *available at* http://www.insidecounsel.com/2012/03/07/5-key -players-you-need-on-your-information-governa.

53. Bertrand Russell, a British philosopher, logician, writer, and mathematician, said this of philosophy, not regulations. However, his philosophic reflection seemed a perfectly good fit for a comment on the obtuseness of many regulations. As an aside, Mr. Russell's statement may explain, in a nutshell, why he was a humanist and believed religion was little more than superstition. Of course, most compliance programs take a little religion in order to be successful.

54. Brian Cabrera, *Five Essential Elements of a Successful International Compliance Program*, CORPORATE COUNSEL, Mar. 1, 2012, *available at* http://www.law.com/jsp/cc/PubArticleCC.jsp?id=1202543899960.

55. What better metaphor for administrative rules and guidelines than legendary sea monsters of giant proportions?

56. For instance, TriComply is a service product offered by TriNovus, LLC. The product concept is to "keep you abreast of the latest regulatory requirements and will provide you with analysis on the best way for your bank to comply and our staff will draft new compliance policies as they are required." *TriComply for Banks*, TRINOVUS, https://www.trinovus.com /tricomply/ (last visited May 12, 2012). For many smaller or regional banks, this kind of service is an instant solution for dealing with the myriad of banking regulations, especially since Dodd-Frank.

57. The White House, *The Cabinet*, *available at* http://www.whitehouse.gov /administration/cabinet (last visited May 12, 2012).

58. It might be a good idea to have the U.S. Government Printing Office's Web site saved as a favorite on your desktop. *Available at* http://www .gpo.gov/fdsys/browse/collectionCfr.action?collectionCode=CFR. For relatively easy research and reference, the Electronic Code of Federal Regulations (e-CFR) is an unofficial database produced by the National Archives and Records Administration's Office of the Federal Register (OFR) and the Government Printing Office. *Available at* http://ecfr .gpoaccess.gov/cgi/t/text/text-idx?c=ecfr&tpl=%2Findex.tpl.

59. OFFICE OF THE FEDERAL REGISTER, FEDERAL REGISTER, *available at* http:// www.gpo.gov/fdsys/browse/collection.action?collectionCode=FR.

60. Exec. Order No. 13,563, 3 Fed. Reg. 3,821 (Jan. 21, 2011).

61. OFFICE OF MGMT. & BUDGET, EXEC. OFFICE OF THE PRESIDENT, *Memorandum for the Heads of Executive Departments and Agencies: Retrospective Analysis of Existing Significant Regulations*, OMB M-11-19 (Apr. 25, 2011).

62. There is an agency within the White House's Office of Management and Budget (OMB) called the Office of Information and Regulatory Affairs (OIRA), created by Congress in 1980 as part of the Paperwork Reduction Act to, among other things, review federal regulations. However, a decades-old debate over the application of a cost-benefit analysis to regulatory decision making has kept the OIRA at the eye of an analytical storm. Empirically, "[r]ulemaking has not been abandoned in the wake

of OIRA's creation, nor have the net benefits of regulations measurably increased. . . . This leads to the question of why economic analysis requirements have neither stopped the regulatory process cold nor lead to more economically efficient regulations." Stuart Shapiro, *Politics and Regulatory Policy Analysis*, Regulation, Summer 2006, at 40–41.

63. The government has made the commenting and tracking processes a bit easier by establishing the online portal, www.regulations.gov.

64. Cabrera, *supra* note 54.

65. ABA Committee on Corporate Counsel, *supra* note 1, at *Corporate Compliance and Ethics*, vol. 3.

66. U.S. Sentencing Commission, Sentencing of Organizations, Federal Sentencing Guidelines Manual § 8B2.1(b) (2011). The entire body of Chapter 8 of the manual is available through the U.S. Sentencing Commission's Web site at http://www.ussc.gov/Guidelines /Organizational_Guidelines/guidelines_chapter_8.htm.

67. OCEG, About, *available at* http://www.oceg.org/view/About (last visited May 3, 2012).

68. Cabrera, *supra* endnote 54.

69. *Id.*

70. I am using the terms *internal auditor* and *external auditor* interchangeably, although the roles and functions can differ, especially in relation to the review of a corporation's financial statements and whether reporting is made to the board or to shareholders. For purposes of this book, those differences are not material.

71. Although internal auditing is not, necessarily, a regulated corporate role, internal auditing has developed its own standards and guidance with which a corporate lawyer should be familiar. These are available through The Institute of Internal Auditors (IIA). The IIA provides "mandatory guidance" to member auditors in the form of a code of ethics and the "International Standards for the Professional Practice of Internal Auditing." *See* www.theiia.org.

72. Shakespeare, *Julius Caesar*, Act 3, Scene 2. Thus observed Mark Antony, Marcus Antonius, as he reflected upon the assassinated Caesar. "Friends, Romans, countrymen, lend me your ears; I come to bury Caesar, not to praise him. The evil that men do . . ."

73. Sarah H. Duggin, *Internal Investigations: Legal Ethics, Professionalism, and the Employee Interview*, 2003 Colum. Bus. L. Rev. 859, 864.

74. *Id.* at 873.

75. *Id.* at 873–74.

76. One of the best I have seen is by Barry McNeil & Brad Brian, Internal Corporate Investigations (3d ed., ABA Publishing 2007). This book provides an excellent, step-by-step guide for "conducting an investigation, clearly describing and advising you on the methods and skills involved, while providing you with practical tips on anticipating, recognizing, and avoiding the traps you are certain to encounter."

77. This may be a good time to review the discussion of privilege issues in Section 2.1.3, and the U.S. Supreme Court's holding in *Upjohn Co. v. United States*, 449 U.S. 383 (1981).

78. For lawyers who are employed by law-enforcement agencies or other public entities, there is a first cousin to the Upjohn warning called a *Garrity* warning. A Garrity warning comes from *Garrity v. New Jersey*, 385 U.S. 493 (1967), in which the U.S. Supreme Court held that law-enforcement officers and other public employees have the right to be free from compulsory self-incrimination. For instance, before an internal investigator (such as internal affairs) can conduct an interview, the public employee must give what is tantamount to a Miranda warning.

79. I have seen sample warnings given that suggest an interviewee may share certain information with his or her own personal lawyer, but I would suggest this right not be stated or suggested. There is currently a healthy debate as to whether an employee can violate a company's privilege, even if doing so is limited to that employee's personal attorney and is used for that employee's own civil purposes (for example, a discrimination lawsuit). No matter where individual courts may come down on this issue, I would advise against a company's legal counsel even suggesting there is any compromise to the company's right of privilege.

80. A medical technology company.

81. Edward Ludwig, *Aim Toward a Higher Calling for Business: Building Purpose—and Value-Driven Enterprises*, 19 METROPOLITAN CORPORATE COUNSEL, no. 12, Dec. 2011.

82. A great bookshelf resource is CYNTHIA M. KRUS, CORPORATE SECRETARY'S ANSWER BOOK (4th ed., Aspen Publishers, Inc., 2007).

83. Melissa Maleske, *Eight Ways That SOX Changed Corporate Governance (10 Years After It Became the Law)*, INSIDECOUNSEL, Jan. 1, 2012, *available at* http://www.insidecounsel.com/2012/01/01/8-ways-sox-changed-corporate-governance?ref=hp.

84. *Id.*

85. *In re* Caremark Int'l Inc. Derivative Litig., 698 A.2d 959 (Del. Ch., New Castle Cnty., 1996).

86. *Standards of Conduct for Directors*, MODEL BUSINESS CORPORATION ACT § 8.30(a)–(e) (American Bar Association, 2002).

87. For forms, suggestions, and notes, I again commend you to the TOOLKIT. ABA COMMITTEE ON CORPORATE COUNSEL, *supra* note 1, at *Corporate Governance*, vol. 2.

88. ABA COMMITTEE ON CORPORATE COUNSEL, *supra* note 1, at *Corporate Governance*, vol. 2, *Introduction*.

89. Aronson v. Lewis, 473 A.2d 805, 812 (Del. 1984) overruled on other grounds, *Brehm v. Eisner*, 746 A.2d 244, 254 (Del. 2000).

90. Burlington Indus., Inc., v. Ellerth, 524 U.S. 742, 756 (1998).

91. Melissa Maleske, *General Counsel's Heightened Influence in the Boardroom*, INSIDECOUNSEL, Apr. 30, 2012, *available at* http://www.insidecounsel.com/2012/04/30/general-counsels-heightened-influence-in-the-board.

92. ABA COMMITTEE ON CORPORATE COUNSEL, *supra* note 1, at *Intellectual Property*, vol. 5, *Introduction*, xv.

93. This refers to the Berne Convention for the Protection of Literary and Artistic Works, first accepted in Bern, Switzerland, in 1886, and which

was agreed to by the United States through the Berne Convention Implementation Act in 1989 (amending the 1976 Copyright Act).

94. Even for purposes of an exclusive licensing agreement in which someone else's component or process is integrated into your client-company's final "original" product, the integrated component or process is still used as a tool, although there might be an asset value (commodity characteristic) to an exclusive licensing agreement.

95. ABA COMMITTEE ON CORPORATE COUNSEL, *supra* note 1, at *Intellectual Property*, vol. 5.

96. Robert Lands, *IP: Don't Let Intellectual Property Be the Deal Breaker*, INSIDECOUNSEL, May 22, 2012, *available at* http://www.insidecounsel.com /2012/05/22/ip-dont-let-intellectual-property-be-the-deal-brea?t=ip.

97. Jumpstart Our Business Startups Act, Pub. L. No. 112-106, 126 Stat. 306 (H.R. 3606) (2012).

98. Not to be confused with the American Jobs Act of 2011 (S. 1549) (H.R. 12) (H. Doc. 112-53).

99. Jumpstart Our Business Startups Act, Pub. L. No. 112-106, §§ 301 *et seq.*, 126 Stat. 306 (H.R. 3606) (2012), *available at* http://www.gpo.gov/fdsys /pkg/PLAW-112publ106/content-detail.html.

100. Scott Popma & Elizabeth Shah, *How to Protect Your Intellectual Property When Using Crowdfunding*, CORPORATE COUNSEL, Sept. 5, 2012, *available at* http://www.law.com/jsp/cc/PubArticleCC.jsp?id=1202570068038&How _to_Protect_Your_Intellectual_Property_When_Using_Crowdfunding.

101. *Id.*

102. *Id.* In case you cannot track down their article, here are their five suggestions in a nutshell:

    1. Quickly follow the Bayh-Dole Act (BDA) requirements, as necessary for government contractors.

    2. "If the company will offer securities, it should elect to retain title to any IP that contributes to the basis for the valuation of a crowdfunding offering before the offering."

    3. "If the company cannot afford to file a patent application before raising funds, it should consider filing a provisional patent application as a filing date placeholder."

    4. "The crowdfunded security offering should clearly inform potential investors of the government's rights or potential rights to the invention."

    5. "To limit the BDA's applicability, businesses should segregate out as much IP as possible by differentiating it from the subject matter covered by any government funding agreements."

103. As an example, a person or company may seek to file a trademark or service mark application, renewal, or assignment with the Texas Secretary of State's Office. *See* TEX. BUS. & COMM. CODE §§ 16.00 *et seq.*

104. The U.S. Patent and Trademark Office, *available at* http://www .uspto.gov/ (last visited May 13, 2012).

105. U.S. Copyright Office, *available at* http://www.copyright.gov/ (last visited May 13, 2012).

106. World Intellectual Property Organization, *available at* http://www.wipo
.int/portal/index.html.en (last visited May 13, 2012).
107. World Trade Organization, *TRIPS [trade-related aspects of intellectual
property rights] material on the WTO website, available at* http://www.wto
.org/english/tratop_e/trips_e/trips_e.htm (last visited May 13, 2012).
108. World Trade Organization, Understanding the WTO: The Agreements,
Intellectual property: protection and enforcement, *available at* http://www
.wto.org/english/thewto_e/whatis_e/tif_e/agrm7_e.htm (last visited May
13, 2012).
109. Ironically, the Candyland (or Candy Land) board game by Hasbro, Inc.,
was involved in one of the first disputes over a relatively new IP issue:
Internet domain names. Hasbro successfully sought an injunction against
an adult content Web site that wanted to use the word *candyland*, and was
eventually awarded ownership of the domain name. *See* Hasbro, Inc., v.
Internet Entm't Grp., Ltd., No. C96-130WD, 1996 WL 84853 (W.D.
Wash. 1996).
110. A *lingua franca* is a working, or bridge, language between people who do
not share a mother tongue. For instance, a person whose native language
is Dutch may converse with a person whose native language is French by
both of them speaking in English, which is a common lingua franca in
Europe.
111. This is not to say that I haven't also seen a few sad examples who seem to
think their only job is to hand everything off to an outside firm, blindly
approve bills, and placidly do whatever the outside counsel suggests.
112. Alvin Lindsay, *E-discovery: Memorializing the E-discovery Process*,
INSIDECOUNSEL, June 5, 2012, *available at* http://www.insidecounsel
.com/2012/06/05/e-discovery-memorializing-the-e-discovery-process.
113. It just so happens the TOOLKIT has a good sample and some equally
good commentary on the matter. *See* ABA COMMITTEE ON CORPORATE
COUNSEL, *supra* note 1, at *Litigation*, vol. 6, 14.
114. Also known as a *Records Management Policy*.
115. *See* ABA COMMITTEE ON CORPORATE COUNSEL, *supra* note 1, at *Corporate
Compliance and Ethics*, vol. 3, 161. Take a look at the TOOLKIT's *Records
Management* policy and commentary.
116. "Banks, for instance, are required by federal statutes and regulations
to maintain customer account data for seven years. Broker-dealers,
financial institutions, the health care industry and certain segments of
the energy industry, among others, need to pay particular attention to
the regulatory requirements of their sectors and tailor their policies to
those requirements. All companies should keep tax records in accordance
with Internal Revenue Service (IRS) dictates." Brian Esser & Judy Selby,
*E-discovery: How to Draft and Implement an Effective Document Retention
Policy*, INSIDECOUNSEL, Jul. 17, 2012, *available at* http://www.insidecounsel
.com/2012/07/17/e-discovery-how-to-draft-and-implement-an-effectiv.
117. Here is a strikingly admonitory anecdote, excerpted from a June 28, 2011,
reprint in INSIDECOUNSEL. INSIDECOUNSEL, Egregious Behavior, *available
at* http://www.insidecounsel.com/2011/06/28/egregious-behavior (last
visited on May 16, 2012).

In *Green v. Blitz U.S.A.*, Judge John Ward of the U.S. District Court for the Eastern District of Texas found the defendant's abuse of the discovery process so egregious that in March he ordered a $250,000 civil contempt sanction. He also ordered the company to provide a copy of the court's order and memorandum to every plaintiff in every lawsuit in which it was a defendant during the two previous years as well as to include a copy with its first pleading in every new lawsuit in which it becomes a party, whether as a plaintiff or defendant, for the next five years. The case serves as another reminder that trial courts have broad discretion in fashioning remedies.

The sole person responsible for e-discovery at Blitz described himself as "computer illiterate as they get." Although multiple products liability lawsuits were pending, he never ordered a litigation hold of documents, performed any searches for e-mails or even asked his IT department about how to do a search. Instead the company was routinely deleting e-mails and backup tapes.

The court found that defendants withheld material internal communications in the products liability cases and ordered the sanctions.

118. Matthew Prewitt, *E-discovery: The Dying Art of Early Case Assessment*, InsideCounsel, Aug. 31, 2012, *available at* http://www.insidecounsel .com/2012/08/31/e-discovery-the-dying-art-of-early-case-assessment?t=e -discovery.
119. CAROLE BASRI AND IRVING KAGAN, CORPORATE LEGAL DEPARTMENTS § 10:5 (4th ed., Practicing Law Institute 2011).
120. *Id.*, citing David Silversteen, *Managing Corporate Social Responsibility in a Changing Legal Environment*, 25 AM. BUS. L. J. 523 (1987).
121. BASRI & KAGAN, *supra* note 119, § 10:5.
122. Howard Scher, *Litigation: The 5 Traits of Highly Effective Trial Lawyers*, INSIDECOUNSEL, Aug. 30, 2012, *available at* http://www.insidecounsel.com /2012/08/30/litigation-the-5-traits-of-highly-effective-trial?t=litigation.
123. *Id.*
124. Mr. Scher practices what he preaches. On the Buchanan, Ingersoll, and Rooney Web site, it offers the following endorsement of Mr. Scher's litigation style and personal characteristics: "Clients interviewed for *Chambers USA 2011* lauded Howard as '[an] incredibly hard-working, aggressive attorney'; 'a strong advocate, professional and extremely good in court'; and 'a rock-solid guy, trustworthy and will stick with his word.'" That is what a client-company *should* be saying about its litigation counsel. BUCHANAN INGERSOLL & ROONEY, http://www.bipc.com/howard-d-scher/.
125. BASRI & KAGAN, *supra* note 119, § 15:7.1.
126. Jan Conlin, *Litigation: Knowing What's Next for In-House Counsel*, INSIDECOUNSEL, Aug. 30, 2012, *available at* http://www.insidecounsel .com/2012/08/30/litigation-knowing-whats-next-for-in-house-counsel ?t=litigation.

127. Basri & Kagan, *supra* note 119, § 10:8. Increasingly, boilerplate disclaimers in legal opinion letters have led to troubled waters. Do not treat an opinion letter as a rubber-stamp project; take your time, review all relevant documents, and give careful consideration to the language of your opinion.

128. Basri & Kagan, *supra* note 119, §§ 4:5.6 and 10:7. Conflicts of interests can arise in house (where particular employees, as well as the organizational client, are being represented), where adverse interests may occur, or outside an organization (through outside counsel), where disqualification can occur. Waivers of conflicts of interest should be thoroughly thought out beforehand, clear, and include clawback provisions for privileged matters.

129. Take a look at Ronald Hicks Jr.'s three-part article series on handling subpoenas. Ronald Hicks Jr., *Litigation: The Do's and Don't's of Responding to a Subpoena*, InsideCounsel, June 14, 2012, *available at* http://www.insidecounsel.com/2012/06/14/litigation-the-dos-and-donts-of-responding-to-a-su. Ronald Hicks Jr., *Litigation: The 5 Risks of Responding to a Subpoena*, InsideCounsel, June 28, 2012, *available at* http://www.insidecounsel.com/2012/06/28/litigation-the-5-risks-of-responding-to-a-subpoena. Ronald Hicks Jr., *Litigation: The 3 Steps of Responding to a Subpoena*, InsideCounsel, Jul. 12, 2012, *available at* http://www.insidecounsel.com/2012/07/12/litigation-the-3-steps-of-responding-to-a-subpoena.

130. Catherine Dunn, *Five Corporate Insurance Tips to Consider before a Storm Strikes*, Corporate Counsel, Aug. 29, 2012, *available at* http://www.dailyreportonline.com/PubArticleDRO.jsp?id=1202569304210&thepage=1.

131. Federal Trade Commission, *Franchise and Business Opportunities Rule*, *available at* http://www.ftc.gov/bcp/franchise/netfran.shtm (last visited on May 9, 2012).

132. Franchise and Business Opportunities Rule, 72 Fed. Reg. 15544 (Mar. 30, 2007) (to be set out in 16 C.F.R. pt. 436). A quick-reference PDF version is available at http://www.ftc.gov/os/fedreg/2007/march/070330franchiserulefrnotice.pdf#page=102.

133. An intriguing situation unfolded when Oracle, Inc., voluntarily disclosed to the SEC that its subsidiary was maintaining a slush fund in India. Oracle's disclosure and its settlement payment of $2 million took care of the matter without any finding of bribery by the SEC. *See* Alexandra Wrage, *Should Companies Turn Themselves in for FCPA Violations?*, Corporate Counsel, Aug. 24, 2012, *available at* http://www.law.com/jsp/cc/PubArticleCC.jsp?id=1202568710892.

134. Shannon Green, *ACC Census Sees Power, Pay, and Prestige for In-House Counsel*, Corporate Counsel, Mar. 30, 2012, *available at* http://www.law.com/jsp/cc/PubArticleCC.jsp?id=1202547396614.

135. Tyler Kingkade, *For-Profit Colleges Spending Millions on Lobbying, Nearly $40 Million Since 2007*, Huffington Post (Aug. 30, 2012, 9:19 A.M.), http://www.huffingtonpost.com/2012/08/30/for-profit-colleges-lobbying_n_1842507.html?utm_hp_ref=education&ir=Education.

136. There are also those stinging situations when it is the corporate counsel's own actions that lead to a media nightmare. Take for instance the public relations mess caused by Safeway's general counsel, Robert Gordon, when

Mr. Gordon made what was reputed to be a sexist joke during Safeway's annual meeting. After an initial public apology, Mr. Gordon also sent two letters of apology to the two targets of his joke: Secretary of State Hillary Clinton and former Speaker of the House Nancy Pelosi. *See* Brian Glaser, *Safeway's GC and CEO Offer Apologies to Clinton and Pelosi*, CORPORATE COUNSEL, May 25, 2012, *available at* http://www.law.com/jsp/cc/PubArticle CC.jsp?id=1202555927374.

137. With a very high recommendation, I would suggest PROFESSOR THOMAS L. HAZEN, SECURITIES REGULATION: CORPORATE COUNSEL GUIDES (1st ed., ABA Publishing 2011).

138. Securities Act of May 27, 1933, ch. 38, tit. I, § 1, 48 Stat. 74 (codified in 15 U.S.C. §§ 77a, *et seq*.). This law is directed predominantly at the distribution of securities through registration requirements.

139. Securities Exchange Act of June 6, 1934, ch. 404, tit. I, § 1, 48 Stat. 881 (codified in 15 U.S.C. §§ 78a, *et seq*.). This law is much broader, encompassing the marketplace of securities (such as exchanges), as well as securities, their issuers, their purchasers, and their brokers. The Securities Exchange Act of 1934 led to the establishment of the Securities Exchange Commission (SEC), which is tasked to oversee all aspects of publicly traded securities.

140. Sarbanes-Oxley Act of 2002, *supra* note 45.

141. My most recent favorite is JAMES W. PRATT & WILLIAM N. KULSRUD, CORPORATE, PARTNERSHIP, ESTATE AND GIFT TAXATION (2013 ed., Cengage Learning 2013). It's a textbook, which is exactly what I need.

142. Also called *multinational enterprises* by some.

143. *Private international law* is a phrase that is quite different, with quite a different meaning, from *public international law*.

144. A ribald and clever exposé on the unrepentant excesses of investment banks and bond traders during the 1980s. MICHAEL LEWIS, LIAR'S POKER (W. W. Norton & Company, Inc., 1989).

145. MICHAEL LEWIS, BOOMERANG: TRAVELS IN THE NEW THIRD WORLD (W. W. Norton & Company, Inc., 2011).

CHAPTER 6

RISK MANAGEMENT— PIN THE TAIL ON THE RIGHT DONKEY

TABLE OF SECTIONS

In his book *Against the Gods: The Remarkable Story of Risk*, Peter L. Bernstein, whose work on the efficient-market hypothesis has made him one of the most well-known authorities on economics, introduces his analysis of risk with this theoretic observation:

> The revolutionary idea that defines the boundary between modern times and the past is the mastery of risk: the notion that the future is more than a whim of the gods and that men and women are not passive before nature. Until human beings discovered a way across that boundary, the future was a mirror of the past or the murky domain of oracles and soothsayers who held a monopoly over knowledge of anticipated events.[1]

Keep Mr. Bernstein's view in mind. If you need to, reread it a few times, and let it sink in. It is reassuring and empowering. You can almost feel your heart rate begin to lower to a contented, rested pace: *we*, the juggernaut human race, have subjugated *risk* into submission. Risk has our lash at its back, and it is ours to predict and prevent.

Now consider another notional observation, this time from Nassim Nicholas Taleb, a Lebanese American scholar with a distinguished career in finance and academia:

> [T]he application of the sciences of uncertainty to real-world problems has had ridiculous effects; I have been privileged to see it in finance and economics. Go ask your portfolio manager for his definition of "risk," and odds are that he will supply you with a measure that excludes the possibility of the Black Swan [that is, a bet-the-company catastrophe or a lottery-wining success]— hence one that has no better predictive value for assessing the total risks than astrology[.][2]

Aha! Your heart rate has leapt back onto its customary racetrack. (Granted, it could simply be because you just read the term *portfolio manager* and all manner of unpleasant financial thoughts came to mind.) Our best efforts to grapple risk into bondage have failed. Spartacus Risk has gathered together an unpredictable, if small, number of rebel scenarios, and they continue to break free from our graphs, charts, measurements, assessments, formulas, and tables of empirical data.

The gods, apparently, do not mind sending black swans to wreck our sense of mastery and calm.

On February 1, 2011, temperatures in El Paso, Texas—a sunny and dry West Texas border city with winter averages usually between 30 and 50 degrees Fahrenheit—suddenly plunged to zero degrees, bringing several days' worth of measurable snowfall and freezing weather.[3] Along with 157 water-main breaks, thousands of dead palm trees and other plants, hundreds of vehicle accidents, low gas pressure (or no gas service at all), closed businesses, closed schools, water shortages, and closed roads, the majority of El Paso residents also lost the key to warmth and security: electrical power.

All eight of El Paso Electric Company's primary generators failed under the unyielding stress of the freezing conditions, and even after power was brought in from other grids, rolling blackouts continued. For over twenty-one years, the border region's infrastructure and way of life had avoided such severe and sudden low temperatures and harsh weather. Ill prepared to cope with the cold, El Paso Electric—a 110-year-old, NYSE-listed company—had an uncomfortable bull's eye on its back for quite some time thereafter.

Eventually, a 357-page report, issued seven months later by the Federal Energy Regulatory Commission and the North American Electric Reliability Corporation, found that more-adequate winterization procedures could have avoided such a massive failure of critical electrical equipment.[4] "Mary Kipp, El Paso Electric's chief compliance officer and general counsel, said the company supports the report's recommendation for plant weatherization standards to be put in state regulations and in the reliability corporation's operating standards."[5] The thousands and thousands of hours of reliable electricity enjoyed by El Paso residents for two decades preceding the 2011 freeze counted for little after that one anomalous February night. El Paso Electric's West Texas services were simply unprepared for the black swan of freezing weather. Among other corporate officers, the general counsel and chief compliance officer found herself part of El Paso Electric's reputational recovery.

Risk had brought along its uglier, meaner stepbrother: Consequences.

Dramatics aside, the recommended heart rate for a corporate lawyer, my dear reader, pitter-patters somewhere between Mr. Bernstein's and Professor Taleb's cerebral positions about risk. However paradoxical their above-quoted observations might at first appear, they are not incompatible positions. Together, they create the pragmatic boundaries for well-informed risk management programs. Indeed, the philosophical key to successful risk management is to recognize that both polarized paradigms are part of every business environment: we *can* control or predict *most* risk, *and* controls and predictions can occasionally be *worthless*.

> Risk means the chance of being wrong, of seeing outcomes different from what we expected. And key to that are the consequences of being wrong. . . . What's critical to risk management, then, is recognizing the consequences of being wrong by a little or a lot, and making decisions to reduce those consequences to an acceptable level.

These remarks by Richard M. Steinberg in his excellent book on managing risk, *Governance, Risk Management, and Compliance: It Can't Happen to Us—Avoiding Corporate Disaster While Driving Success,*[6] reconcile the practical role and reality of every corporate officer—lawyers included—with the black swan calamities of Professor Taleb's observations.

Risk management boils down to three primary components:

1. Identifying the risks (even the remote ones),
2. Identifying and understanding the consequences, and
3. Preparing for avoiding and/or tolerating (accepting) risk consequences.

Managing risk is simply the process by which you and your client-company meet and achieve each of those three components. The processes can be complex—financial-reporting controls that satisfy a SOX 404 top-down review—or they can be extraordinarily simple—remembering to lock the door when you leave a building. All processes, however, should match the type and level of risk they are intended to avoid or tolerate.

Corporate lawyers often struggle with this approach because we are schooled to see risk (or liability) as not only the archenemy but, ironically, also as the basis for our existence. As with most policies, procedures, and processes, the predominant concept is for these mechanisms to complement and strengthen the *business* of a business. A successful risk-management program is not the end goal. A *successful business enterprise* is the end goal. Risk management helps to ensure that success, and a good corporate lawyer learns to balance those, sometimes disparate, interests.

Just like Goldilocks, risk managers and corporate lawyers need to look for the mechanisms that are "just right."

It should come as no surprise that no single process fits each particular company's risk-management needs. Anyone who touts a one-size-fits-all-and-cures-all risk-management process is selling snake oil. Instead, processes should be formulated, vetted, reviewed, and improved in light of the three components we have listed above on a company-by-company basis. Keep it simple, . . . unless it needs to be complex.

As does each risk-management process, risk most often appears in one or more of three manifestations: legal risk, operational risk, and/or reputational risk. As lawyers, we tend to think overwhelmingly in terms of legal risk—the financial or disciplinary impact of lawsuits or compliance issues—but as *corporate* lawyers, we must give equal weight to operational risk (usually internal failures that can thwart a business's output, growth, and efficiency) and reputational risk (what the public, investors, vendors, and lenders may think about a business). No one area of risk is consistently the most risky, but all are capable, in their own right, of bringing a business enterprise to its knees.

The purpose of this chapter is to establish a few fundamental recommendations for preparing for risk and crisis while handling consequences when and if they arise. We will spend several sections briefly perusing a lineup of usual suspects, those dangers that haunt the dreams of corporate lawyers and other risk managers. Many of the suspects will be very familiar to most readers, and the idea is not to belabor their existence as potential threats. Instead, the effort here is to make sure each prospective risk is viewed through the right prism facets: legal concerns, operational concerns, and reputational concerns. As noted previously, the following recommendations and warnings are not designed to be comprehensive, although they should cover most topical bases.

The essential takeaway point for every corporate lawyer is this: train your mind to stretch beyond legal risks, and as you do that, enhance your skills as a proactive *counselor*, even though you will still need to be a quick-to-be-ready *advocate*. Repeatedly, we have already seen that corporate lawyers, in a manner unique to their area of practice, are called upon to be more than event-driven advocates.

> General counsel are responsible at the senior levels of not only asking the first question—is it legal?—but also the last questions: Is it right? ... That means the skills that are required of

them go far beyond being a technical lawyer. They have to be wise counselors and leaders.[7]

UNFORTUNATELY FOR THE VIEWING AUDIENCE OF KACL'S EVENING NEWSCAST, IRWIN WAS NOT THE BEST FIELD REPORTER TO HAVE ON AIR ON THE SAME DAY THE STOCK MARKET CRASHED ...

EVERYONE JUST STAY CALM!! NO ONE PANIC! IT'S JUST A BLACK SWAN, PEOPLE! I MEAN NOT A "BLACK SWAN" BUT JUST A BLACK SWAN ... UM ... LOOK, THIS ISN'T WHAT YOU THINK! .... IT'S AN ACTUAL BLACK SWAN BUT NOT A "BLACK SWAN" ... UM ... I GIVE UP... FORGET IT.

Risk

§ 6.1 RISK AND CRISIS MANAGEMENT—COMBAT TRIAGE

Embedded within the broader topic of risk lies the sudden tragedy of crisis. Because crisis embodies an immediate, active, unavoidable trauma to a client-company (versus risk, which may remain latent or be entirely avoided), a few separate words need to be spent on this kind of unforgiving event.

> Taking short-term pain for long-term gain can sometimes be the best solution to a crisis.[8]

Thankfully, most of us have never faced the kind of gut-wrenching misfortune that requires a caring, knowledgeable, and quick set of hands to salvage a fading human life. However, those men and women who are downrange in harm's way, whether domestically as law-enforcement, emergency-response, or medical personnel or internationally as military personnel, must face the grim likelihood they will be the first and best chance for a fellow human being to stay alive. As with most things in combat-like situations—or in *actual* combat situations—life-saving activity in a moment of crisis is relatively simple, even if the training leading up to that point has been complex. Combat triage is not an intuitive process for most people.

Simple saves. And keeping your head about you keeps it simple.

Years ago, as a Marine recruit sitting with my platoon members in a classroom at the U.S. Marine Recruit Depot, San Diego, I listened to a Navy corpsman—a naval combat medic who accompanied U.S. Marines into hell and back—lecture us on life-saving steps we were to use if a fellow Marine ever went down. Despite our constant state of weariness as we fought to stay awake in the classroom's warmth, I listened intently, and later had the unnerving and unfortunate occasion to put to use what I learned.

Neither the training nor the instructions were necessarily as simple as I now recount them to be, but the essence of how to deal with a full-blown traumatic wound does not change: (1) stop the bleeding, (2) start the breathing, (3) treat the wound, and (4) check for shock. With time and the refinements the war on terror has inevitably brought to combat medicine, there are sure to have been some changes to what I and my fellow recruits were taught that day almost twenty years ago, but the simplicity of the four-step treatment plan remains exquisitely logical. Shock, which is a silent but prevalent killer when a person is traumatically injured, is not as critically important as the immediate threat of a still-exposed wound; but a grotesquely exposed wound is not as important as a lack of oxygen; yet even a lack of oxygen is not as threatening as the speed and finality in which a person can expire if he or she exsanguinates, loses too much blood. Everything else we learned, or would ever learn, about body or vehicle armor, immediate action drills, standard operating procedures, offensive tactics, defensive tactics, gathering intelligence, or using intelligence would mean very little in the terrible space of time after a buddy got hit.

Frankly, the same applies to a business in crisis.

Section 3.3 of this book begins by recalling the swift implosion of Bear Stearns in January of 2008. The booming investment bank had a robust set of risk-management policies and procedures in place at the time. Remember, this was not the rough and tumble decade of greed that was the 1980s. Nor was it the electrifying pace of booms and busts experienced in the 1990s. This was post-SOX, post-Enron, post-Worldcom, post-tech-bubble, toward the end of the first decade of the new millennium. But robust risk-management policies, procedures, and a plethora of regulations were not enough to ward off or handle Bear Stearns' game-ending crisis. Bear Stearns' traders and portfolio managers had moved the venerable investment bank's house to the edge of a fast-eroding seaside cliff consisting of irrationally assembled mortgage-investment tranches. In essence, Bear Stearns was blindly betting its house would not plunge into the sea even if the entire cliff gave way beneath it. Even after having successfully survived the Wall Street Crash of 1929 seventy-nine years earlier, the cliff finally gave way in 2008, and the house of Bear Stearns was swallowed up by a deep blue sea.

Perhaps there was no amount of crisis management that could have salvaged Bear Stearns. Certainly herculean efforts were made. But the lesson is that crisis management—combat triage—eclipses risk management when consequences become all-out trauma. A corporate lawyer has to work immediately in concert with a well-trained team as they go into combat-triage mode.

Businesses, as "living" organizations, are much like people when it comes to trauma. There is a necessary priority when it comes to containing calamitous events, internally or externally. Jobs, reputations, careers, investments, safety, expectant customers, and dependent vendors' businesses are on the line. Beginning our discussion of risk management by talking about crisis triage may seem like putting consequence ahead of risk, but because of those lurking, unpredictable black swans, it is a paramount concern that a corporate lawyer and his or her client-company have a good grasp of crisis management even before the long-term, more comprehensive risk-management policies and procedures are developed and implemented. Crisis management is truly a subset of risk management, but a crisis, unlike repetitive reporting requirements, methodical investigations, or periodic internal reviews, is a full-blown corporate trauma that needs immediate and intelligent attention.

To remind myself of this point, I have taken myself back to another Marine-era experience. My squad and I were going through the final briefing for a building-entry and assault scenario. (The planning and briefing was our "risk management" at work.) The warning order and the patrol order had been thorough, and the briefing was spot on. That is, until the special-operations-training group instructor asked, "So what're you gonna do if your ingress is compromised, and you never even make it to the building?" (This question was asking us about our "crisis management.") What was our plan if the defending forces inside the building, or some other intervening force, stopped us cold before we even began the breach and assault? Did we have a contingency plan to deal with that *and* still take down the building (perhaps using a reserve squad or by tank support or artillery)? We had planned for the objective and for the usual risks, but a *catastrophic* crisis had not entered our minds.

We all struggled for a few moments to come up with an answer to our instructor's black swan.

> The risk of a crisis for most large companies can be diverse, arising from product liability, antitrust issues, industrial accidents, environmental disasters, or sabotage.... The first twenty-four hours are critical, when corporate strategy is initially decided and the first public statements are made.... Corporate counsel should always question any organization's ability to make the best possible judgments about matters of far-reaching importance under extreme pressure in a short time span, which is why planning done before a crisis occurs can be immensely valuable.[9]

Because identifying all possible disasters is a nearly impossible task, the objective for crisis management should be to identify the *types* of disasters (these are risks, but they are of the catastrophic variety) that may befall a client-company and to plan for the unexpected. Do not rest on the laurels of larger risk-management policies or procedures when doing this. Understand most companies, at some time or another, could face sudden crisis. Board involvement, management execution, media-relations preparation, and compliance and ethical considerations must all come into play, and they must do so almost instantaneously, in concert, and with effectiveness. As a professional who has been trained to look for, and deal with, crisis, have you asked the following questions? Can you and your client-company satisfactorily answer them?

- What disasters are likely to befall your client-company?
- How will they impact your client-company's operations, reputation, and financial ability to cope with the crisis? What personnel or groups of stakeholders will they impact in your client-company?
- Is a team in place to deal with each identified disaster and its impact? Are operational contingencies and insurance policies in place?
- Has real-world training taken place? Are procedures reviewed? Is everyone comfortable with his or her own role? Is there a clear order of responsibility and authority?

Businesses may reasonably expect a certain amount of accounting irregularities (hopefully innocent ones), EEOC lawsuits, whistleblower complaints, or shareholder challenges, but most businesses do not routinely expect a manufacturing plant literally to explode, an airliner to crash, a disgruntled employee to begin shooting other employees, a mine shaft to collapse, a train to derail, a cruise liner to sink, employees to be taken hostage, or to face billions in trading losses instead of millions in losses. Crisis management develops a plan to jump outside the usual risk procedures and protocols in order to deal with these kinds of bet-the-company disasters.

The following steps represent practical starting points for putting together and periodically reviewing a crisis-management plan:

1. Identify the type of risk the disaster represents for the client-company, and its likely scope and breadth.
2. Identify who or what constitutes the primarily injured party or operation if the disaster occurs.
3. Create a crisis-management team(s) for that type of disaster.
4. Create a crisis-management plan built on priority objectives for that type of disaster.
5. Train for the unexpected.

Roll up your sleeves and do the heavy lifting now. "Taking short-term pain" will most likely be the order of the day, but that is the reality of a crisis. The proper handling of the crisis will take cool-headed thinking, quick reactions, and a steady eye toward life after the crisis is over. After all, the ultimate goal is not just survival; it is getting back to business as usual. With good crisis management—anticipation, planning, and training—a corporate lawyer will find him- or herself playing a key role in stopping the bleeding, starting the breathing, dressing the wound, and treating for shock.

§ 6.2 PROACTIVE PROCEDURES AND ALLOCATION— PREPARED FOR DISASTER

With a grip on crisis, we can now move on to mainstream risk. Let us begin with a general comment about what risk management practically means to a client-company, procedurally and policy-wise.

The board, or an appropriate committee, should require management to provide and should receive periodic reports describing and assessing the corporation's programs for identifying financial, industry, and other business risks and for managing such risks to protect corporate assets and reputation. In addition, the board must ensure that its risk management overview addresses not just legal and compliance issues, but also devotes time to strategy, product innovations, cyclical risks, and the like.[10]

There you have it. In a nutshell, those actions should result in properly managing a client-company's risk. It sounds simple (and remember, *simple saves*), so what has caused the policies and procedures of risk management to continue to grow in breadth and complexity year after year?

For every corporate lawyer or risk manager who might be asked that question, there are likely to be just as many individual answers. Perhaps, though, the best, most complete answer is merely that business enterprises—and our world—have become more complex, so opportunities for risks to arise have also become more complex and more numerous, thereby creating the need for more-complex and far-reaching management and control systems. Technology, information accessibility, social media platforms, international trade, ease of travel, higher standards of living, byzantine financial and accounting issues and practices, and social activism have all changed the way most businesses govern their conduct and run their operations. In the past, a business might have been able to ignore employee safety; those days are long gone. In the past, a business might have been able to simply lock customer information in a file cabinet for safekeeping; those days are long gone. In the past, a business might have been able to keep a few ledgers and one bookkeeper tucked away in a back office with very little accountability; those days are long gone. The world has permanently changed, as has doing business in it.

Here a few of the broad and fertile fields in which many risk issues take root and erupt:

- Product liability
- Quality assurance
- Information-technology security
- Insurance

- Legal compliance and regulatory lawsuits
- Plant or operational security
- Confidentiality issues
- Intellectual-property security
- Core business risks—strategic and competitive risks
- Financial accounting and reporting
- Marketing campaigns
- Shareholder activism (whether for good or bad)
- Capitalization and debt issues
- Cultural differences

Facing all of this, the questions become

- How should an enterprise-wide risk-management program be developed and implemented?
- How do I know if my client-company's policies and procedures are well structured enough to adequately identify, understand, and avoid or tolerate these likely causes of risk?

To begin with, we should again acknowledge the difficulty—and the foolishness—in attempting to procreate a rigid program to apply to all risk possibilities.

There is no "ideal" risk management program for all corporations. Instead, a board must ensure the corporation's programs address the risks facing their companies in an appropriate manner. The range of risk-management programs is quite broad.[11]

No single set of maps would be able to discern the infinite number of paths your client-company may need to take in order to avoid, or deal with, risk. Because this is the case, a corporate lawyer and his or her client-company need a reliable compass and the ability to read it. In today's environment, there are numerous preprogrammed compasses for businesses to use for various risk-management needs. For instance, the International Organization for Standardization (ISO) published ISO 31000:2009 in November 2009, intending to codify a family of standards for all risk-management controls.[12] An accompanying standard, ISO 31010—Risk Assessment Techniques, soon followed, in December 2009. However, ISO's publications came after the bellwether publication

Enterprise Risk Management—Integrated Framework (ERM Framework), issued in 2004 by the Committee of Sponsoring Organizations of the Treadway Commission (COSO).[13]

The COSO ERM Framework[14] has eight components and four objectives categories. The eight components are as follows:

- Internal environment (Examines how risk is viewed by a company.)
- Objective setting (Objectives are set, are consistent with risk tolerances, and support overall business objectives.)
- Event identification (Internally and externally, risks and opportunities are identified.)
- Risk assessment (Risks are analyzed for probability, scope, and impact.)
- Risk response (Activities of avoiding, reducing, sharing, or accepting risk.)
- Control activities (These are the policies and procedures to establish and implement to ensure that risk responses are carried out.)
- Information and communication (Relevant information is identified and relayed in a form and in a timeframe that enables personnel to carry out their responsibilities.)
- Monitoring (This is accomplished through ongoing management and/or evaluations.)

The four objectives categories are:

- Strategy—high-level goals, aligned with and supporting the organization's mission
- Operations—effective and efficient use of resources
- Financial reporting—reliability of operational and financial reporting
- Compliance—adherence to applicable laws and regulations

In a more methodical way, the ERM Framework takes our three fundamental components of management—identification of risk, identification and understanding of consequences, and preparation for avoidance or tolerance—and provides a repeatable checklist for the development and implementation of almost any kind of enterprise-wide risk-management program. This tailoring quality allows risk-management programs to have the flexibility to be built toward any particular business entity's typical bevy of risk possibilities. Though tailoring a program can be a strength, to be truly effective, enterprise-wide risk management needs to be threaded throughout every operation, division, and office of an entire business. Plugging a leak in the stern of a ship does little good if water continues to pour through a leak in the bow.

> Inherent in all ERM processes, however, is the discipline in the process and that it operates *throughout* the organization.... If it doesn't have the requisite discipline, scope, and function throughout an organization, we call it risk management, not enterprise risk management.[15]

As one of a client-company's top-echelon risk managers—if not *the* risk manager—a corporate lawyer must be able to develop (or help to develop) the policies and procedures, across different divisions and business units, to identify risk, understand its consequences, and plan to avoid or tolerate those consequences. Implementing these policies and procedures, and training others to be the client-company's additional eyes and ears for risk issues, is far easier when the program remains simple, consistent, and supportive of the client-company's business objectives.

If your client-company's program has sprung some leaks, then figure out why, and lead the charge toward fixing those inefficiencies before manageable risk morphs into full-blown crisis.

Risk Prepared

§ 6.3 MINIMIZING ERROR RATES— THE SIX SIGMA ATTORNEY

Understandably, developing, implementing, and supervising a full-blown ERM Framework within most organizations is a formidable and somewhat foreign task for many corporate lawyers. Lawyers, though trained to look for and deal with legal liabilities, are *not* risk managers by trade.[16] They may unconsciously gravitate more toward compliance risks and partially ignore reputational or operational risks, simply because they lack a personal methodology to attack nonlegal risk issues. Or they may not have a repeatable way to articulate their methodology to other personnel in the legal department, or other departments, in order to develop a company-wide risk-management cadre.

Here, then, is where we can hijack one great idea to accomplish another one.

On April 1, 2010, Americanlawyer.com posted a video interview of J. Stephen Poor, a managing partner of the Chicago powerhouse law firm Seyfarth Shaw LLP. The online version of *American Lawyer* introduced the video as follows:

> Five years ago, Chicago law firm Seyfarth Shaw began toying with a business method designed to improve efficiency known as Six Sigma. . . . Since then, the methodology has started to take over at Seyfarth; they want to be known by it.[17]

Though most lawyers and law firms were only dimly aware of the Six Sigma business management strategy (generally because business clients found a way to use the term in every other sentence), Seyfarth Shaw recognized an opportunity. As clients demanded more and more value—efficiency and economy—from their lawyers, Seyfarth Shaw was a savant with its answer: tailor Six Sigma to fit the *business* of law practice. After a lot of innovative effort and hard work, Seyfarth Shaw's current Web site is able to proudly announce the following:

> [W]e have become the only large law firm to build a distinctive client service model—called Seyfarth*Lean*—that combines the core principles of Lean Six Sigma with robust technology, knowledge management, process management techniques, alternative fee structures and practical tools.[18]

With Seyfarth Shaw being one of two megafirms leading the way, there has been an increasing emphasis on Six Sigma strategies for law office, or law department, management and efficiency over the past few years.[19] For our purposes, it does not require much more of an imaginative stretch for a corporate lawyer to apply (even if loosely) Six Sigma strategies to his or her risk-management efforts. And suddenly, a very useable, personal tool—a repeatable and trainable methodology—is born.[20]

Six Sigma was originally born and incubated at Motorola in 1986. The methodology eventually gathered an enormous amount of popular appeal after Jack Welch, the titan of General Electric,[21] made it a core principal of his business strategy in the mid-1990s. It became one of those iconic sound bites of corporate America, as otherwise milquetoast managers bragged about earning martial-arts-sounding things like "green belts" and "black belts."

Essentially, Six Sigma seeks to improve the quality of procedural outputs by identifying and removing causes of errors and minimizing statistical dispersion (variability). Implementing its strategies is intended to encourage efficiency, consistency, and economy, whether financial or procedural. Six Sigma proposes that each project within an organization follow a measurement-based strategy—a sequence of steps—in order to reach a quantified target. This can be accomplished by using one of two submethodologies: DMADV (define, measure, analyze, design, verify) or DMAIC (define, measure, analyze, improve, control).

Assuming we can commandeer the DMAIC submethodology for our risk-management purposes, let us look at a brief example of what kind of play card you could keep handy while tackling your client-company's risk-management program.

Recall that a healthy risk-management program will require each identified risk to be responded to by a particular process to reach a particular result. This is the risk-response component of the EMR Framework. If we apply our Six Sigma submethodology, DMAIC, to this EMR Framework component, we will be able to qualitatively assess whether the implemented component is efficiently working and whether it is meeting its goals.

1. Define the problem (that is, the risk-response component lacks contingencies).
2. Measure key aspects of the response plan and gather data.

3. Analyze the data to determine cause-and-effect relationships (that is, if the risk response is missing important contingencies, why?).
4. Improve the risk responses based on the analyzed data (that is, pilot-run a new risk-response contingency).
5. Control the future risk responses to make sure they do not deviate from the component's objective; put monitoring or control systems in place.

The ERM Framework can provide the components and objectives (and techniques) for devising, implementing, and supervising a business-wide risk-management program, but by supplying a Six Sigma quality-improvement cheat sheet, a corporate lawyer will have a personal methodology to use—or train others to use—when assessing and adjusting risk-management issues. Minimizing error rates minimizes risk exposures.

§ 6.4 POTENTIAL LIABILITIES—THE USUAL SUSPECTS

The fundamental plank work of risk management is to first identify and understand the various risks facing an organization. Consequences cannot be evaluated, tolerances cannot be tested, procedures cannot be properly assessed, and policies cannot be written, unless particular risks—or types of risk—are clearly identified and understood. This imperative must be weighed in balance with our previously stated conclusion that it is virtually *impossible* to identify *every* possible risk to a business, most especially our beloved black swans, which swim about in the same category as predicting when and where lightning will strike.

> "It's just phenomenal the amount of legal exposure faced by directors and management today," says Carrie Hightman, CLO for NiSource, Inc. "It's a different environment than it was 10 to 20 years ago. Because of that change, it's more important than ever that the general counsel is knowledgeable and involved in what's going on in the business."[22]

Indeed, a corporate lawyer may not be able to coax every lurking risk out of the shadows, but like a lineup of roughs at a police station, most of the work can be done when the usual suspects have been identified and dealt with. You do not have to look very far. The identity of most risk suspects is found simply by looking at "what's going on in the business."

As you move through the next several sections, actively think about the three basic risk-management questions:

- Who or what constitutes these latent liabilities—these potential perpetrators of risk—within your client-company?
- What consequences does your client-company likely face if these risks materialize?
- How can your client-company plan for, avoid, or handle these risks? Is a risk-management program already in place? Will it do the job?

Each section will help you by (mercilessly) repeating these evaluative questions, as they are broken apart by the three basic risk categories: legal, operational, and reputational. For each suspect, use these questions as mental, if not literal, reviews. You and your client-company's risk-management program should be able to articulate viable answers to each question.

Risk-management evaluation, like the conjugation of Latin verbs, is best accomplished through rote practice.

EVEN BEFORE THE FEDS SENT A SUBPOENA FOR HIS COMPANY'S ACCOUNTING RECORDS, WILBUR PRIVATELY ADMITTED THAT HIS METHOD OF LEARNING ABOUT THE FOREIGN CORRUPT PRACTICES ACT HAD NOT BEEN AS THOROUGH AS IT SHOULD HAVE BEEN.

Usual Suspects

§ 6.4.1 Government Regulators and Industry Oversight

"In the very olden time there lived a semi-barbaric king, . . ." In this way, Frank R. Stockton began his much-anthologized short story "The Lady, or the Tiger," first written for publication in the American magazine *The Century* in 1882. Mr. Stockton, a humorist and writer who was best known for a series of inventive children's fairy tales, had a delightful way of creating rounded characters in short spurts of prose. His description of this "semi-barbaric king" presents too splendid of an opportunity to pass up as we take a few moments to discuss the risk of government regulators and industry oversight watchdogs.

> He [insert *"the Regulator"* here] was greatly given to self-communing, and, when he and himself agreed upon anything, the thing was done. When every member of his domestic and political systems moved smoothly in its appointed course, his nature was bland and genial; but, whenever there was a little hitch, and some of his orbs got out of their orbits, he was blander and more genial still, for nothing pleased him so much as to make the crooked straight and crush down uneven places.

If that isn't the best, most matter-of-fact description of a faceless regulator or an industry watchdog, I don't know what is. A corporate lawyer can almost bet that whenever a client-company's "orbs [get] out of their orbits," some proxy of the "semi-barbaric king" will be sure to come calling.

In sections 3.1.4, 5.3, and 5.4, we discussed regulation, governance, and compliance issues. Those issues, the agencies who enforce them, the industry watchdogs who report on them, and the individuals who call your client-company's complaint line to insist on them, represent identifiable risks to your client-company. Your client-company's compliance program, which should weave itself in and out of many risk-management issues, will be especially visible when it comes to these categories of risk. Therefore, as a corporate lawyer, you *must* understand who those entities and individuals are and what laws, regulations, and standards apply to your client-company. You must equally understand at what tipping point any one of them moves from being an identified risk to an active consequence.

§ 6.4.1.1 Whistleblowers

> With businesses, public institutions and political leaders around the globe facing growing skepticism about their competence and probity, you'd think leaders would understand . . . covering up

matters in the hope the press won't show up at all [is a] failed [strategy] in a world where anyone with a smartphone or a laptop—including employees, vendors, and shareholders—is a reporter capable of uncovering wrongdoing and telling the story to virtually everyone around the globe.[23]

A person who reveals misconduct occurring within a company is a whistleblower—an increasingly widespread risk to almost every business enterprise. Such a person may blow the whistle *within* the company by filing an internal complaint or calling a company's anonymous whistleblower hotline.[24] Indeed, with practical and workable procedures in place, this kind of risk may be entirely addressed in house with minimal consequences to a client-company. The flipside, of course, is a whistleblower may bypass the internal resources and go *outside* a company, straight to a regulatory agency or law-enforcement authority, and risk management at that point may very well become crisis management, depending on what kind of whistle has been blown.

Whistleblower protections and rewards are the result of a large patchwork of different laws, most recently Dodd-Frank. Though it can be critical to understand how each of those whistleblower laws may relate to your client-company's business operations, it is even more critical to address the risk of whistleblowing by planning to address it before it ever leaves the corporate campus.

Planning for, avoiding, and protecting against this type of risk is often a significant program. In the April 2012 edition of *InsideCounsel*, five steps were suggested to improve the policies and procedures to encourage internal reporting.[25] They were:

1. *Communicate*—Make sure everyone knows that the client-company genuinely believes in, and insists upon, a culture of compliance and ethics, and is open to address concerns.
2. *Appoint an ombudsman*—Create a "channel outside the chain of command" to help resolve issues.
3. *Give supervisors a script*—Train the management on the appropriate words to use when approached with a complaint to avoid creating a further liability.
4. *Consider rewards*—Incentivizing employees, even if nonfinancially, to report concerns or noncompliance uses the same carrot-and-stick principle offered by government regulators.

5. *Proceed with caution*—There is a "fundamental employment aspect to a whistleblower case," so avoid fighting the two-front war of a regulatory charge *and* a retaliation claim.

The second sentence of American Express's Management Policy for Whistleblower Claims clearly sets the recommended tone and defines the intended result for recognizing and understanding this category of risk.

> By appropriately responding to allegations by employees, suppliers, customers or contractors that the Company is not meeting its legal obligations, the Company can better support an environment where compliance is the norm.[26]

As you diagnose potential whistleblower risks, remember to ask the following questions:

- What are the *legal* risks? What are the client-company's tolerances? Is the client-company prepared?
- What are the *operational* risks? What are the client-company's tolerances? Is the client-company prepared?
- What are the *reputational* risks? What are the client-company's tolerances? Is the client-company prepared?

§ 6.4.1.2 Compliance—State and Federal

Section 5.3 took a productive look at compliance issues, programs, and regulatory concerns. Compliance is an area of risk management that is a natural fit for most lawyers. It rests upon interpreting and adhering to a set of statutes, regulations, and/or industry guidelines. Compliance typically has its own department and a distinct set of personnel, routine tasks, and a fairly static chain of reporting and corporate communications. This does not mean, necessarily, the compliance department, by default, has a strong risk-management program for compliance risks.

Oddly enough, I have seen compliance programs and objectives veer so far toward "complying," they nearly ignored what to do about the likely risks of noncompliance. In fact, I have seen an entire board sit there, fairly undisturbed, as critical policies fell further and further out of compliance because of the meddling of the board's chairman. Though everyone was fully aware of compliance issues, no one seemed unnerved about being in noncompliance.

Other than a vague notion that it is bad not to comply with a regulatory requirement, some compliance officers, executives, and board members do not readily understand—or plan for—what to do when such requirements have not been met. They may not appreciate or recognize what a company's tolerances are for noncompliance (this should be zero, but in reality, it rarely is), nor do they have a firm grasp of what preparations need to be made in the event of noncompliance. Their "risk-o-meter" may be lulled into complacency merely as a result of the *existence* of a compliance department or compliance program.

Consider this alarming tale:

> In September 2005, a senior [company] lawyer received an alarming e-mail from a former executive at the company's largest foreign subsidiary[.] In the e-mail and follow-up conversations, the former executive described how [the company] had orchestrated a campaign of bribery to win market dominance. In its rush to build stores, he said, the company had paid bribes to obtain permits in virtually every corner of the country.... [W]ithin days [the company] unearthed evidence of widespread bribery. They found a paper trail of hundreds of suspect payments totaling more than $24 million.... The lead investigator recommended that [the company] expand the investigation. Instead, an examination by the New York Times found, [the company's] leaders shut it down.[27]

You may have already guessed the name of the company, but even if *you've* guessed its name, it would be the *last* company the late Sam Walton would have guessed: Walmart. This bribery scandal—an amazing act of noncompliance with the Foreign Corrupt Practices Act[28]—was allegedly committed and covered up by a company that is the world's third-largest public company, the world's largest private employer, and the world's largest retailer.

Never presume a company has "zero tolerance" for noncompliance risks (Walmart appears to have had plenty of tolerance), or that a compliance program will be strong enough to eradicate all possibility of noncompliance risk. *Never* presume noncompliance risks can simply be brought back into line, quietly contained, and made to fade into a client-company's past. Although some of the ensuing journalistic reporting on the Walmart bribery scandal suggests "it's not a crime not to report violations,"[29] there is a historically overlooked SOX provision that could turn this particular kind of "risk-management strategy" on its head.

Title 18 of the U.S. Code, Section 1519, states:

> [W]hoever knowingly alters, destroys, mutilates, conceals, covers up, falsifies, or makes a false entry in any record, document, or tangible object with the intent to impede, obstruct, or influence the investigation or proper administration of any matter within the jurisdiction of any department or agency of the United States . . . or in relation to or contemplation of any such matter or case, shall be fined . . . imprisoned not more than 20 years, or both.[30]

This provision alone can put a whole new sheen on noncompliance consequences.

As you swivel your head nervously toward your client-company's compliance department, move through your checklist:

- What are the *legal* risks? What are the client-company's tolerances? Is the client-company prepared?
- What are the *operational* risks? What are the client-company's tolerances? Is the client-company prepared?
- What are the *reputational* risks? What are the client-company's tolerances? Is the client-company prepared?

§ 6.4.1.3 False Claims Act—*Qui Tam*

English common law gave us humble colonists the historical precedent for a unique writ of law: a writ of *qui tam*. Its name is the shortened derivative of the Latin phrase *qui tam pro domino rege quam pro se ipso in hac parte sequitur,* meaning "[he] who sues in this matter for the king as [well as] for himself." The essential concept is that an individual can bring a lawsuit on behalf of the government when the government has somehow been swindled by a person or company.

This distinctive civil action was first codified into federal law by President Abraham Lincoln after wearying of unscrupulous defense contractors who made small fortunes by charging the Union's War Department full price for decrepit mules, defective weapons and ammunition, and rancid rations and provisions. Mr. Lincoln's Congress passed the law as the False Claims Act,[31] and it remained largely unchanged until 1986.[32] Thereafter, the Fraud Enforcement and Recovery Act of 2009[33] added to the law's teeth, and in 2010, the Patient Protection and Affordable Care Act filed those teeth to a razor's edge with further amendments.[34]

Mr. Lincoln's law is the first and oldest whistleblower law in the United States.[35] When a person or a company has charged the government for a good or service that it did not deliver, charged the government for a good or service for which it should not have charged, or falsely certified that it qualifies to participate in a government program, it may find itself at the short end of a *qui tam* lawsuit.

Whistleblower risks were raised in Section 6.4.1.1, and a *relator* (the individual who files the false claims lawsuit) is certainly a brand of whistleblower. Then why carve out a separate section for false claims whistleblowers? Because a false claims risk comes with a uniquely insidious twist: the target defendant (that is, your client-company) will probably be *unaware it has been sued* for at least the first six months after the lawsuit has been filed.

A false claims lawsuit is perhaps the only civil lawsuit that is required to be filed *entirely under seal*. Only the U.S. attorney and, in some cases, a state attorney general will be notified of the lawsuit so their offices can conduct their own quasi-criminal, quasi-civil investigations. At the end of the first six months, the notified prosecutorial offices may elect to take over the lawsuit (in which case, the relator remains a party but collects a lesser percentage of any award), or they may allow the relator to proceed with spearheading the lawsuit (in which case, the relator may choose to continue with the lawsuit, and if any damages are recovered, the relator will be entitled to a greater percentage).

Managing risk to avoid potential lawsuits you *can* see is one thing. Managing risk for potential lawsuits you *cannot* see is something entirely different. If your client-company does business with the government, provides certifications to the government (in order to be eligible for participation in certain programs), or benefits from government grants, contracts, or subsidies, then this is an area of risk management that will require singular attention. Focused risk audits for accounting, billing, reporting, or certification discrepancies involving any government-related business activity may need to be built in as a special arm of your client-company's risk-management program. With the kind of statutory awards available to false claims whistleblowers (thousands of dollars for *every occurrence* of fraud), your client-company's efforts to ferret out wrongdoing before a whistleblower files a *qui tam* lawsuit will be competing against a relator's incentive to pursue a financial windfall.

Though the financial impact of a false claims lawsuit presents a significant risk, your client-company also cannot afford to ignore the operational or reputational risks related to being found liable for—or simply being investigated for—having defrauded the government. Identifying and dealing with policies or procedures that might encourage, or may result in, any kind of misrepresentation or false billing (no matter how slight) to the government is a far better price to pay than the butcher's bill that comes with a *qui tam* lawsuit, even if your litigation counsel is ultimately able to successfully ward it off.

Be inventive and be wary. To borrow advice highlighted earlier, in Section 6.1, "Taking short-term pain for long-term gain can sometimes be the best solution[.]"[36]

No less than at any other time, remember to ask the following about any manner of dealings your client-company has with the government:

- What are the *legal* risks? What are the client-company's tolerances? Is the client-company prepared?
- What are the *operational* risks? What are the client-company's tolerances? Is the client-company prepared?
- What are the *reputational* risks? What are the client-company's tolerances? Is the client-company prepared?

§ 6.4.1.4 Are They Friends or Foes?

It can be difficult for a corporate lawyer, or a risk manager, to decide whether regulators, industry watchdogs, and whistleblowers are friends or foes.

At first glance, the weight of the evidence seems to favor the latter. In Section 6.4.1.2, we took note of the SOX provision that can criminalize or harshly penalize any attempt to cover up corporate wrongdoing.[37] There is the Responsible Corporate Officer Doctrine,[38] which allows corporate officers to be held criminally liable for violations of certain laws (some with express provisions and some without), even when there is no evidence of individual culpability, if it is shown that their positions within the corporation gave them responsibility and authority to prevent or correct violations. There is the False Claims Act, civil and criminal penalties under the Foreign Corrupt Practices Act, and dozens of other statutes, regulations, and doctrines by which regulators represent a significant type of risk to almost every organization. A successful risk-management program must vigilantly insulate and protect a client-company from these wolves at the door.

At a second glance, however, regulators, watchdogs, and whistle-blowers also help create a more level playing field for competitive businesses, stabilize financial risks, protect employees, compel safe and socially responsible operations, support self-policing, control information risks, help protect assets, and discourage waste. They are risks that, obversely, can actually *aid* a business, much like a rickety bridge might allow travelers to cross over a deep gorge—but woe to those travelers who are careless as they cross over!

The better tactic for a corporate lawyer (and his or her client-company) is to leave the friend or foe opinion at home. When at work, identify, analyze, and plan for regulatory risks without invective. When animosity toward regulatory risk becomes overt, it can breed a culture of contempt and see-what-we-can-get-away-with resentment. Occasionally, some level of rancor is deserved, but disagreement with particular regulations and regulatory agencies must be aired in an appropriate and professional way. In this, corporate lawyers, who are susceptible to being viewed as the hatchet men for a company, lead the way. Inappropriate antipathy or hostility toward any category of regulatory risk initiates *more* risk. Often as not, businesses run the risk of regulatory violations innocently, not realizing the rickety bridge has begun to sway dangerously from side to side. Do not let yourself, your client-company, or its risk-management program overreact. Many regulatory risks can be greatly mitigated or entirely diffused with transparency, sincere cooperation, and a demonstration that the right protocols were in place, even if those protocols have somehow failed.

On the other hand, do not be too "sweet" on regulatory risks either. They *are* risks after all. They need to be identified and planned for, but they do not need to unnecessarily overwhelm a client-company's business objectives by becoming more important than they actually are. An overemphasis on treating regulatory risks with kid gloves can foster a culture of uneasiness or fear. Or worse, it can breed numerous Chicken

Littles, who will run around clouding the identification of legitimate risks and needlessly draining internal risk-management resources.

§ 6.4.1.5 Remembering Pitfalls of Privilege

As a final comment before we leave the usual-suspect lineup of regulators, industry watchdogs, and whistleblowers, a brief look at privilege issues—privilege *risks*—is in order. It is during encounters with these types of risks that privileges are most likely to be in peril.

Sections 2.1.3 and 5.3.5 both spent time examining the more critical varieties of privilege issues and difficulties faced by corporate lawyers. Those sections were generally concerned with the risk of *losing* or *waiving* privileges. Those concerns rightfully merit alert attention. In fact, lawyers will find that most discussions of privilege will focus on some perspective of those hazards.

It should be no surprise that in risk-management scenarios, or during crisis responses, privilege preservation should be a paramount concern.[39] The hectic and stressful commotion of activity in risk and crisis situations can inadvertently lead to otherwise avoidable losses of privilege that may be difficult, or impossible, to claw back. Though there are several very good strategies for safeguarding privileged information and communications during risk-response and crisis-response situations, the following is simple, straightforward, and effective.

> Use outside counsel as much as practical to quarterback your crisis response. The issues that frustrate the application of privilege to in-house communications—your business functions, your title, your interactions with corporate constituents—usually don't arise with outside counsel, who courts view as adorned with a cloak of independence under which privilege has been protected. Inside counsel, however, face unique threshold inquiries about our status as "attorneys" before the privilege is even considered.[40]

Ironically, an equally relevant concern for risk-management programs is that exercising privileges has a peculiar way of also *creating* risk. For instance, if the preservation of a privilege appears to be at odds with the SOX provision we mentioned in Section 6.4.1.2, then it becomes a gamble (that is, a *risk*) to presume that rights afforded by the privilege will avert a prosecution or civil fines for some kind of interference with a government agency. If the preservation of a privilege runs contrary to the demands of a subpoena—a court order—it is a *risk* to presume a naked assertion of the privilege will avoid a finding of contempt.[41] If the preservation of a privilege depends on a poorly drafted joint-defense agreement, or on an agreement with an investigatory regulator, then it is a *risk* to presume subsequent litigation may not pierce those agreements and expose your client-company to waiver.

The point is simple: privileges are not only thorny issues for purposes of establishing them, maintaining them, and protecting them, they are also uniquely thorny issues for risk-management programs. Asserted privileges can carry or create collateral consequences under their own steam.

Though it may feel odd to do so, examine the privilege issues—the privacy, confidentiality, and secrecy issues—embedded in your client-company's business units, and ask your essential risk-assessment questions:

- What are the *legal* risks? What are the client-company's tolerances? Is the client-company prepared?
- What are the *operational* risks? What are the client-company's tolerances? Is the client-company prepared?
- What are the *reputational* risks? What are the client-company's tolerances? Is the client-company prepared?

ACME, INC., LATER HAD A DIFFICULT TIME CONVINCING THE COURT IT HAD FULLY COOPERATED DURING THE PRE-LITIGATION INVESTIGATION.

Pitfalls

§ 6.4.2 Consumers

In broad strokes, a *consumer* is any person, vendor, entity, or other organization that receives some kind of product, service, or benefit from a business organization. Akin to the risk dichotomy of privilege issues, consumers present a two-fold risk challenge to your client-company: (1) there is the risk a consumer will, in some way, *be harmed* by the service, product, or benefit your client-company provides; or (2) there is the risk a consumer will, directly or indirectly, *cause some kind of harm* to your client-company. Both types of consumer risk need to be conscious parts of your client-company's risk-management program.

The risk of harm *to* a consumer is what might first pop into most people's minds when thinking of consumer risk. The risk of harm to a consumer can manifest itself through physical harm, financial harm, or psychological harm. These risks most often arise from product failures, mislabeling[42] practices or a lack of proper labeling, false advertising, deceptive trade practices, on-site hazards (that is, premise liability), breaches of fiduciary duties, and the failure to successfully manage other risk exposures that, in turn, cause harm to a client-company's consumer base.

The risk of harm *caused by* consumers is less headline sensational but just as potentially devastating to a business. Generally speaking, these risks manifest themselves financially. Most often, this means a consumer poses some kind of credit risk to a company: for example, a credit card is issued to a customer, a vendor is extended delayed-payment terms, a market investor qualifies for a margin account, or a health service is provided based on an expectation of reimbursement by the government. There are also situations in which a consumer can pose other kinds of risks to a business, such as physical risks (as in the case of security or sabotage).

Risk management for consumer goods and services and risk management of consumer-caused risk (when the consumer poses the active threat) are fairly high-profile priorities for most companies. The potential consequence of either type of risk is usually too great, whether to a business's reputation or to its financial health. This, however, does not necessarily mean that any given risk-management program will be prepared to adequately identify, understand, and prepare for these consumer-related risks. Frequently, risk-management programs rely too heavily for preparedness and safety on the posters, signs, forms, informational pamphlets, safety mechanisms, credit checks, formulas, and labels mandated by laws and regulations. Merely meeting the requirements of regulation-imposed checklists is rarely an adequate, or tailored, approach to true consumer-risk management for any business. The effort to identify, understand, and deal with consumer-related risk must be more active and more adapted to a client-company's particular industry, risk tolerances, financial health, and corporate culture.

A corporate lawyer's part in establishing or encouraging an active approach to consumer-related risk begins with—you guessed it—basic risk-assessment questions.

- What are the *legal* risks? What are the client-company's tolerances? Is the client-company prepared?
- What are the *operational* risks? What are the client-company's tolerances? Is the client-company prepared?
- What are the *reputational* risks? What are the client-company's tolerances? Is the client-company prepared?

§ 6.4.2.1 Applicable Laws

If you happen to visit the Web site for the U.S. Federal Trade Commission (www.ftc.gov), you will almost instantly notice the agency's mission phrase, placed immediately to the right of the FTC's seal: "Protecting America's Consumers." Ensuring members of the general public are well informed, fairly informed, and safe are some of the hallmark objectives of the FTC. Interested (or irate) members of the public who visit the FTC Web site are able to click on any one of ten different consumer-related categories to become more informed and/or to learn about their individual rights. The FTC's role in consumer activism is shared with other federal agencies, such as the Food and Drug Administration (www.fda.gov) and the Consumer Product Safety Commission (www.cpsc.gov), and the FTC's enforcement role in consumer protectionism is shared with the Department of Justice (www.doj.gov). Additionally, there are also state-level consumer-protection agencies and regulations in all fifty states that will affect a client-company's risk-management program and consumer-related risks.

A variety of federal statutes incorporate or focus on consumer-protection provisions. For example, there is the Fair Debt Collection

Practices Act,[43] the Fair Credit Reporting Act,[44] the Truth in Lending Act,[45] the Fair Credit Billing Act,[46] the Gramm-Leach-Bliley Act,[47] and, of course, the Dodd–Frank Wall Street Reform and Consumer Protection Act.[48] Most states have their own legislative assortment of codified consumer-protection laws, such as deceptive trade practices acts, "lemon" laws, and health-care patients' bill of rights statutes.

For those types of risks that consumers typically pose to businesses, there are laws that deal with capital regulation and credit-risk management.[49]

Though the area of consumer-protection laws—whether protecting consumers or protecting businesses from consumers—is an area of compliance within a larger enterprise's risk-management program, the assessment of risk remains the same as in other areas. For each law, regulation, or agency guideline that affects your client-company's consumer-related risks, the following questions need thoughtful and practical answers:

- What are the *legal* risks? What are the client-company's tolerances? Is the client-company prepared?
- What are the *operational* risks? What are the client-company's tolerances? Is the client-company prepared?
- What are the *reputational* risks? What are the client-company's tolerances? Is the client-company prepared?

§ 6.4.2.2 Contracts and Torts

Apart from characterizing consumer-related risks by whether they are physical, financial, or psychological, most of these risks can also be characterized as contractual or tortious. This secondary method of characterization can be helpful to a corporate lawyer, or even to a risk manager, because it can assist in the identification of potential consequences, appropriate responses, duties, and relevant laws. The exercise here is not to rehash first-year law school curricula regarding elements of a contract or a tort. Instead, it is to suggest both of these core subjects also represent distinctive mechanisms of consumer-related risk.

For those consumer relationships established through a contract, the management of subsequent risks must take into account the duties, obligations, breach and default mechanisms, and relief provisions expressed within the contracting document. For those consumer-related risks that may arise from a tortious action (or omission), the management of risk must take into account the identification of what duties are involved (statutory or common law), how those duties can be breached, what proofs are necessary to establish causation, and what the possible damage exposure(s) may be (that is, Is there a statutory cap? Can fees be collected? Can interest be collected? Can punitive damages be awarded?). Uniquely, these analyses are areas in which a corporate lawyer can take the forefront and apply his or her knowledge of contracts and torts to the risk management of both categories.

Lest we forget the key objectives of such an analysis, however, the assessment of consumer-related contractual or tortious risks abides by the same fundamental questions:

- What are the *legal* risks? What are the client-company's tolerances? Is the client-company prepared?
- What are the *operational* risks? What are the client-company's tolerances? Is the client-company prepared?
- What are the *reputational* risks? What are the client-company's tolerances? Is the client-company prepared?

§ 6.4.3 Employees and Contractors

Employees and contractors represent an intriguing type of risk to a client-company because they are insiders—allies. Their personal success is, or should be, integrated with the success of their employer, so it seems nonsensical—by strictly theoretical logic—for employees or contractors to be the cause of any damage to "the hand that feeds" them. But the real world does not take its cue from theoretical logic.

Consider the following:

Since the height of the recession in 2008, more workers across the nation have been suing employers under federal and state wage-and-hour laws. The number of lawsuits filed [in 2011] was up 32% vs. 2008[.][50]

[T]he volume of current ADA litigation [in 2012] is averaging 90 percent higher than five years ago.[51]

Accusations of workplace discrimination—which workers file with the commission when they think they have been unfairly treated based on their race, sex or other so-called protected categories—soared to 99,922 in [2010] from 93,277 in the previous year. That was an increase of 7.2 percent, and the highest level of new discrimination cases ever recorded.[52]

Legal risks associated with employees are painfully evident. Employees *sue* employers. Not only do employees sue their employers, but employees can also cause *other* persons to sue their employers. This, of course, is the doctrine of *respondeat superior*, another law school recollection from first-year torts.

The operational and reputational employment-related risks are no better. When employees or contractors refuse to work, or cannot work, a business's operational productivity—its ability to *do* its business—suffers. When employees or contractors are disgruntled, mistreated, or forced to work in avoidably unsafe environments, a business's reputation can suffer enormously. Comprehensive risk-management programs should take into account, and plan for, the risk contingencies attributable to a company's workforce. Because employees and contractors are physically accessible to a company, much can be done in the way of prevention before *risk* becomes *consequence*.

The Federal Bureau of Investigation maintains a Critical Incident Response Group (CIRG), which has developed a seven-step approach to use in crisis situations. One of the seven steps is *active listening*. Active listening, which was mentioned briefly in sections 4.3 and 4.3.4, is a communication technique requiring a listener to paraphrase or restate what he or she heard back to the speaker. This confirms what a listener has heard and confirms and reinforces the understanding of both parties. When any one of us, as human beings, feels ostracized, unhappy, underappreciated, ignored, or marginalized, we need to be *heard*. If it works for the FBI during hostage or crisis negotiations, then it is likely to have significant merit in most employment situations.

Therefore, step one in employment-related risk management is to *listen to your client-company's employees*. If there are grumblings, or looming fissures, in the workforce, it is far better to know they exist before a complaint is lodged, a lawsuit is filed, or a news interview is filmed.

However, active listening should be just one tool—one component—within a portfolio of useful risk-management procedures for diffusing employment-related risks. A company's compliance department and human resources department should be chock-full of various policies, procedures, best practices, and strategies for identifying, avoiding, or dealing with wage and hour issues, discrimination complaints, ADA[53] requirements, medical leave issues, OSHA[54] safety requirements, and union (collective bargaining) matters. But in spite of prodigious amounts of regulations, agency guidelines, consultant resources, formalized training, certifications, and degrees in human resources in corporate America, risks related to employees and contractors have done anything but abate over the past several years.

A corporate lawyer—even if not equipped with a background in employment law—needs to come to the risk-management table as prepared as possible to identify potential risks, identify and understand their consequences, and prepare for avoiding or tolerating those consequences.

The following five sections will start that process for you by identifying some key areas of employment-related risk. The intent is to provide enough of a topical exposure so that you will be ready to seek out and sit down with your client-company's compliance officer, human resources director, union sponsor, or outside employment counsel, and begin to converse with him or her about those particular risks facing your client-company.

I will not burden each section with its own separate refrain, but you cannot forget to challenge your grasp of each employment-related risk by asking the core assessment questions:

- What are the *legal* risks? What are the client-company's tolerances? Is the client-company prepared?
- What are the *operational* risks? What are the client-company's tolerances? Is the client-company prepared?
- What are the *reputational* risks? What are the client-company's tolerances? Is the client-company prepared?

§ 6.4.3.1 Title VII and State Laws

When most people talk about discrimination in the workplace, they are referring to the prohibitions contained in Title VII of the 42nd volume of the U.S. Code. This is the Civil Rights Act of 1964, and its preamble is as follows:

An Act

To enforce the constitutional right to vote, to confer jurisdiction upon the district courts of the United States to provide injunctive relief against discrimination in public accommodations, to authorize the attorney General to institute suits to protect constitutional rights in public facilities and public education, to extend the Commission on Civil Rights, to prevent discrimination in federally assisted programs, to establish a Commission on Equal Employment Opportunity, and for other purposes.[55]

In short, "Title VII prohibits employment discrimination based on race, color, religion, sex and national origin."[56]

Title VII remains a landmark topic of employment law and compliance matters in spite of the civil rights movement's heyday being over forty-five years old. No corporate lawyer worth his or her salt can ignore the role it plays in the daily life of almost every business. There are many very helpful practice manuals on Title VII employment-law issues,[57] and one or more should be part of every corporate lawyer's personal library. As is the case with many OSHA safety issues, there can be specific reporting requirements for Title VII compliance, and a client-company may even have a Title VII compliance officer in place.

So what is the risk we need to identify?

The question seems to suggest a trick answer, but there is none. The risk is simply that an employee will be, or feel like he or she is being, discriminated against on the basis of his or her race, color, religion, gender, or national origin. If or when that occurs, in spite of training, complaint procedures, and zero-tolerance policies, a client-company's risk-management program needs to be in full swing *before* an EEOC (or comparable state agency) complaint is filed, if possible, and before the client-company's relationship with the disgruntled employee hits a sour point of no return.

Any kind of employment-related issue has the potential to be disruptive, but a discrimination issue has the added potential of creating factions among other employees and leading to very negative publicity. This is not to mention the cost and exposure, both financially and legally, involved in conducting an internal investigation, complying with an agency investigation, going through an administrative hearing process, and/or fighting a lawsuit.

However a corporate lawyer may feel about the validity of an employee's complaint, neither the client-company nor its legal counsel can afford to be dismissive of the risk potential.

§ 6.4.3.2 Workplace Safety

Workplace safety can sometimes feel like one of the less stimulating and less lawyerly areas of employment-related risk. Workplace safety issues smack of eyewash stations, ergonomic desk chairs, first-aid kits mounted on a wall, science-lab-like plastic glasses, clearly marked exits, and tedious training requirements—until a human being is hurt. The terrible truth is this: just as the "tree of Liberty must be watered with the blood of Patriots and Tyrants[,]"[58] so too is the tree of Industry—though less noble and less grand—watered with the injury and death of laborers.

Here is a wake-up-call statistic about the ultimate cost of running a business:

> 4,690 workers were killed on the job in 2010 . . . (3.6 per 100,000 full-time equivalent workers)—more than 90 a week or nearly 13 deaths every day. (This is a slight increase from the 4,551 fatal work injuries in 2009, but the second lowest annual total since the fatal injury census was first conducted in 1992).[59]

Nearly 13 deaths every day . . . Workplace safety, by definition, insinuates risk. I am emphasizing the human toll up front for a reason: lawyers, like insurance actuaries, tend to view workplace safety risks largely in terms of legal and financial liabilities. That viewpoint undoubtedly has its place, but a truly successful risk-management program is going to root its risk avoidance strategies and assessments in a much more meaningful—and *real*—way. Corporate lawyers would do well to follow suit.

> Risk management in the workplace is about more than preventing lawsuits or lowering your insurance costs; it's also about showing current and prospective employees, as well as the community, that you're a responsible employer who cares about your worker's well-being. Making workplace health and safety risk management a priority can increase productivity, by minimizing lost hours caused by worker injury.[60]

The point is, effective risk management for workplace safety issues looks at the *human beings* first, not at the accidents likely to befall them.

In turn, this helps to offset future reputational damage and future operational impedance even before legal and financial risks come into play. Corporate lawyers and watchful risk managers can anticipate where the safety-related risks are likely to arise and work to build in preventive measures that will avoid, or lessen, the impact accidents are likely to have.

Workplace safety is a critical (and legally mandatory) part of every business concern, so where should you begin?

Three good starting points for identifying workplace safety risks are: (1) taking note of what safety-related risks are common in your client-company's industry, (2) researching what safety-related risks your client-company has encountered in the past, and (3) ascertaining what protective measures are required by state and federal law. In terms of resources, almost every corporate lawyer should quickly become familiar with the United States Department of Labor's Occupational Safety and Health Administration (OSHA) (www.osha.gov). In addition, most states run their own health and safety programs and agencies, which are allowed to act as proxies for OSHA standards as long as the state-level standards are at least as effective as OSHA's.

The following is a quick starting list of the ten most frequently cited OSHA standards violations in 2011,[61] to get your risk-identification juices flowing:

1. Scaffolding, general requirements, construction (29 CFR § 1926.451)
2. Fall protection, construction (29 CFR § 1926.501)
3. Hazard communication standard, general industry (29 CFR § 1910.1200)
4. Respiratory protection, general industry (29 CFR § 1910.134)
5. Control of hazardous energy (lockout/tagout), general industry (29 CFR § 1910.147)
6. Electrical, wiring methods, components and equipment, general industry (29 CFR § 1910.305)
7. Powered industrial trucks, general industry (29 CFR § 1910.178)
8. Ladders, construction (29 CFR § 1926.1053)
9. Electrical systems design, general requirements, general industry (29 CFR § 1910.303)
10. Machine guarding (machines, general requirements, general industry) (29 CFR § 1910.212)

For your own client-company, you will want to topically consider industry-specific rules, hazard-specific rules, machine-specific rules, and certifications and licenses. Your risk-management efforts should be looking for those situations, items, procedures, processes, machines, and materials that can cause possible injury or death. Those investigations—including an informed assessment of the consequences of each identified risk—should lead to preventive practices, programs, and policies. Some of the more common risk-management actions result in programs and policies, such as

- Accident prevention programs
- Personal protective equipment
- Hazardous-chemical communication program
- Respiratory protection
- Hearing-loss prevention program
- Fall protection work plan

Plunge in. Talk to your client-company's floor managers, dock supervisors, crane operators, safety officers, pipe fitters, welders, chemists, engineers, security officers, maintenance crews, forklift operators, shift managers, roughnecks, and anyone else who comes to mind, and talk to them about safety issues. Go beyond standard reporting programs. Your client-company's employees and managers will greatly appreciate the personal interest you take in their safety, and you will uncover all kinds of helpful information about how to manage those risks more successfully.

Workplace safety is not rocket science (unless you are dealing with the workplace safety of rocket scientists). Remember to ask your three-fold risk-assessment questions and be diligent to revisit workplace-safety issues *often*. Even if a work zone has been accident free for 364 days, it will not mean anything if complacency leads to an accident on the 365th day.

To this day, I can still close my eyes and hear my mother—a dear, sweet woman who had to deal with three seditious sons and one stubborn daughter—utter the single best workplace-safety observation of risk:

It's all fun and games until someone gets hurt.

§ 6.4.3.3 Privacy Issues

Increasingly, *risk* is the first word to come to mind when the issue of employment-related privacy issues is raised. Here again, employees and contractors present a twofold challenge to a corporate lawyer: (1) there are risks that arise as a result of dealing with an employee's privacy boundaries, rights, and expectations; and (2) there are risks that arise as a result of an employee's lack of awareness (or vigilance) for another person's, or a customer's, privacy.

> In an effort to protect themselves from liability, employers are monitoring phone calls, voice mail, e-mail, and Internet site access so they can remedy problems before they escalate into litigation. According to an American Management Association study conducted in April 2000, more than two-thirds of employers use some form of employee surveillance.[62]

Policies and procedures regarding the personal or prohibited use of workplace Internet, email, and other company equipment and communication platforms are an essential part of an overall risk-management (and compliance) program. Employers need to be able to legitimately monitor and control communications and information access, but if those procedures are not carefully developed and carefully followed, they can easily give rise to privacy-related risks.

Take for instance an Internet-usage policy that allows employees to check their private email accounts while at work using workstation desktop computers (that is, company equipment and company-owned software). If an employee takes advantage of the policy and checks his or her personal email, has that employee lost his or her right to keep those personal communications private? Can a company monitor those communications or otherwise access them?

Corporate lawyers, who represent the *company* and not the employee, play a key role in helping a client-company draw these lines and answer these sometimes ambiguous questions, and while doing so, corporate lawyers must be observant of the potential risks that may arise and how tolerant, or intolerant, a client-company's culture will be toward those risks.

Equally important, there must be policies and procedures in place regarding access to, and control of, customer or vendor information. For some industries, such as banking and health care, there are scores of laws and regulations governing these privacy-related issues. For other industries, such as the food-service industry, more complex issues rarely take center stage (although there *are* certain risks; for example, credit card information provided to a cashier carries stringent protections).

Employees—aside from cyber thieves or other external threats—pose an enormous risk of inadvertent, or criminally deliberate, disclosure of confidential information. On the one hand, employees need access to private information, or portions of private information, to do their jobs, but on the other hand, if the information is compromised, the legal, operational, and reputational risks can be severe. Corporate lawyers, as indispensably as compliance officers, must be active participants in the supervision of privacy policies and risks associated with information misuse and unauthorized disclosure.

Document shredding and the tangible security of physical file rooms have been eclipsed, if not replaced, by electronically stored information, software firewalls, passwords, data encryption, user access, and cybersecurity. It can be difficult for a corporate lawyer, or a risk manager, to properly assess privacy-related risk when so much of it lies in the ether-world of computers and electronic technology. However, it is important to keep in mind that the end result can be the same, whether the means are physical or electronic: breach of private information carries risk, which invites consequence.

§ 6.4.3.4 Unions

Entire legal careers are spent in the area of collective bargaining, labor relations, union representation, and other organized employee activities. This section's discussion is not at all designed to tackle the depth and breadth of those practice areas. However, whether these areas of practice are part of a corporate lawyer's daily diet or they are shipped over to outside counsel, it is still important to recognize, at least in generalities, the employment-related risks employee organizations[63] can pose to a client-company.

On August 4, 2011, the DaveFleet blog posted the following observations about American Airlines:

> In January a snowstorm in Chicago caused the cancellation of numerous flights. This week the airline cancelled over 3,000 flights (more than 600 today alone) to conduct wiring checks on the planes, stranding more than a quarter of a million passengers.

To add to the airline's misery, its pilots union went on the offensive as the Allied Pilots' Association took out a big ad in USA Today to attack the airline's management. The ad links to a new site called Tell Your AA Story, which claims to be "produced by a group of concerned American Airlines employees." The site encourages passengers and employees alike to share their stories of dissatisfaction with the union and with American Airlines management, although it warns:

Note: your message will be sent to AA management, but we cannot guarantee that they will read, much less respond, to your concerns.

Double trouble. The airline is facing a major reputation crisis.[64]

Ouch.

American Airlines' labor woes (and other woes) did not stop there, nor have they stopped as of this writing. This unsettling illustration highlights a hat trick of union-related risks: (1) the legal risks of collective bargaining and contracts; (2) the operational risks of losing, or being manipulated by, a critical part of a client-company's workforce; and (3) the reputational risks of being tarred and feathered as an employee-unfriendly company. All three risks can pose full-blown five-alarm fires for all kinds of organizational clients. Nonprofit organizations and governmental entities are certainly not exempt from these risks.[65]

Risks directly related to unions (versus the indirect risks of third-party beneficiaries, which we will discuss in the next section) are varied and can carry interesting consequences. There are obvious risks, as highlighted by American Airlines' situation, but there are also not-so-obvious risks, which can be just as damaging. Consider these possibilities:

- Without workforce attendance systems to manage employee absence, organizations risk failing to comply with collective bargaining agreements and government regulations such as the Family and Medical Leave Act and state leave laws.
- Adverse credit ratings can occur when collective bargaining agreements impose greater debt obligations on an organization than it has planned for fiscally.

- Competitiveness may greatly suffer as a result of product or service price increases in order to offset lower production rates.

Unions have undeniably had their place in the landscape of American
industry over the past seventy to eighty years, and opinions concerning
their positive or negative impact on American industry are often hot or
cold. Very few opinions are tepid. But regardless of what temperature a
corporate lawyer's personal views about unions may be, a necessary part
of his or her job is to assess union-related risks in the same dispassionate
manner as other usual suspects. Risk-management programs must have
preventive measures and contingency plans in place to deal with those
risks as they might arise.

§ 6.4.3.5 Third-Party Beneficiaries

Now that union risks have you thinking of contractual, employment-
related risks, what about *indirect* risks? Many times, these are the risks
that fall in behind whatever frontline consequences your client-company
is dealing with as a result of a union-related event. For example, assume
your client-company has made the hard choice to violate its collective
bargaining agreement with a labor union in order to reduce unsustain-
able insurance costs. Your client-company may or may not be staring
down a union lawsuit or strike, but there is also an *indirect* risk to take
into account: the individual employees who are third-party beneficiaries
to the collective bargaining agreement.

"Third-party beneficiaries usually take contracts as they find them.
They get no more than the signatories provided, and if there is a flaw
in the formation of the contract the third-party beneficiaries get nothing."[66] Third-party beneficiary risks are not exclusive to union-related
situations, of course. They can potentially arise in any situation in
which a contractual arrangement or provision considers, includes, or
has a direct impact upon a non-contracting third party, such as liability-
limitation provisions, pension plans, general contracting, or component
or software supplier agreements.

Theoretically, the potential third-party beneficiary scenarios are
endless, but the risk-assessment process remains the same. Identify the
risk; identify and understand the consequences; and prepare for avoiding or accepting/tolerating the risk. A thorough risk-management program will have a methodology for identifying and categorizing these

kinds of indirect risks. A company's corporate lawyer will many times be the eyes and ears behind those efforts, because third-party beneficiary risks are not always evident and rely greatly on contract-law issues.

Now that we have threshed several kernels of risk out of the rank-and-file workforce, let us turn our attention to the remaining husk: management.

Safety

§ 6.4.4 Officers, Directors, and Shareholders

Members of the board and senior management are the "the aristocracy of our monied corporations,"[67] and like European monarchs who eventually fell victim to the revolutions of the proletariat, corporate aristocrats constantly live in a state of some concern that they will succumb to a similar (but hopefully bloodless) fate. Officers and directors (most especially) bear an enormous amount of fiduciary and legal responsibility in the proper execution of their duties, and that level of responsibility directly correlates to the amount of risk they can potentially face if those duties are negligently, willfully, or, in some circumstances, unwittingly ignored.

These risk issues lie mainly under the umbrella of corporate governance, so our immediate task will not include a repetition of those matters discussed in Chapter 5 but rather will look to foster a few concentrated thoughts about some of the more noteworthy risks faced by, or posed by, a client-company's leadership.

Accountability to shareholders, perhaps above all else, underlies the risks faced by executive management and board members, but the risks of governance are not limited to headline-grabbing class action shareholder lawsuits, high-energy and high-stakes proxy fights, or the sight of an executive walking in handcuffs to his federal sentencing hearing for accounting fraud. The risks of governance may sometimes be more personal to a business than the Wall Street–backdrop theatrics of the evening news. These risks include hazards to livelihoods of employees, to relationships with vendors, to relationships with lenders, to relationships with underwriters, and to expectations and needs of customers and clients.

A client-company that finds itself embroiled in a derivative lawsuit brought against its CEO, or a proxy fight brought by an aggressive hedge-fund shareholder, can become distracted and begin suffering the financial stress of what can be extraordinarily expensive litigation. Corporate lawyers and risk managers alike should make sure there is adequate insurance before disaster strikes. Directors and officers (D&O) insurance policies are a unique underwriting instrument designed specifically to deal with litigation assaults against members of a company's management. The policies are unique and require careful review, demanding close attention to the types of riders that may be needed (perhaps to cover prosecutions based on the Responsible Corporate Officer Doctrine).[68] Here are some of the key elements[69] you will need to read carefully and/or negotiate with your client-company's carrier:

- *Priority of payment*—This deals with the prioritization of payments among various insured parties (usually claims against directors and officers are satisfied before claims against the client-company).
- *Misconduct exclusion*—Negotiate to limit this exclusion to the individual director or officer, or have it taken out altogether.
- *Rescission*—Look closely for severability provisions where the knowledge of one insured is not imputed to others, so the carrier cannot rescind the policy if it finds a material misrepresentation or omission in the coverage application, or have this remedy taken out altogether.
- *Insured vs. insured exclusion*—This is designed to exclude coverage for claims made by one insured against another.

A typical risk-management program will undoubtedly account for the Wall Street–type risks—regulatory and investor-related risks—but many risk-management programs may not do much more than "succession planning" when it comes to risk consequences *within* an organization. A corporate lawyer, however, as legal counsel to the *entity*, must identify, prepare for, and advise on those more-amorphous risks to the best of his or her ability.

§ 6.4.4.1 Fiduciary Duties

In Chapter 5's discussion of governance matters, the best judgment rule and the underlying elements of a director's duty of care were surveyed. The other two ubiquitous fiduciary duties owed by directors of an organization include the duty of loyalty and the duty to act in good faith.[70] Though the fiduciary duties of corporate officers are still a burgeoning subject of litigation, corporate officers' responsibilities to act in good faith and in the company's best interests are a principal area of risk concern. There may also be statutorily imposed duties and standards for both directors and officers, depending on a client-company's industry and/or its structure and status as a public or nonpublic entity.

Legal risks can constitute the more obvious threats when fiduciary or statutory duties are violated. However, a corporate lawyer cannot ignore the operational or reputational risks if such violations have occurred, or if such violations are alleged to have occurred. Regulatory investigations can bring operations to a near standstill, and accusations of wrongdoing, or the failure to satisfy fiduciary responsibilities, can cause horrific reputational damage, all of which hurts the bottom line and a company's ability to go about its normal business routines.

With a constant eye toward these kinds of risks and their consequences, a corporate lawyer, as advisor to management and to the board, will be in a unique position to make or counsel on the corrections necessary to avoid or mitigate risks associated with the breach—inadvertent or otherwise—of fiduciary and statutory duties.

As has been repeated over and over again, examine the activities and decisions of your board members and corporate officers with a very simple framework of risk-assessment questions:

- What are the *legal* risks? What are the client-company's tolerances? Is the client-company prepared?

- What are the *operational* risks? What are the client-company's tolerances? Is the client-company prepared?
- What are the *reputational* risks? What are the client-company's tolerances? Is the client-company prepared?

§ 6.4.4.2 Derivative Suits versus Direct Claims

Two distinctive risks of a director's or an officer's misconduct—real or imagined—are derivative lawsuits and direct-claim lawsuits. Simply because both of these risks are nominally legal risks does not mean they do not also carry operational and reputational risks for a client-company. A corporate lawyer who finds him- or herself looking down the barrel of either type of claim must make sure steps are being taken to avoid, mitigate, or accept the consequences of each category of risk.

Derivative lawsuits are lawsuits brought by shareholders on behalf of a corporation against some third party. This occurs when shareholders believe a claim should be pursued even if the corporation's board or management has decided not to pursue it.[71] Often, the target of a derivative suit is an insider, such as one of the executive officers or board members, and awarded damages are customarily returned to the company instead of to individual shareholders.

Direct-claim lawsuits are lawsuits brought by shareholders directly against a corporation, a board member, an officer, or another shareholder to enforce a shareholder's rights. The same set of facts can, in fact, give rise to both a direct-claim lawsuit and a derivative lawsuit, blurring the line of distinction between the two types of claims.[72]

In their usual manifestation, derivative lawsuits and direct claims have the distressing irony of pitting owners against those persons who run the company. They are family-law lawsuits on a grand, and strange, scale.

Both of these types of lawsuits—many times certified as class actions—because of their typical scope and legal complexity, represent enormous litigation risks to a client-company and to management, who may be held personally liable for breaches of fiduciary duties. Shareholder activism in the form of derivative and direct-claim litigation is nothing new, but recently, boards and officers are facing new kinds of challenges to their traditional managerial functions, such as claims based on executive compensation and "exclusive forum" bylaw provisions.[73]

"Say-on-pay" shareholder fights (over executive compensation) are excellent examples of the layers of reputational and even operational risks involved in derivative and direct-claim litigation risk assessments.

> Executive compensation has long been within the purview of the board of directors' business judgment. However, the advent of the proxy rules requiring "advisory" votes on executive compensation stemming from congressional legislation has spurred many shareholders to push forward derivative suits challenging executive compensation packages and the board of directors' business judgment in recommending and approving executives' compensation.[74]

The resultant risk assessment is as follows:

> Unfortunately for corporate boards, executive compensation is poised to escalate from being a risk to outliers to being a broad risk to all directors. . . . The fight has broadened through regular rounds of enhanced disclosure that foments public outrage, governmental initiatives, and shareholder derivative litigation. This vicious circle challenges board members to stay abreast of best practices and worst risks[.][75]

The principal risk concern raised by derivative and direct-claim litigation is that they could happen at all. Therefore, a risk-management program is going to incorporate processes to diffuse potentially explosive shareholder situations, usually through investor relations programs (communication, communication, communication) and financial transparency. Shareholder "management" is a form of risk management, and its best strategies are those that understand good investor relations must be built on trust, accountability, and sensible (and justifiable) business decisions. Hot-button issues have to be dealt with head on, and boards should "persuasively communicate the reasons for those decisions" to investors.[76]

> The issues requiring special attention will depend on the company, but for most companies will include strategic direction, risk oversight, executive compensation, proxy access, board composition, succession, board leadership, political contributions disclosure, corporate social responsibility and structural defenses.[77]

Even with responsible awareness and constant communication, the reality is that shareholder lawsuits are bound to occur in spite of a client-company's best efforts. Risk management then shifts its focus to litigation management.

§ 6.4.4.3 Proxy Fights and Boardroom Brawls

Proxy season is that time of year—roughly January to June—when companies tell their story to investors: what they've achieved, what they're focused on, and where they're headed. Shareholders, for their part, can vote on what companies have outlined in their proxy statements and put forward proposals of their own.[78]

That sounds nice.

And it can be nice, especially when companies use proxies as another way to engage with shareholders and "to actually tell the story of being more transparent about what they're doing."[79] But they can also be the Roman Forum for proxy fights and proxy access proposals.

A little rebellion is a good thing.

Although elegantly clever in the bravura of our third U.S. president, Thomas Jefferson, this quip is hardly the likely witticism of a corporate lawyer whose client-company is facing a little thing called a proxy fight. A *proxy fight* is a result of shareholder activism when a group, or groups, of corporate activists attempt to convince shareholders to use their proxy votes (that is, votes cast by one person or entity as the authorized representative of another person). *Proxy access proposals* allow shareholders a mechanism to "include their board candidates in a company's proxy materials, saving shareholders the high costs of mounting an outside campaign."[80] These tactics are used to install new management and/or change bylaws.

Incumbent directors and management many times use various tactics to stay in power when under attack through shareholder activism, including staggering the boards (that is, having different election years for different directors), controlling access to the corporation's financial resources, and creating restrictive requirements in the bylaws. Incumbent directors and management may also run their own campaigns against sponsored replacements. As a result, many proxy fights are unsuccessful. Interestingly though, proxy fights waged by hedge funds—typically brought to further an investment strategy that may not be shared with most other shareholders—are successful a majority of the time.

Proxy fights and brawls over boardroom seats can easily set the stage for a number of different risks by shedding light into dark corners or by radically changing a company's leadership profile, strategy, and culture beyond a company's ability to healthily absorb those changes. This can lead to consequences such as derivative or direct claims, publicity nightmares, executive contract litigation, and branding damage. Therefore, when a "run on the bank" is in the air for a client-company's shareholder meeting, prepared legal counsel will run through his or her risk-management assessment.

- What are the *legal* risks? What are the client-company's tolerances? Is the client-company prepared?
- What are the *operational* risks? What are the client-company's tolerances? Is the client-company prepared?
- What are the *reputational* risks? What are the client-company's tolerances? Is the client-company prepared?

§ 6.4.4.4 Infighting—The Hatfields and McCoys

"The committee has met," Bryson continued, "and Tom Murphy and Ray Watson are going to step down." Murphy, the former chairman of Capital Cities/ABC, had joined the board after Disney acquired ABC in 1995; Watson, Disney's chairman before Eisner's arrival in 1984, was, after Roy, the board's longest-serving member. Both were over seventy-two. Roy wasn't surprised, since they had mentioned to him their plans to retire.

"We've concluded that you shouldn't run for reelection," Bryson said. . . .

[Roy E. Disney, the nephew of Walt Disney and the son of co-founder, Roy O. Disney] had only one thing left to say:

"You're making an awful mistake," he said, looking directly at Bryson. "And you're going to regret doing this."

Then he got up and walked out.[81]

In the mid-2000s, James B. Stewart, a Pulitzer Prize–winning journalist and author of *Den of Thieves*,[82] was given unprecedented access into the house of Disney and wrote *Disney Wars*, one of the all-time best nonfiction accounts of boardroom drama, executive power plays, and the general (and very human) dysfunction of some of the most powerful figures in the entertainment industry from 1984 through 2004, the Eisner Era. The above excerpt recounts a fateful exchange between Roy E. Disney, the nephew of Walt Disney, and John Bryson, a member of Disney's board. This effort to tactically remove Roy Disney from the board was the last straw for Roy, who, along with Stanley Gold, another board alumnus, close friend, and business associate, eventually led an all-out, successful proxy assault to oust Chairman Michael Eisner.[83]

When I think of family feuds, I think of the Walt Disney Company. I happen to like Disney, and in a strange way, Mr. Stewart's book and Disney's remarkable story of infighting made the company even more likeable to me. Along with its charismatic magical quality, the Walt Disney Company revealed itself to be wonderfully, agonizingly *real*. The humanity behind its timeless determination to create an ideal utopia is endearing and thought provoking.

Of all threats to a company, the backbiting, wrangling, and bickering among directors and/or executive officers can precipitate some of the greatest risks. When those who are responsible—legally, morally, ethically—for successfully managing a company, instead are consumed with manipulating each other, creating voting alliances, and steamrolling weaker personalities, a company can be in for a very bumpy ride—or ultimate failure. A boardroom's unhealthy atmosphere can even ripple well outside of a company's own shoreline.

Lucy P. Marcus, the founder and CEO of Marcus Venture Consulting, and who serves as a nonexecutive independent director on several boards, made the following observation in September 2011, pointedly on the heels of the boardroom failures of Yahoo! Inc. and Hewlett-Packard:

> The effect is to make everyone watching uneasy. The markets are uneasy, which is never a good thing. It taints how all other businesses and their boards are viewed, casting a pall over other technology companies and the wider business community. . . .
>
> All of this further erodes confidence in the companies as a whole: investors and customers alike begin to think about exit strategies

as they no longer see boards looking after their companies in ways that takes account of stakeholder interests.[84]

The passage of SOX took major steps toward ensuring more accountable, more responsible board composition and duties, but no amount of legislation can eliminate the human factor. A corporate lawyer, perhaps in tandem with outside governance counsel and/or the chief compliance officer, must remain alert to the kinds of chess games played by unstable, irresponsible, or immature board members and executive officers. There is not much direct force to be applied (unless it is circuitously through the mouthpiece of the audit or governance committees, for instance), but a corporate lawyer can still diligently provide the kind of counsel, advice, and warnings that might help keep unpleasant relationships and tactics to a minimum.

If a corporate lawyer—a client-company's legal counsel—is supposed to act as the ethical conscience of a corporation, then Jiminy Cricket needs to be willing to be involved, to speak up, and to lead from the front.

> So, let's take the opportunity of these high profile cases of boards gone awry to speak openly about boards and best practice.

> It is time for all of us—directors, investors, customers, employees, and journalists—to demand something better.[85]

§ 6.4.5 You—*"Thou wretched, rash, intruding fool."*[86]

A chapter on risk management would be shamefully incomplete without holding up a mirror and pointing a finger back at corporate lawyers. Legal counsel, as much as any other working part of a business enterprise, can present significant risks to a client-company. There are innumerable ways by which a lawyer can be the source of risk for his or her client-company. Even the most casual reader could thumb through this book, randomly choose a page, and identify a way for a corporate lawyer's actions, omissions, advice, lack of advice, ignorance, misconduct, or overzealousness to trigger hazard and peril for his or her client-company.

There is no need for further anecdotes, illustrations, or examples. If you are a hard-working, self-aware, and appropriately humble corporate lawyer, then you have a built-in sense—a *healthy* sense—of fear. Fear of messing up—of not delivering for the client when the client really needs you to come through. That unease is your greatest asset (if kept in balance with some confidence and daring). Your quiet anxiety should spur you to constantly self-examine—to make sure you are covering all of the bases, applying yourself, and thereby increasing the value of *you* for your client-company.

Assuming this is the case (each in his or her own way), the following two sections are my parting (and perhaps best) insights into where you can begin when it comes to risk management for your client-company.

§ 6.4.5.1 The Lawyer

Find a notepad so you can take notes. Pick up a mirror. Take a good, long, hard, searching look. As *legal counsel*, ask these questions of *yourself*:

- What *legal* risks do you pose? What are the client-company's tolerances for those risks? Is the client-company prepared? Are you prepared?
- What *operational* risks do you pose? What are the client-company's tolerances for those risks? Is the client-company prepared? Are you prepared?
- What *reputational* risks do you pose? What are the client-company's tolerances for those risks? Is the client-company prepared? Are you prepared?

Read back through your notes. Identify ways to improve. Mitigate the risks you might pose. Accept the ones you cannot change, but then develop a plan for managing those risks if they should arise.

Lead from the front.

§ 6.4.5.2 The Executive

Find a notepad, so you can take notes. Pick up a mirror. Take a good, long, hard, searching look. As *an executive*, ask these questions of *yourself*:

- What *legal* risks do you pose? What are the client-company's tolerances for those risks? Is the client-company prepared? Are you prepared?
- What *operational* risks do you pose? What are the client-company's tolerances for those risks? Is the client-company prepared? Are you prepared?

- What *reputational* risks do you pose? What are the client-company's tolerances for those risks? Is the client-company prepared? Are you prepared?

Read back through your notes. Identify ways to improve. Mitigate the risks you might pose. Accept the ones you cannot change, but then develop a plan for managing those risks if they should arise.

Lead from the front.

As promised, this chapter pitilessly hammered home the three manifestations of risk exposure: legal, operational, and reputational. I apologize for any awkwardness if your colleagues now find you muttering them to yourself unconsciously like a risk-management zombie.

As repetitive as the questions might have been, the idea has been to retrain your lawyerly senses to appreciate the identification, understanding, and consequences of risks faced by your client-company through a broader lens than merely an assessment of legal liabilities. A corporate lawyer's educated ability to troubleshoot legal liability is, undoubtedly, a priceless asset for any organizational client, but the *advisor* role of a corporate lawyer requires an eye to be just as focused on a client-company's operational and reputational exposures.

In an interview of Bob Scott, general counsel for TE Connectivity, Ltd., he explains that part of his role with his board involves his attendance at every board meeting and a discussion of "key risks the company is facing."[87]

> By being very open and transparent with the board about how we view these risks and how we're impacted by them, they don't get surprised or overexcited by issues, because they know they're going to regularly hear about them . . . There's a lot of trust that you're going to tell them about these issues. Without surprises, they can act in a calm manner with us as we try to explain how we can mitigate these risks.[88]

Risks of any stripe can leap out of almost any area of business, and they have a damning tendency to make their leap from being latent to active at the worst times. A well-maintained ERM Framework and the personal use of the Six Sigma efficiency methodology can be a corporate lawyer's ideal tools when working to insulate a client-company from, or prepare a client-company for, the inevitable risks encountered simply by virtue of running an organizational enterprise. And when a black swan occasionally darkens the sky, effective crisis-management procedures will be able to kick in and, with some fair winds, put one over on the gods.

Risk is a natural and sometimes thrilling part of doing business.

Keep its long shadow in proper perspective. A corporate lawyer's objective is not to avoid or prevent all risk; it is to further the business of his or her client-company.

A ship is safe in harbor, but that's not what ships are for.[89]

NOTES

1. PETER L. BERNSTEIN, AGAINST THE GODS: THE REMARKABLE STORY OF RISK 1 (Wiley 1998). Mr. Bernstein takes his reader through game theory, insurance and derivatives, business forecasting, and risk forecasting in a strikingly interesting and historical survey.

2. NASSIM NICHOLAS TALEB, THE BLACK SWAN: THE IMPACT OF THE HIGHLY IMPROBABLE xii–xiii (2nd ed., Random House Trade Paperbacks 2010). This book is one of the recommended materials you will find in Chapter 7. Whether you agree or disagree with Professor Taleb—and I would argue you are very likely to agree with him—BLACK SWAN will have you thinking outside the box, and perhaps finding a better sense of balance when dealing with risk.

3. El Paso's storm was part of the larger North American weather system referred to as the 2011 Groundhog Day Blizzard.

4. Vic Kolenc, *Report: Utilities Could Have Done Better During Freeze*, ELPASOTIMES.COM (Aug. 17, 2011, 12:00 A.M.), http://www.elpasotimes .com/news/ci_18695209?source=pkg.

5. *Id.*

6. This book is recommended reading in CHAPTER 7. RICHARD M. STEINBERG, GOVERNANCE, RISK MANAGEMENT, AND COMPLIANCE: IT CAN'T HAPPEN TO US—AVOIDING CORPORATE DISASTER WHILE DRIVING SUCCESS (John Wiley & Sons, Inc., 2011).

7. Melissa Maleske, *In the Boardroom*, INSIDECOUNSEL, May 2012, at 46.

8. Harris Diamond, *From the Experts: Managing Legal and Reputational Risks*, CORPORATE COUNSEL, Jan. 19, 2012, *available at* http://www.law.com/jsp/cc /PubArticleFriendlyCC.jsp?id=1202538725098.

9. CAROLE BASRI AND IRVING KAGAN, CORPORATE LEGAL DEPARTMENTS §§ 13:3 and 13:4 (4th ed., Practicing Law Institute 2011).

10. ABA CORPORATE LAWS COMMITTEE, *The Business Lawyer* in 66 CORPORATE DIRECTOR'S GUIDEBOOK 975, 998 (6th ed., American Bar Association 2011). The guidebook "provides concise guidance to corporate directors in meeting their responsibilities" by focusing on the role of a director, the

operation and duties of a board, and a board's key committees. If you do not have a copy, then make every effort to get your hands on one.

11. Richard M. Steinberg, *supra* note 6.

12. "ISO 31000:2009 can be applied throughout the life of an organization, and to a wide range of activities, including strategies and decisions, operations, processes, functions, projects, products, services and assets. . . . Although ISO 31000:2009 provides generic guidelines, it is not intended to promote uniformity of risk management across organizations. The design and implementation of risk management plans and frameworks will need to take into account the varying needs of a specific organization, its particular objectives, context, structure, operations, processes, functions, projects, products, services, or assets and specific practices employed." International Organization for Standardization, ISO 3009:2009 (2009). This can be purchased through ISO's Web site: http://www.iso.org/iso/catalogue_detail?csnumber=43170.

13. COSO was organized in 1984 and "was sponsored jointly by five major professional associations headquartered in the United States: the American Accounting Association (AAA), the American Institute of Certified Public Accountants (AICPA), Financial Executives International (FEI), The Institute of Internal Auditors (IIA), and the National Association of Accountants (now the Institute of Management Accountants [IMA])." *About us*, COSO, http://www.coso.org/aboutus.htm (last visited May 25, 2012). "COSO's goal is to provide thought leadership dealing with three interrelated subjects: enterprise risk management (ERM), internal control, and fraud deterrence."

14. COSO, ERM Framework (2004). This can be purchased online, along with other guidance publications by COSO, at http://www.coso.org/guidance.htm.

15. Richard M. Steinberg, *supra* note 6, at 83.

16. This is not to turn a blind eye toward preventive law efforts, but these are focused on identifying and avoiding legal risks before they become legal problems; this represents only a third of the categories of risk faced by businesses, instead of addressing enterprise-wide business-oriented risks.

17. The American Lawyer, *Six Sigma at Seyfarth*, April 1, 2010, *available at* http://www.americanlawyer.com/PubArticleTAL.jsp?id=1202447191899&Six_Sigma_at_Seyfarth&slreturn=20120823201730 (last visited May 20, 2012).

18. *SeyfarthLean*, Seyfarth Shaw LLP, http://www.seyfarth.com/SeyfarthLean (last visited May 20, 2012).

19. In the interests of full disclosure, I am not entirely sold on the process-improvement strategy of Six Sigma for law department management purposes. Chapter 3 passed over it because it has less to do with management per se than it does with quality control. There are a variety of quality or management strategies that, left alone under their own weight, can become too cumbersome or biased: Six Sigma, reverse engineering, value-added focus, performance benchmarking, and decentralization to name a few. They all have strengths and weaknesses, and pet problem

areas they are meant to cure. My intent has been to provide you with practical observations, suggestions, and key points. As such, my admonishment is to use what works for you and your client-company.

20. I wish I could take credit for having been the first to conceptualize the pairing of Six Sigma strategy with risk management, especially ERM Framework, but, alas, I cannot. Others have also noticed, and commented on, the compatibility of the two systems. For instance, Michael Young, *Six Sigma Tools and the Eight Keys to Risk Management*, Six Sigma, http://www.isixsigma.com/tools-templates/risk-management/six-sigma-tools-and-eight-keys-risk-management/ (last visited May 20, 2012). Perhaps, though, this is the first time it has specifically been suggested for use by corporate lawyers. If so, please let me know, and I will try to carve some kind of lucrative intellectual-property rights out of it.

21. During his tenure at GE, between 1981 and 2001, GE's value rose 4,000 percent. Not too bad. Rebecca Leung, *Jack Welch: "I Fell in Love,"* CBSNews.com (Feb. 11, 2009, 7:31 P.M.), http://www.cbsnews.com/stories/2005/03/24/60ii/main682830.shtml.

22. Melissa Maleske, *In the Boardroom: Current and Former General Counsel, Outside Counsel and Other Governance Experts Weigh In on How and Why the GC-Board Dynamic Has Changed*, InsideCounsel, May 2012, at 46.

23. Harris Diamond, *From the Experts: Managing Legal and Reputational Risks*, Corporate Counsel, Jan. 19, 2012, *available at* http://www.law.com/jsp/cc/PubArticleFriendlyCC.jsp?id=1202538725098.

24. Hopefully, you have one or some other kind of reporting mechanism in place if your client-company does not fall under SOX requirements.

25. Mary Swanton, *5 Steps to Protect against Whistleblowers*, InsideCounsel, April 2012.

26. American Express, AEMP17—Whistleblower Claims (September 29, 2010).

27. David Barstow, *Wal-Mart Hushed Up a Vast Mexican Bribery Case*, New York Times, Apr. 21, 2012.

28. Foreign Corrupt Practices Act, 15 U.S.C. § 78dd-1.

29. Sue Reisinger, *Will Wal-Mart Regret Not Disclosing Its Bribery Investigation Sooner?*, Corporate Counsel, Apr. 24, 2012, *available at* http://www.law.com/jsp/cc/PubArticleFriendlyCC.jsp?id=1202549958532.

30. Ashley Post, *A SOX Provision That Could Blindside Your Company*, InsideCounsel, Aug. 23, 2012, *available at* http://www.insidecounsel.com/2012/08/23/a-sox-provision-that-could-blindside-your-company.

31. False Claims Act, 12 Stat. 696 (Mar. 2, 1863). Also known as the "Lincoln Law."

32. False Claims Act Amendments, Pub. L. No. 99-562, 100 Stat. 3153 (enacted October 27, 1986).

33. Fraud Enforcement and Recovery Act, Pub. L. No. 111-21, § 386, 123 Stat. 1617 (enacted May 20, 2009).

34. Patient Protection and Affordable Care Act, Pub. L. No. 111-148, 124 Stat. 119 (enacted March 23, 2010).

35. Most states also have some version of a false claims statute, most often in the area of state-sponsored Medicaid programs.

36. Diamond, *supra* note 8.

37. Post, *supra* note 30.

38. *See* U.S. v. Dotterweich, 320 U.S. 277 (1943) (misbranded drugs); U.S. v. Park, 421 U.S. 658 (1975) (rats in a warehouse).

39. If facing a litigation risk scenario, especially one involving enormous volumes of e-discovery, consider using a privilege nonwaiver order that is subject to the provisions of Federal Rules of Evidence 502, or other applicable state rules of evidence. *See* Fed. R. Civ. P. 502.

40. Brian Martin, *Ensuring Attorney-Client Privilege in Crises*, InsideCounsel, Aug. 23, 2012, *available at* http://www.insidecounsel.com/2012/08/23 /ensuring-attorney-client-privilege-in-crises.

41. Do not ignore a subpoena, but do not answer it immediately either. Cautiously consult with experienced counsel on the matter. If privilege issues are unavoidable, then a privilege log, a protective order, or a disclosure agreement with effective claw-back provisions may be in order.

42. In the pharmaceutical industry, an additional labeling liability can arise from *off-label* marketing, such as marketing a drug to medical practitioners for an unapproved use. Off-label marketing has the potential of resulting in harm to consumers, but beyond giving rise to consumer risks, these marketing schemes have also been the fodder for multi*billion*-dollar *qui tam* lawsuits.

43. Fair Debt Collection Practices Act, 15 U.S.C. §§ 1692–1692P (Sept. 20, 1977).

44. Fair Credit Reporting Act, 15 U.S.C. §§ 1681–1681X (Oct. 26, 1970).

45. Truth in Lending Act, 15 U.S.C. §§ 1601–1616 (Mar. 23, 1976).

46. This is a 1974 amendment to the Truth in Lending Act. Fair Credit Billing Act, 15 U.S.C. §§ 1601–1616 (Oct. 28, 1974).

47. Gramm-Leach-Bliley Act, Pub. L. No. 106-102, 113 Stat. 1338 (Nov. 12, 1999).

48. Consumer Protection Act, Pub. L. No. 111-203, H.R. 4173 (Jul. 21, 2010).

49. These laws are largely focused on banks and investment companies, which is a narrower industry than for purposes of our discussion. Briefly though, from a 50,000-foot view, capital requirements provide a framework on how banks are required to manage their capital in relation to their assets. Internationally, the Bank for International Settlements' Basel Committee on Banking Supervision influences each country's capital requirements, including the United States. In 1988, the Basel Committee introduced a capital measurement system referred to as the Basel Capital Accords. These accords are now in their third adequacy framework revision, commonly known as Basel III.

50. Paul Davidson, *More American Workers Sue Employers for Overtime Pay*, USA Today, Apr. 19, 2012, *available at* http://www.usatoday.com/money /jobcenter/workplace/story/2012-04-15/workers-sue-unpaid-overtime /54301774/1.

51. *See Increase in Employment Discrimination Lawsuits Under the Americans with Disabilities Act*, TRAC Reports, Inc., May 30, 2012.

52. Catherine Rampell, *More Workers Complain of Bias on the Job, a Trend Linked to Widespread Layoffs*, New York Times, Jan. 11, 2011, *available at* http://www.nytimes.com/2011/01/12/business/12bias.html.

53. Americans With Disabilities Act of 1990, 42 U.S.C. § 12101 (Jan. 1, 2009).
54. Occupational Health and Safety Act of 1970, Pub. L. No. 91-596, 84 Stat. 1590.
55. This is the text of Title VII of the Civil Rights Act of 1964, as amended, as it appears in volume 42 of the U.S. Code. Civil Rights Act of 1964, tit. VII, 42 U.S.C. § 2000e (2006), *available at* http://www.eeoc.gov /laws/statutes/titlevii.cfm.
56. *Id.*
57. I provide two other resources in Chapter 7, but I would also highly recommend Gordon Jackson, Labor & Employment Law Handbook (3d ed., Aspen Publishers 2011).
58. Thomas Jefferson said, "Occasionally the tree of Liberty must be watered with the blood of Patriots and Tyrants."
59. U.S. Department of Labor, *Commonly Used Statistics, available at* http:// www.osha.gov/oshstats/commonstats.html (last visited May 28, 2012).
60. Business.com, *Workplace Safety Risk Management, available at* http://www .business.com/human-resources/workplace-safety-risk-management/ (last visited May 28, 2012).
61. *Supra* note 59.
62. *Who Read My E-mail? Employee Privacy in the Electronic Workplace,* EmployerGardian, summer 2002, *available at* http://www.cpai.com/pdfs /EGard_Summer2002.pdf.
63. Which we will dub generally as *unions* for simplicity's sake in this section.
64. Dave Fleet, American Airlines' Reputation Crisis, August 4, 2011, *available at* http://davefleet.com/2008/04/american-airlines-reputation-crisis/ (last visited May 28, 2012).
65. As of this writing, Chicago's teachers have just returned to work after having been on strike for more than a week.
66. Central States, Southeast and Southwest Areas Pension Fund v. Gerber Truck Serv., Inc., 870 F.2d 1148, 1151 (7th Cir. 1989).
67. Thomas Jefferson, in a letter to George Logan dated November 12, 1816, wrote, "I hope we shall take warning from the [British] example and crush in it's [*sic*] birth the aristocracy of our monied corporations which dare already to challenge our government to a trial of strength and bid defiance to the laws our country." Jefferson likely meant something more broad than our modern usage of *corporations,* but it is fascinating that the "challenge [to] our government" by corporate "aristocracy" is still, in many ways, fitting.
68. Increasingly, officers are also facing the risk of prosecution or suspension under the Responsible Corporate Officer Doctrine. *See supra* Section 6.4.1.4. This is a form of strict liability and does not require a showing of personal knowledge.
69. Randy Johnson, *Regulatory: Understanding your D&O Insurance Policy,* InsideCounsel, Mar. 7, 2012, *available at* http://www.insidecounsel .com/2012/03/07/regulatory-understanding-your-do-insurance-policy.
70. The duty of good faith and the duty of loyalty are essentially folded into the best judgment rule, which is, itself, essentially the duty of care. Other not as dogmatized duties, such as the duty not to cause waste, the duty

to act in the best interests of the corporation, and the duty to act on an informed basis, are also folded into the best judgment rule. *See* Grobow v. Perot, 539 A.2d 180 (Del. 1988).

71. Meyer v. Fleming, 327 U.S. 161, 167 (1946) ("[T]he purpose of the derivative action [is] to place in the hands of the individual shareholder a means to protect the interest of the corporation from the misfeasance and malfeasance of faithless directors and mangers").

72. *See* Abelow v. Symonds, 156 A.2d 416, 420 (Del. Ch. 1959) ("[T]he line of distinction between derivative suits and those brought for the enforcement of personal rights asserted on behalf of a class of stockholders is often a narrow one, the latter type of actions being designed to enforce common rights running against plaintiffs' own corporation or those dominating it, while the former are clearly for the purpose of remedying wrongs to the corporation itself").

73. An "exclusive forum" bylaw provision requires shareholders to bring lawsuits exclusively in a particular forum, typically the Delaware Court of Chancery. Shareholders have claimed companies have adopted these bylaws to better shield directors and officers from liability.

74. Mark Poerio, William F. Sullivan & Timothy D. Reynolds, *Staying in Front of Shareholder Litigation Challenges to Executive Compensation*, CORPORATE GOVERNANCE ADVISOR, June 14, 2012, *available at* http://www .paulhastings.com/publicationdetail.aspx?publicationId=2203.

75. *Id.*

76. Ira M. Millstein & Holly J. Gregory, *Rebuilding Trust: The Corporate Governance Opportunity for 2012*, WEIL, GOTSHAL & MANGES, LLP, Dec. 28, 2011, at 3.

77. *Id.*

78. Catherine Dunn, *Compensation, Risk to Dominate the 2012 Proxy Season*, CORPORATE COUNSEL, Dec. 13, 2011, *available at* http://www.law.com/jsp /cc/PubArticleCC.jsp?id=1202535262337.

79. *Id.* quoting Maureen Errity, director of Deloitte LLP's Center for Corporate Governance.

80. Catherine Dunn, *Is Yahoo Proxy Fight a Bellwether for Shareholders in 2012?* CORPORATE COUNSEL, Mar. 20, 2012.

81. James B. Stewart, *Prologue* to DISNEY WAR 6 (Simon & Schuster 2006).

82. I have a well-worn copy of this fantastic book about the rise and fall of the Junk Bond King, Michael Milken, and his coconspirator, Ivan Boesky, who is said to have told a Harvard graduating class, "Greed is good," the piece of advice later immortalized by the character Gordon Gecko in Oliver Stone's 1987 film, WALL STREET. JAMES B. STEWART, DEN OF THIEVES (Touchstone 1992).

83. The board did not immediately remove Eisner as the CEO. Slightly over a year later, Eisner took care of that by resigning.

84. Lucy P. Marcus, *It Is Time to Fix Our Boardrooms*, HARVARD BUSINESS REVIEW, Sept. 23, 2011, *available at* http://blogs.hbr.org/cs/2011/09/it_is _time_to_fix_our_boardroo.html.

85. *Id.*

86. William Shakespeare, *Hamlet*, act 3, sc. 4.

87. Maleske, *supra* note 7, at 50.
88. *Id.*
89. Attributed to William Greenough Thayer Shedd, an American Presbyterian theologian of the nineteenth century.

CHAPTER 7

RESOURCES—"WOULD YOU LIKE TO USE A LIFELINE?"

TABLE OF SECTIONS

Because corporate law, and those who practice it, can become a bit too grim and serious from time to time, I thought it best to provide a parting bit of wisdom in its best form: comedy. Henny Youngman was a British American comedian and accomplished violinist who, for decades, was famous for his one-liners. Therefore, I leave the stage to Mr. Youngman's pithy wit.

A self-taught man usually has a poor teacher and a worse student.

Being self-made in our American society usually conveys a well-deserved aura of fortitude, grit, and determination, but in the legal profession, we journeymen jurists are far more accomplished and far more valuable to our client-companies when we learn our trade, polish our skills, and repeatedly test our expertise through the input, advice, and criticism of other lawyers and professionals.

Corporate law—business law—is a term that covers a multitude of necessary disciplines, and a good corporate lawyer needs to be able to deal fearlessly with each one, whether he or she does so directly or indirectly through supervision and management. This is a formidable task that only grows more complex as our world becomes more complex. The good news is, an abundance of resources are available to educate, assist, and evaluate corporate lawyers.

In 2012, the American Bar Association's Business Law Section boasted approximately fifty-three committees dedicated to distinct areas of substantive corporate law.[1] A quick search of books, using the phrase *business law* on Amazon.com, will result in over a quarter of a million results. In the period of time between September 2012 and December 2013, the Practising Law Institute will offer approximately three hundred seminars and webcasts covering a wide variety of business-law topics. There are numerous organizations, associations, and blogs a corporate lawyer can join or follow, such as the Association of Corporate Counsel (www.acc.com) or Rees Morrison's blog (www.lawdepartment managementblog.com).

Almost every day, something new hits the airwaves, the Internet, or bookshelves that proves useful to practicing corporate lawyers. In fact, developing a daily habit of digesting a certain amount of industry-specific and practice-specific news is a good idea. It will keep you in the loop, and many times, it will bring an issue or a need to the forefront that you might not have thought of before (or have let slip lower and lower on your never-ending to-do list).

The Internet allows a lawyer to do this more easily than ever before, but it has also created an overwhelming superhighway of information to try and pick through. For my own daily diet, I have set my homepage to four Web sites, helping me control my intake but meeting my needs for general news, practice-specific news, and area-of-law-specific news (or research). I usually spend a few minutes each morning scanning through them or using them as initial-research resources for a particular issue, relevant news, or a question I might have.

They are:

The *Wall Street Journal* Online	http://online.wsj.com/home-page
InsideCounsel	http://www.insidecounsel.com/?ref=nav
Law.com / *Corporate Counsel*	http://www.law.com/jsp/cc/index.jsp
Corporate Counsel Section of the State Bar of Texas	http://www.lexology.com/

Both *InsideCounsel* and *Corporate Counsel* also publish periodicals, to which I subscribe, along with the ABA Business Law Section's *The Business Lawyer.* Everyone's needs and areas of interest will, of course, be different and will change over time. You should test-drive different portals and periodicals until you find a good fit.

Honestly though, sifting through a myriad of available resources—whether on the Internet or in hard-copy form—is like facing a big buffet the day after you finish a nothing-but-liquids diet. If you can manage to still think straight, your mind probably formulates only two questions:

Where do I start? And how much should I eat?

Haphazard gorging is rarely the best idea. You might spend too much precious time and appetite on copious amounts of fried chicken and potatoes, only to find you have no room left for the pastries and fruits arranged like a bacchanalian halo around a chocolate-fondue fountain at the dessert bar.

The intent of this chapter is to go to the buffet line in your place, and to attempt to pick and choose some of the best materials and helplines for you. The following sections are meant to provide a bibliography of suggestions to occupy your bookshelf, laptop, and membership subscriptions. They have been chosen for their ease of access, specific expertise, digestibility, and direct application to the variety of topics discussed throughout Chapters 1 through 6.

The following suggestions are *not* intended to exclude many other equally helpful and knowledgeable sources of information or assistance. Use these suggestions as tested springboards; read, absorb, and participate in as much as you are able.

§ 7.1 Networking with Peers

Of all the advice contained in this book, the recommendation to network with other people—reach out for a helping hand or an expert—is probably the most often repeated. From a business-value perspective, picking up the phone or sending an email to a peer or other professional can potentially save your client-company a significant amount of your time and/or avoid costly (even when innocent) mistakes. From a professional development perspective, a variety of input, constructive criticism, suggestions, and advice is the chisel and hammer that can shape each of us into better lawyers—a better end product for our clients.

I never cease to be pleasantly surprised at how easy it is to reach out to someone else with a question, problem, or idea I am wrestling with, and receive thoughtful and supportive advice. As busy as everyone inevitably is, other professionals almost always make the time to send back a helpful email reply, return a phone call, or meet for a quick lunch. It is respectful to do your homework first when you are able to do so—do not ask someone else to do the hard rowing for you simply because you are too lazy to do it yourself—but simple questions, newly navigated waters, or complex or abstruse issues can all be candidates for experienced input sometimes, and most folks are glad to help.

Rest assured,

There are no dumb questions . . . unless they remain unasked.

Here are a few of the best places to network and find answers, both big and small.

www.acc.com

Arguably, the heavyweight in all matters of corporate-law networking organizations is the Association of Corporate Counsel (ACC; www.acc .com). The ACC offers a fantastic database of resources, as well as the Knowledge Network, to help you locate a member with the expertise you might need. There is also the member-to-member virtual community, providing instant access to thousands of other in-house lawyers. The one downside, in my humble opinion, is the ACC limits its membership to "in-house counsel who work for corporations, associations and other private-sector organizations," but the dedication to that demographic, which excludes outside counsel, keeps the ACC's mission statement focused.

www.americanbar.org

For my money, it is tough to beat the membership benefits and scope of the American Bar Association (ABA; http://www.americanbar.org /groups/business_law.html). Though the Business Law Section of the ABA houses the majority of corporate-law-related committees, other sections, such as the Intellectual Property Section, the Litigation Section, and the Employment Law Section, also offer fantastic networking opportunities. The diversity in committee membership and participation, broad assortment of CLE topics and materials (and delivery modes), national exposure, online resources, and advocacy (legislative, judicial, regulatory, and public) are all very valuable features.

http://i-t-h.org

The In the House (ITH; http://i-t-h.org/) networking portal, self-described as "the world's first private social media network exclusively for in-house counsel[.]" At the time of this writing (summer 2012), ITH boasts approximately 1,004 members and is growing. However, like the ACC, ITH limits its membership to lawyers who certify that they are "currently an in-house attorney" for an employer-company.

www.inhouseblog.com

"InhouseBlog (http://www.inhouseblog.com/) was selected as a Top 100 Blawg by the ABA Journal (2008), nominated as a Top 25 Business Law Blog by *LexisNexis* (2010), and selected as the Runner-Up for the Best Practice Specific Blawg in Dennis Kennedy's 2011 Blawggie Awards." This is a great community resource for corporate lawyers, offering an email newsletter, guest posting, and comments posting.

http://www.linkedin.com/

Though I am not necessarily a huge fan of online *social* networking (realizing that, in this, I am apparently alone on an uninhabited, antisocial island), I do feel comfortable recommending LinkedIn for purposes of *professional* (or quasi-social) networking. LinkedIn offers individual membership accounts, company pages, and access to specific networking groups, boasting "executives from all 2011 Fortune 500 companies as members" among its worldwide membership of 175 million.

www.tgcf.org
The General Counsel Forum (http://www.tgcf.org/) was born and bred in Texas, with chapters in Houston, Dallas/Ft. Worth, and Austin/San Antonio, but it expanded its chapters nationally by adding Atlanta in 2010 and Chicago in 2012. "Members are general counsel and senior managing counsel with significant leadership and management responsibilities in a corporation, non-profit organization or government agency."

You might also consider purchasing a recent directory of in-house counsel to use as your white pages for peer contacts. Aspen Publishers (Wolters Kluwer Law & Business) has published a 2011 to 2012 multi-volume directory, which is updated annually. Wolters Kluwer also offers an online "corporate counselor profiler" database service.[2]

§ 7.2 Nightstand Reading

Admittedly, there might not be too many free minutes in your day, and when they are free, you might want to be using them playing golf, watching a movie, going to the park, or simply putting a cold washcloth on your forehead and lying down on the couch. But if you happen to spend some of your precious time with your nose in a book, then there are a few I would recommend.

David J. Parnell, In-House: A Lawyer's Guide to Getting a Corporate Legal Position *(ABA Publishing 2012).*
The book's main focus (no surprise) is on landing the corporate in-house job, but by keeping this focus, Mr. Parnell also does a great job (especially in his first two chapters) providing a frank commentary on some of the realities of in-house counsel work.

Robert Rhee, Essential Concepts of Business for Lawyers *(Aspen Publishers, Inc. 2012).*
It is tough to work *for* a business if you do not understand business. Mr. Rhee's book uses pictures, charts, diagrams, and tables—along with interesting hypotheticals, discussions of recent events, and focus-point summaries—to unpack a variety of business concepts.

Nancy Levit & Douglas O. Linder, The Happy Lawyer: Making a Good Life in the Law *(Oxford University Press 2010).*
This book is not about corporate law per se, but it is about *being* a lawyer—a satisfied lawyer. When we are content—carrying a sense of accomplishment away from every day—then we are far, far better at what we do. This book is definitely worth the read.

Max H. Bazerman & Ann E. Tenbrunsel, Blind Spots: Why We Fail to Do What's Right and What to Do about It *(Princeton University Press 2011).*
If there is a single, overarching role for a corporate lawyer to fulfill, it is to act as a client-company's conscience, legally and ethically, even when the twain don't meet. This well-written book examines "the ways we overestimate our ability to do what is right and how we act unethically without meaning to." We lawyers are accustomed to the slippery slope phenomenon of when moving a "bright line," and few things are more susceptible to that degradation than "doing the right thing." Thankfully, the authors don't just point out the alarming risk; they offer individual and group tactics for improving our judgment.

William Strunk & E. B. White, The Elements of Style *(4th ed., Longman 1999).*
I have sometimes fancied myself to be an overall good writer. That is, until I finally purchased a copy of Strunk and White's classic (and exquisitely thin) manual on how to write well. A lawyer is a wordsmith, and the training and room for improvement never end. *The Elements of Style,* which is actually highly readable, will do a brilliant job fine-tuning and honing your written communication skills. Memorandums, letters, emails, contracts, policies, procedures, briefs, speeches, articles, and even PowerPoint presentations all rely upon the dexterity of a wordsmith to be well communicated and easily understood. Buy it; take the small amount of time required to read it; and apply it as best you can and as often as you can.

§ 7.2.1 *Chapter 1: An Introduction*

E. Norman Veasey and Christine T. Di Guglielmo, Indispensable Counsel: The Chief Legal Officer in the New Reality *(Oxford University Press 2012).*
This is a fantastic, recently published book about the balance-beam nature of a general counsel's role, applicable to most corporate lawyers.

"The ideal of the modern general counsel is a lawyer-statesman who is adept at three distinct legal roles: an acute lawyer, a wise counselor, and a company leader" (from the foreword by Ben W. Heineman Jr.).

Ugo Draetta, On the Side of In-House Counsel *(Juris Publishing, Inc. 2012)*.
Mr. Draetta is currently professor of international law at the Catholic University of Milan, Italy, after having spent thirty years as in-house counsel for General Electric. His book should be assigned reading. *"On the Side of In-House Counsel* highlights the complex relations existing between an in-house counsel and his/her client, who is also his/her manager. Hence, the need for a personal chemistry without which an in-house counsel cannot efficiently operate. The book also describes the managerial skills required of an in-house counsel when he/she is the head of a large legal operation and suggests the appropriate ways to solve issues, such as centralisation versus decentralization of the various company lawyers, and relationships with outside counsel and with the external world (Universities, Institutions)."[3]

Robert Eli Rosen, Lawyers in Corporate Decision-Making *(Quid Pro, LLC 2010)*.
In what was originally an unpublished but frequently cited manuscript, Professor Rosen deciphers the process by which corporate lawyers are assimilated into a company's decision-making processes. This book is a top choice for understanding how corporate lawyers work with an organizational client on legal, ethical, and sociological issues.

§ 7.2.2 Chapter 2: Core Underpinnings

John W. Gergacz, Attorney-Corporate Client Privilege *(3d ed., Clark Boardman Callaghan 2011)*.
This book is an excellent reference for untangling the thorny issues of preserving corporate attorney-client privilege, destroying or losing that privilege, establishing work-product privilege, and discussing the corporate client. There are also helpful chapters on the crime-fraud exception, the waiver exception, and the good-cause exception.

Eric Flamholtz and Yvonne Randle, Corporate Culture: The Ultimate Strategic Asset *(Stanford Business Books 2011)*.
Understanding and translating an organization's culture from an intangible into a perceptible asset is a challenge for any executive.

For corporate lawyers, a compliant, responsible, and communicative culture is downright essential. "Eric Flamholtz and Yvonne Randle provide a new understanding of the need to not just assess corporate culture, but to actively manage culture toward the end of improved performance. In doing so, they create an innovative, uniquely comprehensive framework to guide business leaders."[4]

§ 7.2.3 *Chapter 3: Starting Your Job*

The reading and reference suggestions in this section are not mutually exclusive. Because the nature of almost every business enterprise is to be constantly dynamic, several of these recommended materials will overlap with each other. At the same time a business is dissolving one of its subsidiary units, it may be launching a new business unit, merging its remaining units with another company, or acquiring other operations in order to grow in a different or more expanded direction. Chances are, at some time or other, you will have a practical need for each of the following books.

New Ventures

JAMES D. COX AND THOMAS LEE HAZEN, CORPORATE COUNSEL GUIDES: CORPORATION LAW *(ABA Publishing 2012)*.
This book, which is one of the titles in the ABA's Corporate Counsel Guides series, "examines the key rules, regulations, and duties governing a corporation, and includes completely up-to-date information on recent Delaware and other leading decisions focused on fiduciary obligations and duties in corporate acquisitions; state and statutory developments affecting corporations, including the Dodd-Frank Act; the changing landscape of securities fraud suits in the federal courts; and insightful explanations of such news-making issues as corporate governance and director liabilities."[5]

DAVID H. FATER, ESSENTIALS OF CORPORATE AND CAPITAL FORMATION *(1st ed., Wiley 2010)*.
This book is a hands-on tool to use when launching new businesses and addressing capital concerns. It is not written just for lawyers, which makes it perfect. Most corporate lawyers can find their way to law books on formation issues, but far fewer lawyers properly appreciate all the other aspects of starting, organizing, and financing new business ventures from a *business* perspective.

GREGORY C. SMITH, START-UP & EMERGING COMPANIES: PLANNING, FINANCING & OPERATING THE SUCCESSFUL BUSINESS *(Law Journal Press 1997)*.

This thorough, loose-leaf, two-volume set now comes with a CD-ROM and has annual subscriptions for printed updates. It features numerous forms, clauses, agreements, checklists, and term sheets, and covers a multitude of topics, such as negotiating strategies, tax, registration and investor rights, venture capital financing, governance, joint ventures, employee benefit plans, accounting procedures, exit strategies, and limited liability companies. It is a must-have bookshelf reference.

Ongoing Business Concerns

WILLIAM M. PRIDE, ROBERT J. HUGHES & JACK R. KAPOOR, BUSINESS *(11th ed., South-Western College/West 2011)*.

The one-word title says it all. When a corporate lawyer (or any professional) jumps midstream into a vibrant, working business organization, full immersion is begins on day one. Because lawyers typically lack the educational business background to hit the ground running, this book is an ideal fit for researching and understanding the functional areas of almost every business: management, marketing, accounting, finance, and information technology, along with the core topics of ethics, social responsibility, and sustainability.

Transitions, Dissolutions, and Mergers and Acquisitions

WEIL, GOTSHAL & MANGES, LLP, REORGANIZING FAILING BUSINESSES, REVISED EDITION: A COMPREHENSIVE REVIEW AND ANALYSIS OF FINANCIAL RESTRUCTURING AND BUSINESS REORGANIZATION *(ABA Publishing 2006)*.

"Reorganizing Failing Businesses, offering the totality on restructurings in and out of bankruptcy, is written for [a] broad spectrum of professionals who engage in Restructurings, including corporate lawyers and litigators, executives, bankers, and accountants. Its coverage of the many interactive specialties that constitute the Restructuring process makes this publication a unique and valuable resource."[6] I could not have said it better myself.

SHANNON PRATT, THE LAWYER'S BUSINESS VALUATION HANDBOOK: UNDERSTANDING FINANCIAL STATEMENTS, APPRAISAL REPORTS, AND EXPERT TESTIMONY *(ABA Publishing 2003)*.

Mr. Pratt, a preeminent expert on all manner of business valuation issues, wrote this book specifically with lawyers in mind—lawyers who are unlikely to be well versed in appraisal techniques and methodologies. When you need the fundamentals from a reliable source, you will be very comfortable working from Mr. Pratt's text.

ABA COMMITTEE ON NEGOTIATED ACQUISITIONS, THE M&A PROCESS: A PRACTICAL GUIDE FOR THE BUSINESS LAWYER *(ABA Publishing 2006).* Mergers and acquisitions represent one of the more specialized areas of law. This book, compiled by those in the know, provides all the customary structures of acquisition transactions and addresses the purchase of both public and private organizations, although the weighted emphasis is on private deals.

§ 7.2.4 *Chapter 4: The Legal Department*

CAROLE L. BASRI AND IRVING KAGAN, CORPORATE LEGAL DEPARTMENTS *(4th ed., Practising Law Institute 2012).*
This two-volume set is, perhaps, my favorite go-to manual for almost anything and everything to do with practicing corporate law as a corporate lawyer. I have cited to the third edition throughout this book, but nothing beats having an up-to-date edition, so I recommend purchasing the fourth edition.

Rees Morrison, LAW DEPARTMENT MANAGEMENT, *http://www .lawdepartment managementblog.com/.*
If you overlook Rees Morrison's blog on law department management, then shame on you. Mr. Morrison's site is very navigable and provides copious amounts of practical advice, references, and current issues for corporate lawyers. Comments are also welcome on almost every blogged article.

§ 7.2.5 *Chapter 5: Areas of Practice*

ABA COMMITTEE ON CORPORATE COUNSEL, THE IN-HOUSE COUNSEL'S ESSENTIAL TOOLKIT *(ABA Publishing 2007).*
This is *the Toolkit* to have on your bookshelf and in your CD drive. Compiled by a thoughtful and very experienced group of corporate lawyers, this practical resource is chock-full of forms, samples, notes, suggestions, and commentary on all of the seven core areas of practice of corporate law.

Employment and Labor Law
ORRICK, HERRINGTON & SUTCLIFFE, LLP, EMPLOYMENT LAW YEARBOOK 2012 *(Practising Law Institute 2012).*
The title sounds as though the book will be full of whimsical pictures, sloppy signatures, and blurbs about "2012, our senior year" . . . not so.

Actually, this weighty tome is an extraordinarily solid resource for just about every employment-law issue a corporate lawyer could run into. I highly recommend keeping it within reach, highlighted, tabbed, and dog eared.

RANDY FREKING, THE REAL EMPLOYEE HANDBOOK: A TOP LAWYER REVEALS WHAT YOU NEED TO KNOW—AND WHAT YOUR BOSS WON'T TELL YOU *(CreateSpace Independent Publishing Platform 2012).*
The title and the viewpoint of this book suggest that it is from the dark side, arming employees with arrows to shoot into your client-company's carefully crafted employment policies, procedures, and practices. In a way, it is. And what *better* way to draft even better policies, procedures, and practices than to know where the holes are? Your first-tier concern is your client-company's workforce; having a down-to-earth understanding of how they see things, and what their anxieties and frustrations are (and how their personal lawyers might think), is priceless.

Contract and Transactional Law
LEENÉ EIDSON ESPENSCHIED, CONTRACT DRAFTING: POWERFUL PROSE IN TRANSACTIONAL PRACTICE *(ABA Publishing 2010).*
This is the first book in the ABA's Fundamental Series, and it delivers. Ms. Espenschied's book provides "fourteen lessons, [where] readers will learn how to work from prior documents to produce effective and complete legal documents that protect the client's interests. The book also features techniques for avoiding ambiguity by making better word choices, crafting strong sentences, and eliminating contextual ambiguity, and includes exercises and example documents."[7]

COMMERCIAL CONTRACTS: STRATEGIES FOR DRAFTING AND NEGOTIATING *(Morton Moskin ed., Wolters Kluwer Law & Business 2011).*
This two-volume set is a crème-de-la-crème resource for in-depth drafting suggestions, detailed checklists, sample documents and forms, extracts from relevant laws and regulations, and case and statutory references. Everything from opinion letters to leasing transactions is well covered and expertly examined.

Regulations, Compliance, and Investigations

MARTIN T. BIEGLMAN, BUILDING A WORLD-CLASS COMPLIANCE PROGRAM: BEST PRACTICES AND STRATEGIES FOR SUCCESS *(John Wiley & Sons, Inc. 2008).*

This is a very practical, thorough resource on all manner of compliance-program issues and concerns. Its appendices include a summary of the Federal Sentencing Guidelines and a sample compliance-program charter.

LOUIS BRAIOTTA JR., R. TRENT GAZZAWAY, ROBERT COLSON, SRIDHAR RAMAMOORTI, THE AUDIT COMMITTEE HANDBOOK *(5th ed., John Wiley & Sons, Inc. 2010).*

Having been improved and updated over several editions, and having been vetted by those whose business it is to work with, advise, and manage corporate audit committees, this resource is an absolutely reliable reference for corporate lawyers and their client-companies' audit committee members.

INTERNAL CORPORATE INVESTIGATIONS *(Barry F. McNeil and Brad D. Brian eds., 3d ed., ABA Publishing 2007).*

This book brings a very practical, informative approach to the spiderweb area of internal investigations. It "guides you through the steps necessary to conduct a proper and thorough legal investigation. Each chapter covers one aspect of conducting an investigation, clearly describing and advising you on the methods and skills involved, while providing you with practical tips on anticipating, recognizing, and avoiding the traps you are certain to encounter."[8]

Governance and Corporate Ethics

CYNTHIA M. KRUS, CORPORATE SECRETARY'S ANSWER BOOK *(4th ed., Aspen Publishers, Inc. 2007).*

This, in my opinion, works as the single-stop shop for corporate lawyers who also bear the role of corporate secretaries and/or work closely with their boards and governance committees (or audit committees) on governance issues. This book has everything you need to know and how to get it done.

DAVID F. LARCKER AND BRIAN TAYAN, CORPORATE GOVERNANCE MATTERS: A CLOSER LOOK AT ORGANIZATIONAL CHOICES AND THEIR CONSEQUENCES *(Pearson Education, Inc., publishing as FT Press 2011).*
The title of this book belies its practical usefulness for everyday corporate-law practitioners. Even though the book has an academic approach, its advice, observations, data, and thoroughness make it a very useful resource, especially as many corporations face not only sundry regulatory issues but actual governance ratings by organizations such as Standard & Poor's.

HARVARD LAW SCHOOL FORUM ON CORPORATE GOVERNANCE AND FINANCIAL REGULATION, *http://blogs.law.harvard.edu/corpgov/.*
Subscribing is relatively painless, and the amount of critical resources, which are cosponsored by Harvard Law School's Program on Corporate Governance and the Harvard Law School Program on Institutional Investors, makes this forum/blog a fantastic favorite for your Web browser.

Intellectual Property
WILLIAM A. FINKELSTEIN & JAMES R. SIMS III, THE INTELLECTUAL PROPERTY HANDBOOK: A PRACTICAL GUIDE FOR FRANCHISE, BUSINESS, AND IP COUNSEL *(ABA Publishing 2005).*
"A single-volume resource on all major components of intellectual property. Written by intellectual property and franchise lawyers, this book synthesizes difficult concepts and offers 'plain-English' treatment of arcane and complex intellectual property issues. It features an overview of domestic and international trademarks, domain name and 'cyberlaw' issues, copyrights, patents, trade secrets, and the important analysis of the intersection of intellectual property issues and cutting-edge technology."

ALAN R. THIELE, JUDITH R. BLAKEWAY & CHARLES M. HOSCH, THE PATENT INFRINGEMENT LITIGATION HANDBOOK *(ABA Publishing 2009).*
"Our mandate and goal as editors was to provide both substantive and practical guidance to a wide audience of non-IP specialists: franchise practitioners and general practitioners; in-house corporate counsel who regularly address IP issues; paralegals and budding intellectual property practitioners looking for a practical overview of IP; and IP specialists in one area who need a refresher or grounding in another."[9]

Litigation

RACHEL GIESBER CLINGMAN, LITIGATION MANAGEMENT *(Law Journal Press 2010).*

Any corporate lawyer would be hard-pressed to find a litigation management topic not well-covered by this book. You can purchase a "combo" subscription, which will give you one year of online access for one user, as well as one copy of all print releases during the year, or you can simply purchase the book. There are an increasing number of litigation-management resources for corporate lawyers, but if you have to have just one shelf reference that will cover just about every issue—including views on costs, risks, and standards—then this is it.

Other Support Services

FRANCHISE LAW COMPLIANCE MANUAL *(Jeffrey A. Brimer ed., 2nd ed., ABA Publishing 2011).*

One of the most compelling endorsements for obtaining a copy of this book is that each of its chapters was prepared by an in-house corporate counsel and an outside counsel to franchisors. From "franchise disclosure and sales compliance" to operational issues to "mergers and acquisitions of franchise systems" to "international franchising," you will be able to glean information and experience from corporate lawyers whose careers have focused on each of this book's topics.

OTTO LERBINGER, CORPORATE PUBLIC AFFAIRS: INTERACTING WITH INTEREST GROUPS, MEDIA, AND GOVERNMENT *(Lea's Communication Series, Routledge Communication Series, Lawrence Erlbaum Associates 2005).* Though this book is not specifically directed toward legal counsel, neither is the realm of public affairs and media relations. Corporate lawyers have to act the apprentice role to respond, or assist in responding, to issues and concerns arising from interfaces with "primary constituencies"—interest groups, media, customers, and government. This book does a great job providing an overview of the corporate public affairs function and the strategies and processes involved in successful public affairs management.

THOMAS LEE HAZEN, CORPORATE COUNSEL GUIDES: SECURITIES REGULATION *(ABA Publishing 2011).*

Professor Hazen's book is an excellent, accessible bookshelf reference for nonsecurities corporate lawyers who need a general understanding of federal securities laws with an emphasis on "those areas of the law that are likely to be confronted in a general or corporate practice, while at the same time giving some coverage to market regulation, broker-dealers, and the regulation of investment companies and investment advisers."[10]

DENNIS UNKOVIC, CORPORATE COUNSEL GUIDES: UNDERSTANDING ASIA *(ABA Publishing 2011)*.
As another title in the ABA's Corporate Counsel Guides series, Mr. Unkovic's decades' worth of personal experiences "in deciding deal structures, conducting negotiations, hiring . . . overseas staff, and all the other intricacies of conducting business" in "12 of the most important countries, from China and Japan, to Vietnam," provides very sound advice for those corporate lawyers who need insights and tips on Asian "negotiation, arbitration, and general business etiquette."[11] (As a bonus, you will greatly enjoy this book's cartoons.)

§ 7.2.6 *Chapter 6: Risk Management*

RICHARD M. STEINBERG, GOVERNANCE, RISK MANAGEMENT, AND COMPLIANCE: IT CAN'T HAPPEN TO US—AVOIDING CORPORATE DISASTER WHILE DRIVING SUCCESS *(John Wiley & Sons, Inc. 2011)*.
Though this book does an excellent job opening with a discussion of compliance and governance issues, its weight is in the area of risk management. This has been one of my go-to books on risk-management issues because of its easy-to-read discussions about internal controls, supervision strategies, succession planning, crisis management, performance measures, and board governance and effectiveness.

FREDERICK D. LIPMAN, WHISTLEBLOWERS: INCENTIVES, DISINCENTIVES, AND PROTECTION STRATEGIES *(1st ed., Wiley 2011)*.
After the passage of SOX, whistleblowing took on a whole new life. That life was expanded after the Dodd-Frank Wall Street Reform and Consumer Protection Act was signed into law. One of the preeminent academics in corporate governance holds this opinion of the book: "As with his prior writings, Mr. Lipman has created a thoughtful and comprehensive guide. Following the passing of the Dodd-Frank corporate governance reform bill, the whistleblower issue has taken on significant prominence. This is why this book's subject has such relevance."[12] This book provides case studies, federal and state statutory incentives to

whistleblowing, and best practices for corporations in light of SOX and Dodd-Frank.

NASSIM NICHOLAS TALEB, THE BLACK SWAN: THE IMPACT OF THE HIGHLY IMPROBABLE *(2d ed., Random House Trade Paperbacks 2010).* If there is a single truism about risk, it is that all risk cannot always be eliminated at all times. Good management eliminates most risk, most of the time, so the event to prepare for—organizationally and mentally—is the black swan. Think of BP's Deepwater Horizon oil spill in the Gulf in 2010. Though it would have been manageable to prevent the risk of a blowout preventer's failure, it was not on anyone's radar to manage the risk for the largest marine oil spill in the history of the petroleum industry. If you spend any time thinking about risk (which you should), then this is simply an absolute must-read.

By now, your bookshelf, magazine rack, email inbox, and list of Internet browser favorites should be well occupied. If that proves insufficient, give me a call or drop me a line. I will be happy to help in any way I can.

NOTES

1. The actual number of committees is higher, but this rough count excludes administrative committees.
2. http://corporatecounselprofiler.wolterskluwerlb.com/?gclid=CMKskL -wuLICFeY7MgodZh8AjA
3. Amazon.com, *Book Description*, http://www.amazon.com/Side—House -Counsel-Ugo-Draetta/dp/1578233674/ref=sr_1_3?s=books&ie=UTF8 &qid=1352580078&sr=1-3&keywords=Ugo+Draetta (last visited May 30, 2012).
4. Amazon.com, *Editorial Reviews*, Jeff Cornwall, President, USASBE, and Director, Center for Entrepreneurship and the Jack C. Massey Chair of Entrepreneurship, Belmont University, http://www.amazon.com /Corporate-Culture-Ultimate-Strategic-Stanford/dp/080476364X/ref=sr _1_3?s=books&ie=UTF8&qid=1352580336&sr=1-3&keywords=corporate +culture (last visited May 30, 2012).
5. JAMES D. COX AND THOMAS LEE HAZEN, CORPORATE COUNSEL GUIDES: CORPORATION LAW (ABA Publishing 2012) (blurb).
6. American Bar Association, *About the Book*, http://apps.americanbar.org /abastore/index.cfm?section=main&fm=Product.AddToCart&pid=5070531 (last visited May 30, 2012).
7. American Bar Association, *About Contract Drafting: Powerful Prose in Transactional Practice*, http://apps.americanbar.org/abastore/index.cfm

?section=main&fm=Product.AddToCart&pid=1620424B (last visited May 30, 2012).

8. American Bar Association, *About the Book*, http://apps.americanbar.org /abastore/index.cfm?section=main&fm=Product.AddToCart&pid=5310367 (last visited on May 30, 2012).

9. Alan R. Thiele, Judith R. Blakeway & Charles M. Hosch, The Patent Infringement Litigation Handbook (ABA Publishing 2009), *Preface*, xix (co-editors, August 2005).

10. Thomas Lee Hazen, Corporate Counsel Guides: Securities Regulation (ABA Publishing 2011) (blurb).

11. Dennis Unkovic, Corporate Counsel Guides: Understanding Asia (ABA Publishing 2011) (blurb).

12. Frederick D. Lipman, Whistleblowers: Incentives, Disincentives, and Protection Strategies (1st ed., Wiley 2011) (back cover) Professor Charles M. Elson, Woolard Chair in Corporate Governance and Director of the Weinberg Center for Corporate Governance, University of Delaware.

INDEX

ABOUT THE AUTHOR

Steven L. Lovett is a senior attorney with the Carrillo Law Firm, P.C., in Las Cruces, New Mexico. After holding corporate counsel positions in the banking industry, his concentration is in general corporate matters, including governance, compliance, and litigation. He is also an adjunct professor of business law and ethics at the University of Texas at El Paso's College of Business Administration.